THE
RELIGIONS OF JAPAN

FROM THE DAWN OF HISTORY
TO THE ERA OF MÉIJI

BY

WILLIAM ELLIOT GRIFFIS

"I came not to destroy, but to fulfil."—THE SON OF MAN

Essay Index Reprint Series

 BOOKS FOR LIBRARIES PRESS
FREEPORT, NEW YORK

First Published 1895
Reprinted 1972

Library of Congress Cataloging in Publication Data

Griffis, William Elliot, 1843-1928.
    The religions of Japan, from the dawn of history
to the era of Méiji.

    (Essay index reprint series)
    Reprint of the 1895 ed., issued in the series Morse
lectures, 1894.
    1. Japan--Religion. I. Title. II. Series: The
Morse lectures, 1894.
BL2201.G8 1972   299'.56   70-37469
ISBN 0-8369-2550-5

PRINTED IN THE UNITED STATES OF AMERICA
BY
NEW WORLD BOOK MANUFACTURING CO., INC.
HALLANDALE, FLORIDA 33009

IN GLAD RECOGNITION OF THEIR SERVICES TO THE WORLD
AND
IN GRATEFUL ACKNOWLEDGMENT OF MY OWN GREAT DEBT TO BOTH
I DEDICATE THIS BOOK
SO UNWORTHY OF ITS GREAT SUBJECT
TO
THOSE TWO NOBLE BANDS OF SEEKERS AFTER TRUTH
THE FACULTY OF UNION THEOLOGICAL SEMINARY
OF WHOM
CHARLES A. BRIGGS AND GEORGE L. PRENTISS
ARE THE HONORED SURVIVORS
AND TO
THAT TRIO OF ENGLISH STUDENTS
ERNEST M. SATOW, WILLIAM G. ASTON AND BASIL H. CHAMBERLAIN
WHO LAID THE FOUNDATIONS OF CRITICAL SCHOLARSHIP IN JAPAN

———————

"IN UNCONSCIOUS BROTHERHOOD, BINDING THE SELF-SAME SHEAF

PREFACE

THIS book makes no pretence of furnishing a mirror of contemporary Japanese religion. Since 1868, Japan has been breaking the chains of her intellectual bondage to China and India, and the end is not yet. My purpose has been, not to take a snap-shot photograph, but to paint a picture of the past. Seen in a lightning-flash, even a tempest-shaken tree appears motionless. A study of the same organism from acorn to seed-bearing oak, reveals not a phase but a life. It is something like this—" *to* the era of Meiji " (A.D. 1868 –1894+) which I have essayed. Hence I am perfectly willing to accept, in advance, the verdict of smart inventors who are all ready to patent a brand-new religion for Japan, that my presentation is " antiquated."

The subject has always been fascinating, despite its inherent difficulties and the author's personal limitations. When in 1867, the polite lads from Satsuma and Kiōto came to New Brunswick, N. J., they found at least one eager questioner, a sophomore, who, while valuing books, enjoyed at first hand contemporaneous human testimony.

When in 1869, to Rutgers College, came an application through Rev. Dr. Guido F. Verbeck, of Tōkiō, from Fukui for a young man to organize schools upon the

American principle in the province of Echizen (ultra-Buddhistic, yet already so liberally leavened by the ethical teachings of Yokoi Héishiro), the Faculty made choice of the author. Accepting the honor and privilege of being one of the " beginners of a better time," I caught sight of peerless Fuji and set foot on Japanese soil December 29, 1870. Amid a cannonade of new sensations and fresh surprises, my first walk was taken in company with the American missionary (once a marine in Perry's squadron, who later invented the jinriki-sha), to see a hill-temple and to study the wayside shrines around Yokohama. Seven weeks' stay in the city of Yedo --then rising out of the débris of feudalism to become the Imperial capital, Tōkiō, enabled me to see some things now so utterly vanished, that by some persons their previous existence is questioned. One of the most interesting characters I met personally was Fukuzawa, the reformer, and now " the intellectual father of half of the young men of . . . Japan." On the day of the battle of Uyéno, July 11, 1868, this far-seeing patriot and inquiring spirit deliberately decided to keep out of the strife, and with four companions of like mind, began the study of Wayland's Moral Science. Thus were laid the foundations of his great school, now a university.

Journeying through the interior, I saw many interesting phenomena of popular religions which are no longer visible. At Fukui in Echizen, one of the strongholds of Buddhism, I lived nearly a year, engaged in educational work, having many opportunities of learning both the scholastic and the popular forms of Shintō and of Buddhism. I was surrounded by monasteries, temples, shrines, and a landscape richly embroidered with myth and legend. During my four years' residence and travel in the Empire, I perceived that in all things the people of Japan were *too* re- ·ligious.

In seeking light upon the meaning of what I saw before me and in penetrating to the reasons behind the phenomena, I fear I often made myself troublesome to both priests and lay folk. While at work in Tōkiō, though under obligation to teach only physical science, I voluntarily gave instruction in ethics to classes in the University. I richly enjoyed this work, which, by questioning and discussion, gave me much insight into the minds of young men whose homes were in every province of the Empire. In my own house I felt free to teach to all comers the religion of Jesus, his revelation of the fatherhood of God and the ethics based on his life and words. While, therefore, in studying the subject, I have great indebtedness to acknowledge to foreigners, I feel that first of all I must thank the natives who taught me so much both by precept and practice. Among the influences that have helped to shape my own creed and inspire my own life, have been the beautiful lives and noble characters of Japanese officers, students and common people who were around and before me. Though freely confessing obligation to books, writings, and artistic and scholastic influences, I hasten first to thank the people of Japan, whether servants, superior officers, neighbors or friends. He who seeks to learn what religion is from books only, will learn but half.

Gladly thanking those, who, directly or indirectly, have helped me with light from the written or printed page, I must first of all gratefully express my especial obligations to those native scholars who have read to me, read for me, or read with me their native literature.

The first foreign students of Japanese religions were the Dutch, and the German physicians who lived with them, at Déshima. Kaempfer makes frequent references, with text and picture, in his Beschryving van Japan. Von Siebold, who was an indefatigable collector rather than a critical student, in Vol. V. of his invaluable *Archiv* (Pantheon von Nippon), devoted over forty pages to the religions of Japan. Dr. J. J. Hoffman translated into Dutch, with notes and explanations, the Butsu-zō-dzu-i, which, besides its 163 figures of Buddhist holy men, gives a bibliography of the works mentioned by the native author. In visiting the Japanese museum on the Rapenburg, Leyden, one of the oldest, best and most intelligently arranged in Europe, I have been interested with the great work done by the Dutchmen, during two centuries, in leavening the old lump for that transformation which in our day as New Japan, surprises the world. It requires the shock of battle to awaken the western nations to that appreciation of the racial and other differences between the Japanese and Chinese, which the student has already learned.

The first praises, however, are to be awarded to the English scholars, Messrs. Satow, Aston, Chamberlain, and others, whose profound researches in Japanese history, language and literature have cleared the path for others to tread in. I have tried to acknowledge my debt to them in both text and appendix.

To several American missionaries, who despite their trying labors have had the time and the taste to study critically the religions of Japan, I owe thanks and appreciation. With rare acuteness and learning, Rev. Dr. George Wm. Knox has opened on its philosophical, and Rev. Dr. J. H. DeForest on its practical side, the subject of Japanese Confucianism. By his lexicographical work, Dr. J. C. Hepburn has made debtors to him both the native and the alien. To our knowledge of Buddhism in Japan, Dr. J. C. Berry and Rev. J. L. Atkinson have made noteworthy contributions. I have been content to quote as authorities and illustrations, the names of those who have thus wrought on the soil, rather than of those, who, even though world-famous, have been but slightly familiar with the ethnic and the imported faith of Japan. The profound misunderstandings of Buddhism, which some very eminent men of Europe have shown in their writings, form one of the literary curiosities of the world.

In setting forth these Morse lectures, I have purposely robbed my pages of all appearance of erudition, by using as few uncouth words as possible, by breaking up the matter into paragraphs of moderate length, by liberally introducing subject-headings in italics, and by relegating all notes to the appendix. Since writing the lectures, and even while reading the final proofs, I have ransacked my library to find as many references, notes, illustrations and authorities as possible, for the benefit of the general student. I have purposely avoided recondite and inaccessible books and have named those easily obtainable from American or European publishers, or from Messrs. Kelly & Walsh, of Yokohama, Japan. In using oriental words I have followed, in the main, the spelling of the Century Dictionary. The Japanese names are expressed according to that uniform system of transliteration used by

Hepburn, Satow and other standard writers, wherein consonants have the same general value as in English (except that initial g is always hard), while the vowels are pronounced as in Italian.   Double vowels must be pronounced double, as in Méiji (mā-ē-jē) ; those which are long are marked, as in ō or ū ; i before o or. u is short.   Most of the important Japanese, as well as Sanskrit and Chinese, terms used, are duly expressed and defined in the Century Dictionary.

I wish also to thank especially my friends, Riu Watanabe, Ph.D., of Cornell University, and William Nelson Noble, Esq., of Ithaca.   The former kindly assisted me with criticisms and suggestions, while to the latter, who has taken time to read all the proofs, I am grateful for considerable improvement in the English form of the sentences.

In closing, I trust that whatever charges may be brought against me by competent critics, lack of sympathy will not be one.   I write in sight of beautiful Lake Cayuga, on the fertile and sloping shores of which in old time the Iroquois Indian confessed the mysteries of life.   Having planted his corn, he made his pregnant squaw walk round the seed-bed in hope of receiving from the Source of life increased blessing and sustenance for body and mind.   Between such a truly religious act of the savage, and that of the Christian sage, Joseph Henry, who uncovered his head while investigating electro-magnetism to "ask God a question," or that of Samuel F. B. Morse, who sent as his first telegraphic message "What hath God wrought," I see no essential difference.   All three were acts of faith and acknowledgment of a power greater than man.   Religion is one, though religions are many.

As Principal Fairbairn, my honored predecessor in the Morse lectureship, says : " What we call superstition of the savage is not superstition *in him.* Superstition is the perpetuation of a low form of belief along with a higher knowledge. . . . Between fetichism and Christian faith there is a great distance, but a great affinity—the recognition of a supra-sensible life."

" For the earnest expectation of the creation waiteth for the revealing of the sons of God . . . The creation itself shall be delivered from the bondage of corruption into the liberty of the glory of the children of God."

W. E. G.

Itɦaca, N. Y., October 27, 1894.

TABLE OF CONTENTS

CHAPTER I

Salutatory.—The Morse Lectureship and its provisions.—The Science of Comparative Religion is Christianity's own child.—The Parliament of Religions.—The Study of Religion most appropriate in a Theological Seminary.—Shortening weapons and lengthening boundaries.—The right missionary spirit that of the Master, who "came not to destroy but to fulfil."- Characteristics of Japan.—Bird's-eye view of Japanese history and religion.—Popularly, not three religions but one religion.—Superstitions which are not organically parts of the "book-religions."—The boundary line between the Creator and his creation not visible to the pagan.— Shamanism : Fetichism.—Mythical monsters, Kirin, Phœnix, Tortoise, Dragon.—Japanese mythical zoölogy. —The erection of the stone fetich.— Insurance by amulets upon house and person.—Phallicism.—Tree-worship.—Serpent-worship.—These unwritten superstitions condition the "book-religions."—Removable by science and a higher religion.

CHAPTER II

Japan is young beside China and Korea.—Japanese history is comparatively modern.—The oldest documents date from A.D. 712.—The Japanese archipelago inhabited before the Christian era.—Faith, worship and ritual are previous to written expression.—The Kojiki, Manyōshu and Norito.— Tendency of the pupil nations surrounding China to antedate their civilization.—Origin of the Japanese people and their religion.—Three distinct lines of tradition from Tsukushi, Idzumo and Yamato.—War of the invaders against the aborigines —Mikadoism is the heart of Shintō.—Illustrations from the liturgies.—Phallicism among the aborigines and common people.—The mind or mental climate of the primæval man.—Representa-

CHAPTER V

CHAPTER VI

CHAPTER VII

The experience of two centuries and a half of Buddhism in Japan.—
Necessity of using more powerful means for the conversion of the Japanese.—Popular customs nearly ineradicable.—Analogy from European history.—Syncretism in Christian history.—In the Arabian Nights.—How far
is the process of Syncretism honest?—Examples not to be recommended
for imitation.—The problem of reconciling the Kami and the Buddhas.—
Northern Buddhism ready for the task.—The Tantra or Yoga-chara system.—Art and its influence on the imagination.—The sketch replaced by
the illumination and monochrome by colors.—Japanese art.—Mixed
Buddhism rather than mixed Shintō.—Kōbō the wonder-worker who made
all Japanese history a transfiguration of Buddhism.—Legends about his
extraordinary abilities and industry.—His life, and studies in China.—The
kata-kana syllabary.—Kōbō's revelation from the Shintō goddess Toyo-
Ukè-Bimé.—The gods of Japan were avatars of Buddha.—Kōbō's plan of
propaganda.—Details of the scheme.—A clearing-house of gods and
Buddhas.—Relative rise and fall of the native and the foreign deities.—

CHAPTER VIII

CHAPTER IX

CHAPTER X

The missionary history of Japanese Buddhism is the history of Japan.—
The first organized religion of the Japanese.—Professor Basil Hall Chamberlain's testimony.—A picture of primeval life in the archipelago.—What
came in the train of the new religion from "the West."—Missionary civil-
izers, teachers, road-makers, improvers of diet.—Language of flowers and
gardens.—The house and home.—Architecture.—The imperial capital.—
Hiyéizan.—Love of natural scenery.—Pilgrimages and their fruits.—The
Japanese æsthetic.—Art and decoration in the temples.—Exterior resemblances between the Roman form of Christianity and of Buddhism.—Quotation from "The Mikado's Empire."—Internal vital differences.—Enlightenment and grace.—Ingwa and love.—Luxuriance of the art of Northern
Buddhism.—Variety in individual treatment.—Place of the temple in the
life of Old Japan.—The protecting trees.—The bell and its note.—The
graveyard and the priests' hold upon it.—Japanese Buddhism as a political
power.—Its influence upon military history.—Abbots on horseback and
monks in armor.—Battles between the Shin and Zen sects.—Nobunaga.—
Influence of Buddhism in literature and education.—The temple school.—
The *kana* writing.—Survey and critique of Buddhist history in Japan.—
Absence of organized charities.—Regard for animal and disregard for
human life.—The Eta.—The Aino.—Attitude to women.—Nuns and nunneries.—Polygamy and concubinage.—Buddhism compared with Shintō.—
Influence upon morals.—The First Cause.—Its leadership among the sects.
—Unreality of Amida Buddha.—Nichiren.—His life and opinions.—Idols
and avatars.—The favorite scripture of the sect, the Saddharma Pundarika.—Its central dogma, everything in the universe capable of Buddhaship.—The Salvation Army of Buddhism.—Kōbō's leaven working.—
Buddhism ceases to be an intellectual force.—The New Buddhism.—Are
the Japanese eager for reform ?

CHAPTER XI

The many-sided story of Japanese Christianity.—One hundred years of
intercourse between Japan and Europe.—State of Japan at the introduction
of Portuguese Christianity.—Xavier and Anjiro.—Xavier at Kiōto and in

CHAPTER XII

PRIMITIVE FAITH: RELIGION BEFORE BOOKS

"The investigation of the beginnings of a religion is never the work of infidels, but of the most reverent and conscientious minds."

"We, the forty million souls of Japan, standing firmly and persistently upon the basis of international justice, await still further manifestations as to the morality of Christianity."—Hiraii, of Japan.

"When the Creator [through intermediaries that were apparently animals] had finished creating this world of men, the good and the bad Gods were all mixed together promiscuously, and began disputing for the possession of this world."—The Aino Story of the Creation.

"If the Japanese have few beast stories, the Ainos have apparently no popular tales of heroes. . . . The Aino mythologies . . . lack all connection with morality. . . . Both lack priests and prophets. . . . Both belong to a very primitive stage of mental development. . . . Excepting stories . . . and a few almost metreless songs, the Ainos have no other literature at all."—Aino Studies.

"I asked the earth, and it answered, 'I am not He;' and whatsoever are therein made the same confession. I asked the sea and the deep and the creeping things that lived, and they replied, 'We are not thy God; seek higher than we.' . . . And I answered unto all things which stand about the door of my flesh, 'Ye have told me concerning my God, that ye are not he; tell me something about him.' And with a loud voice they exclaimed, 'It is He who hath made us!'"—Augustine's Confessions.

"Seek Him that maketh the seven stars and Orion, and turneth the shadow of death into the morning, and maketh the day dark with night; that calleth for the waters of the sea, and poureth them out upon the face of the earth: The LORD is his name."—Amos.

"That which hath been made was life in Him."—John.

CHAPTER I

The Morse Lectureship and the Study of Comparative Religion

As a graduate of the Union Theological Seminary in the city of New York, in the Class of 1877, your servant received and accepted with pleasure the invitation of the President and Board of Trustees to deliver a course of lectures upon the religions of Japan. In that country and in several parts of it, I lived from 1870 to 1874. I was in the service first of the feudal daimiō of Echizen and then of the national government of Japan, helping to introduce that system of public schools which is now the glory of the country. Those four years gave me opportunities for close and constant observation of the outward side of the religions of Japan, and facilities for the study of the ideas out of which worship springs. Since 1867, however, when first as a student in Rutgers College at New Brunswick, N. J., I met and instructed those students from the far East, who, at risk of imprisonment and death had come to America for the culture of Christendom, I have been deeply interested in the study of the Japanese people and their thoughts.

To attempt a just and impartial survey of the religions of Japan may seem a task that might well appall even a life-long Oriental scholar. Yet it may be that an honest purpose, a deep sympathy and a gladly avowed desire to help the East and the West, the Japanese and the English-speaking people, to understand each other, are not wholly useless in a study of religion, but for our purpose of real value. These lectures are upon the Morse [1] foundation which has these specifications written out by the founder :

The general subject of the lectures I desire to be : "The Relation of the Bible to any of the Sciences, as Geography, Geology, History, and Ethnology, . . . and the relation of the facts and truths contained in the Word of God, to the principles, methods, and aims of any of the sciences."

Now, among the sciences which we must call to our aid are those of geography and geology, by which are conditioned history and ethnology of which we must largely treat ; and, most of all, the science of Comparative Religion.

This last is Christianity's own child. Other sciences, such as geography and astronomy, may have been born among lands and nations outside of and even before Christendom. Other sciences, such as geology, may have had their rise in Christian time and in Christian lands, their foundation lines laid and their main processes illustrated by Christian men, which yet cannot be claimed by Christianity as her children bearing her own likeness and image ; but the science of Comparative Religion is the direct offspring of the religion of Jesus. It is a distinctively Christian science. "It is so because it is a product of Christian civilization, and because it finds its impulse in that freedom of inquiry which Christianity fosters." [2] Christian scholars began

the investigations, formulated the principles, collected
the materials and reared the already splendid fabric of
the science of Comparative Religion, because the spirit
of Christ which was in them did signify this. Jesus
bade his disciples search, inquire, discern and compare.
Paul, the greatest of the apostolic Christian college,
taught: "Prove all things; hold fast that which is
good." In our day one of Christ's loving followers [3]
expressed the spirit of her Master in her favorite motto,
"Truth for authority, not authority for truth." Well
says Dr. James Legge, a prince among scholars, and
translator of the Chinese classics, who has added several portly volumes to Professor Max Müller's series of
the "Sacred Books of the East," whose face to-day is
bronzed and whose hair is whitened by fifty years of
service in southern China where with his own hands
he baptized six hundred Chinamen: [4]

> The more that a man possesses the Christian spirit, and is
> governed by Christian principle, the more anxious will he be to
> do justice to every other system of religion, and to hold his
> own without taint or fetter of bigotry. [5]

It was Christianity that, in a country where the religion of Jesus has fullest liberty, called the Parliament
of Religions, and this for reasons clearly manifest.
Only Christians had and have the requisites of success,
viz.: sufficient interest in other men and religions; the
necessary unity of faith and purpose; and above all, the
brave and bold disregard of the consequences. Christianity calls the Parliament of Religions, following out
the Divine audacity of Him who, so often, confronting
worldly wisdom and priestly cunning, said to his disciples, "Think not, be not anxious, take no heed, be

careful for nothing—only for love and truth. I am not come to destroy, but to fulfil."

Of all places therefore, the study of comparative religion is most appropriate in a Christian theological seminary. We must know how our fellow-men think and believe, in order to help them. It is our duty to discover the pathways of approach to their minds and hearts. We must show them, as our brethren and children of the same Heavenly Father, the common ground on which we all stand. We must point them to the greater truth in the Bible and in Christ Jesus, and demonstrate wherein both the divinely inspired library and the truth written in a divine-human life fulfil that which is lacking in their books and masters.

To know just how to do this is knowledge to be coveted as a most excellent gift. An understanding of the religion of our fellow-men is good, both for him who goes as a missionary and for him who at home prays, " Thy kingdom come."

The theological seminary, which begins the systematic and sympathetic study of Comparative Religion and fills the chair with a professor who has a vital as well as academic interest in the welfare of his fellow-men who as yet know not Jesus as Christ and Lord, is sure to lead in effective missionary work. The students thus equipped will be furnished as none others are, to begin at once the campaign of help and warfare of love.

It may be that insight into and sympathy with the struggles of men who are groping after God, if haply they may find him, will shorten the polemic sword of the professional converter whose only purpose is destructive hostility without tactics or strategy, or whose chief idea of missionary success is in statistics, in blackening the character of "the heathen," in sensational letters for home consumption and reports properly cooked and served for the secretarial and sectarian palates. Yet, if true in history, Greek, Roman, Japanese, it is also true in the missionary wars, that "the race that shortens its weapons lengthens its boundaries."[6]

Apart from the wit or the measure of truth in this sentence quoted, it is a matter of truth in the generalizations of fact that the figure of the "sword of the spirit, which is the word of God," used by Paul, and also the figure of the "word of God, living and active, sharper than any two-edged sword, and piercing even to the dividing of the soul and spirit, of both joints and marrow, and quick to discern the thoughts and intents of the heart," of the writer to the Hebrews, had for their original in iron the victorious *gladium* of the Roman legionary—a weapon both short and sharp. We may learn from this substance of fact behind the shadow of the figure a lesson for our instant application. The disciplined Romans scorned the long blades of the barbarians, whose valor so often impetuous was also impotent against discipline. The Romans measured their blades by inches, not by feet. For ages the Japanese sword has been famed for its temper more than its weight.[7] The Christian entering upon his Master's campaigns with as little impediments of sectarian dogma as possible, should select a weapon that is short, sure and divinely tempered.

To know exactly the defects of the religion we seek to abolish, modify, supplement, supplant or fulfil, means wise economy of force. To get at the secrets of its hold upon the people we hope to convert leads to a right use of power. In a word, knowledge of the opposing religion, and especially of alien language, literature and ways of feeling and thinking, lengthens missionary life. A man who does not know the moulds of thought of his hearers is like a swordsman trying to fight at long range but only beating the air. Armed with knowledge and sympathy, the missionary smites with effect at close quarters. He knows the vital spots.

Let me fortify my own convictions and conclude this preliminary part of my lectures by quoting again, not from academic authorities, but from active missionaries who are or have been at the front and in the field. [8]

The Rev. Samuel Beal, author of "Buddhism in China," said (p. 19) that "it was plain to him that no real work could be done among the people [of China and Japan] by missionaries until the system of their belief was understood."

The Rev. James MacDonald, a veteran missionary in Africa, in the concluding chapter of his very able work on "Religion and Myth," says :

The Church that first adopts for her intending missionaries the study of Comparative Religion as a substitute for subjects now taught will lead the van in the path of true progress.

The People of Japan.

In this faith then, in the spirit of Him who said, "I come not to destroy but to fulfil," let us cast our eyes upon that part of the world where lies the empire of Japan with its forty-one millions of souls. Here we have not a country like India—a vast conglomeration of nations, languages and religions occupying a peninsula itself like a continent, whose history consists of a stratification of many civilizations. Nor have we here a seemingly inert mass of humanity in a political structure blending democracy and imperialism, as in China, so great in age, area and numbers as to weary the imagination that strives to grasp the details. On the contrary, in Dai Nippon, or Great Land of the Sun's Origin, we have a little country easy of study. In geology it is one of the youngest of lands. Its known history is comparatively modern. Its area roughly reckoned as 150,000 square miles, is about that of our Dakotas or of Great Britain and Ireland. The census completed December 31, 1892, illustrates here, as all over the world, nature's argument against polygamy. It tells us that the relation between the sexes is, numerically at least, normal. There were 20,752,366 males and 20,337,574 females, making a population of 41,089,940 souls. All these people are subjects of the one emperor, and excepting fewer than twenty thousand savages in the northern islands called Ainos, speak one language and form substantially one race. Even the Riu Kiu islanders are Japanese in language, customs and religion. In a word, except in minor differences appreciable or at least important only to the special student, the modern Japanese are a homogeneous people.

In origin and formation, this people is a composite of many tribes. Roughly outlining the ethnology of Japan, we should say that the aborigines were immigrants from the continent with Malay reinforcement in the south, Koreans in the centre, and Ainos in the east and north, with occasional strains of blood at different periods from various parts of the Asian mainland. In brief, the Japanese are a very mixed race. Authentic history before the Christian era is unknown. At some point of time, probably later than A.D. 200, a conquering tribe, one of many from the Asian main-land, began to be paramount on the main island. About the fourth century something like historic events and personages begin to be visible, but no Jap-anese writings are older than the early part of the eighth century, though almanacs and means of measur-ing time are found in the sixth century. Whatever Japan may be in legend and mythology, she is in fact and in history younger than Christianity. Her line of rulers, as alleged in old official documents and ostenta-tiously reaffirmed in the first article of the constitution of 1889, to be "unbroken for ages eternal," is no older than that of the popes. Let us not think of Aryan or Chinese antiquity when we talk of Japan. Her his-tory as a state began when the Roman empire fell. The Germanic nations emerged into history long be-fore the Japanese.

Roughly outlining the political and religious life of the ancient Japanese, we note that their first system of government was a rude sort of feudalism imposed by the conquerors and was synchronous with aborig-inal fetichism, nature worship, ancestral sacrifices, sun-worship and possibly but not probably, a very rude sort of monotheism akin to the primitive Chinese cult-us.[9]   Almost contemporary with Buddhism, its intro-duction and missionary development, was the struggle for centralized imperialism borrowed from the Chinese and consolidated in the period from the seventh to the twelfth century. During most of this time Shintō, or the primitive religion, was overshadowed while the

Confucian ethics were taught. From the twelfth to this nineteenth century feudalism in politics and Buddhism in religion prevailed, though Confucianism furnished the social laws or rules of daily conduct. Since the epochal year of 1868, with imperialism re-established and the feudal system abolished, Shintō has had a visible revival, being kept alive by government patronage. Buddhism, though politically disestablished, is still the popular religion with recent increase of life,[10] while Confucianism is decidedly losing force. Christianity has begun its promising career.

The Amalgam of Religios.

Yet in the imperial and constitutional Japan of our day it is still true of probably at least thirty-eight millions of Japanese that their religion is not one, Shintō, Confucianism or Buddhism, but an amalgam of all three. There is not in every-day life that sharp distinction between these religions which the native or foreign scholar makes, and which both history and philosophy demand shall be made for the student at least. Using the technical language of Christian theologians, Shintō furnishes theology, Confucianism anthropology and Buddhism soteriology. The average Japanese learns about the gods and draws inspiration for his patriotism from Shintō, maxims for his ethical and social life from Confucius, and his hope of what he regards as salvation from Buddhism. Or, as a native scholar, Nobuta Kishimoto,[11] expresses it,

In Japan these three different systems of religion and morality are not only living together on friendly terms with one another, but, in fact, they are blended together in the minds

of the people, who draw necessary nourishment from all of these
sources. One and the same Japanese is both a Shintoist, a
Confucianist, and a Buddhist. He plays a triple part, so to
speak. . . . Our religion may be likened to a triangle.
. . . Shintoism furnishes the object, Confucianism offers
the rules of life, while Buddhism supplies the way of salvation ;
so you see we Japanese are eclectic in everything, even in religion.

These three religious systems as at present constituted, are "book religions." They rest, respectively, upon the Kojiki and other ancient Japanese literature and the modern commentators ; upon the Chinese
classics edited and commented on by Confucius and
upon Chu Hi and other mediæval scholastics who
commented upon Confucius ; and upon the shastras
and sutras with which Gautama, the Buddha, had
something to do. Yet in primeval and prehistoric
Nippon neither these books nor the religions growing
out of the books were extant. Furthermore, strictly
speaking, it is not with any or all of these three religions that the Christian missionary comes first, oftenest
or longest in contact. In ancient, in mediæval, and in
modern times the student notices a great undergrowth
of superstition clinging parasitically to all religions,
though formally recognized by none. Whether we call
it fetichism, shamanism, nature worship or heathen-
ism in its myriad forms, it is there in awful reality.
It is as omnipresent, as persistent, as hard to kill as
the scrub bamboo which both efficiently and sufficiently takes the place of thorns and thistles as the
curse of Japanese ground.

The book-religions can be more or less apprehended by those alien to them, but to fully appreciate the

depth, extent, influence and tenacity of these archaic, unwritten and unformulated beliefs requires residence upon the soil and life among the devotees. Disowned it may be by the priests and sages, indignantly disclaimed or secretly approved in part by the organized religions, this great undergrowth of superstition is as apparent as the silicious bamboo grass which everywhere conditions and modifies Japanese agriculture. Such prevalence of mental and spiritual disease is the sad fact that confronts every lover of his fellow-men. This paganism is more ancient and universal than any one of the religions founded on writing or teachers of name and fame. Even the applied science and the wonderful inventions imported from the West, so far from eradicating it, only serve as the iron - clad man - of - war in warm salt water serves the barnacles, furnishing them food and hold.

We propose to give in this our first lecture, a general or bird's-eye view of this dead level of paganism above which the systems of Shintō, Confucianism and Buddhism tower like mountains. It is by this omnipresent superstition that the respectable religions have been conditioned in their history and are modified at present, even as Christianity has been influenced in its progress by ethnic or local ideas and temperaments, and will be yet in its course of victory in the Mikado's empire.

Just as the terms " heathen " (happily no longer, in the Revised Version of the English Bible) and " pagan " suggest the heath-man of Northern Europe and the isolated hamlet of the Roman empire, while the cities were illuminated with Christian truth, so, in the main, the matted superstitions of Chinese Asia are more suggestive of distances from books and centres of knowledge, though still sufficiently rooted in the crowded cities.

One to whom the boundary line between the Creator and his world is perfectly clear, one who knows the eternal difference between mind and matter, one born amid the triumphs of science can but faintly realize the mental condition of the millions of Japan to whom there is no unifying thought of the Creator-Father. Faith in the unity of law is the foundation of all science, but the average Asiatic has not this thought or faith. Appalled at his own insignificance amid the sublime mysteries and awful immensities of nature, the shadows of his own mind become to him real existences. As it is affirmed that the human skin, sensitive to the effects of light, takes the photograph of the tree riven by lightning, so, on the pagan mind lie in ineffaceable and exaggerated grotesqueness the scars of impressions left by hereditary teaching, by natural phenomena and by the memory of events and of landmarks. Out of the soil of diseased imagination has sprung up a growth as terrible as the drunkard's phantasies. The earthquake, flood, tidal wave, famine, withering or devastating wind and poisonous gases, the geological monsters and ravening bird, beast and fish, have their representatives or supposed incarnations in mythical phantasms.

Frightful as these shadows of the mind appear, they are both very real and, in a sense, very necessary to the ignorant man. He must have some theory by which to explain the phenomena of nature and soothe his own terrors. Hence he peoples the earth and water, not only with invisible spirits more or less malevolent, but also with bodily presences usually in terrific bestial form. To those who believe in one Spirit pervading, ordering, governing all things, there is unity amid all phenomena, and the universe is all order and beauty. To the mind which has not reached this height of simplicity, instead of one cause there are many. The diverse phenomena of nature are brought about by spirits innumerable, warring and discordant. Instead of a unity to the mind, as of sun and solar system, there is nothing but planets, asteroids and a constant rain of shooting-stars.

Shamanism.

Glancing at some phases of the actual unwritten religions of Japan we name Shamanism, Mythical Zoology, Fetichism, Phallicism, and Tree and Serpent Worship.

In actual Shamanism or Animism there may or there may not be a belief in or conception of a single all-powerful Creator above and beyond all.[12] Usually there is not such a belief, though, even if there be, the actual government of the physical world and its surroundings is believed to lie in the hands of many spirits or gods benevolent and malevolent. Earth, air, water, all things teem with beings that are malevolent and constantly active. In time of disaster, famine, epidemic the universe seems as overcrowded with them as stagnant water seems to be when the solar microscope throw its contents into apparition upon the screen. It is absolutely necessary to propitiate these spirits by magic rites and incantations.

Among the tribes of the northern part of the Chinese

Empire and the Ainos of Japan this Shamanism exists as something like an organized cultus. Indeed, it would he hard to find any part of Chinese Asia from Korea to Annam or from Tibet to Formosa, not dominated by this belief in the power and presence of minor spirits. The Ainos of Yezo may be called Shamanists or Animists; that is, their minds are cramped and confused by their belief in a multitude of inferior spirits whom they worship and propitiate by rites and incantations through their medicine-man or sorcerer. How they whittle sticks, keeping on the fringe of curled shavings, and set up these, called *inao*, in places whence evil is suspected to lurk, and how the shaman conducts his exorcisms and works his healings, are told in the works of the traveller and the missionary.[13] In the wand of shavings thus reared we see the same motive as that which induced the Mikado in the eighth century to build the great monasteries on Hiyéizan, northeast of Kiōto, this being the quarter in which Buddhist superstition locates the path of advancing evil, to ward off malevolence by litanies and incense. Or, the *inao* is a sort of lightning-rod conductor by which impending mischief may be led harmlessly away.

Yet, besides the Ainos,[14] there are millions of Japanese who are Shamanists, even though they know not the name or organized cult. And if we make use of the term Shamanism instead of the more exact one of Animism, it is for the very purpose of illustrating our contention that the underlying paganisms of the Japanese archipelago, unwritten and unformulated, are older than the religions founded on books; and that these paganisms, still vital and persistent, constantly modify and corrupt the recognized religions. The term Shaman, a Pali word, was originally a pure Buddhist term meaning one who has separated from his family and his passions. One of the designations of the Buddha was Shamana-Gautama. The same word, Shamon, in Japanese still means a bonze, or Buddhist priest. Its appropriation by the sorcerers, medicine-men, and lords of the misrule of superstition in Mongolia and Manchuria shows decisively how indigenous paganism has corrupted the Buddhism of northern Asia even as it has caused its decay in Japan.

As out of Animism or Shamanism grows Fetichism in which a visible object is found for the abode or medium of the spirit, so also, out of the same soil arises what we may call Imaginary Zoölogy. In this mental growth, the nightmare of the diseased imagination or of the mind unable to draw the line between the real and the unreal, Chinese Asia differs notably from the Aryan world. With the mythical monsters of India and Iran we are acquainted, and with those of the Semitic and ancient European cycle of ideas which furnished us with our ancients and classics we are familiar. The lovely presences in human form, the semi-human and bestial creations, sphinxes, naiads, satyrs, fauns, harpies, griffins, with which the fancy of the Mediterranean nations populated glen, grotto, mountain and stream, are probably outnumbered by the less beautiful and even hideous mind-shadows of the Turanian world. Chief among these are what in Chinese literature, so slavishly borrowed by the Japanese, are called the four supernatural or spiritually endowed creatures—the Kirin or Unicorn, the Phœnix, the Tortoise and the Dragon.[15]

2

Mythical Zoölogy.

Of the first species the *ki* is the male, the *lin* is the female, hence the name Kilin. The Japanese having no *l*, pronounce this Kirin. Its appearance on the earth is regarded as a happy portent of the advent of good government or the birth of men who are to prove virtuous rulers. It has the body of a deer, the tail of an ox, and a single, soft horn. As messenger of mercy and benevolence, the Kirin never treads on a live insect or eats growing grass. Later philosophy made this imaginary beast the incarnation of those five primordial elements—earth, air, water, fire and ether—of which all things, including man's body, are made and which are symbolized in the shapes of the cube, globe, pyramid, saucer and tuft of rays in the Japanese gravestones. It is said to attain the age of a thousand years, to be the noblest form of the animal creation and the emblem of perfect good. In Chinese and Japanese art this creature holds a prominent place, and in literature even more so. It is not only part of the repertoire of the artist's symbols in the Chinese world of ideas, but is almost a necessity to the moulds of thought in eastern Asia. Yet it is older than Confucius or the book-religions, and its conception shows one of the nobler sides of Animism.

The Feng-hwang or Phœnix, Japanese Hō-wō, the second of the incarnations of the spirits, is of wondrous form and mystic nature. The rare advent of this bird upon the earth is, like that of the kirin or unicorn, a presage of the advent of virtuous rulers and good government. It has the head of a pheasant, the beak of a swallow, the neck of a tortoise, and the features of the dragon and fish. Its colors and streaming feathers are gorgeous with iridian sheen, combining the splendors of the pheasant and the peacock. Its five colors symbolize the cardinal virtues of uprightness of mind, obedience, justice, fidelity and benevolence. The male bird *Hō*, and female *wō*, by their inseparable fellowship furnish the artist, poet and literary writer with the originals of the ten thousand references which are found in Chinese and its derived literatures. Of this mystic Phœnix a Chinese dictionary thus gives description :

> The Phœnix is of the essence of water ; it was born in the vermilion cave ; it perches not but on the most beautiful of all trees ; it eats not but of the seed of the bamboo ; its body is adorned with the five colors ; its song contains the five notes ; as it walks it looks around ; as it flies hosts of birds follow it.

Older than the elaborate descriptions of it and its representations in art, the Hō-wō is one of the creations of primitive Chinese Animism.

The Kwei or Tortoise is not the actual horny reptile known to naturalists and to common experience, but a spirit, an animated creature that ages ago rose up out of the Yellow River, having on its carapace the mystic writing out of which the legendary founder of Chinese civilization deciphered the basis of moral teachings and the secrets of the unseen. From this divine tortoise which conceived by thought alone, all other tortoises sprang. In the elaboration of the myths and legends concerning the tortoise we find many varieties of this scaly incarnation. It lives a thousand years, hence it is emblem of longevity in art and literature. It is the attendant of the god of the waters. It has some of the qualities and energies of the dragon, it has the power of transformation. In pictures and sculptures we are familiar with its figure, often of colossal size, as forming the curb of a well, the base of a monument or tablet. Yet, whatever its form in literature or art, it is the later elaborated representation of ancient Animism which selected the tortoise as one of the manifold incarnations or media of the myriad spirits that populate the air.

Chief and leader of the four divinely constituted beasts is the Lung, Japanese Riō, or Dragon, which has the power of transformation and of making itself visible or invisible. At will it reduces itself to the size of a silk-worm, or is swollen until it fills the space of heaven and earth. This is the creature especially pre-eminent in art, literature and rhetoric. There are nine kinds of dragons, all with various features and functions, and artists and authors revel in their representation. The celestial dragon guards the mansions of the gods and supports them lest they fall; the spiritual dragon causes the winds to blow and rain to descend for the service of mankind; the earth dragon marks out the courses of rivers and streams; the dragon of the hidden treasures watches over the wealth concealed from mortals, etc. Outwardly, the dragon of superstition resembles the geological monsters brought to resurrection by our paleontologists. He seems to incarnate all the attributes and forces of animal life—vigor, rapidity of motion, endurance, power of offence in horn, hoof, claw, tooth, nail, scale and fiery breath. Being the embodiment of all force the dragon is especially symbolical of the emperor. Usually associated with malevolence, one sees, besides the conventional art and literature of civilization, the primitive animistic idea of men to whose mind this mysterious universe had no unity, who believed in myriad discordant spirits but knew not of "one Law-giver, who is able both to save and to destroy." An enlargement, possibly, of prehistoric man's reminiscence of now extinct monsters, the dragon is, in its artistic development, a mythical embodiment of all the powers of moisture to bless and to harm. We shall see how, when Buddhism entered China, the cobra-de-capello, so often figured in the Buddhistic representations of India, is replaced by the dragon.

Yet besides these four incarnations of the spirits that misrule the world there is a host, a menagerie of mythical monsters. In Korea, one of the Asian countries richest in demonology, beast worship is very prevalent. Mythical winged tigers and flying serpents with attributes of fire, lightning and combinations of forces not found in any one creature, are common to the popular fancy. In Japan, the *kappa*, half monkey half tortoise, which seizes children bathing in the rivers, as real to millions of the native common folk as is the shark or porpoise; the flying-weasel, that moves in the whirlwind with sickle-like blades on his claws, which cut the face of the unfortunate; the wind-god or imp that lets loose the gale or storm; the thunder-imp or hairy, cat-like creature that on the cloud-edges beats his drums in crash, roll, or rattle; the earthquake-fish or subterranean bull-head or cat-fish that wriggles and writhes, causing the earth to shiver, shudder and open; the *ja* or dragon centipede; the *tengu* or long-nosed and winged mountain sprite, which acts as the messenger of the gods, pulling out the tongues of fibbing, lying children; besides the colossal spiders and mythical creatures of the old story-books; the foxes, badgers, cats and other creatures which transform themselves and " possess " human beings, still influence the popular mind. These, once the old *kami* of the primitive Japanese, or *kamui* of the aboriginal Aino, show the mental soil and climate [16] which were to condition the growth of the seed imported from other lands, whether of Buddhism or Christianity. It is very hard to kill a god while the old mind that grew and nourished him still remains the same. Banish or brand a phantom or mind-shadow once worshipped as divine, and it will appear as a fairy, a demon, a mythical animal, or an *oni;* but to annihilate it requires many centuries of higher culture.

As with the superstitions and survival of Animism and Fetichism from our pagan ancestors among ourselves, many of the lingering beliefs may be harmless, but over the mass of men in Japan and in Chinese Asia they still exert a baleful influence. They make life full of distress; they curtail human joy; they are a hindrance to spiritual progress and to civilization.

Fetichism.

The animistic tendency in that part of Asia dominated by the Chinese world of ideas shows itself not only in a belief in messengers or embodiments of divine malevolence or benevolence, but also in the location of the spiritual influence in or upon an inanimate object or fetich. Among men in Chinese Asia, from the clodhopper to the gentleman, the inheritance of Fetichism from the primeval ages is constantly noticeable. Let us glance at the term itself.

As the Chinaman's "Joss" is only his own pronunciation of the Portuguese word *Deos*, or the Latin *Deus*, so the word "fetich" is but the Portuguese modification of the Latin word *facticius*, that is *feitiço*. Portugal, beginning nearly five hundred years ago, had the honor of sending the first ships and crews to explore the coasts of Africa and Asia, and her sailors by this word, now Englished as fetich, described the native charms or talismans. The word "fetichism" came into the European languages through the work of Charles de Brosses, who, in 1760, wrote on "Du Culte des Dieux Fétiches." In Fetichism, the "object is treated as having personal consciousness and power, is talked with, worshipped, prayed to, sacrificed to, petted or ill-treated with reference to its past or future behavior to its votaries."

Let me draw a picture from actual observation. I look out of the windows of my house in Fukui. Here is a peasant who comes back after the winter to prepare his field for cultivation. The man's horizon of ideas, like his vocabulary, is very limited. His view of actual life is bounded by a few rice-fields, a range of hills, and the village near by. Possibly one visit to a city or large town has enriched his experience. More probably, however, the wind and clouds, the weather, the soil, crops and taxes, his family and food and how to provide for them, are the main thoughts that occupy his mind. Before he will strike mattock or spade in the soil, lay axe to a tree, collect or burn underbrush, he will select a stone, a slab of rock or a stick of wood, set it upon hill side or mud field-boundary, and to this he will bow, prostrate himself or pray. To him, this stone or stick is consecrated. It has power to placate

the spirits and ward off their evil. It is the medium
of communication between him and them. Now, having attended, as he thinks, to the proprieties in the
case, he proceeds to dig, plough, drain, put in order
and treat soil or water, tree or other growth as is most
convenient for his purpose. His fetich is erected to
"the honorable spirits." Were this not attended to,
some known or unknown bad luck, sinister fortune, or
calamity would befall him. Here, then, is a fetich-wor-
shipper. The stick or stone is the medium of communication between the man and the spirits who can bless
or harm him, and which to his mind are as countlessly
numerous as the swarms of mosquitoes which he drives
out of and away from his summer cottage by smudge
fires in August.

One need not travel in Yezo or Saghalin to see practical Fetichism. Go where you will in Japan, there are
fetich worshippers. Among the country folk, the
"*inaka*" of Japanese parlance, Fetichism is seen in its
grossest forms. Yet among probably millions of Buddhists, especially of certain sects, the Nichiren for example, and even among the rationalistic Confucians,
there are fetich-worshippers. Rare is the Japanese
farmer, laborer, mechanic, ward-man, or *hei-min* of any
trade who does not wear amulet, charm or other object
which he regards with more or less of reverence as having relation to the powers that help or harm.[17] In
most of the Buddhist temples these amulets are sold
for the benefit of the priests or of the shrine or monastery. Not a few even of the gentry consider it best to
be on the safe side and wear in pouch or purse these
protectors against evil.

Of the 7,817,570 houses in the empire, enumerated

in the census of 1892, it is probable that seven millions
of them are subjects of insurance by fetich.[18] They
are guaranteed against fire, thieves, lightning, plague
and pestilence. It is because of money paid to the
priests that the wooden policies are duly nailed on
the walls, and not on account of the wise application
of mathematical, financial or medical science. Examine also the paper packages carefully tied and af-
fixed above the transom, decipher the writing in ink or
the brand left by the hot iron on the little slabs of
pine-wood—there may be one or a score of them—and
what will you read? Names of the temples with date
of issue and seal of certificate from the priests, mottoes
or titles from sacred books, often only a Sanskrit letter
or monogram, of which the priest-pedler may long
since have forgotten the meaning. To build a house,
select a cemetery or proceed to any of the ordinary
events of life without making use of some sort of material fetich, is unusual, extraordinary and is voted
heterodox.

Long after the brutish stage of thought is past the
fetichistic instinct remains in the sacredness attached
to the mere letter or paper or parchment of the sacred
book or writing, when used as amulet, plaster or medicine. The survivals, even in Buddhism, of ancient and
prehistoric Fetichism are many and often with undenied
approval of the religious authorities, especially in
those sects which are themselves reversions to primitive
and lower types of religion.

Among the Ainos of Yezo and Saghalin the medicine-man or shaman is decorated with fetichistic bric-
à-brac of all sorts, and these bits of shells, metals, and
other clinking substances are believed to be media of

communication with mysterious influences and forces. In Korea thousands of trees bedecked with fluttering rags, clinking scraps of tin, metal or stone signify the same thing.   In Japan these primitive tinkling scraps and clinking bunches of glass have long since become the *suzu* or wind-bells seen on the pagoda which tintinabulate with every passing breeze.   The whittled sticks of the Aino, non-conductors of evil and protectors of those who make and rear them, stuck up in every place of awe or supposed danger, have in the slow evolution of centuries become the innumerable flagpoles, banners and streamers which one sees at their *matsuris* or temple festivals.   Millions of towels and handkerchiefs still flutter over wells and on sacred trees.   In old Japan the banners of an army almost outnumbered the men who fought beneath them.   To-day, at times they nearly conceal the temples from view.

The civilized Japanese, having passed far beyond the Aino's stage of religion, still show their fetichistic instincts in the veneration accorded to priestly inventions for raising revenue.[19]   This instinct lingers in the faith accorded to medicine in the form of decoction, pill, bolus or poultice made from the sacred writing and piously swallowed; in the reverence paid to the idol for its own sake, and in the charm or amulet worn by the soldier in his cap or by the gentleman in his pill-box, tobacco-pouch or purse.

As the will of the worshipper who selects the fetich makes it what it is, so also, by the exercise of that will he imagines he can in a certain measure be the equal or superior of his god.   Like the Italian peasant who beats or scolds his bambino when his prayers are not

answered or his wishes gratified, so the fetich is punished or not allowed to know what is going on, by being covered up or hidden away. Instances of such
rough handling of their fetiches by the people are far
from unknown in the Land of Great Peace. At such
childishness we may wonder and imagine that fetich-
worship is the very antipodes of religion; and yet it requires but little study of the lower orders of mind and
conduct in Christendom to see how fetich-worship still
lingers among people called Christians, whether the
fetich be the image of a saint or the Virgin, or a verse
of the Bible found at random and used much as is
a penny-toss to decide minor actions. Or, to look
farther south, what means the rabbit's foot carried in
the pocket or the various articles of faith now hanging
in the limbo between religion and folk-lore in various
parts of our own country ?

Phallicism.

Further illustrations of far Eastern Animism and
Fetichism are seen in forms once vastly more prevalent
in Japan than now. Indeed, so far improved off the face
of the earth are they, that some are already matters of
memory or archæology, and their very existence even
in former days is nearly or wholly incredible to the
generation born since 1868—when Old Japan began to
vanish in dissolving views and New Japan to emerge.
What the author has seen with his own eyes, would
amaze many Japanese born since 1868 and the readers
of the rhapsodies of tourists who study Japan from the
jin-riki-sha. Phases of tree and serpent worship are
still quite common, and will be probably for genera-

ations to come; but the phallic shrines and emblems abolished by the government in 1872 have been so far invisible to most living travellers and natives, that their once general existence and use are now scarcely suspected. Even profound scholars of the Japanese language and literature whose work dates from after the year 1872 have scarcely suspected the universality of phallic worship. Yet what we could say of this cult and its emblems, especially in treating of Shintō, the special ethnic faith of Japan, would be from sight of our own eyes besides the testimony of many witnesses.[20]

The cultus has been known in the Japanese archipelago from Riu Kiu to Yezo. Despite official edicts of abolition it is still secretly practised by the "heathen," the *inaka* of Japan. "Government law lasts three days," is an ancient proverb in Nippon. Sharp eyes have, within three months of the writing of this line, unearthed a phallic shrine within a stone's-throw of Shintō's most sacred temples at Isé. Formerly, however, these implements of worship were seen numerously—in the cornucopia distributed in the temples, in the *matsuris* or religious processions and in representation by various plastic material—and all this until 1872, to an extent that is absolutely incredible to all except the eye-witnesses, some of whose written testimonies we possess. What seems to our mind shocking and revolting was once a part of our own ancestors' faith, and until very recently was the perfectly natural and innocent creed of many millions of Japanese and is yet the same for tens of thousands of them.

We may easily see why and how that which to us is a degrading cult was not only closely allied to Shintō, but directly fostered by and properly a part of it, as soon as we read the account of the creation of the world, as contained in the national " Book of Ancient Traditions," the " Kojiki." Several of the opening paragraphs of this sacred book of Shintō are phallic myths explaining cosmogony. Yet the myths and the cult are older than the writing and are phases of primitive Japanese faith. The mystery of fatherhood is to the primitive man the mystery of creation also. To him neither the thought nor the word was at hand to put difference and transcendental separation between him and what he worshipped as a god.

Into the details of the former display and carriage of these now obscene symbols in the popular celebrations; of the behavior of even respectable citizens during the excitement and frenzy of the festivals; of their presence in the wayside shrines; of the philosophy, hideousness or pathos of the subject, we cannot here enter. We simply call attention to their existence, and to a form of thought, if not of religion, properly so-called, which has survived all imported systems of faith and which shows what the native or indigenous idea of divinity really is—an idea that profoundly affects the organization of society. To the enlightened Buddhist, Confucian, and even the modern Shintoist the phallus-worshipper is a " heathen," a "pagan," and yet he still practises his faith and rites. It is for us to hint at the powerful influence such persistent ideas have upon Japanese morals and civilization. Still further, we illustrate the basic fact which all foreign religions and all missionaries, Confucian, Buddhist, Mahometan or Christian must deal with, viz.: That the Eastern Asiatic mind runs to panthe-

ism as surely as the body of flesh and blood seeks
food.

Tree and Serpent Worship.

In prehistoric and mediæval Japan, as among the
Ainos to-day, trees and serpents as well as rocks,
rivers and other inanimate objects were worshipped,
because such of them as were supposed for reasons
known and felt to be awe-inspiring or wonderful were
"kami," that is, above the common, wonderful.[21] This
word kami is usually translated god or deity, but the
term does not conform to our ideas, by a great gulf
of difference. It is more than probable that the Japanese term kami is the same as the Aino word *kamui*,
and that the despised and conquered aboriginal savage
has furnished the mould of the ordinary Japanese idea
of god—which even to-day with them means anything
wonderful or extraordinary.[22] From the days before
history the people have worshipped trees, and do so
yet, considering them as the abodes of and as means of
communication with supernatural powers. On them
the people hang their votive offerings, twist on the
branches their prayers written on paper, avoid cutting
down, breaking or in any way injuring certain trees.
The *sakaki* tree is especially sacred, even to this day,
in funeral or Shintō services. To wound or defile a
tree sacred to a particular god was to call forth the
vengeance of the insulted deity upon the insulter, or
as the hearer of prayer upon another to whom guilt
was imputed and punishment was due.

Thus, in the days older than this present generation, but still within this century, as the writer has
witnessed, it was the custom of women betrayed by

their lovers to perform the religious act of vengeance called *Ushi toki mairi,* or going to the temple at the hour of the ox, that is at 2 A.M. First making an image or manikin of straw, she set out on her errand of revenge, with nails held in her mouth and with hammer in one hand and straw figure in the other, sometimes also having on her head a reversed tripod in which were stuck three lighted candles. Arriving at the shrine she selected a tree dedicated to a god, and then nailed the straw simulacrum of her betrayer to the trunk, invoking the kami to curse and annihilate the destroyer of her peace. She adjures the god to save his tree, impute the guilt of desecration to the traitor and visit him with deadly vengeance. The visit is repeated and nails are driven until the object of the incantation sickens and dies, or is at least supposed to do so. I have more than once seen such trees and straw images upon them and have observed others in which the large number of rusted nails and fragments of straw showed how tenaciously the superstition lingered.[23]

In instances more pleasant to witness, may be seen trees festooned with the symbolical rice-straw in cords and fringes. With these the people honor the trees as the abode of the kami, or as evidence of their faith in the renown accredited in the past.

In common with most human beings the Japanese consider the serpent an object of mystery and awe, but most of them go further and pay the ophidian a reverence and awe which is worship. Their oldest literature shows how large a part the serpent played in the so-called divine age, how it acted as progenitress of the Mikado's ancestry, and how it afforded means of incarnation for the kami or gods. Ten species of ophidia are known in the Japanese islands, but in the larger number of more or less imaginary varieties which figure in the ancient books we shall find plenty of material for fetich-worship. In perusing the "Kojiki" one scarcely knows, when he begins a story, whether the character which to all appearance is a man or woman is to end as a snake, or whether the mother after delivering her child will or will not glide into the marsh or slide away into the sea, leaving behind a trail of slime. A dragon is three-fourths serpent, and both the dragon and the serpent are prominent figures, per-haps the most prominent of the kami or gods in human or animal form in the "Kojiki" and other early legends of the gods, though the crocodile, crow, deer, dog, and other animals are kami.[24] It is therefore no wonder that serpents have been and are still worshipped by the people, that some of their gods and goddesses are liable at any time to slip away in scaly form, that famous temples are built on sites noted as being the abode or visible place of the actual water or land snake of natural history, and that the spot where a serpent is seen to-day is usually marked with a sacred emblem or a shrine.[25] We shall see how this snake-worship became not only a part of Shintō but even a notable feature in corrupt Buddhism.

Pantheism's Destruction of Boundaries.[26]

In its rudest forms, this pantheism branches out into animism or shamanism, fetichism and phallicism. In its higher forms, it becomes polytheism, idolatry and defective philosophy. Having centuries ago corrupted

Buddhism it is the malaria which, unseen and unfelt, is ready to poison and corrupt Christianity. Indeed, it has already given over to disease and spiritual death more than one once hopeful Christian believer, teacher and preacher in the Japan of our decade.

To assault and remove the incubus, to replace and refill the mind, to lift up and enlighten the Japanese peasant, science as already known and faith in one God, Creator and Father of all things, must go hand in hand. Education and civilization will do much for the ignorant *inaka* or boors, but for the cultured whose minds waver and whose feet flounder, as well as for the unlearned and priest-ridden, there is no surer help and healing than that faith in the Heavenly Father which gives the unifying thought to him who looks into creation.

Keep the boundary line clear between God and his world and all is order and discrimination. Obliterate that boundary and all is pathless morass, black chaos and on the mind the phantasms which belong to the victim of *delirium tremens.*

There is one Lawgiver. In the beginning, God. In the end, God, all in all.

3

SHINTŌ : MYTHS AND RITUAL

" In the great days of old,
   When o'er the land the gods held
     sov'reign sway,
Our fathers lov'd to say
That the bright gods with tender
   care enfold
The fortunes of Japan,
Blessing the land with many an
   holy spell :

And what they loved to tell,
We of this later age ourselves do
   prove ;
For every living man
May feast his eyes on tokens of their
   love."
—Poem of Yamagami-no Okura,
   A.D. 733.

   Baal : " While I on towers and hanging terraces,
   In shaft and obelisk, beheld my sign
   Creative, shape of first imperious law."
                   —Bayard Taylor's " Masque of the Gods."

" Thou hast also taken thy fair jewels of my gold and of my silver, which I had given thee, and madest to thyself images of men, and didst commit whoredom with them, and tookest thy broidered garments, and coveredst them : and thou hast set mine oil and mine incense before them. My meat also which I gave thee, fine flour, and oil, and honey, wherewith I fed thee, thou hast even set it before them for a sweet savor : and thus it was, saith the Lord GOD."—Ezekiel.

" If it be said (as has been the case), ' Shintoism has nothing in it,' we should be inclined to answer, ' So much the better, there is less error to counteract.' But there *is* something in it, and that . . . of a kind of which we may well avail ourselves when making known the second commandment, and the ' fountain of cleansing from all sin.' "—E. W. Syle.

" If Shintō has a dogma, it is purity."—Kaburagi.

" I will wash my hands in innocency, O Lord : and so will I go to thine altar."—Ps. xxvi. 6.

CHAPTER II

The Japanese a Young Nation

WHAT impresses us in the study of the history of
Japan is that, compared with China and Korea, she is
young. Her history is as the story of yesterday.
The nation is modern. The Japanese are as younger
children in the great family of Asia's historic people.
Broadly speaking, Japan is no older than England,
and authentic Japanese history no more ancient than
British history. In Albion, as in the Honorable
Country, there are traditions and mythologies that
project their shadows æons back of genuine records ;
but if we consider that English history begins in the
fifth, and English literature in the eighth century, then
there are other reasons besides those commonly given
for calling Japan " the England of the East."

No trustworthy traditions exist which carry the
known history of Japan farther back than the fifth
century. The means for measuring and recording
time were probably not in use until the sixth century.
The oldest documents in the Japanese language, excepting a few fragments of the seventh century, do not
antedate the year 712, and even in these the Chinese
characters are in many instances used phonetically, because the meaning of the words thus transliterated had

already been forgotten. Hence their interpretation in detail is still largely a matter of conjecture.

Yet the Japanese Archipelago was inhabited long before the dawn of history. The concurrent testimony of the earliest literary monuments, of the indigenous mythology, of folk-lore, of shell-heaps and of kitchen-middens shows that the occupation by human beings of the main islands must be ascribed to times long before the Christian era. Before written records or ritual of worship, religion existed on its active or devotional side, and there were mature growths of thought preserved and expressed orally. Poems, songs, chants and *norito* or liturgies were kept alive in the human memory, and there was a system of worship, the *name* of which was given long after the introduction of Buddhism. This descriptive term, Kami no Michi in Japanese, and Shin-tō in the Chinese as pronounced by Japanese, means the Way of the Gods, the tō or final syllable being the same as tao in Taoism. We may say that Shintō means, literally, theoslogos, theology. The customs and practices existed centuries before contact with Chinese letters, and long previous to the Shintō literature which is now extant.

Whether Kami no Michi is wholly the product of Japanese soil, or whether its rudimentary ideas were imported from the neighboring Asian continent and more or less allied to the primitive Chinese religion, is still an open question. The preponderance of argument tends, however, to show that it was an importation as to its origin, for not a few events outlined in the Japanese mythology cast shadows of reminiscence upon Korea or the Asian mainland. In its development, however, the cultus is almost wholly Japanese.

The modern forms of Shintō, as moulded by the revivalists of the eighteenth century, are at many points
notably different from the ancient faith. At the
World's Parliament of Religions at Chicago, Shintō
seemed to be the only one, and probably the last, of
the purely provincial religions.

In order to gain a picture of life in Japan before the
introduction of Chinese civilization, we must consult
those photographs of the minds of the ancient islanders which still exist in their earliest literature. The
fruits of the study of ethnology, anthropology and
archæology greatly assist us in picturing the day-
break of human life in the Morning Land. In preparing materials for the student of the religions of
Japan many laborers have wrought in various fields,
but the chief literary honors have been taken by the
English scholars, Messrs. Satow,[1] Aston,[2] and Chamberlain.[3] These untiring workers have opened the
treasures of ancient thought in the Altaic world.[4]

Although even these archaic Japanese compositions,
readable to-day only by special scholars, are more or
less affected by Chinese influences, ideas and modes of
expression, yet they are in the main faithful reflections
of the ancient life before the primitive faith of the
Japanese people was either disturbed or reduced to
system in presence of an imported religion. These
monuments of history, poetry and liturgies are the
"Kojiki," or Notices of Ancient Things; the "Manyōshu" or Myriad Leaves or Poems, and the "Norito,"
or Liturgies.

The Ancient Documents.

The first book, the " Kojiki," gives us the theology, cosmogony, mythology, and very probably, in its later portions, some outlines of history of the ancient Japanese. The " Kojiki " is the real, the dogmatic exponent, or, if we may so say, the Bible, of Shintō. The " Many-ōshu," or Book of Myriad Poems, expresses the thoughts and feelings; reflects the manners and customs of the primitive generations, and, in the same sense as do the Sagas of the Scandinavians, furnishes us un-chronological but interesting and more or less real narratives of events which have been glorified by the poets and artists. The ancient codes of law and of cere-monial procedure are of great value, while the "Norito " are excellent mirrors in which to see reflected the relig-ion called Shintō on the more active side of worship.

In a critical study, either of the general body of national tradition or of the ancient documents, we must continually be on our guard against the usual assump-tion that Chinese civilization came in earlier than it really did. This assumption colors all modern Japanese popular ideas, art and literature. The vice of the pu-pil nations surrounding the Middle Kingdom is their desire to have it believed that Chinese letters and cult-ure among them is as nearly coeval with those of China as can be made truly or falsely to appear. The Koreans, for example, would have us believe that their civilization, based on letters and introduced by Kishi, is, " four thousand years old " and contemporaneous with China's own, and that " the Koreans are among the oldest people of the world." [5]   The average modern

Japanese wishes the date of authentic or official history projected as far back as possible. Yet he is a modest man compared with his mediæval ancestor, who constructed chronology out of ink-stones. Over a thousand years ago a deliberate forgery was officially put on paper. A whole line of emperors who never lived was canonized, and clever penmen set down in ink long chapters which describe what never happened.[6] Furthermore, even after, and only eight years after the fairly honest "Kojiki" had been compiled, the book called "Nihongi," or Chronicles of Japan, was written. All the internal and not a little external evidence shows that the object of this book is to give the impression that Chinese ideas, culture and learning had long been domesticated in Japan. The "Nihongi" gives dates of events supposed to have happened fifteen hundred years before, with an accuracy which may be called villainous; while the "Kojiki" states that Wani, a Korean teacher, brought the "Thousand Character Classic" to Japan in A.D. 285, though that famous Chinese book was not composed until the sixth century, or A.D. 550.[7]

Even to this day it is nearly impossible for an American to get a Korean "frog in the well"[8] to understand why the genuine native life and history, language and learning of his own peninsular country is of greater value to the student than the pedantry borrowed from China. Why these possess any interest to a "scholar" is a mystery to the head in the horsehair net. Anything of value, he thinks, *must* be on the Chinese model. What is not Chinese is foolish and fit for women and children only. Furthermore, Korea "always had" Chinese learning. This is the sum of the arguments of the Korean literati, even as it used to be of the old-time hatless Yedo scholar of shaven skull and topknot.

Despite Japanese independence and even arrogance in certain other lines, the thought of the demolition of cherished notions of vast antiquity is very painful. Critical study of ancient traditions is still dangerous, even in parliamentary Nippon. Hence the unbiassed student must depend on his own reading of and judgment upon the ancient records, assisted by the thorough work done by the English scholars Aston, Satow, Chamberlain, Bramsen and others.

It was the coming of Buddhism in the sixth century, and the implanting on the soil of Japan of a system of religion in which were temples with all that was attractive to the eye, gorgeous ritual, scriptures, priesthood, codes of morals, rigid discipline, a system of dogmatics in which all was made positive and clear, that made the variant myths and legends somewhat uniform. The faith of Shaka, by winning adherents both at the court and among the leading men of intelligence, reacted upon the national traditions so as to compel their collection and arrangement into definite formulas. In due time the mythology, poetry and ritual was, as we have seen, committed to writing and the whole system called Shintō, in distinction from Butsu-dō, the Way of the Gods from the Way of the Buddhas. Thus we can see more clearly the outward and visible manifestations of Shintō. In forming our judgment, however, we must put aside those descriptions which are found in the works of European writers, from Marco Polo and Mendez Pinto down to the year 1870. Though these were good observers, they were often necessarily mistaken in their deductions. For,

as we shall see in our lecture on Riyōbu or Mixed
Buddhism, Shintō was, from the ninth century until
late into the nineteenth century, absorbed in Buddhism so as to be next to invisible.

Origins of the Japanese People.

Without detailing processes, but giving only results,
our view of the origin of the Japanese people and of
their religion is in the main as follows :

The oldest seats of human habitation in the Japanese Archipelago lie between the thirtieth and thirty-
eighth parallels of north latitude. South of the thirty-
fourth parallel, it seems, though without proof of
writing or from tradition, that the Malay type and
blood from the far south probably predominated, with,
however, much infusion from the northern Asian main-
land.

Between the thirty-fourth and thirty-sixth parallels,
and west of the one hundred and thirty-eighth meridian
of longitude, may be found what is still the choicest,
richest and most populous part of The Country Between Heaven and Earth. Here the prevailing element was Korean and Tartar.

To the north and east of this fair country lay the
Emishi savages, or Ainos.

In "the world" within the ken of the prehistoric
dwellers in what is now the three islands, Hondo, Kiushiu and Shikoku, there was no island of Yezo and no
China ; while Korea was but slightly known, and the
lands farther westward were unheard of except as the
home of distant tribes.

Three distinct lines of tradition point to the near

peninsula or the west coast of Japan as the "Heaven" whence descended the tribe which finally grew to be dominant. The islands of Tsushima and Iki were the stepping-stones of the migration out of which rose what may be called the southern or Tsukushi cycle of legend, Tsukushi being the ancient name of Kiushiu.

Idzumo is the holy land whence issued the second stream of tradition.

The third course of myth and legend leads us into Yamato, whence we behold the conquest of the Mikado's home-land and the extension of his name and influence into the regions east of the Hakoné Mountains, including the great plain of Yedo, where modern Tōkiō now stands.

We shall take the term "Yamato" as the synonym of the prehistoric but discernible beginnings of national life. It represents the seat of the tribe whose valor and genius ultimately produced the Mikado system. It was through this house or tribe that Japanese history took form. The reverence for the ruler long afterward entitled "Son of Heaven" is the strongest force in the national history. The spirit and prowess of these early conquerors have left an indelible impress upon the language and the mind of the nation in the phrase Yamato Damashi—the spirit of (Divine and unconquerable) Japan.

The story of the conquest of the land, in its many phases, recalls that of the Aryans in India, of the Hebrews in Canaan, of the Romans in Europe and of the Germanic races in North America. The Yamato men gradually advanced to conquest under the impulse, as they believed, of a divine command.[9] They were sent from Takama - no - hara, the High Plain of Heaven.

Theirs was the war, of men with a nobler creed, having agriculture and a feudal system of organization which furnished resources for long campaigns, against hunters and fishermen. They had improved artillery and used iron against stone. Yet they conquered and pacified not only by superior strategy, tactics, weapons and valor, but also by advanced fetiches and dogma. They captured the religion of their enemies as well as their bodies, lands and resources. They claimed that their ancestors were from Heaven, that the Sun was their kinswoman and that their chief, or Mikado, was vicegerent of the Heavenly gods, but that those whom they conquered were earth-born or sprung from the terrestrial divinities.

Mikadoism the Heart of Shintō.

As success came to their arms and their chief's power was made more sure, they developed further the dogma of the Mikado's divinity and made worship centre in him as the earthly representative of the Sun and Heaven. His fellow-conquerors and ministers, as fast as they were put in lordship over conquered provinces, or indigenous chieftains who submitted obediently to his sway or yielded graciously to his prowess, were named as founders of temples and in later generations worshipped and became gods.[10] One of the motives for, and one of the guiding principles in the selections of the floating myths, was that the ancestry of the chieftains loyal to the Mikado might be shown to be from the heavenly gods. Both the narratives of the "Kojiki" and the liturgies show this clearly.

The nature-worship, which was probably practised throughout the whole archipelago, became part of the system as government and society were made uniform on the Yamato model. It seems at least possible, if Buddhism had not come in so soon, that the ordinary features of a religion, dogmatic and ethical codes, would have been developed. In a word, the Kami no Michi, or religion of the islanders in prehistoric times before the rise of Mikadoism, must be carefully distinguished from the politico-ecclesiasticism which the system called Shintō reveals and demands. The early religion, first in the hands of politicians and later under the pens and voices of writers and teachers at the Imperial Court, became something very different from its original form. As surely as Kōbō later captured Shintō, making material for Buddhism out of it and overlaying it in Riyōbu, so the Yamato men made political capital out of their own religion and that of the subject tribes. The divine sovereign of Japan and his political church did exactly what the state churches of Europe, both pagan and Christian, have done before and since the Christian era.

Further, in studying the "Kojiki," we must remember that the sacred writings sprang out of the religion, and that the system was not an evolution from the book. Customs, ritual, faith and prayer existed long before they were written about or recorded in ink. Moreover, the philosophy came later than the practice, the deeds before the myths, and the joy and terror of the visible universe before the cosmogony or theogony, while the book-preface was probably written last of all.

The sun was first, and then came the wonder, admiration and worship of men. The personification and pedigree of the sun were late figments. To connect their ancestors with the sun-goddess and the heavenly gods, was a still later enterprise of the "Mikado reverencers" of this earlier time. Both the god-way in its early forms and Shintō in its later development, were to them political as well as ecclesiastical institutes of dogma. Both the religion which they themselves brought and cultivated and the aboriginal religion which the Yamato men found, were used as engines in the making of Mikadoism, which is the heart of Shintō.

Not until two centuries after the coming of Buddhism and of Asiatic civilization did it occur to the Japanese to reduce to writing the floating legends and various cycles of tradition which had grown up luxuriantly in different parts of "the empire," or to express in the Chinese character the prayers and thanksgivings which had been handed down orally through many generations. These norito had already assumed elegant literary form, rich in poetic merit, long before Chinese writing was known. They, far more than the less certain philosophy of the "Kojiki," are of undoubted native origin. It is nearly certain that the prehistoric Japanese did not borrow the literary forms of the god-way from China, as any one familiar with the short, evenly balanced and antithetical sentences of Chinese style can see at once. The norito are expressions, in the rhythmical and rhetorical form of worship, of the articles of faith set forth in the historic summary which we have given. We propose to illustrate the dogmas by quoting from the rituals in Mr. Satow's masterly translation. The following was addressed to the sun-goddess (Amatérasu no Mikami, or the From-

Heaven-Shining-Great-Deity) by the priest-envoy of the priestly Nakatomi family sent annually to the temples at Isé, the Mecca of Shintō. The *sovran* referred to in the ritual is the Mikado. This word and all the others printed in capitals are so rendered in order to express in English the force of "an untranslatable honorific syllable, supposed to be originally identical with a root meaning 'true,' but no longer possessing that signification." Instead of the word "earth," that of " country " (Japan) is used as the correlative of Heaven.

Ritual in Praise of the Sun-goddess.

He (the priest-envoy) says : Hear all of you, ministers of the gods and sanctifiers of offerings, the great ritual, the heavenly ritual, declared in the great presence of the From-Heaven-Shining-Great-DEITY, whose praises are fulfilled by setting up the stout pillars of the great HOUSE, and exalting the cross-beams to the plain of high heaven at the sources of the Isuzu River at Uji in Watarai.

He says : It is the sovran's great WORD. Hear all of you, ministers of the gods and sanctifiers of offerings, the fulfilling of praises on this seventeenth day of the sixth moon of this year, as the morning sun goes up in glory, of the Oho-Nakatomi, who —having abundantly piled up like a range of hills the TRIBUTE thread and sanctified LIQUOR and FOOD presented as of usage by the people of the deity's houses attributed to her in the three departments and in various countries and places, so that she deign to bless his [the Mikado's] LIFE as a long LIFE, and his AGE as a luxuriant AGE eternally and unchangingly as multitudinous piles of rock; may deign to bless the CHILDREN who are born to him, and deigning to cause to flourish the five kinds of grain which the men of a hundred functions and the peasants of the countries in the four quarters of the region under heaven long and peacefully cultivate and

eat, and guarding and benefiting them to deign to bless them
—is hidden by the great offering-wands.

In the Imperial City the ritual services were very
imposing. Those in expectation of the harvest were
held in the great hall of the Jin-Gi-Kuan, or Council of
the Gods of Heaven and Earth. The description of
the ceremonial is given by Mr. Satow.[11] In the prayers
offered to the sun-goddess for harvest, and in thanksgiving to her for bestowing dominion over land and
sea upon her descendant the Mikado, occurs the following passage:

I declare in the great presence of the From-Heaven-Shining-
Great-DEITY who sits in Isé. Because the sovran great GODDESS
bestows on him the countries of the four quarters over which
her glance extends, as far as the limit where heaven stands up
like a wall, as far as the bounds where the country stands up
distant, as far as the limit where the blue clouds spread flat, as
far as the bounds where the white clouds lie away fallen—the
blue sea plain as far as the limit whither come the prows of the
ships without drying poles or paddles, the ships which continuously crowd on the great sea plain, and the road which men
travel by land, as far as the limit whither come the horses' hoofs,
with the baggage-cords tied tightly, treading the uneven rocks
and tree-roots and standing up continuously in a long path without a break—making the narrow countries wide and the hilly
countries plain, and as it were drawing together the distant
countries by throwing many tens of ropes over them—he will
pile up the first-fruits like a range of hills in the great presence
of the sovran great GODDESS, and will peacefully enjoy the re-
mainder.

Phallic Symbols.

To form one's impression of the Kami no Michi
wholly from the poetic liturgies, the austere simplicity
of the miyas or shrines, or the worship at the palace or

4

capital, would be as misleading as to gather our ideas of the status of popular education from knowing only of the scholars at court. Among the common people the real basis of the god-way was ancestor-worship. From the very first this trait and habit of the Japanese can be discerned. Their tenacity in holding to it made the Confucian ethics more welcome when they came. Furthermore, this reverence for the dead profoundly influenced and modified Buddhism, so that to-day the altars of both religions exist in the same house, the dead ancestors becoming both kami and buddhas.

Modern taste has removed from sight what were once the common people's symbols of the god-way, that is of ancestor worship. The extent of the phallus cult and its close and even vital connection with the god-way, and the general and innocent use of the now prohibited emblems, tax severely the credulity of the Occidental reader. The processes of the ancient mind can hardly be understood except by vigorous power of the imagination and by sympathy with the primeval man. To the critical student, however, who has lived among the people and the temples devoted to this worship, who knows how innocent and how truly sincere and even reverent and devout in the use of these symbols the worshippers are, the matter is measurably clear. He can understand the soil, root and flower even while the most strange specimen is abhorrent to his taste, and while he is most active in destroying that mental climate in which such worship, whether native or exotic, can exist and flourish.

In none of the instances in which I have been eye-witness of the cult, of the person officiating or of the emblem, have I had any reason to doubt the sincerity

of the worshipper. I have never had reason to look
upon the implements or the system as anything else
than the endeavor of man to solve the mystery of Being and Power. In making use of these emblems, the
Japanese worshipper simply professes his faith in such
solution as has seemed to him attainable.

That this cultus was quite general in pre-Buddhistic Japan, as in many other ancient countries, is certain from the proofs of language, literature, external
monuments and relics which are sufficiently numerous.
Its organic connection with the god-way may be clearly
shown.

To go farther back in point of time than the "Kojiki,"
we find that even before the development of art in very
ancient Japan, the male gods were represented by a
symbol which thus became an image of the deity himself. This token was usually made of stone, though
often of wood, and in later times of terra-cotta, of cast
and wrought iron and even of gold.[12]

Under the direct influence of such a cult, other objects appealed to the imagination or served the temporary purpose of the worshipper as *ex-voto* to hang up
in the shrines, such as the mushroom, awabi, various
other shells and possibly the fire-drill. It is only in
the decay of the cultus, in the change of view and
centre of thought compelled by another religion, that
representations of the old emblems ally themselves
with sensualism or immorality. It is that natural
degradation of one man's god into another man's
devil, which conversion must almost of necessity bring,
that makes the once revered symbol "obscene," and
talk about it become, in a descending scale, dirty, foul,
filthy, nasty. That the Japanese suffer from the moral

effluvia of a decayed cult which was once as the very
vertebral column of the national body of religion, is
evident to every one who acquaints himself with their
popular speech and literature.

How closely and directly phallicism is connected
with the god-way, and why there were so many Shintō
temples devoted to this latter cult and furnished with
symbols, is shown by study of the " Kojiki." The two
opening sections of this book treat of kami that were
in the minds even of the makers of the myths little
more than mud and water[13]—the mere bioplasm of
deity. The seven divine generations are " born," but
do nothing except that they give Izanagi and Izanami
a jewelled spear. With this pair come differentiation
of sex. It is immediately on the apparition of the consciousness of sex that motion, action and creation
begin, and the progress of things visible ensues. The
details cannot be put into English, but it is enough, besides noting the conversation and union of the pair, to
say that the term meaning giving birth to, refers to
inanimate as well as animate things. It is used in
reference to the islands which compose the archipelago
as well as to the various kami which seem, in many
cases, to be nothing more than the names of things or
places.

Fire-myths and Ritual.

Fire is, in a sense, the foundation and first necessity
of civilization, and it is interesting to study the myths
as to the origin of fire, and possibly even more interesting to compare the Greek and Japanese stories. As we
know, old-time popular etymology makes Prometheus
the fore-thinker and brother of Epimetheus the after-

thinker. He is the stealer of the fire from heaven, in order to make men share the secret of the gods. Comparative philology tells us, however, that the Sanskrit *Pramantha* is a stick that produces fire. The "Kojiki" does indeed contain what is probably the later form of the fire-myth about two brothers, Prince Fire-Shine and Fire-Fade, which suggests both the later Greek myth of the fore- and after-thinker and a tradition of a flood. The first, and most probably older, myth in giving the origin of fire does it in true Japanese style, with details of parturition. After numerous other deities had been born of Izanagi and Izanami, it is said "that they gave birth to the Fire-Burning-Swift-Male-Deity, another name for whom is the Deity-Fire-Shining-Prince, and another name is the Deity-Fire-Shining-Elder." In the other ancient literature this fire-god is called Ho-musubi, the Fire-Producer.

Izanami yielded up her life upon the birth of her son, the fire-god; or, as the sacred text declares, she "divinely retired"[14] into Hades. From her corpse sprang up the pairs of gods of clay, of metal, and other kami that possessed the potency of calming or subduing fire, for clay resists and water extinguishes. Between the mythical and the liturgical forms of the original narrative there is considerable variation.

The Norito entitled the "Quieting of Fire" gives the ritual form of the myth. It contains, like so many Norito, less the form of prayer to the Fire-Producer than a promise of offerings. Not so much by petitions as by the inducements of gifts did the ancient worshippers hope to save the palace of the Mikado from the fire-god's wrath. We omit from the text those details which are offensive to modern and western taste.

I declare with the great ritual, the heavenly ritual, which was bestowed on him at the time when, by the WORD of the Sovran's dear progenitor and progenitrix, who divinely remain in the plain of high heaven, they bestowed on him the region under heaven, saying :

"Let the Sovran GRANDCHILD's augustness tranquilly rule over the country of fresh spikes which flourishes in the midst of the reed-moor as a peaceful region."

When . . . Izanami . . . had deigned to bear the many hundred myriads of gods, she also deigned to bear her dear youngest child of all, the Fire-producer god, . . . and said :

". . . My dear elder brother's augustness shall rule the upper country ; I will rule the lower country," she deigned to hide in the rocks ; and having come to the flat hills of darkness, she thought and said : "I have come hither, having borne and left a bad-hearted child in the upper country, ruled over by my illustrious elder brother's augustness," and going back she bore other children. Having borne the water-goddess, the gourd, the river-weed, and the clay-hill maiden, four sorts of things, she taught them with words, and made them to know, saying : "If the heart of this bad-hearted child becomes violent, let the water-goddess take the gourd, and the clay-hill maiden take the river-weed, and pacify him."

In consequence of this I fulfil his praises, and say that for the things set up, so that he may deign not to be awfully quick of heart in the great place of the Sovran GRANDCHILD's augustness, there are provided bright cloth, glittering cloth, soft cloth, and coarse cloth, and the five kinds of things ; as to things which dwell in the blue-sea plain, there are things wide of fin and narrow of fin, down to the weeds of the shore ; as to LIQUOR, raising high the beer-jars, filling and ranging in rows the bellies of the beer-jars, piling the offerings up, even to rice in grain and rice in ear, like a range of hills, I fulfil his praises with the great ritual, the heavenly ritual.

Izanagi, after shedding tears over his consort, whose death was caused by the birth of the fire-god, slays the fire-god, and follows her into the Root-land, or Hades, whereupon begins another round of wonderful stories of the birth of many gods. Among these, though evidently out of another cycle of legends, is the story of the birth of the three gods—Fire-Shine, Fire Climax and Fire-Fade, to which we have already referred.

The fire-drill mentioned in the "Kojiki" suggests easily the same line of thought with the myths of cosmogony and theogony, and it is interesting to note that this archaic implement is still used at the sacred temples of Isé to produce fire. After the virgin priestesses perform the sacred dances in honor of local deities the water for their bath is heated by fires kindled by heaps of old *harai* or amulets made from temple-wood bought at the Mecca of Japan. It is even probable that the retention of the fire-drill in the service of Shintō is but a survival of phallicism.

The liturgy for the pacification of the gods of fire is worth noticing. The full form of the ritual, when compared with a legend in the "Nihongi," shows that a myth was "partly devised to explain the connection of an hereditary family of priests with the god whose shrine they served ; it is possible that the claim to be directly descended from the god had been disputed."[15] The Norito first recites poetically the descent of Ninigi, the grandchild of the sun-goddess from heaven, and the quieting of the turbulent kami.

I (the diviner), declare: When by the WORD of the progenitor and progenitrix, who divinely remaining in the plain of high heaven, deigned to make the beginning of things, they divinely deigned to assemble the many hundred myriads of gods in the high city of heaven, and deigned divinely to take counsel in council, saying : " When we cause our Sovran GRAND-CHILD'S augustness to leave heaven's eternal seat, to cleave a path with might through heaven's manifold clouds, and to descend from heaven, with orders tranquilly to rule the country of fresh spikes, which flourishes in the midst of the reed-moor as a peaceful country, what god shall we send first to divinely sweep away, sweep away and subdue the gods who are turbulent in the country of fresh spikes;" all the gods pondered and declared: "You shall send Aménohohi's augustness, and subdue them," declared they. Wherefore they sent him down from heaven, but he did not declare an answer; and having next sent Takémikuma's augustness, he also, obeying his father's words, did not declare an answer. Amé-no-waka-hiko also, whom they sent, did not declare an answer, but immediately perished by the calamity of a bird on high. Wherefore they pondered afresh by the WORD of the heavenly gods, and having deigned to send down from heaven the two pillars of gods, Futsunushi and Takémika-dzuchi's augustness, who having deigned divinely to sweep away, and sweep away, and deigned divinely to soften, and soften the gods who were turbulent, and silenced the rocks, trees, and the least leaf of herbs likewise that had spoken, they caused the Sovran GRAND-CHILD's augustness to descend from heaven.

I fulfil your praises, saying : As to the OFFERINGS set up, so that the sovran gods who come into the heavenly HOUSE of the Sovran GRANDCHILD's augustness, which, after he had fixed upon as a peaceful country—the country of great Yamato where the sun is high, as the centre of the countries of the four quarters bestowed upon him when he was thus sent down from heaven—stoutly planting the HOUSE-pillars on the bottom-most rocks, and exalting the cross-beams to the plain of high heaven, the builders had made for his SHADE from the heavens and SHADE from the sun, and wherein he will tranquilly rule the country as a peaceful country—may, without deigning to be turbulent, deigning to be fierce, and deigning to hurt, knowing, by virtue of their divinity, the things which were begun in the plain of high heaven, deigning to correct with Divine-correcting and Great-correcting, remove hence out to the clean places of the mountain-streams which look far away over the four quarters, and rule them as their own place. Let the Sovran gods tranquilly take with clear HEARTS, as peaceful OFFERINGS and sufficient OFFERINGS the great OFFERINGS which I set up, piling them upon the tables like a range of hills, providing bright cloth, glittering cloth, soft cloth, and coarse cloth ; as a thing to see plain in—a mirror : as things to play with—beads : as things to shoot off with—a bow and arrows : as a thing to strike and cut with—a sword : as a thing which gallops out—a horse ; as to LIQUOR—raising high the beer jars, filling and ranging in rows the bellies of the beer-jars, with grains of rice and ears ; as to the things which dwell in the hills—things soft of hair, and things rough of hair ; as to the things which grow in the great field plain—sweet herbs and bitter herbs ; as to the things which dwell in the blue sea plain—things broad of fin and things narrow of fin, down to weeds of the offing and weeds of the shore, and without deigning to be turbulent, deigning to be fierce, and deigning to hurt, remove out to the wide and clean places of the mountain-streams, and by virtue of their divinity be tranquil.

In this ritual we find the origin of evil attributed to wicked kami, or gods. To get rid of them is to be free from the troubles of life. The object of the ritual worship was to compel the turbulent and malevolent kami to go out from human habitations to the mountain solitudes and rest there. The dogmas of both god-possession and of the power of exorcism were not, however, held exclusively by the high functionaries of the official religion, but were part of the faith of all the people. To this day both the tenets and the practices are popular under various forms.

Besides the twenty-seven Norito which are found in the Yengishiki, published at the opening of the tenth century, there are many others composed for single occasions. Examples of these are found in the Government Gazettes. One celebrates the Mikado's removal from Kiōto to Tōkiō, another was written and recited to add greater solemnity to the oath which he took to govern according to modern liberal principles and to form a national parliament. To those Japanese whose first idea of duty is loyalty to the emperor, Shintō thus becomes a system of patriotism exalted to the rank of a religion. Even Christian natives of Japan can use much of the phraseology of the Norito while addressing their petitions on behalf of their chief magistrate to the King of kings.

The primitive worship of the sun, of light, of fire, has left its impress upon the language and in vernacular art and customs. Among scores of derivations of Japanese words (often more pleasing than scientific), in which the general term *hi* enters, is that which finds in the word for man, *hito*, the meaning of "light-bearer." On the face of the broad terminal tiles of the house-roofs, we still see moulded the river-weed, with which the Clay-Hill Maiden pacified the Fire-God. On the frontlet of the warrior's helmet, in the old days of arrow and armor, glittered in brass on either side of his crest the same symbol of power and victory.

Having glanced at the ritual of Shintō, let us now examine the teachings of its oldest book.

"THE KOJIKI" AND ITS TEACHINGS

> " Japan is not a land where men need pray,
> For 'tis itself divine :
> Yet do I lift my voice in prayer. . . ."
>
> Hitomaro, † A.D. 737.

" Now when chaos had begun to condense, but force and form were not yet manifest, and there was naught named, naught done, who could know its shape ? Nevertheless Heaven and Earth first parted, and the three Deities performed the commencement of creation ; the Passive and Active Essences then developed, and the Two Spirits became the ancestors of all things."—Preface of Yasumarō (A.D. 712) to the "Kojiki."

" These, the ' Kojiki ' and ' Nihongi ' are their [the Shintōists] canonical books, . . . and almost their every word is considered undeniable truth."

" The Shintō faith teaches that God inspired the foundation of the Mikadoate, and that it is therefore sacred."—Kaburagi.

" We now reverently make our prayer to Them [Our Imperial Ancestors] and to our Illustrious Father [Komei, † 1867], and implore the help of Their Sacred Spirits, and make to Them solemn oath never at this time nor in the future to fail to be an example to Our subjects in the observance of the Law [Constitution] hereby established."—Imperial oath of the Emperor Mutsuhito in the sanctuary in the Imperial Palace, Tōkiō, February 11, 1889.

" Shintō is not our national religion A faith existed before it, which was its source. It grew out of superstitious teaching and mistaken tradition. The history of the rise of Shintō proves this."—T. Matsugami.

" Makoto wo moté KAMI NO MICHI wo oshiyuréba nari." (Thou teachest the way of God in truth.)—Mark xii. 14.

" Ware wa MICHI nari, Makoto nari, Inochi nari."—John xiv. 6.—The New Testament in Japanese.

CHAPTER III

"The Kojiki" and its Myths of Cosmogony

As to the origin of the "Kojiki," we have in the closing sentences of the author's preface the sole documentary authority explaining its scope and certifying to its authenticity. Briefly the statement is this: The "Heavenly Sovereign" or Mikado, Temmu (A.D. 673–686), lamenting that the records possessed by the chief families were "mostly amplified by empty falsehoods," and fearing that "the grand foundation of the monarchy" would be destroyed, resolved to preserve the truth. He therefore had the records carefully examined, compared, and their errors eliminated. There happened to be in his household a man of marvellous memory, named Hiyéda Aré, who could repeat, without mistake, the contents of any document he had ever seen, and never forgot anything which he had heard. This person was duly instructed in the genuine traditions and old language of former ages, and made to repeat them until he had the whole by heart. "Before the undertaking was completed," which probably means before it could be committed to writing, "the emperor died, and for twenty-five years Aré's memory was the sole depository of what afterwards received the title of 'Kojiki.' . . . At the end of this interval the Empress Gemmiō ordered Yasumarō to write it down from the mouth of Aré, which accounts for the completion of the manuscript in so short a time as four months and a half,"[1] in A.D. 712.

It is from the "Kojiki" that we obtain most of our ideas of ancient life and thought. The "Nihongi," or Chronicles of Japan, expressed very largely in Chinese phrases and with Chinese technical and philosophical terms, further assists us to get a measurably correct idea of what is called The Divine Age. Of the two books, however, the "Kojiki" is much more valuable as a true record, because, though rude in style and exceedingly naïve in expression, and by no means free from Chinese thoughts and phrases, it is marked by a genuinely Japanese cast of thought and method of composition. Instead of the terse, carefully measured, balanced, and antithetical sentences of correct Chinese, those of the "Kojiki" are long and involved, and without much logical connection. The "Kojiki" contains the real notions, feelings, and beliefs of Japanese who lived before the eighth century.

Remembering that prefaces are, like porticos, usually added last of all, we find that in the beginning all things were in chaos. Heaven and earth were not separated. The world substance floated in the cosmic mass, like oil on water or a fish in the sea. Motion in some way began. The ethereal portions sublimed and formed the heavens; the heavier residuum became the present earth. In the plain of high heaven, when the heaven and earth began, were born three kami who "hid their bodies," that is, passed away or died. Out of the warm mould of the earth a germ sprouted, and from this were born two kami, who also were born

alone, and died. After these heavenly kami came forth
what are called the seven divine generations, or line
of seven kami.[2]

To express the opening lines of the "Kojiki" in terms
of our own speech and in the moulds of Western
thought, we may say that matter existed before mind
and the gods came forth, as it were, by spontaneous
evolution. The first thing that appeared out of the
warm earth-muck was like a rush-sprout, and this became a kami, or god. From this being came forth
others, which also produced beings, until there were
perfect bodies, sex and differentiation of powers. The
"Nihongi," however, not only gives a different view of
this evolution basing it upon the dualism of Chinese
philosophy—that is, of the active and passive principles—and uses Chinese technical terminology, but
gives lists of kami that differ notably from those in
the "Kojiki." This latter fact seems to have escaped
the attention of those who write freely about what
they imagine to be the early religion of the Japanese.[3]

After this introduction, in which "Dualities, Trini-
ties, and Supreme Deities " have been discovered by
writers unfamiliar with the genius of the Japanese language, there follows an account of the creation of the
habitable earth by Izanami and Izanagi, whose names
mean the Male - Who - Invites and the Female-Who-
Invites. The heavenly kami commanded these two
gods to consolidate and give birth to the drifting
land. Standing on the floating bridge of heaven,
the male plunged his jewel-spear into the unstable
waters beneath, stirring them until they gurgled and
congealed. When he drew forth the spear, the drops
trickling from its point formed an island, ever after-

ward called Onokoro-jima, or the Island of the Congealed Drop. Upon this island they descended. The creative pair, or divine man and woman, now separated to make a journey round the island, the male to the left, the female to the right. At their meeting the female spoke first: "How joyful to meet a lovely man!" The male, offended that the woman had spoken first, required the circuit to be repeated. On their second meeting, the man cried out: "How joyful to meet a lovely woman!" This island on which they had descended was the first of several which they brought into being. In poetry it is the Island of the Congealed Drop. In common geography it is identified as Awaji, at the entrance of the Inland Sea. Thence followed the creation of the other visible objects in nature.

Izanagi's Visit to Hades and Results.

After the birth of the god of fire, which nearly destroyed the mother's life, Izanami fled to the land of roots or of darkness, that is into Hades. Izanagi, like a true Orpheus, followed his Eurydice and beseeched her to come back to earth to complete with him the work of creation. She parleyed so long with the gods of the underworld that her consort, breaking off a tooth of his comb, lighted it as a torch and rushed in. He found her putrefied body, out of which had been born the eight gods of thunder. Horrified at the awful foulness which he found in the underworld, he rushed up and out, pursued by the Ugly-Female-of-Hades. By artifices that bear a wonderful resemblance to those in Teutonic fairy tales, he blocked up the way. His head-dress, thrown at his pursuer,

turned into grapes which she stopped to eat. The
teeth of his comb sprouted into a bamboo forest, which
detained her. The three peaches were used as pro-
jectiles; his staff which stuck up in the ground became
a gate, and a mighty rock was used to block up the
narrow pass through the mountains. Each of these
objects has its relation to place-names in Idzumo or
to superstitions that are still extant. The peaches and
the rocks became gods, and on this incident, by which
the beings in Hades were prevented from advance and
successful mischief on earth, is founded one of the norito which Mr. Satow gives in condensed form. The
names of the three gods,[1] Youth and Maiden of the
Many Road-forkings, and Come-no-further Gate, are
expressed and invoked in the praises bestowed on them
in connection with the offerings.

He (the priest) says : I declare in the presence of the sovran
gods, who like innumerable piles of rocks sit closing up the
way in the multitudinous road-forkings . . . I fulfil your
praises by declaring your NAMES, Youth and Maiden of the
Many Road-forkings and Come-no-further Gate, and say : for
the OFFERINGS set up that you may prevent [the servants of the
monarch] from being poisoned by and agreeing with the things
which shall come roughly-acting and hating from the Root-
country, the Bottom-country, that you may guard the bottom
(of the gate) when they come from the bottom, guard the
top when they come from the top, guarding with nightly
guard and with daily guard, and may praise them — peacefully take the great OFFERINGS which are set up by piling them up like a range of hills, that is to say, providing bright cloth, etc., . . . and sitting closing-up the
way like innumerable piles of rock in the multitudinous road-
forkings, deign to praise the sovran GRANDCHILD'S augustness
eternally and unchangingly, and to bless his age as a luxuriant AGE.

5

Retreating to another part of the world—that is, into southwestern Japan—Izanami purified himself by bathing in a stream. While washing himself,[5] many kami were born from the rinsings of his person, one of them, from the left eye (the left in Japanese is always the honorable side), being the far-shining or heaven-illuminating kami, whose name, Amatérasu, or Heaven-shiner, is usually translated "The Sun-goddess." This personage is the centre of the system of Shintō. The creation of gods by a process of cleansing has had a powerful effect on the Japanese, who usually associate cleanliness of the body (less moral, than physical) with godliness.

It is not necessary to detail further the various stories which make up the Japanese mythology. Some of these are lovely and beautiful, but others are horrible and disgusting, while the dominant note throughout is abundant filthiness.

Professor Basil Hall Chamberlain, who has done the world such good service in translating into English the whole of the Kojiki, and furnishing it with learned commentary and notes, has well said:

" The shocking obscenity of word and act to which the ' Records ' bear witness is another ugly feature which must not quite be passed over in silence. It is true that decency, as we understand it, is a very modern product, and it is not to be looked for in any society in the barbarous stage. At the same time, the whole range of literature might perhaps be ransacked for a parallel to the naïve filthiness of the passage forming Sec. IV. of the following translation, or to the extraordinary topic which the hero Yamato-Také and his mistress Miyadzŭ are made to select as the theme of poetical repartee. One passage likewise would lead us to suppose that the most beastly crimes were commonly committed." [6]

Indeed, it happens in several instances that the thread by which the marvellous patchwork of unrelated and varying local myths is joined together, is an indecent love story.

A thousand years after the traditions of the Kojiki had been committed to writing, and orthodox Shintō commentators had learned science from the Dutch at Nagasaki, the stirring of the world mud by Izanagi's spear[7] was gravely asserted to be the cause of the diurnal revolution of the earth upon its axis, the point of the axis being still the jewel spear.[8] Onogoro-jima, or the Island of the Congealed Drop, was formerly at the north pole,[9] but subsequently removed to its present position. How this happened is not told.

Life in Japan During the Divine Age.

Now that the Kojiki is in English and all may read it, we can clearly see who and what were the Japanese in the ages before letters and Chinese civilization; for these stories of the kami are but legendary and mythical accounts of men and women. One could scarcely recognize in the islanders of eleven or twelve hundred years ago, the polished, brilliant, and interesting people of to-day. Yet truth compels us to say that social morals in Dai Nippon, even with telegraphs and railways, are still more like those of ancient days than readers of rhapsodies by summer tourists might suppose. These early Japanese, indeed, were possibly in a stage of civilization somewhat above that of the most advanced of the American Indians when first met by Europeans, for they had a rude system of agriculture and knew the art of fashioning iron into tools and weapons. Still, they were very barbarous, certainly as much so as our Germanic "forbears." They lived in huts. They were without writing or commerce, and were able to count only to ten.[10] Their cruelty was as revolting as that of the savage tribes of America. The family was in its most rudimentary stage, with little or no restraint upon the passions of men. Children of the same father, but not of the same mother, could intermarry. The instances of men marrying their sisters or aunts were very common. There was no art, unless the making of clay images, to take the place of the living human victims buried up to their necks in earth and left to starve on the death of their masters,[11] may be designated as such.

The Magatama, or curved jewels, being made of ground and polished stone may be called jewelry; but since some of these prehistoric ornaments dug up from the ground are found to be of jade, a mineral which does not occur in Japan, it is evident that some of these tokens of culture came from the continent. Many other things produced by more or less skilled mechanics, the origin of which is poetically recounted in the story of the dancing of Uzumé before the cave in which the Sun-goddess had hid herself,[12] were of continental origin. Evidently these men of the god-way had passed the "stone age," and, probably without going through the intermediate bronze age, were artificers of iron and skilled in its use. Most of the names of metals and of many other substances, and the terms used in the arts and sciences, betray by their tell-tale etymology their Chinese origin. Indeed, it is evident that some of the leading kami were born in Korea or Tartary.

Then as now the people in Japan loved nature, and
were quickly sensitive to her beauty and profoundly
in sympathy with her varied phenomena. In the mediæval ages, Japanese Wordsworths are not unknown.[13]
Sincerely they loved nature, and in some respects they
seemed to understand the character of their country
far better than the alien does or can. Though a land
of wonderful beauty, the Country of Peaceful Shores is
enfolded in powers of awful destructiveness. With
the earthquake and volcano, the typhoon and the tidal
wave, beauty and horror alternate with a swiftness
that is amazing.

Probably in no portion of the earth are the people
and the land more like each other or apparently better
acquainted with each other. Nowhere are thought
and speech more reflective of the features of the landscape. Even after ten centuries, the Japanese are, in
temperament, what the Kojiki reveals them to have
been in their early simplicity. Indeed, just as the
modern Frenchman, down beneath his outward envi-
ronments and his habiliments cut and fitted yesterday,
is intrinsically the same Gaul whom Julius Cæsar described eighteen hundred years ago, so the gentleman
of Tōkiō or Kiōto is, in his mental make-up, wonderfully like his ancestors described by the first Japanese
Stanley, who shed the light of letters upon the night
of unlettered Japan and darkest Dai Nippon.

The Kojiki reveals to us, likewise, the childlike religious ideas of the islanders. Heaven lay, not about
but above them in their infancy, yet not far away. Although in the "Notices," it is "the high plain of
heaven," yet it is just over their heads, and once a
single pillar joined it and the earth. Later, the idea

was, that it was held up by the pillar-gods of the wind, and to them norito were recited. " The great plain of the blue sea " and " the land of luxuriant reeds " form " the world "—which means Japan. The gods are only men of prowess or renown. A kami is anything wonderful—god or man, rock or stream, bird or snake, whatever is surprising, sensational, or phenomenal, as in the little child's world of to-day. There is no sharp line dividing gods from men, the natural from the supernatural, even as with the normal uneducated Japanese of to-day. As for the kami or gods, they have all sorts of characters; some of them being rude and ill-mannered, many of them beastly and filthy, while others are noble and benevolent. The attributes of moral purity, wisdom and holiness, cannot be, and in the original writings are not, ascribed to them ; but they were strong and had power. In so far as they had power they were called kami or gods, whether celestial or terrestrial. Among the kami—the one term under which they are all included— there were heavenly bodies, mountains, rivers, trees, rocks and animals, because these also were supposed to possess force, or at least some kind of influence for good or evil. Even peaches, as we have seen, when transformed into rocks, became gods.[14]

That there was worship with awe, reverence, and fear, and that the festivals and sacrifices had two purposes, one of propitiating the offended Kami and the other of purifying the worshipper, may be seen in the norito or liturgies, some of which are exceedingly beautiful.[15] In them the feelings of the gods are often referred to. Sometimes their characters are described. Yet one looks in vain in either the " No-

tices," poems, or liturgies for anything definite in
regard to these deities, or concerning morals or doctrines to be held as dogmas. The first gods come into
existence after evolution of the matter of which they
are composed has taken place. The later gods are
sometimes able to tell who are their progenitors, sometimes not. They live and fight, eat and drink, and
give vent to their appetites and passions, and then
they die; but exactly what becomes of them after they
die, the record does not state. Some are in heaven,
some on the earth, some in Hades. The underworld
of the first cycle of tradition is by no means that of
the second.[16] Some of the kami are in the water, or
on the water, or in the air. As for man, there is no
clear statement as to whether he is to have any future
life or what is to become of him, though the custom
or jun-shi, or dying with the master, points to a sort
of immortality such as the early Greeks and the Iroquois believed in.

It would task the keenest and ablest Shintōist to
deduce or construct a system of theology, or of ethics,
or of anthropology from the mass of tradition so full
of gaps and discord as that found in the Kojiki, and
none has done it. Nor do the inaccurate, distorted,
and often almost wholly factitious translations, so-
called, of French and other writers, who make versions which hit the taste of their occidental readers
far better than they express the truth, yield the desired information. Like the end strands of a new
spider's web, the lines of information on most vital
points are still " in the air."

The Ethics of the God-way.

There are no codes of morals inculcated in the god-way, for even its modern revivalists and exponents consider that morals are the invention of wicked people like the Chinese ; while the ancient Japanese were pure in thought and act. They revered the gods and obeyed the Mikado, and that was the chief end of man, in those ancient times when Japan was the world and Heaven was just above the earth. Not exactly on Paul's principle of " where there is no law there is no transgression," but utterly scouting the idea that formulated ethics were necessary for these pure-minded people, the modern revivalists of Shintō teach that all that is " of faith " now is to revere the gods, keep the heart pure, and follow its dictates.[17] The naïveté of the representatives of Shintō at Chicago in A.D. 1893, was almost as great as that of the revivalists who wrote when Japan was a hermit nation.

The very fact that there was no moral commandments, not even of loyalty or obedience such as Confucianism afterward promulgated and formulated, is proof to the modern Shintōist that the primeval Japanese were pure and holy ; they did right, naturally, and hence he does not hesitate to call Japan, the Land of the Gods, the Country of the Holy Spirits, the Region Between Heaven and Earth, the Island of the Congealed Drop, the Sun's Nest, the Princess Country, the Land of Great Peace, the Land of Great Gentleness, the Mikado's Empire, the Country ruled by a Theocratic Dynasty. He considers that only with the vice brought over from the Continent of Asia were ethics both imported and made necessary.[18]

All this has been solemnly taught by famous Shintō scholars of the eighteenth and nineteenth centuries, and is still practically promulgated in the polemic Shintō literature of to-day, even after the Kojiki has been studied and translated into European languages. The Kojiki shows that whatever the men may have been or done, the gods were abominably obscene, and both in word and deed were foul and revolting, utterly opposed in act to those reserves of modesty or standards. of shame that exist even among the cultivated Japanese to-day.[19] Even among the Ainos, whom the Japanese look upon as savages, there is still much of the obscenity of speech which belongs to all society [20] in a state of barbarism ; but it has been proved that genuine modesty is a characteristic of the Aino women.[21] A literal English translation of the Kojiki, however, requires an abundant use of Latin in order to protect it from the grasp of the law in English-speaking Christendom. In Chamberlain's version, the numerous cesspools are thus filled up with a dead language, and the road is constructed for the reader, who likes the language of Edmund Spencer, of William Tyndale and of John Ruskin kept unsoiled.

The cruelty which marks this early stage shows that though moral codes did not exist, the Buddhist and Confucian missionary were for Japan necessities of the first order. Comparing the result to-day with the state of things in the early times, one must award high praise to Buddhism that it has made the Japanese gentle, and to Confucianism that it has taught the proprieties of life, so that the polished Japanese gen-

tleman, as to courtesy, is in many respects the peer
and at some external points the superior, of his European confrère.

Another fact, made repulsively clear, about life in
ancient Japan, is that the high ideals of truth and
honor, characteristic at least of the Samurai of modern
times, were utterly unknown in the days of the kami.
Treachery was common. Instances multiply on the
pages of the Kojiki where friend betrayed friend. The
most sacred relations of life were violated. Altogether
these were the darkest ages of Japan, though, as
among the red men of America, there were not wanting
many noble examples of stoical endurance, of courage,
and of power nobly exerted for the benefit of others.

The Rise of Mikadoism.

Nevertheless we must not forget that the men of the
early age of the Kami no Michi conquered the aborigines by superior dogmas and fetiches, as well as by
superior weapons. The entrance of these heroes, invaders from the highlands of the Asian continent, by
way of Korea, was relatively a very influential factor
of progress, though not so important as was the Aryan
descent upon India, or the Norman invasion of England, for the aboriginal tribes were vastly lower in the
scale of humanity than their subduers. Where they
found savagery they introduced barbarism, which,
though unlettered and based on the sword, was a vast
improvement over what may be called the geological
state of man, in which he is but slightly raised above
the brutes.

For the proofs from the shell heaps, combined with

the reflected evidences of folk-lore, show, that cannibal-
ism [22] was common in the early ages, and that among
the aboriginal hill tribes it lingered after the inhabitants of the plain and shore had been subdued. The
conquerors, who made themselves paramount over the
other tribes and who developed the Kami religion,
abolished this relic of savagery, and gave order where
there had been chronic war. Another thing that impresses us because of its abundant illustrations, is the
prevalence of human sacrifices. The very ancient
folk-lore shows that beautiful maidens were demanded
by the "sea-gods" in propitiation, or were devoured
by the "dragons." These human victims were either
chosen or voluntarily offered, and in some instances
were rescued from their fate by chivalrous heroes [23]
from among the invaders.

These gods of the sea, who anciently were propiti-
ated by the sacrifice of human beings, are the same to
whom Japanese sailors still pray, despite their Buddhism. The title of the efficient victims was *hitoga-
shira*, or human pillars. Instances of this ceremony,
where men were lowered into the water and drowned
in order to make the sure foundation for bridges, piers
or sea-walls, or where they were buried alive in the
earth in order to lay the right bases for walls or castles,
are quite numerous, and most of the local histories contain specific traditions.[24] These traditions, now transfigured, still survive in customs that are as beautiful as
they are harmless. To reformers of pre-Buddhistic
days, belongs the credit of the abolition of jun-shi, or
dying with the master by burial alive, as well as of the
sacrifice to dragons and sea-gods.

Strange as it may seem, before Buddhism captured

and made use of Shintō for its own purposes (just as
it stands ready to-day to absorb Christianity by making Jesus one of the Palestinian avatars of the Buddha),
the house or tribe of Yamato, with its claim to descent
from the heavenly gods, and with its Mikado or god-
ruler, had given to the Buddhists a precedent and
potent example. Shintō, as a state religion or union
of politics and piety, with its system of shrines and
festivals, and in short the whole Kami no Michi, or
Shintō as we know it, from the sixth to the eighth century, was in itself (in part at least), a case of the absorption of one religion by another.

In short, the Mikado tribe or Yamato clan did, in
reality, capture the aboriginal religion, and turn it into
a great political machine. They attempted syncretism and succeeded in their scheme. They added to
their own stock of dogma and fetich that of the natives. Only, while recognizing the (earth) gods of the
aborigines they proclaimed the superiority of the Mikado as representative and vicegerent of Heaven, and
demanded that even the gods of the earth, mountain,
river, wind, and thunder and lightning should obey
him. Not content, however, with absorbing and cor-
rupting for political purposes the primitive faith of the
aborigines, the invaders corrupted their own religion
by carrying the dogma of the divinity and infallibility
of the Mikado too far. Stopping short of no absurdity,
they declared their chief greater even than the heavenly gods, and made their religion centre in him rather
than in his alleged heavenly ancestors, or "heaven."
In the interest of politics and conquest, and for the
sake of maintaining the prestige of their tribe and
clan, these "Mikado-reverencers" of early ages ad-

vanced from dogma to dogma, until their leader was
virtually chief god in a great pantheon.

A critical native Japanese, student of the Kojiki
and of the early writings, Professor Kumi, formerly of
the Imperial University in Tōkiō, has brought to light
abundant evidence to show that the aboriginal religion
found by the Yamato conquerors was markedly different at many vital points, from that which was long afterward called Shintō.

If the view of recent students of anthropology be
correct, that the elements dominating the population in
ancient Japan were in the south, Malay ; in the north,
Aino; and in the central region, or that occupied by
the Yamato men, Korean ; then, these continental invaders may have been worshippers of Heaven and have
possessed a religion closely akin to that of ancient
China with its monotheism. It is very probable also
that they came into contact with tribes or colonies of
their fellow-continentals from Asia. These tribes,
hunters, fishermen, or rude agriculturists—who had
previously reached Japan—practised many rites and
ceremonies which were much like those of the new invaders. It is certain also, as we have seen, that the
Yamato men made ultimate conquest and unification of
all the islanders, not merely by the superiority of their
valor and of their weapons of iron, but also by their
dogmas. After success in battle, and the first beginnings of rude government, they taught their conquered
subjects or over-awed vassals, that they were the descendants of the heavenly gods ; that their ancestors
had come donw from heaven ; and that their chief or
Mikado was a god. According to the same dogmatics,
the aborigines were descendants of the earth-born

gods, and as such must obey the descendants of the heavenly gods, and their vicegerent upon the earth, the Mikado.

Purification of Offences.

These heaven-descended Yamato people were in the main agriculturists, though of a rude order, while the outlying tribes were mostly hunters and fishermen ; and many of the rituals show the class of crimes which nomads, or men of unsettled life, would naturally commit against their neighbors living in comparatively settled order. It is to be noted that in the god-way the origin of evil is to be ascribed to evil gods. These kami pollute, and pollution is iniquity. From this iniquity the people are to be purged by the gods of purification, to whom offerings are duly made.

He who would understand the passion for cleanliness which characterizes the Japanese must look for its source in their ancient religion. The root idea of the word *tsumi*, which Mr. Satow translated as "offence," is that of pollution. On this basis, of things pure and things defiling, the ancient teachers of Shintō made their classification of what was good and what was bad. From the impression of what was repulsive arose the idea of guilt.

In rituals translated by Mr. Satow, the list of offences is given and the defilements are to be removed to the nether world, or, in common fact, the polluted objects and the expiatory sacrifices are to be thrown into the rivers and thence carried to the sea, where they fall to the bottom of the earth. The following norito clearly shows this. Furthermore, as Mr. Satow, the translator, points out, this ritual contains the germ of criminal law, a whole code of which might have been

evolved and formulated under Shintō, had not Buddhism arrested its growth.

Amongst the various sorts of offences which may be committed in ignorance or out of negligence by heaven's increasing
people, who shall come into being in the country, which the
Sovran GRANDCHILD'S augustness, hiding in the fresh RESI-
DENCE, built by stoutly planting the HOUSE-pillars on the bottom-most rocks, and exalting the cross-beams to the plain of
high heaven, as his SHADE from the heavens and SHADE from
the sun, shall tranquilly rule as a peaceful country, namely, the
country of great Yamato, where the sun is seen on high, which
he fixed upon as a peaceful country, as the centre of the countries of the four quarters thus bestowed upon him—breaking
the ridges, filling up water-courses, opening sluices, double-
sowing, planting stakes, flaying alive, flaying backwards, and
dunging; many of such offences are distinguished as heavenly
offences, and as earthly offences ; cutting living flesh, cutting
dead flesh, leprosy, proud-flesh, . . . calamities of crawl-
ing worms, calamities of a god on high, calamities of birds on
high, the offences of killing beasts and using incantations ;
many of such offences may be disclosed.

When he has thus repeated it, the heavenly gods will push
open heaven's eternal gates, and cleaving a path with might
through the manifold clouds of heaven, will hear ; and the
country gods, ascending to the tops of the high mountains, and
to the tops of the low hills, and tearing asunder the mists of the
high mountains and the mists of the low hills, will hear.

And when they have thus heard, the Maiden-of-Descent-into-
the-Current, who dwells in the current of the swift stream
which boils down the ravines from the tops of the high mountains, and the tops of the low hills, shall carry out to the great
sea plain the offences which are cleared away and purified, so
that there be no remaining offence ; like as Shinato's wind
blows apart the manifold clouds of heaven, as the morning wind
and the evening wind blow away the morning mist and the
evening mist, as the great ships which lie on the shore of a
great port loosen their prows, and loosen their sterns to push

out into the great sea-plain ; as the trunks of the forest trees, far and near, are cleared away by the sharp sickle, the sickle forged with fire : so that there ceased to be any offence called an offence in the court of the Sovran GRANDCHILD'S augustness to begin with, and in the countries of the four quarters of the region under heaven.

And when she thus carries them out and away, the deity called the Maiden-of-the-Swift-cleansing, who dwells in the multitudinous meetings of the sea waters, the multitudinous currents of rough sea-waters shall gulp them down.

And when she has thus gulped them down, the lord of the Breath-blowing-place, who dwells in the Breath-blowing-place, shall utterly blow them away with his breath to the Root-country, the Bottom-country.

And when he has thus blown them away, the deity called the Maiden-of-Swift-Banishment, who dwells in the Root-country, the Bottom-country, shall completely banish them, and get rid of them.

And when they have thus been got rid of, there shall from this day onwards be no offence which is called offence, with regard to the men of the offices who serve in the court of the Sovran, nor in the four quarters of the region under heaven.

Then the high priest says :

Hear all of you how he leads forth the horse, as a thing that erects its ears towards the plain of high heaven, and deigns to sweep away and purify with the general purification, as the evening sun goes down on the last day of the watery moon of this year.

O diviners of the four countries, take (the sacrifices) away out to the river highway, and sweep them away.

Mikadoism Usurps the Primitive God-way.

A further proof of the transformation of the primitive god-way in the interest of practical politics, is shown by Professor Kumi in the fact that some of the festivals now directly connected with the Mikado's house, and even in his honor,were originally festivals with which he had nothing to do, except as leader of the worship, for the honor was paid to Heaven, and not to his ancestors. Professor Kumi maintains that the thanksgivings of the court were originally to Heaven itself, and not in honor of Amatérasŭ, the sun-goddess, as is now popularly believed. It is related in the Kojiki that Amatérasŭ herself celebrated the feast of Niinamé. So also, the temple of Isé, the Mecca of Shintō, and the Holy shrine in the imperial palace were originally temples for the worship of Heaven. The inferior gods of earthly origin form no part of primitive Shintō.

Not one of the first Mikados was deified after death, the deification of emperors dating from the corruption which Shintō underwent after the introduction of Buddhism. Only by degrees was the ruler of the country given a place in the worship, and this connection was made by attributing to him descent from Heaven. In a word, the contention of Professor Kumi is, that the ancient religion of at least a portion of the Japanese and especially of those in central Japan, was a rude sort of monotheism, coupled, as in ancient China, with the worship of subordinate spirits.

It is needless to say that such applications of the higher criticism to the ancient sacred documents proved to be no safer for the applier than if he had lived in the United States of America. The orthodox Shintōists were roused to wrath and charged the learned critic with " degrading Shintō to a mere branch of Christianity." The government, which, despite its Constitution and Diet, is in the eyes of the people

6

really based on the myths of the Kojiki, quickly put the professor on the retired list.[25]

It is probably correct to say that the arguments adduced by Professor Kumi, confirm our theory of the substitution in the simple god-way, of Mikadoism, the centre of the primitive worship being the sun and nature rather than Heaven.

Between the ancient Chinese religion with its abstract idea of Heaven and its personal term for God, and the more poetic and childlike system of the godway, there seems to be as much difference as there is racially between the people of the Middle Kingdom and those of the Land Where the Day Begins. Indeed, the entrance of Chinese philosophical and abstract ideas seemed to paralyze the Japanese imagination. Not only did myth-making, on its purely æsthetic and non-utilitarian side cease almost at once, but such myths as were formed were for direct business purposes and with a transparent tendency. Henceforth, in the domain of imagination the Japanese intellect busied itself with assimilating or re-working the abundant material imported by Buddhism.

Ancient Customs and Usages.

In the ancient god-way the temple or shrine was called a miya. After the advent of Buddhism the keepers of the shrine were called kannushi, that is, shrine keepers or wardens of the god. These men were usually descendants of the god in whose honor the temples were built. The gods being nothing more than human founders of families, reverence was paid to them as ancestors, and so the basis of Shintō is ancestor

worship. The model of the miya, in modern as in ancient times, is the primitive hut as it was before Buddhism introduced Indian and Chinese architecture. The
posts, stuck in the ground, and not laid upon stones as
in after times, supported the walls and roof, the latter
being of thatch. The rafters, crossed at the top, were
tied along the ridge-pole with the fibres of creepers or
wistaria vines. No paint, lacquer, gilding, or ornaments of any sort existed in the ancient shrine, and
even to-day the modern Shintō temple must be of pure
hinoki or sun-wood, and thatched, while the use of
metal is as far as possible avoided. To the gods, as
the norito show, offerings of various kinds were made,
consisting of the fruits of the soil, the products of the
sea, and the fabrics of the loom.

Inside modern temples one often sees a mirror, in
which foreigners with lively imaginations read a great
deal that is only the shadow of their own mind, but
which probably was never known in Shintō temples
until after Buddhist times. They also see in front of
the unpainted wooden closets or casements, wands or
sticks of wood from which depend masses or strips of
white paper, cut and notched in a particular way.
Foreigners, whose fancy is nimble, have read in these
the symbols of lightning, the abode of the spirits and
various forthshadowings unknown either to the Japanese or the ancient writings. In reality these *gohei*, or
honorable offerings, are nothing more than the paper
representatives of the ancient offerings of cloth which
were woven, as the arts progressed, of bark, of hemp
and of silk.

The chief Shintō ministers of religion and shrine-
keepers belonged to particular families, which were often

honored with titles and offices by the emperor. In ordinary life they dressed like others of their own rank or station, but when engaged in their sacred office were robed in white or in a special official costume, wearing upon their heads the *éboshi* or peculiar cap which we associate with Japanese archæology. They knew nothing of celibacy; but married, reared families and kept their scalps free from the razor, though some of the lower order of shrine-keepers dressed their hair in ordinary style, that is, with shaven poll and topknot. At some of the more important shrines, like those at Isé, there were virgin priestesses who acted as custodians both of the shrines and of the relics.[26]

In front of the miyas stood what we should suppose on first seeing was a gateway. This was the *torii* or bird-perch, and anciently was made only of unpainted wood. Two upright tree-trunks held crosswise on a smooth tree-trunk the ends of which projected somewhat over the supports, while under this was a smaller beam inserted between the two uprights. On the torii, the birds, generally barn-yard fowls which were sacred to the gods, roosted. These creatures were not offered up as sacrifices, but were chanticleers to give notice of day-break and the rising of the sun. The cock holds a prominent place in Japanese myth, legend, art and symbolism. How this feature of pure Japanese architecture, the torii, afterward lost its meaning, we shall show in our lecture on Riyōbu or mixed Buddhism.

Shintō's Emphasis on Cleanliness.

One of the most remarkable features of Shintō was the emphasis laid on cleanliness. Pollution was calam-

ity, defilement was sin, and physical purity at least,
was holiness. Everything that could in any way soil
the body or the clothing was looked upon with abhor-
rence and detestation. Disease, wounds and death
were defiling, and the feeling of disgust prevailed over
that of either sympathy or pity. Birth and death were
especially polluting. Anciently there were huts built
both for the mother about to give birth to a child, or
for the man who was dying or sure to die of disease or
wounds. After the birth of the infant or the death of
the patient these houses were burned. Cruel as this
system was to the woman at a time when she needed
most care and comfort, and brutal as it seems in regard
to the sick and dying, yet this ancient custom was continued in a few remote places in Japan as late as the
year 1878.[27] In modern days with equal knowledge of
danger and defilement, tenderness and compassion
temper the feeling of disgust, and prevail over it.
Horror of uncleanliness was so great that the priests
bathed and put on clean garments before making the
sacred offerings or chanting the liturgies, and were accustomed to bind a slip of paper over their mouths lest
their breath should pollute the offering. Numerous
were the special festivals, observed simply for purification. Salt also was commonly used to sprinkle over
the ground, and those who attended a funeral must
free themselves from contamination by the use of salt.[28]
Purification by water was habitual and in varied forms.
The ancient emperors and priests actually performed
the ablution of the people or made public lustration
in their behalf.

Afterwards, and probably because population increased and towns sprang up, we find it was custom-

ary at the festivals of purification to perform public ablution, vicariously, as it were, by means of paper mannikins instead of making applications of water to the human cuticle. Twice a year paper figures representing the people were thrown into the river, the typical meaning of which was that the nation was thereby cleansed from the sins, that is, the defilements, of the previous half - year. Still later, the Mikado made the chief minister of religion at Kiōto his deputy to perform the symbolical act for the people of the whole country.

Prayers to Myriads of Gods.

In prayer, the worshipper, approaching the temple but not entering it, pulls a rope usually made of white material and attached to a peculiar-shaped bell hung over the shrine, calling the attention of the deity to his devotions. Having washed his hands and rinsed out his mouth, he places his hands reverently together and offers his petition.

Concerning the method and words of prayer, Hirata, a famous exponent of Shintō, thus writes :

As the number of the gods who possess different functions is so great, it will be convenient to worship by name only the most important and to include the rest in a general petition. Those whose daily affairs are so multitudinous that they have not time to go through the whole of the following morning prayers, may content themselves with adoring the residence of the emperor, the domestic kami-dana, the spirits of their ancestors, their local patron god and the deity of their particular calling in life.

In praying to the gods the blessings which each has it in his power to bestow are to be mentioned in a few words, and they are not to be annoyed with greedy petitions, for the Mikado in his palace offers up petitions daily on behalf of his people, which are far more effectual than those of his subjects.

Rising early in the morning, wash your face and hands, rinse out the mouth and cleanse the body. Then turn toward the province of Yamato, strike the palms of the hands together twice, and worship, bowing the head to the ground. The proper posture is that of kneeling on the heels, which is ordinarily assumed in saluting a superior.

PRAYER.

From a distance I reverently worship with awe before Amé no Mi-hashira (Heaven-pillar) and Kuni no Mi-hashira (Country-pillar), also called Shinatsu-hiko no kami and Shinatsu-himé no kami, to whom is consecrated the Palace built with stout pillars at Tatsuta no Tachinu in the department of Héguri in the province of Yamato.

I say with awe, deign to bless me by correcting the unwitting faults which, seen and heard by you, I have committed, by blowing off and clearing away the calamities which evil gods might inflict, by causing me to live long like the hard and lasting rock, and by repeating to the gods of heavenly origin and to the gods of earthly origin the petitions which I present every day, along with your breath, that they may hear with the sharp-earedness of the forth-galloping colt.

To the common people the sun is actually a god, as none can doubt who sees them worshipping it morning and evening. The writer can never forget one of many similar scenes in Tōkiō, when late one afternoon after O Tentō Sama (the sun-Lord of Heaven), which had been hidden behind clouds for a fortnight, shone out on the muddy streets. In a moment, as with the promptness of a military drill, scores of people rushed out of their houses and with faces westward, kneeling, squatting, began prayer and worship before the great luminary. Besides all the gods, supreme, subordi-

nate and local, there is in nearly every house the
Kami-dana or god-shelf. This is usually over the
door inside. It contains images with little paper-cov-
ered wooden tablets having the god's name on them.
Offerings are made by day and a little lamp is lighted
at night. The following is one of several prayers
which are addressed to this kami-dana.

Reverently adoring the great god of the two palaces of Isé, in
the first place, the eight hundred myriads of celestial gods, the
eight hundred myriads of terrestrial gods, all the fifteen hundred myriads of gods to whom are consecrated the great and
small temples in all provinces, all islands and all places of the
Great Land of Eight Islands, the fifteen hundreds of myriads
of gods whom they cause to serve them, and the gods of branch
palaces and branch temples, and Sohodo no kami, whom I have
invited to the shrine set up on this divine shelf, and to whom I
offer praises day by day, I pray with awe that they will deign
to correct the unwitting faults, which, heard and seen by them,
I have committed, and blessing and favoring me according to
the powers which they severally wield, cause me to follow the
divine example, and to perform good works in the Way.

Shintō Left in a State of Arrested Development.

Thus from the emperor to the humblest believer, the
god-way is founded on ancestor worship, and has had
grafted upon its ritual system nature worship, even to
phallicism.[29] In one sense it is a self-made religion of
the Japanese. Its leading characteristics are seen in
the traits of the normal Japanese character of to-day.
Its power for good and evil may be traced in the education of the Japanese through many centuries. Knowing Shintō, we to a large degree know the Japanese,
their virtues and their failings.

What Shintō might have become in its full evolution

had it been left alone, we cannot tell. Whether in the growth of the nation and without the pressure of Buddhism, Confucianism or other powerful influences from outside, the scattered and fragmentary mythology might have become organized into a harmonious system, or codes of ethics have been formulated, or the doctrines of a future life and the idea of a Supreme Being with personal attributes have been conceived and perfected, are questions the discussion of which may seem to be vain. History, however, gives no uncertain answer as to what actually did take place. We do but state what is unchallenged fact, when we say, that after commitment to writing of the myths, poems and liturgies which may be called the basis of Shintō, there came a great flood of Chinese and Buddhistic literature and a tremendous expansion of Buddhist missionary activity, which checked further literary growth of the kami system. These prepared the way for the absorption of the indigenous into the foreign cultus under the form called by an enthusiastic emperor, Riyōbu Shintō, or the "two-fold divine doctrine." Of this, we shall speak in another lecture.

Suffice it here to say that by the scheme of syncretism propounded by Kōbō in the ninth century, Shintō was practically overlaid by the new faith from India, and largely forgotten as a distinct religion by the Japanese people. As late as A.D. 927, there were three thousand one hundred and thirty-two enumerated metropolitan and provincial temples, besides many more unenumerated village and hamlet shrines of Shintō. These are referred to in the revised codes of ceremonial law set forth by imperial authority early in the tenth century. Probably by the twelfth century the pure rites of the god-way were celebrated, and the unmixed traditions maintained, in families and temples, so few as to be counted on the fingers. The ancient language in which the archaic forms had been preserved was so nearly lost and buried, that out of the ooze of centuries of oblivion, it had to be rescued by the skilled divers of the seventeenth century. Mabuchi, Motöori and the other revivalists of pure Shintō, like the plungers after orient pearls, persevered until they had first recovered much that had been supposed irretrievably lost. These scholars deciphered and interpreted the ancient scriptures, poetry, prose, history, law and ritual, and once more set forth the ancient faith, as they believed, in its purity.

Whether, however, men can exactly reproduce and think for themselves the thoughts of others who have been dead for a millennium, is an open question. The new system is apt to be transparent. Just as it is nearly impossible for us to restore the religious life, thoughts and orthodoxy of the men who lived before the flood, so in the writings of the revivalists of pure Shintō we detect the thoughts of Dutchmen, of Chinese, and of very modern Japanese. Unconsciously, those who would breathe into the dry bones of dead Shintō the breath of the nineteenth century, find themselves compelled to use an oxygen and nitrogen generator made in Holland and mounted with Chinese apparatus ; withal, lacquered and decorated with the art of to-day. To change from metaphor to matter of fact, modern "pure Shintō " is mainly a mass of speculation and philosophy, with a tendency of which the ancient god-way knew nothing.

The Modern Revivalists of Kami no Michi.

Passing by further mention of the fifteen or more corrupt sects of Shintōists,[30] we name with honor the native scholars of the seventeenth century, who followed the illustrious example of Iyéyasŭ, the political unifier of Japan. They ransacked the country and purchased from temples, mansions and farm-houses, old manuscripts and books, and forming libraries began anew the study of ancient language and history. Kéichu (1640–1701), a Buddhist priest, explored and illumined the poems of the Manyōshu. Kada Adzumarō, born in 1669 near Kiōto, the son of a shrine-keeper at Inari, attempted the mastery of the whole archaic native language and literature. He made a grand beginning. He is unquestionably the founder of the school of Pure Shintō. He died in 1736. His successor and pupil was Mabuchi (1697–1769), who claimed direct descent from that god which in the form of a colossal crow had guided the first chief of the Yamato tribe as he led his invaders through the country to found the line of Mikados. After Mabuchi came Motoöri (1730–1801) a remarkable scholar and critic, who, with erudition and acuteness, analyzed the ancient literature and showed what were Chinese or imported elements and what was of native origin. He summarized the principles of the ancient religion, reasserted and illuminated with amazing learning and voluminous commentary the archaic documents, expounded and defended the ancient cosmogony, and in the usual style of Japanese polemics preached anew the doctrines of Shintō. With wonderful naïveté and enthusiasm, Motoöri taught that Japan was the first part of the earth created, and that it is therefore The Land of the Gods, the Country of the Holy Spirits. The stars were created from the muck which fell from the spear of Izanagi as he thrust it into the warm earth, while the other countries were formed by the spontaneous consolidation of the foam of the sea. Morals were invented by the Chinese because they were an immoral people, but in Japan there is no necessity for any system of morals, as every Japanese acts aright if he only consults his own heart. The duty of a good Japanese consists in obeying the Mikado, without questioning whether his commands are right or wrong. The Mikado is god and vicar of all the gods, hence government and religion are the same, the Mikado being the centre of Church and State, which are one. Did the foreign nations know their duty they would at once hasten to pay tribute to the Son of Heaven in Kiōto.

It is needless here to dwell upon the tremendous power of Shintō as a political system, especially when wedded with the forces, generated in the minds of the educated Japanese by modern Confucianism. The Chinese ethical system, expanded into a philosophy as fascinating as the English materialistic school of to-day, entered Japan contemporaneously with the revival of the Way of the Gods and of native learning. In full rampancy of their vigor, in the seventeenth century these two systems began that generation of national energy, which in the eighteenth century was consolidated and which in the nineteenth century, though unknown and unsuspected by Europeans or Americans, was all ready for phenomenal manifestation and tremendous eruption, even while Perry's fleet was bearing the olive branch to Japan. As we all know, this consolidation of forces from the inside, on meeting, not with collision but with union, the exterior forces of western civilization, formed a resultant in the energies which have made New Japan.

The Great Purification of 1870.

In 1870, with the Shōgun of Yedo deposed, the dual system abolished, feudalism in its last gasp and Shintō in full political power, with the ancient council of the gods (Jin Gi Kuan) once more established, and purified Shintō again the religion of state, thousands of Riyōbu Shintō temples were at once purged of all their Buddhist ornaments, furniture, ritual, and everything that might remind the Japanese of foreign elements. Then began, logically and actually, the persecution of those Christians, who through all the centuries of repression and prohibition had continued their existence, and kept their faith however mixed and clouded. Theoretically, ancient belief was re-established, yet it was both physically and morally impossible to return wholly to the baldness and austere simplicity of those early ages, in which art and literature were unknown. For a while it seemed as though the miracle would be performed, of turning back the dial of the ages and of plunging Japan into the fountain of her own youth. Propaganda was instituted, and the attempts made to convert all the Japanese to Shintō tenets and practice were for a while more lively than edifying ; but the scheme was on the whole a splendid failure, and bitter disappointment succeeded the first exultation of victory. Confronted by modern problems of society and government, the Mikado's ministers found themselves unable, if indeed willing, to entomb politics in religion, as in the ancient ages. For a little while, in 1868, the Jin Gi Kuan, or Council of the Gods of Heaven and Earth, held equal authority with the Dai Jō Kuan, or Great Council of the Government. Pretty soon the first step downward was taken, and from a supreme council it was made one of the ten departments of the government. In less than a year followed another retrograde movement and the department was called a board. Finally, in 1877, the board became a bureau. Now, it is hard to tell what rank the Shintō cultus occupies in the government, except as a system of guardianship over the imperial tombs, a mode of official etiquette, and as one of the acknowledged religions of the country.

Nevertheless, as an element in that amalgam of religions which forms the creed of most Japanese, Shintō is a living force, and shares with Buddhism the arena against advancing Christianity, still supplying much of the spring and motive to patriotism.

The Shintō lecturers with unblushing plagiarism rifled the storehouses of Chinese ethics. They enforced their lessons from the Confucian classics. Indeed, most of their homiletical and illustrative material is still derived directly therefrom. Their three main official theses and commandments were :

1. Thou shalt honor the Gods and love thy country.

2 Thou shalt clearly understand the principles of Heaven, and the duty of man.

3. Thou shalt revere the Emperor as thy sovereign and obey the will of his Court.

For nearly twenty years this deliverance of the Japanese Government, which still finds its strongest support in the national traditions and the reverence of the
people for the throne, sufficed for the necessities of
the case. Then the copious infusion of foreign ideas,
the disintegration of the old framework of society, and
the weakening of the old ties of obedience and loyalty,
with the flood of shallow knowledge and education
which gave especially children and young people just
enough of foreign ideas to make them dangerous,
brought about a condition of affairs which alarmed the
conservative and patriotic. Like fungus upon a dead
tree strange growths had appeared, among others that
of a class of violently patriotic and half-educated young
men and boys, called *Soshi*. These hot-headed youths
took it upon themselves to dictate national policy to
cabinet ministers, and to reconstruct society, religion
and politics. Something like a mania broke out all
over the country which, in certain respects, reminds us
of the Children's Crusade, that once afflicted Europe
and the children themselves. Even Christianity did
not escape the craze for reconstruction. Some of the
young believers and pupils of the missionaries seemed
determined to make Christianity all over so as to suit
themselves. This phase of brain-swelling is not yet
wholly over. One could not tell but that something
like the Tai Ping rebellion, which disturbed and devastated China, might break out.

These portentous signs on the social horizon called
forth, in 1892, from the government an Imperial Re-
script, which required that the emperor's photograph
be exhibited in every school, and saluted by all teachers and scholars whatever their religious tenets and

scruples might be. Most Christians as well as Buddhists, saw nothing in this at which to scruple. A few, however, finding in it an offence to conscience, resigned their positions. They considered the mandate an unwarrantable interference with their rights as conferred by the constitution of 1889, which in theory is the gift of the emperor to his people.

The radical Shintōist, to this day, believes that all political rights which Japanese enjoy or can enjoy are by virtue of the Mikado's grace and benevolence. It is certain that all Japanese, whatever may be their religious convictions, consider that the constitution depends for its safeguards and its validity largely upon the oath which the Mikado swore at the shrine of his heavenly ancestors, that he would himself be obedient to it and preserve its provisions inviolate. For this solemn ceremony a special norito or liturgy was composed and recited.

Summary of Shintō.

Of Shintō as a system we have long ago given our opinion. In its higher forms, "Shintō is simply a cultured and intellectual atheism; in its lower forms it is blind obedience to governmental and priestly dictates." "Shintō," says Mr. Ernest Satow, "as expounded by Motoöri is nothing more than an engine for reducing the people to a condition of mental slavery." Japan being a country of very striking natural phenomena, the very soil and air lend themselves to support in the native mind this system of worship of heroes and of the forces of nature. In spite, however, of the conservative power of the ancestral influences, the patriotic incentives and the easy morals of Shintō under which lying and licentiousness shelter themselves, it is doubtful whether with the pressure of Buddhism, and the spread of popular education and Christianity, Shintō can retain its hold upon the Japanese people. Yet although this is our opinion, it is but fair, and it is our duty, to judge every religion by its ideals and not by its failings. The ideal of Shintō is to make people pure and clean in all their personal and household arrangements ; it is to help them to live simply, honestly and with mutual good will ; it is to make the Japanese love their country, honor their imperial house and obey their emperor. Narrow and local as this religion is, it has had grand exemplars in noble lives and winning characters.

So far as Shintō is a religion, Christianity meets it not as destroyer but fulfiller, for it too believes that cleanliness is not only next to godliness but a part of it. Jesus as perfect man and patriot, Captain of our salvation and Prince of peace, would not destroy the Yamato damashii—the spirit of unconquerable Japan —but rather enlarge, broaden, and deepen it, making it love for all humanity. Reverence for ancestral virtue and example, so far from being weakened, is strengthened, and as for devotion to king and ruler, law and society, Christianity lends nobler motives and grander sanctions,[31] while showing clearly, not indeed the way of the eight million or more gods, but the way to God— the one living, only and true, even through **Him** who said "I am the **Way**."

7

THE CHINESE ETHICAL SYSTEM IN JAPAN

"Things being investigated, knowledge became complete; knowledge being complete, thoughts were sincere; thoughts being sincere, hearts were rectified; hearts being rectified, persons were cultivated; persons being cultivated, families were regulated; families being regulated, states were rightly governed; states being rightly governed, the whole nation was made tranquil and happy."

"When you know a thing to hold that you know it; and when you do not know a thing to allow that you do not know it; this is knowledge."

"Old age sometimes becomes second childhood; why should not filial piety become parental love?"

"The superior man accords with the course of the mean. Though he may be all unknown, unregarded by the world, he feels no regret. He is only the sage who is able for this."—Sayings of Confucius.

"There is, in a word, no bringing down of God to men in Confucianism in order to lift them up to Him. Their moral shortcomings, when brought home to them, may produce a feeling of shame, but hardly a conviction of guilt."—James Legge.

"Do not to others what you would not have them do to you."—The Silver Rule.

"All things whatsoever ye would that men should do to you, do ye even so to them."—The Golden Rule.

"In respect to revenging injury done to master or father, it is granted by the wise and virtuous (Confucius) that you and the injurer cannot live together under the canopy of heaven."—Legacy of Iyéyasū, Cap. lii., Lowder's translation.

"But I say unto you forgive your enemies."—Jesus.

"Thou, O Lord, art our father, our redeemer, thy name is from everlasting."—Isaiah.

CHAPTER IV

THE CHINESE ETHICAL SYSTEM IN JAPAN

Confucius a Historical Character

IF the greatness of a teacher is to be determined by
the number of his disciples, or to be measured by the
extent and diversity of his influence, then the foremost
place among all the teachers of mankind must be
awarded to The Master Kung (or Confucius, as the
Jesuit scholars of the seventeenth century Latinized
the name). Certainly, he of all truly historic personages is to-day, and for twenty-three centuries has been,
honored by the largest number of followers.

Of the many systems of religion in the world, but
few are based upon the teachings of one person. The
reputed founders of some of them are not known in
history with any certainty, and of others—as in the
case of Buddhism—have become almost as shadows
among a great throng of imaginary Buddhas or other
beings which have sprung from the fancies of the brain
and become incorporated into the systems, although
the original teachers may indeed have been historical.

Confucius is a clear and distinct historic person.
His parentage, place of birth, public life, offices, work
and teaching, are well known and properly authenti-
cated. He used the pen freely, and not only compiled,
edited and transmitted the writings of his predecessors,

but composed an historical and interpretative book.
He originated nothing, however, but on the contrary
disowned any purpose of introducing new ideas, or of
expressing thoughts of his own not based upon or in
perfect harmony with the teaching of the ancients. He
was not an original thinker. He was a compiler, an
editor, a defender and reproclaimer of the ancient religion, and an exemplar of the wisdom and writings of
the Chinese fathers. He felt that his duty was exactly that which some Christian theologians of to-day
conscientiously feel to be theirs—to receive intact a
certain "deposit" or "system" and, adding nothing to
it, simply to teach, illuminate, defend, enforce and
strongly maintain it as "the truth." He gloried in
absolute freedom from all novelty, anticipating in this
respect a certain illustrious American who made it a
matter for boasting, that his school had never originated a new idea.[1]   Whether or not the Master Kung
did nevertheless, either consciously or unconsciously,
modify the ancient system by abbreviating or enlarging it, we cannot now inquire.

Confucius was born into the world in the year 551
B.C., during that wonderful century of religious revival
which saw the birth of Ezra, Gautama, and Lao Tsze,
and in boyhood he displayed an unusually sedate temperament which made him seem to be what we would
now call an "old-fashioned child." The period during
which he lived was that of feudal China. From the
age of twenty-two, while holding an office in the state
of Lu within the modern province of Shan-Tung, he
gathered around him young men as pupils with whom,
like Socrates, he conversed in question and answer.
He made the teachings of the ancients the subjects of

his research, and he was at all times a diligent student of the primeval records. These sacred books are called King, or Kiō in Japanese, and are: Shu King, a collection of historic documents; Shih King, or Book of Odes; Hsiao King, or Classic of Filial Piety, and Yi King, or Book of Changes.[2] This division of the old sacred canon, resembles the Christian or non-Jewish arrangement of the Old Testament scriptures in the four parts of Law, History, Poetry and Prophesy, though in the Chinese we have History, Poetry, Ethics and Divination.[3]

His own table-talk, conversations, discussions and notes were compiled by his pupils, and are preserved in the work entitled in English, "The Confucian Analects," which is one of the four books constituting the most sacred portion of Chinese philosophy and instruction. He also wrote a work named "Spring and Autumn, or Chronicles of his Native State of Lu from 722 B.C., to 481[4] B.C." He "changed his world," as the Buddhists say, in the year 478 B.C., having lived seventy-three years.

Primitive Chinese Faith.

The pre-Confucian or primitive faith was monotheistic, the forefathers of the Chinese nation having been believers in one Supreme Spiritual Being. There is an almost universal agreement among scholars in translating the term " Shang Ti " as God, and in reading from these classics that the forefathers " in the ceremonies at the altars of Heaven and earth . . . served God." Concurrently with the worship of one Supreme God there was also a belief in subordinate spirits and in the idea of revelation or the communication of God with men. This restricted worship of God was accompanied by reverence for ancestors and the honoring of spirits by prayers and sacrifices, which resulted, however, neither in deification nor polytheism. But, as the European mediæval schoolmen have done with the Bible, so, after the death of Confucius the Chinese scholastics by metaphysical reasoning and commentary, created systems of interpretation which greatly altered the apparent form and contents of his own and of the ancient texts. Thus, the original monotheism of the pre-Confucian documents has been completely obscured by the later webs of sophistry which have been woven about the original scriptures. The ancient simplicity of doctrine has been lost in the mountains of commentary which were piled upon the primitive texts. Throughout the centuries, the Confucian system has been conditioned and greatly modified by Taoism, Buddhism and the speculations of the Chinese wise men.

Confucius, however, did not change or seriously modify the ancient religion except that, as is more than probable, he may have laid unnecessary emphasis upon social and political duties, and may not have been sufficiently interested in the honor to be paid to Shang Ti or God. He practically ignored the Godward side of man's duties. His teachings relate chiefly to duties between man and man, to propriety and etiquette, and to ceremony and usage. He said that "To give one's self to the duties due to men and while respecting spiritual beings to keep aloof from them, may be called wisdom. "[5]

We think that Confucius cut the tap-root of all true progress, and therefore is largely responsible for the arrested development of China. He avoided the personal term, God (Ti), and instead, made use of the abstract term, Heaven (Tien). His teaching, which is so often quoted by Japanese gentlemen, was, " Honor the Gods and keep them far from you." His image stands in thousands of temples and in every school, in China, but he is only revered and never deified.

China has for ages suffered from agnosticism; for no normal Confucianist can love God, though he may learn to reverence him. The Emperor periodically worships for his people, at the great marble altar to Heaven in Peking, with vast holocausts, and the prayers which are offered may possibly amount to this: " Our Father who art in Heaven, Hallowed be thy name." But there, as it seems to a Christian, Chinese imperial worship stops. The people at large, cut off by this restricted worship from direct access to God, have wandered away into every sort of polytheism and idolatry, while the religion of the educated Chinese is a mediæval philosophy based upon Confucianism, of which we shall speak hereafter.

The Confucian system as a religion, like a giant with a child's head, is exaggerated on its moral and ceremonial side as compared with its spiritual development. Some deny that it is a religion at all, and call it only a code. However, let us examine the Confucian ethics which formed the basis and norm of all government in the family and nation, and are summed up in the doctrine of the "Five Relations." These are: Sovereign and Minister; Father and Son; Husband and Wife; Elder Brother and Younger Brother; and Friends. The relation being stated, the correlative duty arises at once. It may perhaps be truly said by Christians that Confucius might have made a religion of his system of ethics, by adding a sixth and supreme relation—that between God and man. This he declined to do, and so left his people without any aspiration toward the Infinite. By setting before them only a finite goal he sapped the principles of progress.[6]

Vicissitudes of Confucianism.

After the death of Confucius (478 B.C.) the teachings of the great master were neglected, but still later they were re-enforced and expounded in the time (372–289 B.C.) of Meng Ko, or Mencius (as the name has been Latinized) who was likewise a native of the State of Lu. At one time a Chinese Emperor attempted in vain to destroy not only the writings of Confucius but also the ancient classics. Taoism increased as a power in the religion of China, especially after the fall of its feudal system. The doctrine of ancestral worship as commended by the sage had in it much of good, both for kings and nobles. The common people, however, found that Taoism was more satisfying. About the beginning of the Christian era Buddhism entered the Middle Kingdom, and, rapidly becoming popular, supplied needs for which simple Confucianism was not adequate. It may be said that in the sixth century—which concerns us especially—although Confucianism continued to be highly esteemed, Buddhism had become supreme in China—that venerable State which is the mother of civilization in all Asia east of the Ganges, and the Middle Kingdom among pupil nations.

Confucianism overflowed from China into Korea,

where to this day it is predominant even over Buddhism. Thence, it was carried beyond sea to the Japanese Archipelago, where for possibly fifteen hundred years it has shaped and moulded the character of a brave and chivalrous people. Let us now turn from China and trace its influence and modifications in the Land of the Rising Sun.

It must be remembered that in the sixth century of the Christian Era, Confucianism was by no means the fully developed philosophy that it is now and has been for five hundred years. In former times, the system of Confucius had been received in China not only as a praiseworthy compendium of ceremonial observances, but also as an inheritance from the ancients, illumined by the discourses of the great sage and illustrated by his life and example. It was, however, very far from being what it is at present—the religion of the educated men of the nation, and, by excellence, the religion of Chinese Asia. But in those early centuries it did not fully satisfy the Chinese mind, which turned to the philosophy of Taoism and to the teachings of the Buddhist for intellectual food, for comfort and for inspiration.

The time when Chinese learning entered Japan, by the way of Korea, has not been precisely ascertained.[7] It is possible that letters [8] and writings were known in some parts of the country as early as the fourth century, but it is nearly certain, that, outside the Court of the Emperor, there was scarcely even a sporadic knowledge of the literature of China until the Korean missionaries of Buddhism had obtained a lodgement in the Mikado's capital. Buddhism was the real purveyor of the foreign learning and became the vehicle by means of which Confucianism, or the Chinese ethical principles, reached the common people of Japan. The first missionaries in Japan were heartily in sympathy with the Confucian ethics, from which no effort was made to alienate them. They were close allies, and for a thousand years wrought as one force in the national life. They were not estranged until the introduction, in the seventeenth century, of the metaphysical and scholastic forms given to the ancient system by the Chinese schoolmen of the Sung dynasty (A.D. 960–1333).

Japanese Confucianism and Feudalism Contemporary.

The intellectual history of the Japanese prior to their recent contact with Christendom, may be divided into three eras :

1. The period of early insular or purely native thought, from before the Christian era until the eighth century ; by which time, Shintō, or the indigenous system of worship—its ritual, poetry and legend having been committed to writing and its life absorbed in Buddhism—had been, as a system, relegated from the nation and the people to a small circle of scholars and archæologists.

2. The period from 800 A.D. to the beginning of the seventeenth century ; during which time Buddhism furnished to the nation its religion, philosophy and culture.

3. From about 1630 A.D. until the present time ; during which period the developed Confucian philosophy, as set forth by Chu Hi in the twelfth century, has been the creed of a majority of the educated men of Japan.

The political history of the Japanese may also be divided into three eras:

1. The first extends from the dawn of history until the seventh century. During this period the system of government was that of rude feudalism. The conquering tribe of Yamato, having gradually obtained a rather imperfect supremacy over the other tribes in the middle and southern portions of the country now called the Empire of Japan, ruled them in the name of the Mikado.

2. The second period begins in the seventh century, when the Japanese, copying the Chinese model, adopted a system of centralization. The country was divided into provinces and was ruled through boards or ministries at the capital, with governors sent out from Kiōto for stated periods, directly from the emperor. During this time literature was chiefly the work of the Buddhist priests and of the women of the imperial court.

While armies in the field brought into subjection the outlying tribes and certain noble families rose to prominence at the court, there was being formed that remarkable class of men called the Samurai, or servants of the Mikado, which for more than ten centuries has exercised a profound influence upon the development of Japan.

In China, the pen and the sword have been kept apart; the civilian and the soldier, the man of letters and the man of arms, have been distinct and separate. This was also true in old Loo Choo (now Riu Kiu), that part of Japan most like China. In Japan, however, the pen and the sword, letters and arms, the civilian and the soldier, have intermingled. The unique product of this union is seen in the Samurai, or servant of the Mikado. Military-literati, are unknown in China, but in Japan they carried the sword and the pen in the same girdle.

3. This class of men had become fully formed by the end of the twelfth century, and then began the new feudal system, which lasted until the epochal year 1868 A.D.—a year of several revolutions, rather than of restoration pure and simple. After nearly seven hundred years of feudalism, supreme magistracy, with power vastly increased beyond that possessed in ancient times, was restored to the emperor. Then also was abolished the duarchy of Throne and Camp, of Mikado and Shōgun, and of the two capitals Kiōto and Yedo, with the fountain of honor and authority in one and the fountain of power and execution in the other. Thereupon, Japan once more presented to the world, unity.

Practically, therefore, the period of the prevalence of the Confucian ethics and their universal acceptance by the people of Japan nearly coincides with the period of Japanese feudalism or the dominance of the military classes.

Although the same ideograph, or rather logogram, was used to designate the Chinese scholar and the Japanese warrior as well, yet the former was man of the pen only, while the latter was man of the pen and of two swords. This historical fact, more than any other, accounts for the striking differences between Chinese and Japanese Confucianism. Under this state of things the ethical system of the sage of China suffered a change, as does almost everything that is imported into Japan and borrowed by the islanders, but whether for the better or for the worse we shall not inquire too carefully. The point upon which we now lay emphasis is this : that, although the Chinese teacher had made filial piety the basis of his system, the Japanese gradually but surely made loyalty (Kun-Shin), that is, the allied relations of sovereign and minister, of lord and retainer, and of master and servant, not only first in order but the chief of all. They also infused into this term ideas and associations which are foreign to the Chinese mind. In the place of filial piety was Kun-shin, that new growth in the garden of Japanese ethics, out of which arose the white flower of loyalty that blooms perennial in history.

In Japan, Loyalty Displaces Filial Piety.

This slow but sure adaptation of the exotic to its new environment, took place during the centuries previous to the seventeenth of the Christian era. The completed product presented a growth so strikingly different from the original as to compel the wonder of those Chinese refugee scholars, who, at Mito [9] and Yedo, taught the later dogmas which are orthodox but not historically Confucian.

Herein lies the difference between Chinese and Japanese ethical philosophy. In old Japan, loyalty was above filial obedience, and the man who deserted parents, wife and children for the feudal lord, received unstinted praise. The corner-stone of the Japanese edifice of personal righteousness and public weal, is loyalty. On the other hand, filial piety is the basis of Chinese order and the secret of the amazing national longevity, which is one of the moral wonders of the world, and sure proof of the fulfilment of that promise which was made on Sinai and wrapped up in the fourth commandment.

This master passion of the typical Samurai of old Japan made him regard life as infinitely less than nothing, whenever duty demanded a display of the virtue of loyalty. " The doctrines of Koshi and Moshi " (Confucius and Mencius) formed, and possibly even yet form, the gospel and the quintessence of all wordly wisdom to the Japanese gentleman; they became the basis of his education and the ideal which inspired his conceptions of duty and honor; but, crowning all his doctrines and aspirations was his desire to be loyal. There might abide loyal, marital, filial, fraternal and various other relations, but the greatest of all these was loyalty. Hence the Japanese calendar of saints is not filled with reformers, alms-givers and founders of hospitals or orphanages, but is over-crowded with canonized suicides and committers of *hara-kiri*. Even to-day, no man more quickly wins the popular regard during his life or more surely draws homage to his tomb, securing even apotheosis, than the suicide, though he may have committed a crime. In this era of Meiji or enlightened peace, most appalling is the list of assassinations beginning with the murder in Kiōto of Yokoi Héishiro, who was slain for recommending the toleration of Christianity, down to the last cabinet minister who has been knifed or dynamited. Yet in every case the murderers considered themselves consecrated men and ministers of Heaven's righteous vengeance.[10] For centuries, and until constitutional times, the government of Japan was " despotism tempered by assassination." The old-fashioned way of moving a vote of censure upon the king's ministers was to take off their heads. Now, however, election by ballot has been substituted for this, and two million swords have become bric-à-brac.

A thousand years of training in the ethics of Confucius — which always admirably lends itself to the possessors of absolute power, whether emperors, feudal lords, masters, fathers, or older brothers—have so tinged and colored every conception of the Japanese mind, so dominated their avenues of understanding and shaped their modes of thought, that to-day, notwithstanding the recent marvellous development of their language, which within the last two decades has made it almost a new tongue,[11] it is impossible with perfect accuracy to translate into English the ordinary Japanese terms which are congregated under the general idea of Kun-shin.

Herein may be seen the great benefit of carefully studying the minds of those whom we seek to convert. The Christian preacher in Japan who uses our terms "heaven," "home," "mother," "father," "family," "wife," "people," "love," "reverence," "virtue," "chastity," etc., will find that his hearers may indeed receive them, but not at all with the same mental images and associations, nor with the same proportion and depth, that these words command in western thought and hearing. One must be exceedingly careful, not only in translating terms which have been used by Confucius in the Chinese texts, but also in selecting and rendering the current expressions of the Japanese teachers and philosophers. In order to understand each other, Orientals and Occidentals need a great deal

8

of mutual intellectual drilling, without which there will be waste of money, of time, of brains and of life.

The Five Relations.

Let us now glance at the fundamentals of the Confucian ethics—the Five Relations—as they were taught in the comparatively simple system which prevailed before the new orthodoxy was proclaimed by Sung schoolmen.

First. Although, each of the Chinese and Japanese emperors is supposed to be, and is called, "father of the people," yet it would be entirely wrong to imagine that the phrase implies any such relation, as that of William the Silent to the Dutch, or of Washington to the American nation. In order to see how far the emperor was removed from the people during a thousand years, one needs but to look upon a brilliant painting of the Yamato-Tosa school, in which the Mikado is represented as sitting behind a cloud of gold or a thick curtain of fine bamboo, with no one before the matting-throne but his prime ministers or the empress and his concubines. For centuries, it was supposed that the Mikado did not touch the ground with his feet. He went abroad in a curtained car; and he was not only as mysterious and invisible to the public eye as a dragon, but he was called such. The attributes of that monster with many powers and functions, were applied to him, with an amazing wealth of rhetoric and vocabulary. As well might the common folks to-day pre· sume to pray unto one of the transcendent Buddhas, between whom and the needy suppliant there may be hosts upon hosts of interlopers or mediators, as for an ordinary subject to petition the emperor or even to gaze upon his dragon countenance. The change in the constitutional Japan of our day is seen in the fact that the term "Mikado" is now obsolete. This description of the relation of sovereign and minister (inaccurately characterized by some writers on Confucianism as that of "King and subject," a phrase which might almost fit the constitutional monarchy of to-day) shows the relation, as it did exist for nearly a thousand years of Japanese history. We find the same imitation of procedure, even when imperialism became only a shadow in the government and the great Shōgun who called himself "Tycoon," the ruler in Yedo, aping the majesty of Kiōto, became so powerful as to be also a dragon. Between the Yedo Shōgun and the people rose a great staircase of numberless subordinates, and should a subject attempt to offer a petition in person he must pay for it by crucifixion.[12]

As, under the emperor there were court ministers, heads of departments, governors and functionaries of all kinds before the people were reached, so, under the Shōgun in the feudal days, there were the Daimiōs or great lords and the Shomiōs or small lords with their retainers in graduated subordination, and below these were the servants and general humanity. Even after the status of man was reached, there were gradations and degradations through fractions down to ciphers and indeed to minus quantities, for there existed in the Country of Brave Warriors some tens of thousands of human beings bearing the names of *eta* (pariah) and *hi-nin* (non-human), who were far below the pale of humanity.

The Paramount Idea of Loyalty.

The one idea which dominated all of these classes,[13] —in Old Japan there were no masses but only many classes—was that of loyalty. As the Japanese language shows, every faculty of man was subordinated to this idea. Confucianism even conditioned the development of Japanese grammar, as it also did that of the Koreans, by multiplying honorary prefixes and suffixes and building up all sociable and polite speech on perpendicular lines. Personality was next to nothing and individuality was in a certain sense unknown. In European languages, the pronoun shows how clearly the ideas of personality and of individuality have been developed ; but in the Japanese language there really are no pronouns, in the sense of the word as used by the Germanic nations, at least, although there are hundreds of impersonal and topographical substitutes for them.[14] The mirror, of the language itself, reflects more truth upon this point of inquiry than do patriotic assertions, or the protests of those who in the days of this Meiji era so handsomely employ the Japanese language as the medium of thought. Strictly speaking, the ego disappears in ordinary conversation and action, and instead, it is the servant speaking reverently to his master ; or it is the master condescending to the object which is " before his hand " or " to the side " or " below " where his inferior kneels ; or it is the " honorable right " addressing the " esteemed left."

All the terms which a foreigner might use in speaking of the duties of sovereign and minister, of lord and retainer and of master and servant, are comprehended in the Japanese word, Kun-shin, in which is crystallized but one thought, though it may relate to three grades of society. The testimony of history and of the language shows, that the feelings which we call loyalty and reverence are always directed upward, while those which we term benevolence and love invariably look downward.

Note herein the difference between the teachings of Christ and those of the Chinese sage. According to the latter, if there be love in the relation of the master and servant, it is the master who loves, and not the servant who may only reverence. It would be inharmonious for the Japanese servant to love his master; he never even talks of it. And in family life, while the parent may love the child, the child is not expected to love the parent but rather to reverence him. So also the Japanese wife, as in our old scriptural versions, is to "see that she *reverence* her husband." Love (not *agapé*, but *eros*) is indeed a theme of the poets and of that part of life and of literature which is, strictly speaking, outside of the marriage relation, but the thought that dominates in marital life, is reverence from the wife and benevolence from the husband. The Christian conception, which requires that a woman should love her husband, does not strictly accord with the Confucian idea.

Christianity has taught us that when a man loves a woman purely and makes her his wife, he should also have reverence for her, and that this element should be an integral part of his love. Christianity also teaches a reverence for children; and Wordsworth has but followed the spirit of his great master, Christ, when expressing this beautiful sentiment in his melodious numbers. Such ideas as these, however, are discords in Japanese social life of the old order. So also the Christian preaching of love to God, sounds outlandish to the men of Chinese mind in the middle or the pupil kingdom, who seem to think that it can only come from the lips of those who have not been properly trained. To "love God" appears to them as being an unwarrantable patronage of, and familiarity with "Heaven," or the King of Kings. The same difficulty, which to-day troubles Christian preachers and translators, existed among the Roman Catholic missionaries three centuries ago.[15] The moulds of thought were not then, nor are they even now, entirely ready for the full truth of Christian revelation.

Suicide Made Honorable.

In the long story of the Honorable Country, there are to be found many shining examples of loyalty, which is the one theme oftenest illustrated in popular fiction and romance. Its well-attested instances on the crimson thread of Japanese history are more numerous than the beads on many rosaries. The most famous of all, perhaps, is the episode of the Forty-Seven Rōnins, which is a constant favorite in the theatres, and has been so graphically narrated or pictured by scores of native poets, authors, artists, sculptors and dramatists, and told in English by Mitford, Dickens and Greey.[16]

These forty-seven men hated wife, child, society, name, fame, food and comfort for the sake of avenging the death of their master. In a certain sense, they ceased to be persons in order to become the impersonal instruments of Heaven's retribution. They gave up everything—houses, lands, kinsmen — that they might have in this life the hundred-fold reward of vengeance, and in the world-life of humanity throughout the centuries, fame and honor. Feeding the hunger of their hearts upon the hope of glutting that hunger with the life-blood of their victim, they waited long years. When once their swords had drunk the consecrated blood, they laid the severed head upon their master's tomb and then gladly, even rapturously, delivered themselves up, and ripping open their bowels they died by that judicially ordered seppuku which cleansed their memory from every stain, and gave to them the martyr's fame and crown forever. The tombs of these men, on the hillside overlooking the Bay of Yedo, are to this day ever fragrant with fresh flowers, and to the cemetery where their ashes lie and their memorials stand, thousands of pilgrims annually wend their way. No dramas are more permanently popular on the stage than those which display the virtues of these heroes, who are commonly spoken of as "The righteous Samurai." Their tombs have stood for two centuries, as mighty magnets drawing others to self-impalement on the sword—as multipliers of suicides.

Yet this alphabetic number, this *i-ro-ha* of self-murder, is but one of a thousand instances in the Land of Noble Suicides. From the pre-historic days when the custom of *Jun-shi*, or dying with the master, required the interment of the living retainers with the dead lord, down through all the ages to the Revolution of 1868, when at Sendai and Aidzu scores of men and boys opened their bowels, and mothers slew their infant sons and cut their own throats, there has been flowing through Japanese history a river of suicides' blood [17] having its springs in the devotion of retainers to masters, and of soldiers to a lost cause as represented by the feudal superior. Shigémori, the son of the prime minister Kiyomori, who protected the emperor even against his own father, is a model of that Japanese kun-shin which placed fidelity to the sovereign above filial obedience; though even yet Shigémori's name is the synonym of both virtues. Kusunoki Masashigé,[18] the white flower of Japanese chivalry, is but one, typical not only of a thousand but of thousands of thousands of soldiers, who hated parents, wife, child, friend in order to be disciple to the supreme loyalty. He sealed his creed by emptying his own veins. Kiyomori,[19] like King David of Israel, on his dying bed ordered the assassination of his personal enemy.

The common Japanese novels read like records of slaughter-houses. No Moloch or Shiva has won more victims to his shrine than has this idea of Japanese loyalty which is so beautiful in theory and so hideous in practice. Despite the military clamps and frightful despotism of Yedo, which for two hundred and fifty years gave to the world a delusive idea of profound quiet in the Country of Peaceful Shores, there was in fact a chronic unrest which amounted at many times and in many places to anarchy. The calm of despotism was, indeed, rudely broken by the aliens in the "black ships" with the "flowery flag"; but, without regarding influences from the West, the indications of history as now read, pointed in 1850 toward the bloodiest of Japan's many civil wars. Could the statistics of the suicides during this long period be collected, their publication would excite in Christendom the utmost incredulity.

Nevertheless, this qualifying statement should be made. A study of the origin and development of the national method of self-destruction shows that suicide by seppuku, or opening of the abdomen, was first a custom, and then a privilege. It took, among men of honor, the place of the public executions, the massacres in battle and siege, decimation of rebels and similar means of killing at the hands of others, which so often mar the historical records of western nations. Undoubtedly, therefore, in the minds of most Japanese, there are many instances of *hara-kiri* which should not be classed as suicide, but technically as execution of judicial sentence. And yet no sentence or process of death known in western lands had such influence in glorifying the victim, as had seppuku in Japan.

The Family Idea.

The Second Relation is that of father and son, thus preceding what we should suppose to be the first of human relations—husband and wife—but the arrangement entirely accords with the Oriental conception that the family, the house, is more important than the individual. In Old Japan the paramount idea in marriage, was not that of love or companionship, or of mutual assistance with children, but was almost wholly that of offspring, and of maintaining the family line.[20] The individual might perish but the house must live on.

Very different from the family of Christendom, is the

family in Old Japan, in which we find elements that would not be recognized where monogamy prevails and children are born in the home and not in the herd. Instead of father, mother and children, there are father, wife, concubines, and various sorts of children who are born of the wife or of the concubine, or have been adopted into the family. With us, adoption is the exception, but in Japan it is the invariable rule whenever either convenience or necessity requires it of the house. Indeed it is rare to find a set of brothers bearing the same family name. Adoption and concubinage keep the house unbroken.[21] It is the house, the name, which must continue, although not necessarily by a blood line. The name, a social trade-mark, lives on for ages. The line of Japanese emperors, which, in the Constitution of 1889, by adding mythology to history is said to rule " unbroken from ages eternal," is not one of fathers and sons, but has been made continuous by concubinage and adoption. In this view, it is possibly as old as the line of the popes.

It is very evident that our terms and usages do not have in such a home the place or meaning which one not familiar with the real life of Old Japan would suppose. The father is an absolute ruler. There is in Old Japan hardly any such thing as " parents," for practically there is only one parent, as the woman counts for little. The wife is honored if she becomes a mother, but if childless she is very probably neglected. Our idea of fatherhood implies that the child has rights and that he should love as well as be loved. Our customs excite not only the merriment but even the contempt of the old-school Japanese. The kiss and the embrace, the linking of the child's arm around its father's neck, the address on letters "My dear Wife" or "My beloved Mother" seem to them like caricatures of propriety. On the other hand, it is undoubtedly true that in reverence toward parents—or at least toward one of the parents—a Japanese child is apt to excel the one born even in a Christian home.

This so-called filial "piety" becomes in practice, however, a horrible outrage upon humanity and especially upon womanhood. During centuries the despotic power of the father enabled him to put an end to the life of his child, whether boy or girl.

Under this abominable despotism there is no protection for the daughter, who is bound to sell her body, while youth or beauty last or perhaps for life, to help pay her father's debts, to support an aged parent or even to gratify his mere caprice. In hundreds of Japanese romances the daughter, who for the sake of her parents has sold herself to shame, is made the theme of the story and an object of praise. In the minds of the people there may be indeed a feeling of pity that the girl has been obliged to give up her home life for the brothel, but no one ever thinks of questioning the right of the parent to make the sale of the girl's body, any more than he would allow the daughter to rebel against it. This idea still lingers and the institution remains,[22] although the system has received stunning blows from the teaching of Christian ethics, the preaching of a better gospel and the improvements in the law of the land.

The Marital Relation.

The Third Relation is that of husband and wife. The meaning of these words, however, is not the same

with the Japanese as with us. In Confucius there is
not only male and female, but also superior and inferior, master and servant.[23] Without any love-making
or courtship by those most interested, a marriage between two young people is arranged by their parents
through the medium of what is called a " go-between."
The bride leaves her father's house forever—that is,
when she is not to be subsequently divorced—and entering into that of her husband must be subordinate
not only to him but also to his parents, and must obey
them as her own father and mother. Having all her
life under her father's roof reverenced her superiors,
she is expected to bring reverence to her new domicile,
but not love. She must always obey but never be jealous. She must not be angry, no matter whom her husband may introduce into his household. She must
wait upon him at his meals and must walk behind him,
but not with him. When she dies her children go to
her funeral, but not her husband.

A foreigner, hearing the Japanese translate our word
chastity by the term *téiso* or *misao*, may imagine that
the latter represents mutual obligation and personal
purity for man and wife alike, but on looking into the
dictionary he will find that *téiso* means "Womanly
duties." A circumlocution is needed to express the
idea of a chaste man.

Jealousy is a horrible sin, but is always supposed to
be a womanish fault, and so an exhibition of folly and
weakness. Therefore, to apply such a term to God—
—to say "a jealous God"—outrages the good sense of
a Confucianist,[24] almost as much as the statement that
God "cannot lie" did that of the Pundit, who wondered
how God could be Omnipotent if He could not lie,

How great the need in Japanese social life of some
purifying principle higher than Confucianism can afford, is shown in the little book entitled "The Japanese
Bride,"[25] written by a native, and scarcely less in the
storm of native criticism it called forth. Under the
system which has ruled Japan for a millennium and a
half, divorce has been almost entirely in the hands of
the husband, and the document of separation, entitled
in common parlance the "three lines and a half," was
invariably written by the man. A woman might indeed nominally obtain a divorce from her husband,
but not actually; for the severance of the marital tie
would be the work of the house or relatives, rather
than the act of the wife, who was not "a person" in the
case. Indeed, in the olden time a woman was not a
person in the eye of the law, but rather a chattel. The
case is somewhat different under the new codes,[26] but
the looseness of the marriage tie is still a scandal to
thinking Japanese. Since the breaking up of the
feudal system and the disarrangement of the old social
and moral standards, the statistics made annually from
the official census show that the ratio of divorce to
marriage is very nearly as one to three.[27]

The Elder and the Younger Brother.

The Fourth Relation is that of Elder Brother and
Younger Brother. As we have said, foreigners in
translating some of the Chinese and Japanese terms
used in the system of Confucius are often led into errors by supposing that the Christian conception of
family life prevails also in Chinese Asia. By many
writers this relation is translated "brother to brother;"

but really in the Japanese language there is no term meaning simply "brother" or "sister,"[28] and a circumlocution is necessary to express the ideas which we convey by these words. It is always "older brother" or "younger brother," and "older sister" or "younger sister"—the male or female "*kiyodai*," as the case may be. With us—excepting in lands where the law of primogeniture still prevails—all the brothers are practically equal, and it would be considered a violation of Christian righteousness for a parent to show more favor to one child than to another. In this respect the "wisdom that cometh from above" is "without partiality." The Chinese ethical system, however, disregards the principle of mutual rights and duties, and builds up the family on the theory of the subordination of the younger brother to the elder brother, the predominant idea being not mutual love, but, far more than in the Christian household, that of rank and order. The attitude of the heir of the family toward the other children is one of condescension, and they, as well as the widowed mother, regard the oldest son with reverence. It is as though the commandment given on Sinai should read, "Honor thy father and thy elder brother."

The mother is an instrument rather than a person in the life of the house, and the older brother is the one on whom rests the responsibility of continuing the family line. The younger brothers serve as subjects for adoption into other families, especially those where there are daughters to be married and family names to be continued. In a word, the name belongs to the house and not to the individual. The habit of naming children after relatives or friends of the parents, or illustrious men and women, is unknown in Old Japan, though an approach to this common custom among us is made by conferring or making use of part of a name, usually by the transference of one ideograph forming the name-word. Such a practice lays stress upon personality, and so has no place in the country without pronouns, where the idea of continuing the personal house or semi-personal family, is predominant. The customs prevalent in life are strong even in death, and the elder brother or sister, in some provinces, did not go to the funeral of the younger. This state of affairs is reflected in Japanese literature, and produces in romance as well as in history many situations and episodes which seem almost incredible to the Western mind.

In the lands ruled by Confucius the grown-up children usually live under the parental roof, and there are few independent homes as we understand them. The so-called family is composed both of the living and of the dead, and constitutes the unit of society.

Friendship and Humanity.

The Fifth Relation—Friends. Here, again, a mistake is often made by those who import ideas of Christendom into the terms used in Chinese Asia, and who strive to make exact equivalent in exchanging the coins of speech. Occidental writers are prone to translate the term for the fifth relation into the English phrase "man to man," which leads the Western reader to suppose that Confucius taught that universal love for man, as man, which was instilled and exemplified by Jesus Christ. In translating Confucius they often make the same mistake that some have done who read in Terence's "Self-Tormentor" the line, "I am a man, and nothing human is foreign to me," [29] and imagine that this is the sentiment of an enlightened Christian, although the context shows that it is only the boast of a busybody and parasite. What Confucius taught under the fifth relation is not universality, and, as compared to the teachings of Jesus, is moonlight, not sunlight. The doctrine of the sage is clearly expressed in the Analects, and amounts only to courtesy and propriety. He taught, indeed, that the stranger is to be treated as a friend ; and although in both Chinese and Japanese history there are illustrious proofs that Confucius had interpreters nobler than himself, yet it is probable that the doctrine of the stranger's receiving treatment as a friend, does not extend to the foreigner. Confucius framed something like the Golden Rule— though it were better called a Silver Rule, or possibly a Gilded Rule, since it is in the negative instead of being definitely placed in the positive and indicative form. One may search his writings in vain for anything approaching the parable of the Good Samaritan, or the words of Him who commended Elijah for replenishing the cruse and barrel of the widow of Sarepta, and Elisha for healing Naaman the Syrian leper, and Jonah for preaching the good news of God to the Assyrians who had been aliens and oppressors. Lao Tsze, however, went so far as to teach "return good for evil." When one of the pupils of Confucius interrogated his Master concerning this, the sage answered : "What then will you return for good? Recompense injury with justice, and return good for good."

But if we do good only to those who do good to us,

what thanks have we? Do not the publicans the same? Behold how the Heavenly Father does good alike unto all, sending rain upon the just and unjust!

How Old Japan treated the foreigner is seen in the repeated repulse, with powder and ball, of the relief ships which, under the friendly stars and stripes, attempted to bring back to her shores the shipwrecked natives of Nippon.[30] Granted that this action may have been purely political and the Government alone responsible for it—just as our un-Christian anti-Chinese legislation is similarly explained—yet it is certain that the sentiment of the only men in Japan who made public opinion,—the Samurai of that day,—was in favor of this method of meeting the alien.

In 1852 the American expedition was despatched to Japan for the purpose of opening a lucrative trade and of extending American influence and glory, but also unquestionably with the idea of restoring shipwrecked Japanese as well as securing kind treatment for shipwrecked American sailors, thereby promoting the cause of humanity and international courtesy ; in short, with motives that were manifestly mixed.[31] In the treaty pavilion there ensued an interesting discussion between Commodore Perry and Professor Hayashi upon this very subject.

Perry truthfully complained that the dictates of humanity had not been followed by the Japanese, that unnecessary cruelty had been used against shipwrecked men, and that Japan's attitude toward her neighbors and the whole world was that of an enemy and not of a friend.

Hayashi, who was then probably the leading Confucianist in Japan, warmly defended his countrymen

9

and superiors against the charge of intentional cruelty, and denounced the lawless character of many of the foreign sailors. Like most Japanese of his school and age, he wound up with panegyrics on the pre-eminence in virtue and humanity, above all nations, of the Country Ruled by a Theocratic Dynasty, and on the glory and goodness of the great Tokugawa family, which had given peace to the land during two centuries or more.[32]

It is manifest, however, that so far as this hostility to foreigners, and this blind bigotry of " patriotism " were based on Chinese codes of morals, as officially taught in Yedo, they belonged as much to the old Confucianism as to the new. Wherever the narrow philosophy of the sage has dominated, it has made Asia Chinese and nations hermits. As a rule, the only way in which foreigners could come peacefully into China or the countries which she intellectually dominated was as vassals, tribute-bearers, or " barbarians." The mental attitude of China, Korea, Annam and Japan has for ages been that of the Jews in Herodian times, who set up, between the Court of Israel and the Court of the Gentiles, their graven stones of warning which read : [33]

> " No foreigner to proceed
> within the partition wall
> and enclosure around the
> sanctuary ; whoever is
> caught in the same
> will on that account be liable
> to incur death,"

CONFUCIANISM IN ITS PHILOSOPHICAL FORM

"After a thousand years the pine decays; the flower has its glory in blooming for a day."—Hakkyoi, Chinese Poet of the Tang Dynasty.

"The morning-glory of an hour differs not in heart from the pine-tree of a thousand years."—Matsunaga of Japan.

"The pine's heart is not of a thousand years, nor the morning-glory's of an hour, but only that they may fulfil their destiny."

"Since Iyéyasú, his hair brushed by the wind, his body anointed with rain, with lifelong labor caused confusion to cease and order to prevail, for more than a hundred years there has been no war. The waves of the four seas have been unruffled and no one has failed of the blessing of peace. The common folk must speak with reverence, yet it is the duty of scholars to celebrate the virtue of the Government."—Kyusō, of Yedo.

"A ruler must have faithful ministers. He who sees the error of his lord and remonstrates, not fearing his wrath, is braver than he who bears the foremost spear in battle."—Iyéyasú.

"The choice of the Chinese philosophy and the rejection of Buddhism was not because of any inherent quality in the Japanese mind. It was not the rejection of supernaturalism or the miraculous. The Chinese philosophy is as supernaturalistic as some forms of Buddhism. The distinction is not between the natural and the supernatural in either system, but between the seen and the unseen."

"The Chinese philosophy is as religious as the original teaching of Gautama. Neither Shushi nor Gautama believed in a Creator, but both believed in gods and demons. . . . It has little place for prayer, but has a vivid sense of the Infinite and the Unseen, and fervently believes that right conduct is in accord with the 'eternal verities.'"—George William Knox.

"In him is the yea."—Paul.

CHAPTER V

CONFUCIANISM IN ITS PHILOSOPHICAL FORM

Japan's Millennium of Simple Confucianism

HAVING seen the practical working of the ethics of Confucianism, especially in the old and simple system, let us now glance at the developed and philosophical forms, which, by giving the educated man of Japan a creed, made him break away from Buddhism and despise it, while becoming often fanatically Confucian.

For a thousand years (from 600 to 1600 A.D.) the Buddhist religious teachers assisted in promulgating the ethics of Confucius; for during all this time there was harmony between the various Buddhisms imported from India, Tibet, China and Korea, and the simple undeveloped system of Chinese Confucianism. Slight modifications were made by individual teachers, and emphasis was laid upon this or that feature, while out of the soil of Japanese feudalism were growths of certain virtues as phases of loyalty, phenomenal beyond those in China. Nevertheless, during all this time, the Japanese teachers of the Chinese ethic were as students who did but recite what they learned. They simply transmitted, without attempting to expand or improve.

Though the apparatus of distribution was early known, block printing having been borrowed from the

Chinese after the ninth century, and movable types learned from the Koreans and made use of in the sixteenth century,[1] the Chinese classics were not printed as a body until after the great peace of Genna (1615). Nor during this period were translations made of the classics or commentaries, into the Japanese vernacular. Indeed, between the tenth and sixteenth centuries there was little direct intercourse, commercial, diplomatic or intellectual, between Japan and China, as compared with the previous eras, or the decades since 1870.

Suddenly in the seventeenth century the intellect of Japan, all ready for new surprises in the profound peace inaugurated by Iyéyasŭ, received, as it were, an electric thrill. The great warrior, becoming first a unifier by arms and statecraft, determined also to become the architect of the national culture. Gathering up, from all parts of the country, books, manuscripts, and the appliances of intellectual discipline, he encouraged scholars and stimulated education. Under his supervision the Chinese classics were printed, and were soon widely circulated. A college was established in Yedo, and immediately there began a critical study of the texts and principal commentaries. The fall of the Ming dynasty in China, and the accession of the Manchiu Tartars, became the signal for a great exodus of learned Chinese, who fled to Japan. These received a warm welcome, both at the capital and in Yedo, as well as in some of the castle towns of the Daimiōs, among whom stand illustrious those of the province of Mito.[2]

These men from the west brought not only ethics but philosophy; and the fertilizing influences of these scholars of the Dispersion, may be likened to those of the exodus of the Greek learned men after the capture of Constantinople by the Turks. Confucian schools were established in most of the chief provincial cities. For over two hundred years this discipline in the Chinese ethics, literature and history constituted the education of the boys and men of Japan. Almost every member of the Samurai classes was thoroughly drilled in this curriculum. All Japanese social, official, intellectual and literary life was permeated with the new spirit. Their "world" was that of the Chinese, and all outside of it belonged to "barbarians." The matrices of thought became so fixed and the Japanese language has been so moulded, that even now, despite the intense and prolonged efforts of thirty years of acute and laborious scholarship, it is impossible, as we have said, to find English equivalents for terms which were used for a century or two past in every - day Japanese speech. Those who know most about these facts, are most modest in attempting with English words to do justice to Japanese thought; while those who know the least seem to be most glib, fluent and voluminous in showing to their own satisfaction, that there is little difference between the ethics of Chinese Asia and those of Christendom.

Survey of the Intellectual History of China.

The Confucianism of the last quarter-millennium in Japan is not that of her early centuries. While the Japanese for a thousand years only repeated and recited—merely talking aloud in their intellectual sleep but not reflecting—China was awake and thinking hard.

Japan's continued civil wars, which caused the almost total destruction of books and manuscripts, secured also the triumph of Buddhism which meant the atrophy of the national intellect. When, after the long feuds and battles of the middle ages, Confucianism stepped the second time into the Land of *Brave* Scholars, it was no longer with the simple rules of conduct and ceremonial of the ancient days, nor was it as the ally of Buddhism. It came like an armed man in full panoply of harness and weapons. It entered to drive Buddhism out, and to defend the intellect of the educated against the wiles of priestcraft. It was a full-blown system of pantheistic rationalism, with a scheme of philosophy that to the far-Oriental mind seemed perfect as a rule both of faith and practice. It came in a form that was received as religion, for it was not only morality " touched " but infused with motion. Nor were the emotions kindled, those of the partisan only, but rather also those of the devotee and the martyr. Henceforth Buddhism, with its inventions, its fables, and its endless dogmatism, was for the common people, for women and children, but not for the Samurai. The new Confucianism came to Japan as the system of Chu Hi. For three centuries this system had already held sway over the intellect of China. For two centuries and a half it has dominated the minds of the Samurai so that the majority of them to-day, even with the new name Shizoku, are Confucianists so far as they are anything.

To understand the origin of Buddhism we must know something of the history and the previous religious and philosophical systems of India, and so, if we are to appreciate modern " orthodox " Confucianism, we must review the history of China, and see, in outline, at least, its literature, politics and philosophy during the middle ages.

" Four great stages of literary and national development may be pointed to as intervening (in the fifteen hundred years) between the great sage and the age called that of the Sung-Ju,"[3] from the tenth to the fourteenth century, in which the Confucian system received its modern form. Each of them embraced the course of three or four centuries.

I. From the sixth to the third century before Christ the struggle was for Confucian and orthodox doctrine, led by Mencius against various speculators in morals and politics, with Taoist doctrine continually increasing in acceptance.

II. The Han age (from B.C. 206 to A.D. 190) was rich in critical expositors and commentators of the classics, but "the tone of speculation was predominantly Taoist."

III. The period of the Six Dynasties (from A.D. 221 to A.D. 618) was the golden age of Buddhism, when the science and philosophy of India enriched the Chinese mind, and the wealth of the country was lavished on Buddhist temples and monasteries. The faith of Shaka became nearly universal and the Buddhists led in philosophy and literature, founding a native school of Indian philosophy.

IV. The Tang period (from A.D. 618 to 905) marked by luxury and poetry, was an age of mental inaction and enervating prosperity.

V. The fifth epoch, beginning with the Sung Dynasty (from A.D. 960 to 1333) and lasting to our own time, was ushered in by a period of intense mental energy.

Strange to say (and most interesting is the fact to Americans of this generation), the immediate occasion of the recension and expansion of the old Confucianism was a Populist movement.[4] During the Tang era of national prosperity, Chinese socialists questioned the foundations of society and of government, and there grew up a new school of interpreters as well as of politicians. In the tenth century the contest between the old Confucianism and the new notions, broke out with a violence that threatened anarchy to the whole empire.

One set of politicians, led by Wang (1021–1086), urged an extension of administrative functions, including agricultural loans, while the brothers Cheng (1032–1085, 1033–1107) reaffirmed, with fresh intellectual power, the old orthodoxy.

The school of writers and party agitators, led by Szma Kwang (1009–1086)[5] the historian, contended that the ancient principles of the sages should be put in force. Others, the Populists of that age and land, demanded the entire overthrow of existing institutions.

In the bitter contest which ensued, the Radicals and Reformers temporarily won the day and held power. For a decade the experiment of innovation was tried. Men turned things social and political upside down to see how they looked in that position. So these stood or oscillated for thirteen years, when the people demanded the old order again. The Conservatives rose to power. There was no civil war, but the Radicals were banished beyond the frontier, and the country returned to normal government.

This controversy raised a landmark in the intellec-

tual history of China.[6] The thoughts of men were
turned toward deep and acute inquiry into the nature
and use of things in general. This thinking resulted
in a literature which to-day is the basis of the opinions
of the educated men in all Chinese Asia. Instead of a
sapling we now have a mighty tree. The chief of the
Chinese writers, the Calvin of Asiatic orthodoxy, who
may be said to have wrought Confucianism into a developed philosophy, and who may be called the greatest teacher of the mind, of modern China, Korea and
Japan, is Chu Hi, who reverently adopted the criticisms on the Chinese classics of the brothers Cheng.[7]
It is evident that in Chu Hi's system, we have a body
of thought which may be called the result of Chinese
reflection during a millennium and a half. It is the
ethics of Confucius transfused with the mystical elements of Taoism and the speculations of Buddhism.
As the common people of China made an amalgam of
the three religions and consider them one, so the philosophers have out of these three systems made one,
calling that one Confucianism. The dominant philosophy in Japan to-day is based upon the writings of Chu
Hi (in Japanese, Shu Shi) and called the system of Téi-
Shu, which is the Japanese pronunciation of the names
of the Cheng brothers and of Chu (Hi). It is a medley
which the ancient sage could no more recognize than
would Jesus know much of the Christianity that casts
out devils in his name.

Contrast between the Chinese and Japanese Intellect.

Here we must draw a contrast between the Chinese
and Japanese intellect to the credit of the former ;

China made, Japan borrowed. While history shows that the Chinese mind, once at least, possessed mental initiative, and the power of thinking out a system of philosophy which to-day satisfies largely, if not wholly, the needs of the educated Chinaman, there has been in the Japanese mind, as shown by its history, apparently no such vigor or fruitfulness. From the literary and philosophical points of view, Confucianism, as it entered Japan, in the sixth century, remained practically stationary for a thousand years. Modifications, indeed, were made upon the Chinese system, and these were striking and profound, but they were less developments of the intellect than necessities of the case. The modifications were made, as molten metal poured into a mould shaped by other hands than the artist's own, rather than as clay made plastic under the hand of a designer. Buddhism, being the dominant force in the thoughts of the Japanese for at least eight hundred years, furnished the food for the requirements of man on his intellectual and religious side.

Broadly speaking, it may be said that the Japanese, receiving passively the Chinese classics, were content simply to copy and to recite what they had learned. As compared with their audacity in not only going beyond the teachings of Buddha, but in inventing systems of Buddhism which neither Gautama nor his first disciples could recognize, the docile and almost slavish adherence to ancient Confucianism is one of the astonishing things in the history of religions in Japan. In the field of Buddhism we have a luxuriant growth of new and strange species of colossal weeds that overtower and seem to have choked out whatever furze of original Buddhism there was in Japan, while in the domain of

Confucianism there is a barren heath. Whereas, in China, the voluminous literature created by commentators on Confucius and the commentaries on the commentators suggests the hyperbole used by the author of John's Gospel,[8] yet there is probably nothing on Confucianism from the Japanese pen in the thousand years under our review which is worth the reading or the translation.[9] In this respect the Japanese genius showed its vast capabilities of imitation, adoption and assimilation.

As of old, Confucianism again furnished a Chinese wall, within which the Japanese could move, and wherein they might find food for the mind in all the relations of life and along all the lines of achievement permitted them. The philosophy imported from China, as shown again and again in that land of oft-changing dynasties, harmonizing with arbitrary government, accorded perfectly with the despotism of the Tokugawas, the "Tycoons" who in Yedo ruled from 1603 to 1868. Nothing new was permitted, and any attempt at modification, enlargement, or improvement was not only frowned and hissed down as impious innovation, but usually brought upon the daring innovator the ban of the censor, imprisonment, banishment, or death by enforced suicide.[10] In Yedo, the centre of Chinese learning, and in other parts of the country, there were, indeed, thinkers whose philosophy did not always tally with what was taught by the orthodox,[11] but as a rule even when these men escaped the ban of the censor, or the sword of the executioner, they were but as voices crying in the wilderness. The great mass of the gentry was orthodox, according to the standards of the Séido College, while the common people re-

mained faithful to Buddhism. In the conduct of daily
life they followed the precepts which had for centuries
been taught them by their fathers.

Philosophical Confucianism the Religion of the Samurai.

What were the features of this modern Confucian
philosophy, which the Japanese Samurai exalted to a
religion ? [12] We say philosophy and religion, because
while the teachings of the great sage lay at the bottom
of the system, yet it is not true since the early seventeenth century, that the thinking men of Japan have
been satisfied with only the original simple ethical
rules of the ancient master. Though they have craved
a richer mental pabulum, yet they have enjoyed less
the study of the original text, than acquaintance with
the commentaries and communion with the great philosophical exponents, of the master. What, then, we ask,
are the features of the developed philosophy, which,
imported from China, served the Japanese Samurai not
only as morals but for such religion as he possessed or
professed ?

We answer : The system was not agnostic, as many
modern and western writers assert that it is, and as
Confucius, transmitting and probably modifying the
old religion, had made the body of his teachings to be.
Agnostic, indeed, in regard to many things wherein
a Christian has faith, modern Confucianism, besides
being bitterly polemic and hostile to Buddhism, is
pantheistic.

Certain it is that during the revival of Pure Shintō
in the eighteenth century, the scholars of the Shintō
school, and those of its great rival, the Chinese, agreed

in making loyalty[13] take the place of filial duty in the Confucian system. To serve the cause of the Emperor became the most essential duty to those with culti-vated minds. The newer Chinese philosophy mightily influenced the historians, Rai Sanyo and those of the Mito school, whose works, now classic, really began the revolution of 1868. By forming and setting in motion the public opinion, which finally overthrew the Shō-gun and feudalism, restored the Emperor to supreme power, and unified the nation, they helped, with mod-ern ideas, to make the New Japan of our day. The Shintō and the Chinese teachings became amalgamated in a common cause, and thus the philosophy of Chu Hi, mingling with the nationalism and patriotism in-culcated by Shintō, brought about a remarkable result. As a native scholar and philosopher observes, " It certainly is strange to see the Tokugawa rule much shaken, if not actually overthrown, by that doctrine which generations of able Shōguns and their ministers had earnestly encouraged and protected. It is perhaps still more remarkable to see the Mito clan, under many able and active chiefs, become the centre of the Kinno[14] movement; which was to result in the overthrow of the Tokugawa family, of which it was itself a branch."

A Medley of Pantheism.

The philosophy of modern Confucianism is wholly pantheistic. There is in it no such thing or being as God. The orthodox pantheism of Old Japan means that everything in general is god, but nothing in par-ticular is God ; that All is god, but not that God is all. It is a " pantheistic medley." [15]

Chu Hi and his Japanese successors, especially **Kyū-so**, argue finely and discourse volubly about *Ki* [16] or spirit; but it is not Spirit, or spiritual in the sense of Him who taught even a woman at the well-curb at Sychar. It is in the air. It is in the earth, the trees, the flowers. It comes to consciousness in man. His *Ri* is the Tao of Lao Tsze, the Way, Reason, Law. It is formless, invisible.

"**Ri** is not separate from **Ki**, for then it were an empty abstract thing. It is joined to **Ki**, and may be called, by nature, one decreed, changeless Norm. It is the rule of **Ki**, the **very** centre, the reason why **Ki** is **Ki**."

Ten or Heaven is not God or the abode of God, but an abstraction, a sort of Unknowable, or Primordial Necessity.

"The doctrine of the Sages knows and worships Heaven, and without faith in it there is no truth. For men and things, the universe, are born and nourished by Heaven, and the 'Way,' the 'ri,' that is in all, is the 'Way,' the 'ri' of Heaven. Distinguishing root and branch, the heart is the root of Heaven and the appearance, the revolution of the sun and moon, the order of the stars, is the branch. The books of the sages teach us to conform to the heart of Heaven and deal not with appearances."

"The teaching of the sages is the original truth and, given to men, it forms both their nature and their relationships. With it complete, naught else is needed for the perfect following of the 'Way.' Let then the child make its parents Heaven, the retainer, his Lord, the wife her husband, and let each give up life for righteousness. Thus will each serve for Heaven. But if we exalt Heaven above parent or Lord, we shall come to think we can serve it though they be disobeyed and like tiger or wolf shall rejoice to kill them. To such fearful end does the Western learning lead. . . . Let each one die for duty, there is naught else we can do."

Thus wrote Ohashi Junzo, as late as 1857 A.D., the same year in which Townsend Harris entered Yedo to teach the practical philosophy of Christendom, and the brotherhood of man as expressed in diplomacy. Ohashi Junzo bitterly opposed the opening of Japan to modern civilization and the ideas of Christendom. His book was the swan-song of the dying Japanese Confucianism. Slow as is the dying, and hard as its death may be, the mind of new Japan has laid away to dust and oblivion the Téi-shu philosophy. "At present they (the Chinese classics) have fallen into almost total neglect, though phrases and allusions borrowed from them still pass current in literature, and even to some extent in the language of every-day life." Séido, the great temple of Confucius in Tokyo, is now utilized as an educational Museum.[17]

A study of this subject and of comparative religion, is of immediate practical benefit to the Christian teacher. The preacher, addressing an audience made up of educated Japanese, who speaks of God without describing his personality, character, or attributes as illustrated in Revelation, will find that his hearers receive his term as the expression for a bundle of abstract principles, or a system of laws, or some kind of regulated force. They do, indeed, make some reference to a "creator" by using a rare word. Occasionally, their language seems to touch the boundary line on the other side of which is conscious intelligence, but nothing approaching the clearness and definiteness of the early Chinese monotheism of the pre-Confucian classics is to be distinguished.[18] The modern Japan-

10

ese long ago heard joyfully the words, "Honor the gods, but keep them far from you," and he has done it. To love God would no more occur to a Japanese gentleman than to have his child embrace and kiss him. Whether the source and fountain of life of which they speak has any Divine Spirit, is very uncertain, but whether it has, or has not, man need not obey, much less worship him. The universe is one, the essence is the same. Man must seek to know his place in the universe; he is but one in an endless chain; let him find his part and fulfil that part; all else is vanity. One need not inquire into the origins or the ultimates. Man is moved by a power greater than himself; he has no real independence of his own; everything has its rank and place; indeed, its rank and place is its sole title to a separate existence. If a man mistakes his place he is a fool, he deserves punishment.

The Ideals of a Samurai.

Out of his place, man is not man. Duty is more important than being. Nearly everything in our life is fixed by fate; there may seem to be exceptions, because some wicked men are prosperous and some righteous men are wretched, but these are not real exceptions to the general rule that we are made for our environment and fitted to it. And then, again, it may be that our judgments are not correct. Let the heart be right and all is well. Let man be obedient and his outward circumstance is nothing, having no relation to his joy or happiness. Even when as to his earthly body man passes away, he is not destroyed; the drop again becomes part of the sea, the spark re-enters the flame, and his life continues, though it be not a conscious life. In this way man is in harmony with the original principle of all things. He outlasts the universe itself.

Hence to a conscientious Samurai there is nothing in this world better than obedience, in the ideal of a true man. What he fears most and hates most is that his memory may perish, that he shall have no seed, that he shall be forgotten or die under a cloud and be thought treacherous or cowardly or base, when in reality his life was pure and his motives high. " Better," sang Yoshida Shoin, the dying martyr for his principles, "to be a crystal and to be broken, than to be a tile upon the housetop and remain."

So, indeed, on a hundred curtained execution grounds, with the dirk of the suicide firmly grasped and about to shed their own life-blood, have sung the martyrs who died willingly for their faith in their idea of Yamato Damashii.[19] In untold instances in the national history, men have died willingly and cheerfully, and women also by thousands, as brave, as unflinching as the men, so that the story of Japanese chivalry is almost incredible in its awful suicides. History reveals a state of society in which cool determination, desperate courage and fearlessness of death in the face of duty were quite unique, and which must have had their base in some powerful though abnormal code of ethics.

This leads us to consider again the things emphasized by Japanese as distinct from Chinese and Korean[20] Confucianism, and to call attention to its fruits, while at the same time we note its defects, and show wherein it failed. We shall then show how this old system has already waxed old and is passing away. Christ has come to Japan, and behold a new heaven and a new earth!

New Japan Makes Revision.

First. For sovereign and minister, there are coming into vogue new interpretations. This relation, if it is to remain as the first, will become that of the ruler and the ruled. Constitutional government has begun ; and codes of law have been framed which are recognizing the rights of the individual and of the people. Even a woman has rights before the law, in relation to husband, parents, brothers, sisters and children. It is even beginning to be thought that children have rights. Let us hope that as the rights are better understood the duties will be equally clear.

It is coming to pass in Japan that even in government, the sovereign must consult with his people on all questions pertaining to their welfare. Although thus far the constitutional government makes the ministers responsible to the Sovereign instead of to the Diet, yet the contention of the enlightened men and the liberal parties is, that the ministers shall be responsible to the Diet. The time seems at hand when the sovereign's power over his people will not rest on traditions more or less uncertain, on history manufactured by governmental order, on mythological claims based upon the so-called "eternal ages," on prerogatives upheld by the sword, or on the supposed grace of the gods, but will be "broad-based upon the people's will." The power of the rulers will be derived from the consent of the governed. The Emperor will become the first and chief servant of the nation.

Revision and improvement of the Second Relation will make filial piety something more real than that unto which China has attained, or Japan has yet seen, or which is yet universally known in Christendom. The tyranny of the father and of the older brother, and the sale of daughters to shame, will pass away; and there will arise in the Japanese house, the Christian home.

It would be hard to say what Confucianism has done for woman. It is probable that all civilizations, and systems of philosophy, ethics and religion, can be well tested by this criterion—the position of woman. Confucianism virtually admits two standards of morality, one for man, another for woman.[21] In Chinese Asia adultery is indeed branded as one of the vilest of crimes, but in common idea and parlance it is a woman's crime, not man's. So, on the other hand, chastity is a female virtue, it is part of womanly duty, it has little or no relation to man personally. Right revision and improvement of the Third Relation will abolish concubinage. It will reform divorce. It will make love the basis of marriage. It will change the state of things truthfully pictured in such books as the Genji Monogatari, or Romance of Prince Genji, with its examples of horrible lust and incests; the Kojiki or Ethnic scripture, with its naïve accounts of filthiness among the gods; the Onna Dai Gaku, Woman's Great Study, with its amazing subordination and moral slavery of wife and daughter; and The Japanese Bride, of yesterday—all truthful pictures of Japanese life, for the epoch in which each was written. These books will become the forgotten curiosities of literature, known only to the archæologist.

Improvement and revision of the Fourth Relation,

will bring into the Japanese home more justice, righteousness, love and enjoyment of life. It will make
possible, also, the cheerful acceptance and glad practice of those codes of law common in Christendom,
which are based upon the rights of the individual and
upon the idea of the greatest good to the greatest number. It will help to abolish the evils which come from
primogeniture and to release the clutch of the dead
hand upon the living. It will decrease the power of
the graveyard, and make thought and care for the living the rule of life. It will abolish sham and fiction,
and promote the cause of truth. It will hasten the
reign of righteousness and love, and beneath propriety
and etiquette lay the basis of "charity toward all,
malice toward none."

Revision with improvement of the Fifth Relation
hastens the reign of universal brotherhood. It lifts
up the fallen, the down-trodden and the outcast. It
says to the slave " be free," and after having said " be
free," educates, trains, and lifts up the brother once
in servitude, and helps him to forget his old estate
and to know his rights as well as his duties, and develops in him the image of God. It says to the hi-
nin or not-human, " be a man, be a citizen, accept the
protection of the law." It says to the eta, " come into
humanity and society, receive the protection of law,
and the welcome of your fellows ; let memory forget
the past and charity make a new future." It will
bring Japan into the fraternity of nations, making her
people one with the peoples of Christendom, not
through the empty forms of diplomacy, or by the craft
of her envoys, or by the power of her armies and navies
reconstructed on modern principles, but by patient

education and unflinching loyalty to high ideals. Thus
will Japan become worthy of all the honors, which the
highest humanity on this planet can bestow.

The Ideal of Yamato Damashii Enlarged.

In this our time it is not only the alien from Christendom, with his hostile eye and mordant criticism,
who is helping to undermine that system of ethics
which permitted the sale of the daughter to shame, the
introduction of the concubine into the family and the
reduction of woman, even though wife and mother, to
nearly a cipher. It is not only the foreigner who assaults that philosophy which glorified the vendetta,
kept alive private war, made revenge in murder the
sweetest joy of the Samurai and suicide the gate to
honor and fame, subordinated the family to the house,
and suppressed individuality and personality. It is the
native Japanese, no longer a hermit, a "frog in the
well, that knows not the great ocean " but a student,
an inquirer, and a critic, who assaults the old ethical
and philosophical system, and calls for a new way
between heaven and earth, and a new kind of Heaven
in which shall be a Creator, a Father and a Saviour.
The brain and pen of New Japan, as well as its heart,
demand that the family shall be more than the house
and that the living members shall have greater rights
as well as duties, than the dead ancestors. They claim
that the wife shall share responsibility with the husband, and that the relation of husband and wife shall
take precedence of that of the father and son ; that the
mother shall possess equal authority with the father ;
that the wife, whether she be mother or not, shall

not be compelled to share her home with the concubine; and that the child in Japan shall be born in the home and not in the herd. The sudden introduction of the Christian ideas of personality and individuality has undoubtedly wrought peril to the framework of a society which is built according to the Confucian principles; but faith in God, love in the home, and absolute equality before the law will bring about a reign of righteousness such as Japan has never known, but toward the realization of which Christian nations are ever advancing.

Even the old ideal of the Samurai embodied in the formula Yamato Damashii will be enlarged and improved from its narrow limits and ferocious aspects, when the tap-root of all progress is allowed to strike into deeper truth, and the Sixth Relation, or rather the first relation of all, is taught, namely, that of God to Man, and of Man to God. That this relation is understood, and that the Samurai ideal, purified and enlarged, is held by increasing numbers of Japan's brightest men and noblest women, is shown in that superb Christian literature which pours from the pens of the native men and women in the Japanese Christian churches., Under this flood of truth the old obstacles to a nobler society are washed away, while out of the enriched soil rises the new Japan which is to be a part of the better Christendom that is to come. Christ in Japan, as everywhere, means not destruction, but fulfilment.

THE BUDDHISM OF NORTHERN ASIA

" LIFE IS A DREAM is what the pilgrim learns,
Nor asks for more, but straightway home returns."
—Japanese mediæval lyric drama.

"The purpose of Buddha's preaching was to bring into light the permanent truth, to reveal the root of all suffering, and thus to lead all sentient beings into the perfect emancipation from all passions."—Outlines of the Mahayana.

" Buddhism will stand forth as the embodiment of the eternal verity that as a man sows he will reap, associated with the duties of mastery over self and kindness to all men, and quickened into a popular religion by the example of a noble and beautiful life."—Dharmapala of Ceylon.

"Buddhism teaches the right path of cause and effect, and nothing which can supersede the idea of cause and effect will be accepted and believed. Buddha himself cannot contradict this law which is the Buddha of Buddhas, and no omnipotent power except this law is believed to be existent in the universe.

" Buddhism does not quarrel with other religions about the truth . . . Buddhism is truth common to every religion regardless of the outside garment."—Horin Toki, of Japan.

" Death we can face ; but knowing, as some of us do, what is human life, which of us is it that without shuddering could (if we were summoned) face the hour of birth ? "—De Quincey.

The prayer of Buddhism, " Deliver us from existence."
The prayer of the Christian, " Deliver us from evil."

" In the beginning, God created the heavens and the earth."—Genesis.

" I am come that they might have life and that they might have it more abundantly."—Jesus.

CHAPTER VI

THE BUDDHISM OF NORTHERN ASIA

Pre-Buddhistic India

DOES the name of Gautama, the Buddha, stand for
a sun-myth or for a historic personage ? One set of
scholars and writers, represented by Professor Kern,[1]
of Leyden, thinks the Buddha a mythical personage.
Another school, represented by Professor T. Rhys
Davids,[2] declares that he lived in human flesh and
breathed the air of earth. We accept the historical
view as best explaining the facts.

In order to understand a religion, in its origin at
least, we must know some of the conditions out of
which it arose. Buddhism is one of the protestant-
isms of the world. Yet, is not every religion, in one
sense, protestant ? Is it not a protest against something to which it opposes a difference ? Every new
religion, like a growing plant, ignores or rejects certain elements in the soil out of which it springs. It
takes up and assimilates, also, other elements not
used before, in order to produce a flower or fruit different from other growths out of the same soil. Yet
whether the new religion be considered as a development, fulfilment, or protest, we must know its historical perspective or background. To understand the
origin of Buddhism, one of the best preparations is to

read the history of India and especially of the thought
of her many generations; for the landmarks of the
civilizations of India, as a Hindu may proudly say,
are its mighty literatures. At these let us glance.[3]

The age of the Vedas extends from the year 2000
to 1400 B.C., and the history of this early India is
wonderfully like that of America. During this era, the
Hindus, one of the seven Aryan tribes of which the
Persian, Greek, Latin, Celtic, Sclav and Teutonic
form the other six, descending from the mid-Asian
plateau, settled the Punjab in Northwest India. They
drove the dark-skinned aborigines before them and re-
claimed forest and swamp to civilization, making the
land of the seven rivers bright with agriculture and
brilliant with cities. This was the glorious heroic age
of joyous life and conquest, when men who believed in
a Heavenly Father[4] made the first epoch of Hindu
history.

Then followed the epic age, 1400–1000 B.C., when
the area of civilization was extended still farther down
the Ganges Valley, the splendor of wealth, learning,
military prowess and social life excelling that of the
ancestral seats in the Punjab. Amid differences of
wars and diplomacy with rivalries and jealousies, a
common sacred language, literature and religion with
similar social and religious institutions, united the
various nations together. In this time the old Vedas
were compiled into bodies or collections, and the
Brahmanas and the Upanishads, besides the great epic
poems, the Mahabharata and the Ramayana were composed.

The next, or rationalistic epoch, covers the period
from 1000 B.C. to 320 B.C., when the Hindu expansion

had covered all India, that is, the peninsula from the Himalayas to Cape Comorin. Then, all India, including Ceylon, was Hinduized, though in differing degrees; the purest Aryan civilization being in the north, the less pure in the Ganges Valley and south and east, while the least Aryan and more Dravidian was in Bengal, Orissa, and India south of the Kistna River.

This story of the spread of Hindu civilization is a brilliant one, and seems as wonderful as the later European conquest of the land, and of the other "Indians" of North America from the Atlantic to the Pacific. Beside the conquests in material civilization of these our fellow-Aryans (who were the real Indians, and who spoke the language which is the common ancestor of our own and of most European tongues), what impresses us most of all, in these Aryans, is their intellectual energy. The Hindus of the rationalistic age made original discoveries. They invented grammar, geometry, arithmetic, decimal notation, and they elaborated astronomy, medicine, mental philosophy and logic (with syllogism) before these sciences were known or perfected in Greece. In the seventh century before Christ, Kapila taught a system of philosophy, of which that of the Europeans, Schopenhaur and Hartmann, seems largely a reproduction.

Following this agnostic scheme of thought, came, several centuries later, the dualistic Yoga[5] system in which the chief feature is the conception of Deity as a means of final emancipation of the human soul from further transmigration, and of union with the Universal Spirit or World Soul. There is, however, perhaps no sadder chapter in the history of human thought than the story of the later degeneration of the Yoga system into one of bloody and cruel rites in India, and of superstition in China.

Still other systems followed : one by Gautama, of the same clan or family of the later Buddha, who develops inference by the construction of syllogism ; while Kanada follows the atomic philosophy in which the atoms are eternal, but the aggregates perishable by disintegration.

Against these schools, which seemed to be dangerous "new departures," orthodox Hindus, anxious for their ancient beliefs and practices as laid down in the Vedas, started fresh systems of philosophy, avowedly more in consonance with their ancestral faith. One system insisted on the primitive Vedic ritual, and another laid emphasis on the belief in a Universal Soul first inculcated in the Upanishads.

Conditions out of which Buddhism Arose.

Whatever we may think of these schools of philosophy, or the connection with or indebtedness of Gautama, the Buddha, to them, they reveal to us the conceptions which his contemporaries had of the universe and the beings inhabiting it. These were honest human attempts to find God. In them the various beings or six conditions of sentient existence are devas or gods ; men ; asuras or monsters ; pretas or demons ; animals ; and beings in hell. Furthermore, these schools of Hindu philosophy show us the conditions out of which Buddhism arose, furnish us with its terminology and technical phrases, reveal to us what the reformer proposed to himself to do, and, what is perhaps still more important, show us the types to which

Buddhism in its degeneration and degradation reverted. The strange far-off oriental words which to-day scholars discuss, theosophists manipulate, and charlatans employ as catchpennies were common words in the every-day speech of the Hindu people, two or three thousand years ago.

Glancing rapidly at the condition of religion in the era ushering in the birth of Buddha, we note that the old joyousness of life manifested in the Vedic hymns is past, their fervor and glow are gone. In the morning of Hindu life there was no caste, no fixed priest-hood, and no idols ; but as wealth, civilization, easy and settled life succeeded, the taste for pompous sacrifices conducted by an hereditary priestly caste increased. Greater importance was laid upon the detail of the ceremonies, the attention of the worshipper being turned from the deities " to the minutiæ of rites, the erection of altars, the fixing of the proper astronomical moments for lighting the fire, the correct pronunciation of prayers, and to the various requisite acts accompanying a sacrifice." [6] In the chapter of decay which time wrote and literature reflects, we find " grotesque reasons given for every minute rite, dogmatic explanation of texts, penances for every breach of form and rule, and elaborate directions for every act and moment of the worshipper."

The literature shows a degree of credulity and submission on the part of the people and of absolute power on the part of the priests, which reminds us of the Middle Ages in Europe. The old inspiring wars with the aborigines are over. The time of bearing a noble creed, meaning culture and civilization as against savagery and idolatry, is past, and only intestine quarrels and local strife have succeeded. The age of creative literature is over, and commentators, critics and grammarians have succeeded. Still more startling are the facts disclosed by literary history. The liquid poetry has become frozen prose : the old flaming fuel of genius is now slag and ashes. We see Hindus doing exactly what Jewish rabbis, and after them Christian schoolmen and dogma-makers, did with the old Hebrew poems and prophecies. Construing literally the prayers, songs and hopes of an earlier age, they rebuild the letter of the text into creeds and systems, and erect an amazing edifice of steel-framed and stone-cased tradition, to challenge which is taught to be heresy and impiety. The poetical similes used in the Rig Vedas have been transformed into mythological tales. In the change of language the Vedas themselves are unreadable, except by the priests, who fatten on popular beliefs in the transmigration of souls and in the power of priestcraft to make that transmigration blissful—provided liberal gifts are duly forthcoming. Idolatry and witchcraft are rampant. Some saviour, some light was needed.

Buddhism a Logical Product of Hindu Thought.

At such a time, probably 557 B.C., was born Shaka, of the Muni clan, at Kapilavastu, one hundred miles northeast of Benares. We pass over the details[7] of the life of him called Prince, Lord, Lion of the Tribe of Shaka, and Saviour ; of his desertion of wife and child, called the first Great Renunciation ; of his struggles to obtain peace ; of his enlightenment or Buddhahood ; of his second or Greater Renunciation ; of merit on account of austerities; and give the story told in a mountain of books in various tongues, but condensed in a paragraph by Romesh Chunder Dutt.

"At an early age, Prince Gautama left his royal home, and his wife, and new-born child, and became a wanderer and a mendicant, to seek a way of salvation for man. Hindu rites, accompanied by the slaughter of innocent victims, repelled his feelings. Hindu philosophy afforded him no remedy, and Hindu penances and mortifications proved unavailing after he had practised them for years. At last, by severe contemplation, he discovered the long coveted truth ; a holy and calm life, and benevolence and love toward all living creatures seemed to him the essence of religion. Self-culture and universal love—this was his discovery—this is the essence of Buddhism." [8]

From one point of view Buddhism was the logical continuance of Aryan Hindoo philosophy; from another point of view it was a new departure. The leading idea in the Upanishads is that the object of the wise man should be to know, inwardly and consciously, the Great Soul of all; and by this knowledge his individual soul would become united to the Supreme Being, the true and absolute self. This was the highest point reached in the old Indian philosophy [9] before Buddha was born.

So, looking at Buddhism in the perspective of Hindu history and thought, we may say that it is doubtful whether Gautama intended to found a new religion. As, humanly speaking, Saul of Tarsus saved Christianity from being a Jewish sect and made it universal, so Gautama extricated the new enthusiasm of humanity from the priests. He made Aryan religion the property of all India. What had been a rare monopoly as narrow as Judaism, he made the inheri-

11

tance of all Asia. Gautama was a protestant and a reformer, not an agnostic or skeptic. It is more probable that he meant to shake off Brahmanism and to restore the pure and original form of the Aryan religion of the Vedas, as far as it was possible to do so. In one sense, Buddhism was a revolt against hereditary and sacerdotal privilege—an attack of the people against priestcraft. The Buddha and his disciples were levellers. In a different age and clime, but along a similar path, they did a work analogous to that of the so-called Anabaptists in Europe and Independents in England, centuries later.

It is certain, however, that Buddhism has grown logically out of ancient Hinduism. In its monastic feature—one of its most striking characteristics—we see only the concentration and reduction to system, of the old life of the ascetics and religious mendicants recognized and respected by Hinduism. For centuries the Buddhist monks and nuns were regarded in India as only a new sect of ascetics, among many others which flourished in the land.

The Buddhist doctrine of karma, or in Japanese, *ingwa*, of cause and effect, whereby it is taught that each effect in this life springs from a cause in some previous incarnation, and that each act in this life bears its fruit in the next, has grown directly out of the Hindu idea of the transmigration of souls. This idea is first inculcated in the Upanishads, and is recognized in Hindu systems of philosophy.

So also the Buddhist doctrine of Nirvana, or the attainment of a sinless state of existence, has grown out of the idea of final union of the individual soul with the Universal Soul, which is also inculcated in the

Upanishads. Yet, as we shall see, the Buddhists were, in the eyes of the Brahmans, atheists, because in the ken of these new levellers gods and men were put on the same plane. Brahmanism has never forgiven Buddhism for ignoring the gods, and the Hindoos finally drove out the followers of Gautama from India. It eventuated that after a millenium or so of Buddhism in India, the old gods, Brahma, Indra, etc., which at first had been shut out from the ken of the people, by Gautama, found their places again in the popular faith of the Buddhists, who believed that the gods as well as men, were all progressing toward the blessed Nirvana —that sinless life and holy calm, which is the Buddhist's heaven and salvation.

It is certainly very curious, and in a sense amusing, to find flourishing in far-off Japan the old gods of India, that one would suppose to have been utterly dead and left behind in oblivion. As acknowledged devas or kings and bodhisattvas or soon-to-be Buddhas, not a few once defunct Hindu gods, utterly unknown to early Buddhism, have forced their way into the company of the elect. Though most of them have not gained the popularity of the indigenous deities of Nippon, they yet attract many worshippers. They remind one that amid the coming of the sons of Elohim before Jehovah, " the satan " came also.[10]

From another point of view Buddhism was a new religion ; for it swept away and out of the field of its vision the whole of the World or Universal Soul theory. " It proclaimed a salvation which each man could gain for himself and by himself, in this world during this life, without the least reference to God, or to gods, either great or small." " It placed the first importance on knowledge ; but it was no longer a knowledge of God, it was a clear perception of the real nature as they supposed it to be of men and things." In a word, Gautama never reached the idea of a personal self-existent God, though toward that truth he groped. He was satisfied too soon.[11] His followers were even more easily satisfied with abstractions. When Gautama saw the power over the human heart of inward culture and of love to others, he obtained peace, he rested on certainty, he became the Buddha, that is, the enlightened. Perhaps he was not the first Buddhist. It may be that the historical Gautama, if so he is worthy to be called, merely made the sect or the new religion famous. Hardly a religion in the full sense of the word, Buddhism did not assume the rôle of theology, but sought only to know men and things. In one sense Buddhism is atheism, or rather, atheistic humanism. In one sense, also, the solution of the mystery of God, of life, and of the universe, which Gautama and his followers attained, was one of skepticism rather than of faith. Buddhism is, relatively, a very modern religion ; it is one of the new faiths. Is it paradoxical to say that the Buddhists are " religious atheists ? "

The Buddhist Millennium in India.

Let us now look at the life of the Founder. Day after day, the pure-souled teacher attracted new disciples while he with alms-bowl went around as mendicant and teacher. Salvation merely by self-control, and love without any rites, ceremonies, charms, priestly powers, gods or miracles, formed the burden of his teachings. "Thousands of people left their homes, embraced the holy order and became monks, ignoring caste, and relinquishing all worldly goods except the bare necessaries of life, which they possessed and enjoyed in common." Probably the first monastic *system* of the world, was that of the Indian Buddhists.

The Buddha preached the good news during forty-five years. After his death, five hundred of his followers assembled at Rajagriha and chanted together the teachings of Gautama, to fix them in memory. A hundred years later, in 377 B.C., came the great schism among the Buddhists, out of which grew the divisions known as Northern and Southern Buddhism. There was disagreement on ten points. A second council was therefore called, and the disputed points determined to the satisfaction of one side. Thereupon the seceders went away in large numbers, and the differences were never healed; on the contrary, they have widened in the course of ages.

The separatists began what may be called the Northern Buddhisms of Nepal, Tibet, China, Korea and Japan. The orthodox or Southern Buddhists are those of Ceylon, Burma and Siam. The original canon of Southern Buddhism is in Pali; that of Northern Buddhism is in Sanskrit. The one is comparatively small and simple; the other amazingly varied and voluminous. The canon of Southern scripture is called the Hinayana, the Little or Smaller Vehicle; the canon of Northern Buddhism is named the Mahayana or Great Vehicle. Possibly, also, besides the Southern and Northern Buddhisms, the Buddhism of Japan may be treated by itself and named Eastern Buddhism.

In the great council called in 242 B.C., by King Asoka,

who may be termed the Constantine of Buddhism, the sacred texts were again chanted. It was not until the year 88 B.C. in Ceylon, six hundred years after Gautama, that the three Pitakas, Boxes or Baskets, were committed to writing in the Pali language. In a word, Buddhism knows nothing of sacred documents or a canon of scripture contemporary with its first disciples.

The splendid Buddhist age of India lasted nearly a thousand years, and was one of superb triumphs in civilization. It was an age of spiritual emancipation, of freedom from idol worship, of nobler humanity and of peace.[12] It was followed by the Puranic epoch and the dark ages. Then Buddhism was, as some say, "driven out" from the land of its birth, finding new expansion in Eastern and Northern Asia, and again, a still more surprising development in the ultima-Thule of the Asiatic continent, Japan. There is now no Buddhism in India proper, the faith being represented only in Ceylon and possibly also on the main land, by the sect of the Jains, and peradventure in Persia by Babism which contains elements from three religions.[13] Like Christianity, Buddhism was "driven out" of its old home to bless other nations of the world. It is probably far nearer the truth to say that Buddhism was never expelled from India, but rather that it died by disintegration and relapse.[14] It had become Brahmanism again. The old gods and the old idol-worship came back. It is in Japan that the ends of the earth, eastern and western civilization, and the freest and fullest or at least the latest developments of Christianity and of Buddhism, have met.

In its transfer to distant lands and its developments throughout Eastern Asia, the faith which had originated in India suffered many changes. Dividing into two great branches, it became a notably different religion according as it moved along the southern, the northern, or the eastern channel. By the vehicle of the Pali language it was carried to Ceylon, Siam, Burma, Cambodia and the islands of the south; that is, to southern or peninsular and insular Asia. Here there is little evidence of any striking departure from the doctrines of the Pali Pitakas; and, as Southern Buddhism does not greatly concern us in speaking of the religions of Japan, we may pass it by. For although the books and writings belonging to Southern Buddhism, and comprehended under the formula of the Hinayana or Smaller Vehicle, have been studied in China, Korea and Japan, yet they have had comparatively little influence upon doctrinal, ritualistic, or missionary development in Chinese Asia.

Astonishingly different has been the case with the Northern Buddhisms which are those of Nepal, Tibet, Mongolia, Manchuria, China, Korea and Japan. As luxuriant as the evolutions of political and dogmatic Christianity and as radical in their departures from the primitive simplicity of the faith, have been these forms of Buddhist doctrine, ritual and organization. We cannot now dwell upon the wonderful details of the vast and complicated system, differing so much in various countries. We pass by, or only glance at, the philosophy of the Punjaub; the metaphysics of Nepal —with its developments into what some writers consider to be a close approach to monotheism, and others, indeed, monotheism itself; the system of Lamaism in Tibet, which has paralleled so closely the development of the papal hierarchy; the possibly two thousand years' growth and decay of Chinese Buddhism; the varieties of the Buddhism of Mongolia—almost swamped in the Shamanistic superstitions of these dwellers on the plains; the astonishing success, quick ripening, decay, and almost utter annihilation, among the learned and governing classes, of Korean Buddhism;[15] and study in detail only Eastern or Japanese Buddhism.

We shall in this lecture attempt but two things:

I. A summary of the process of thought by which the chief features of the Northern Buddhisms came into view.

II. An outline of the story of Japanese Buddhism during the first three centuries of its existence.

The Development of Northern Buddhism.

Leaving the early Buddha legends and the solid ground of history, the makers of the newer Buddhist doctrines in Nepal occupied themselves with developing the theory of Buddhahood and of the Buddhas;[16] for we must ever remember that Buddha[17] is not a proper name, but a common adjective meaning enlightened, from the root to know, perceive, etc. They made constant and marvellous additions to the primitive doctrine, giving it a momentum which gathered force as the centuries went on; and, as propaganda, it moved against the sun.

This development theory ran along the line of *personification*. Not being satisfied with "the wheel of the law," it personified both the hub and the spokes. It began with the spirit of kindness out of which all human virtues rise, and by the power of which the

Buddhist organization will conquer all sin and unbelief and become victorious throughout the world. This personification is called the Maitreya Buddha, the unconquerable one, or the future Buddha of benevolence, the Buddha who is yet to come. Here was a tremendous and revolutionary movement in the new faith, the beginning of a long process. It was as though the Christians had taken the particular attributes, justice, mercy, etc., of God and, after personifying each one, deified it, thus multiplying gods.

What was the soil for the new sowing, and what was the harvest to be reaped in due time?

With many thousands of India Buddhists whose minds were already steeped in Brahministic philosophy and mythology, who were more given to speculation and dreaming than to self-control and moral culture, and who mourned for the dead gods of Hinduism, the soil was already prepared for a growth wholly abnormal to true Buddhism, but altogether in keeping with the older Brahministic philosophies from which these dreamers had been but partially converted to Buddhism.[18]

The seed is found in the doctrine which already forms part of the system of the Little Vehicle, when it tells of the personal Buddhas and the Buddhas elect, or future Buddhas. In the Jataka stories, or Birth tales, "the Buddha elect" is the title given to each of the beings, man, angel, or animal, who is held to be a Bodhisattva, or the future Buddha in one of his former births. The title Bodhisattva [19] is the name given to a being whose Karma will produce other beings in a continually ascending scale of goodness until it becomes vested in a Buddha. Or, in the more common use of the word, a Bodhisattva (Japanese bosatsu) is a being whose essence has become intelligence, and who will have to pass through human existence once more only before entering Nirvana.

In Southern Buddhist temples, the pure white image of Maitreya is sometimes found beside the idol representing Gautama or the historical Buddha. While in Southern Buddhism the idea of this possibility of development seems to have been little seized upon and followed up, in Northern Buddhism as early as 400 A.D. the worship of two Buddhas elect named Manjusri and Avalokitesvara, or personified Wisdom and Power, had already become general. Manjusri,[20] the Great Being or " Prince Royal," is the personification of wisdom, and especially of the mystic religious insight which has produced the Great Vehicle or canon of Northern Buddhism ; or, as a Japanese author says, the third collection of the Tripitaka was that made by Manjusri and Maitreya. Avalokitesvara,[21] the Lord of View or All-sided One, is the personification of power, the merciful protector and preserver of the world and of men. Both are frequently and voluminously mentioned in the Saddharma Pundarika,[22] in which the good law is made plain by flowers of rhetoric, and of which we shall have occasion frequently to speak. Manjusri is the mythical author of this influential work,[23] the twenty-fourth chapter being devoted to a glorification of the character, the power, and the advantages to be derived from the worship of Avalokitesvara.

The Creation of Gods.

Possibly the name of Manjusri may be derived from that of the Indian mendicant, the traditional introducer of Buddhism and its accompanying civilization into Nepal. The Tibetans identify him with the minister of a great King Strongstun, who lived in the seventh century of our era and who was the great patron of Buddhism into Tibet. He is the founder of that school of thought which ended in the Great Vehicle, — the literature of Northern Buddhism.[24] From Nepal to Japan, in the books of the Northern Buddhists there is certainly much confusion between the metaphysical being and the legendary civilizer and teacher of Nepal. The other name, Avalokitesvara, which means the Lord of View, "the lord who looks down from on high," instead of being a purely metaphysical invention, may be only an adaptation of one epithet of Shiva, which meant Master of View.

Later and by degrees the attributes were separated and each one was personified. For example, the power of Avalokitesvara was separated from his protecting care and providence. His power was personified as the bearer of the thunder-bolt, or the lightning-handed one; and this new personification added to the two other Buddhas elect, made a triad, the first in Northern Buddhism. In this triad, the thunder-bolt holder was Vagrapani; Manjusri was the deified teacher; and Avalokitesvara was the Spirit of the Buddhas present in the church. Before many centuries had elapsed, these imaginary beings, with a few others, had become gods to whom men prayed; and thus Buddhism became a religion with some kind of theism,—which Gautama had expressly renounced.

If any one wants proof of this reversion into the old religions of India, he has only to notice that the name, given to the new god made by personification of the attribute of power, Vagrapani, or Vadjradhara, or the bearer of the thunder-bolt, had formerly been used as an epithet of the old fire-god of the Vedas, Indra.

It were tedious to recount all the steps in the further development of Northern Buddhism.[25] Suffice it to say, that out of ideas and principles set forth in the earlier Buddhism, and under the generating force reborn from old Brahminism, the Dhyani Buddhas (that is the Buddhas evolved out of the mind in mystic trance) were given their elect Buddhas; and so three sets of five were co-ordinated.[26] That is, first, five pre-penultimate Buddhas; then their Bodhisattvas or penultimate Buddhas; and then the ultimate or human Buddhas, of which Gautama was one. Or, first abstraction; then pre-human effluence; then emanation.

All this multiplication of beings is unknown to Southern Buddhism, unknown to the Saddharma Pundarika, and very probably unknown also to the Chinese pilgrims who visited India in the fifth and seventh centuries. Professor Rhys Davids, in his compact little manual of Buddhism, says:[27]

" Among those hypothetical beings—the creations of a sickly scholasticism, hollow abstractions without life or reality—the fourth Amitabha. 'Immeasurable Light,' whose Bodhisatwa is Avalokitesvara, and whose emanation is Gautama, occupies of course the highest and most important rank. Surrounded by innumerable Bodhisatwas, he sits enthroned under a Bo-tree in Sukhavati, *i.e.*, the Blissful, a paradise of heavenly joys, whose description occupies whole tedious books of the so-called Great Vehicle. By this theory, each of the five Buddhas has become three, and the fourth of these five sets of three is the second Buddhist Trinity, the belief in which must have arisen after the seventh century of our era."

Buddhism has been called the light of Asia, and Gautama its illuminator; but certainly the light has not been pure, nor the products of its illumination wholesome. Pardon an illustration. In Christian churches and cathedrals of Europe, there is still a great prejudice against the use of pipes, and of gas made from coal, because of the machinery and of the impure emanations. The prejudice is a wholesome one; for we all know that most of the elements forming common illuminating gas are worthless except to convey the very small amount of light-giving material, and that these elements in combustion vitiate the air and give off deleterious products which corrode, tarnish and destroy. Now though Buddhist doctrine may have been the light of India, yet to reach the Northern and Eastern nations of Asia it had, apparently, to be adulterated for conveyance, as much as is the illuminating gas in our cities. From the first, Northern Buddhism showed a wonderful affinity, not only for Brahministic superstitions and speculations, but for almost everything else with which it came in contact in countries beyond India. Instead of combating, it absorbed. It adapted itself to circumstances, and finding certain beliefs prevalent among the people, it imbibed them, and thus gained by accretion until its bulk, both of beliefs and of disciples, was in the inverse ratio of its purity. Even to-day, the occult theosophy of " Isis Unveiled," and of the school of writers such as Blavatsky, Olcott, etc., seems to be a perfectly logical product of the Northern Buddhisms, and may be called one of them; yet it is simply a repetition of what took place centuries ago. Most of the primitive beliefs and superstitions of Nepal and Tibet were absorbed in the ever hungry and devouring system of Buddhistic scholasticism.

The Making of a Pantheon.

Let us glance again at this Nepal Buddhism. In the tenth century we find what at first seems to be a growth out of Polytheism into Monotheism, for a new Being, to whom the attributes of infinity, self-existence and omniscience are ascribed, is invented and named Adi-Buddha, or the primordial Buddha. According to the speculations of the thinkers, he had evolved himself out of the five Dhyani-Buddhas by the exercise of the five meditations, while each of these had evolved out of itself by wisdom and contemplation, the corresponding Buddhas elect. Again, each of the latter evolved out of his own essence a material world, —our present world being the fourth of these, that is of Avaloki. One almost might consider that this setting forth of the primordial Buddha was real Monotheism; but on looking more carefully one sees that it is as little real Monotheism as was possible in the system of Gnosticism. Indeed the force of evolution could not stop here ; for, since even this primordial Buddha rested upon Ossa of hypothesis piled upon Pelion of hypothesis, there must be other hypotheses yet to come, and so the Tantra system, a compound of old Brahminism with the magic and witchcraft and Shamanism of

Northern Asia burst into view. As this was to travel into Japan and be hailed as purest Buddhism, let us note how this tenth century Tantra system grew up. To see this clearly, is to look upon the parable of the man with the unclean spirit being acted out on a vast scale in history.

In the sixth century of our era, one Asanga, or Asamga, wrote the Shastra, called the Shastra Yogachara Bhumi.[28] With great dexterity he erected a sort of clearing-house for both the corrupt Brahminism and corrupt Buddhism of his day, and exchanging and rearranging the gods and devils in both systems, he represented them as worshippers and supporters of the Buddha and Avalokitesvara. In such a system, the old primitive Buddhism of the noble eight-fold path of self-conquest and pure morals was utterly lost. Instead of that, the worshipper gave his whole powers to obtaining occult potencies by means of magic phrases and magic circles. Then grew up whole forests of monasteries and temples, with an outburst of devilish art representing many-headed and many-eyed and many-handed idols on the walls, on books, on the roadside, with manifold charms and phrases the endless repetitions of which were supposed to have efficacy with the hypothetical being who filled the heavens. That was *the* age of idols for China as well as for India; and the old Chinese house, once empty, swept and garnished by Confucianism, was now filled with a mob of unclean spirits each worse than the first. With more courageous logic than the more matter-of-fact Chinese, the Tibetan erected his prayer-mills [29] and let the winds of heaven and the flowing waters continually multiply his prayers and holy syllables. And these inventions were duly imported into Japan, and even now are far from being absent.[30]

Passing over for the present the history of Buddhism in China,[31] suffice it to say that the Buddhism which entered Japan from Korea in the sixth century, was not the simple atheism touched with morality, the bald skepticism or benevolent agnosticism of Gautama, but a religion already over a thousand years old. It was the system of the Northern Buddhists. These, dissatisfied, or unsatisfied, with absorption into a passionless state through self-sacrifice and moral discipline, had evolved a philosophy of religion in which were gods, idols and an apparatus of conversion utterly unknown to the primitive faith.

Buddhism Already Corrupted when brought to Japan.

This sixth century Buddhism in Japan was not the army with banners, which was introduced still later with the luxuriances of the fully developed system, its paradise wonderfully like Mohammed's and its over-populated pantheon. It was, however, ready with the necessary machinery, both material and mental, to make conquest of a people which had not only religious aspirations, but also latent æsthetic possibilities of a high order. As in its course through China this Northern Buddhism had acted as an all-powerful absorbent of local beliefs and superstitions, so in Japan it was destined to make a more remarkable record, and, not only to absorb local ideas but actually to cause the indigenous religion to disappear.

Let us inquire who were the people to whom Buddhism, when already possessed of a millenium of history, entered its Ultima Thule in Eastern Asia. At what stage of mutual growth did Buddhism and the Japanese meet each other?

Instead of the forty millions of thoroughly homogeneous people in Japan—according to the census of December 31, 1892—all being loyal subjects of one Emperor, we must think of possibly a million of hunters, fishermen and farmers in more or less warring clans or tribes. These were made up of the various migrations from the main land and the drift of humanity brought by the ocean currents from the south; Ainos, Koreans, Tartars and Chinese, with probably some Malay and Nigrito stock. In the central part of Hondo, the main island, the Yamato tribe dominated, its chief being styled Suméru-mikoto, or Mikado. To the south and southwest, the Mikado's power was only more or less felt, for the Yamato men had a long struggle in securing supremacy. Northward and eastward lay great stretches of land, inhabited by unsubdued and uncivilized native tribes of continental and most probably of Korean origin, and thus more or less closely akin to the Yamato men. Still northward roamed the Ainos, a race whose ancestral seats may have been in far-off Dravidian India. Despite the constant conflicts between the Yamato people who had agriculture and the beginnings of government, law and literature, and their less civilized neighbors, the tendency to amalgamation was already strong. The problem of the statesman, was to extend the sway of the Mikado over the whole Archipelago.

Shintō was, in its formation, made use of as an engine to conquer, unify and civilize all the tribes. In one sense, this conquest of men having lower forms of

12

faith, by believers in the Kami no Michi, or Way of the
Gods, was analogous to the Aryan conquest of India
and the Dravidians. However this may be, the energy
and valor displayed in these early ages formed the ideal
of Yamato Damashii (The Spirit of unconquerable
Japan), which has so powerfully influenced the modern Japanese. We shall see, also, how grandly Buddhism also came to be a powerful force in the unification of the Japanese people. At first, the new faith
would be rejected as an alien invader, stigmatized as a
foreign religion, and, as such, sure to invoke the wrath
of the native gods. Then later, its superiority to the
indigenous cult would be seen both by the wise and
the practically minded, and it would be welcomed and
enjoyed.

The Inviting Field.

Never had a new religion a more inviting field or
one more sure of success, than had Buddhism on step-
ping from the Land of Morning Dawn to the Land of
the Rising Sun. Coming as a gorgeous, dazzling and
disciplined array of all that could touch the imagination, stimulate the intellect and move the heart of the
Japanese, it was irresistible. For the making of a
nation, Shintō was as a donkey engine, compared to
the system of furnaces, boilers, shaft and propeller of
a ten-thousand-ton steel cruiser, moved by the energies
of a million years of sunbeam force condensed into
coal and released again through transmigration by fire.

All accounts in the vernacular Japanese agree, that
their Butsu-dō or Buddhism was imported from
Korea. In the sixteenth year of Kéitai, the twenty-

seventh Mikado (of the list made centuries after, and
the eleventh after the impossible line of the long-lived
or mythical Mikados), A.D. 534, it is said that a man
from China brought with him an image of Buddha into Yamato, and setting it up in a thatched cottage worshipped it. The people called it "foreign-country
god." Visitors discussed with him the religion of Shaka, as the Japanese call Shakyamuni, and some little
knowledge of Buddhism was gained, but no notable
progress was made until A.D. 552, which is generally
accepted and celebrated as the year of the introduction of the faith into Japan. Then a king of Hiaksai
in Korea, sent over to the court and to the Mikado
golden images of the Buddha and of the triad of
"precious ones," with Sutras and sacred books. These
holy relics are believed to be still preserved in the
famous temple of Zenkōji,[32] belonging to the temple of
the Tendai Sect at Nagano in Northern Japan, this
shrine being dedicated to Amida and his two followers
Kwannon (Avalokitesvara) and Dai-séi-shi (Mahastana-
prapta). This group of idols, as the custodian of the
shrine will tell you, was made by Shaka himself out of
gold, found at the base of the tree which grows at the
centre of the universe. After remaining in Korea for
eleven hundred and twelve years, it was brought to
Japan. Mighty is the stream of pilgrims which continually sets toward the holy place. A common proverb declares that even a cow can find her way thither.

In A.D. 572 and again in 584, new images, sutras and
teachers came over from another part of Korea. The
Mikado called a council to determine what should be
done with the idols, to the worship of which he was
himself inclined; but a majority were against the

idea of insulting the native gods by receiving the presents and thus introducing a foreign religion. The minister of state, however, one Soga no Iname, expressed himself in favor of Buddhism, and put the images in his country house which he converted into a temple. When, soon after, the land was afflicted with a pestilence, the opponents of the new faith attributed it to the wrath of the gods at the hospitality given to the new idols. War broke out, fighting took place, and the Buddhist temple was burned and the idols thrown into the river, near Osaka. Great portents followed, and the enemies of Buddhism were, it is said, burned up by flames descending from heaven.

The tide then turned in favor of the Indian faith, and Soga rebuilt his temple. Priests and missionaries were invited to come over from Korea, being gladly furnished by the allies of Japan from the state of Shinra, and Buddhism again flourished at the court, but not yet among the people. Once more, fighting broke out; and again the temple of the alien gods was destroyed, only to be rebuilt again. The chief champion of Buddhism was the son of a Mikado, best known by his posthumous title, Shōtoku,[33] who all his life was a vigorous defender and propagator of the new faith. Through his influence, or very probably through the efforts of the Korean missionaries, the devastating war between the Japanese and Koreans was ended. In the peace which followed, notable progress was made through the vigor of the missionaries encouraged by the regent Shōtoku, so that at his death in the year A.D. 621, there were forty-six temples, and thirteen hundred and eighty-five priests, monks and nuns in Japan. Many of the most famous temples, which are now full of wealth and renown, trace their foundations to this era of Shōtoku and of his aunt, the Empress Suiko (A.D. 593–628), who were friendly to the new religion. Shōtoku may be almost called the founder of Japanese Buddhism. Although a layman, he is canonized and stands unique in the Pantheon of Eastern Buddhism, his image being prominently visible in thousands of Japanese temples.

Legend, in no country more luxurious than in Japan, tells us that the exotic religion made no progress until Amida, the boundlessly Merciful One, assuming the shape of a concubine of the imperial prince who afterward became the Mikado Yomé, gave birth to Shōtoku, who was himself Kwannon or the goddess of mercy in human form; and that when he grew up, he took to wife an incarnation of the Buddha elect, Mahastana-prapta, or in Japanese Dai-séi-shi, whose idol is honored at Zenkōji.

The New Faith Becomes Popular.

Then Buddhism became popular, passing out from the narrow circle of the court to be welcomed by the people. In A.D. 623, monks came over directly from China, and we find mentioned two sects, the Sanron and the Jōjitsu, which are no longer extant in Japan. In about A.D. 650 the fame of Yuan Chang (Hiouen Thsang) the Chinese pilgrim to India, or the holy land, reached Japan; and his illustrious example was enthusiastically followed. History now frequently repeated itself. The Japanese monk, Dōshō, crossed the seas to China to gaze upon the face and become the pupil of that illustrious Chinese pilgrim, who had seen

Buddha Land. Later on, other monks crossed over to the land of Sinim, until we find that in this and succeeding centuries, hundreds of Japanese in their frail junks, braved the dangers of the stormy ocean, in order to study Sanskrit, to read the old scriptures, to meet the new lights of learning or revelation, and to become versed in the latest fashions of religion. We find the pilgrims returning and founding new sects or sub-sects, and stimulating by their enthusiasm the monks and the home missionaries. In the year A.D. 700 the custom of cremation was introduced. This wrought not only a profound change in customs, but also became the seed of a rich crop of superstitions; since out of the cremated bodies of the saints came forth the *shari* or, in Sanskrit, *sarira*. These hard substances or pellets, preserved in crystal cabinets, are treated as holy gems or relics. Thus venerated, they become the nuclei of cycles of fairy lore.

In A.D. 710, the great monastery at Nara was founded; and here we must notice or at least glance at the great throng of civilizing influences that came in with Buddhism, and at the great army of artists, artisans and skilled men and women of every sort of trade and craft. We note that with the building of this great Nara monastery came another proof of im- provement and the added element of stability in Japan- ese civilization. The ancient dread which the Japanese had, of living in any place where a person had died was passing away. The nomad life was being given up. The successor of a dead Mikado was no longer com- pelled to build himself a new capital. The traveller in Japan, familiar with the ancient poetry of the Manyō-shu, finds no fewer than fifty-eight sites [34] as

the early homes of the Japanese monarchy. Once occupying the proud position of imperial capitals, they
are now for the most part mere hamlets, oftentimes
mere names, with no visible indication of former human habitation ; while the old rivers or streams once
gay with barges filled with silken-robed lords and ladies, have dried up to mere washerwomen's runnels.
For the first time after the building of this Buddhist
monastery, the capital remained permanent, Nara being the imperial residence during seventy-five years.
Then beautiful Kiōto was chosen, and remained the
residence of successive generations of emperors until
1868. In A.D. 735, we read of the Kégon sect. Two
years later a large monastery, with a seven-storied pagoda alongside of it, was ordered to be built in every
province. These, with the temples and their surroundings, and with the wayside shrines beginning to spring
up like exotic flowers, made a striking alteration in the
landscape of Japan. The Buddhist scriptures were
numerously copied and circulated among the learned
class, yet neither now nor ever, except here and there
in fragments, were they found among the people. For,
although the Buddhist canon has been repeatedly imported, copied by the pen and in modern times printed,
yet no Japanese translation has ever been made. The
methods of Buddhism in regard to the circulation of
the scriptures are those, not of Protestantism but of
Roman Catholicism.

In the same year, the Mikado called for contributions from all the people for the building of a colossal
image of the Buddha, which was to be of bronze and
gilded. Yet, fearing that the Shintō gods might be
offended, a skilful priest named Giyoku, — probably

the same man who introduced the potter's wheel into Japan,—was sent to the shrine of the Sun-goddess in Isé to present her with a shari or relic of the Buddha, and find out how she would regard his project. After seven days and nights of waiting, the chapel doors flew open and the loud-voiced oracle was interpreted in a favorable sense. The night following the return of the priest, the Mikado dreamed that the sun-goddess appeared to him in her own form and said " The sun is Birushana " (Vairokana). This meant that the chief deity of the Japanese proclaimed herself an avatar or incarnation of one of the old Hindu gods.[35] She also approved the project of the image ; and in this same year, 759, native gold was found in Japan, which sufficed for the gilding of the great idol that, after eleven hundred years and many vicissitudes, still stands, the glory of a multitude of pilgrims.

In A.D. 754 a famous priest, who introduced the new Ritsu Sect, was able to convert the Mikado and obtain four hundred converts in the imperial court. Thirteen years later, another tremendous triumph of Buddhism was scored and a deadly blow at Shintō was struck. The Buddhist priests persuaded the Mikados to abandon their ancient title of Suméru and adopt that of Tennō (Heavenly King or Tenshi) Son of Heaven, after the Chinese fashion. At the same time it was taught that the emperor could gain great merit and sooner become a Buddha, by retiring from the active cares of the throne and becoming a monk, with the title of Hō-ō, or Cloistered Emperor. This innovation had far-reaching consequences, profoundly altering the status of the Mikado, giving sensualism on the one hand and priestcraft on the other, their coveted opportunity, changing the ruler of the nation from an active statesman into a recluse and the recluse into a pious monk, or a licentious devotee, as the case might be. It paved the way for the usurpation of the government by the unscrupulous soldier, " the man on horseback," who was destined to rule Japan for seven hundred years, while the throne and its occupant were in the shadow. One of a thousand proofs of the progress of the propaganda scheme is seen in the removal of the Shintō temple which had stood at Nikkō, and the erection in its place of a Buddhist temple. In A.D. 805 the famous Tendai, and in 806 the powerful Shingon Sect were introduced. All was now ready in Japan for the growth not only of one new Buddhism, but of several varieties among the Northern Buddhisms which so arouse the astonishment of those who study the simple Pali scriptures that contain the story of Gautama, and who know only the southern phase of the faith, that is to Asia, relatively, what Christianity is to Europe. We say relatively, for while Buddhism made Chinese Asia gentle in manners and kind to animals, it covered the land with temples, monasteries and images; on the other hand the religion of Jesus filled Europe not only with churches, abbeys, monasteries and nunneries, but also with hospitals, orphan asylums, lighthouses, schools and colleges. Between the fruits of Christendom and Buddhadom, let the world judge.

Survey and Summary.

To sum up: Buddhism is the humanitarian's, and also the skeptic's, solution of the problem of the universe. Its three great distinguishing characteristics are

atheism, metempsychosis and absence of caste.   It was
in its origin pure democracy.   As against despotic priesthood and oppressive hierarchy, it was congregational.
Theoretically it is so yet, though far from being so practically.   It is certainly sacerdotal and aristocratic in organization.   As in any other system which has so vast
a hierarchy with so many grades of honor and authority, its theory of democracy is now a memory.   First
preached in a land accursed by caste and under spiritual and secular oppressions, it acknowledged no caste,
but declared all men equally sinful and miserable, and
all equally capable of being freed from sin and misery
through Buddhahood, that is, knowledge or enlightenment.[36]

The three-fold principle laid down by Gautama,
and now in dogma, literature, art and worship, a
triad or formal trinity, is, Buddha, the attainment of
Buddha-hood, or perfect enlightenment, through meditation and benevolence; Karma, the law of cause
and effect; and Dharma, discipline or order; or, the
Lord, the Law and the Church.   Paying no attention
to questions of cosmogony or theogony, the universe
is accepted as an ultimate fact.   Matter is eternal.
Creation exists but not a Creator.   All is god, but God
is left out of consideration.   The gods are even less
than Buddhas.   Humanity is glorified and the stress of
all teaching is upon this life.   In a word: a sinless life,
attainable by man, through his own exertions in this
world, above all the powers or beings of the universe,
is the essence of original Buddhism.   Original Nirvana
meant death which ends all, extinction of existence.

Gautama's immediate purpose was to emancipate
himself and his followers from the fetters of Brahmin-

ism. He tried to leave the world of Hindu philosophy behind him and to escape from it.

Did he succeed ? Partially.

Buddha hoped also to rise above the superstitions of the common people, but in this he was again only partially successful.[37] "The clouds returned after the rain." The old dead gods of Brahminism came back under new names and forms. The malarial exhalations of corrupt Brahmanistic philosophy, continually poisoned the atmosphere which Buddha's disciples breathed. Still worse, as his religion transmigrated into other lands, it became itself a history of transformation, until to-day no religion on earth seems to be such a kaleidoscopic phantasmagoria. Polytheism is rampant over the greater part of the Buddhist world to-day. In the larger portion of Chinese Asia, pantheism dominates the mind. In modern Babism,—a mixture of Mohammedanism, Christianity and Buddhism, — there are streaks of dualism. If Monotheism has ever dawned on the Buddhist world, it has been in fitful pulses as in auroral flashes, soon to leave darkness darker.

For us is this lessson : Buddhism, brought face to face with the problem of the world's evil and possible improvement, evades it ; begs the whole question at the outset ; prays : "Deliver us from existence. Save us from life and give us as little as possible of it." Christianity faces the problem and flinches not ; orders advance all along the line of endeavor and prays : "Deliver us from evil ; " and is ever of good cheer, because Captain and leader says : "I have overcome the world." Go, win it for me. "I have come that they might have life, and that they might have it more abundantly."

RIYŌBU, OR MIXED BUDDHISM

"All things are nothing but mind."

"The doctrines of Buddhism have no fixed forms."

"There is nothing in things themselves that enables us to distinguish in them either good or evil, right or wrong. It is but man's fancy that weighs their merits and causes him to choose one and reject the other."

"Non-individuality is the general principle of Buddhism."—Outlines of the Mahāyāna.

"It (Shintō) was smothered before reaching maturity, but Buddhism and Confucianism had to disguise and change in order to enter Japan."

"Life has a limited span and naught may avail to extend it. This is manifested by the impermanence of human beings. But yet whenever necessary I will hereafter make my appearance from time to time as a god, a sage, or a Buddha."—Last words of Shaka the Buddha, in Japanese biography.

"It is our opinion that Buddhism cannot long hold its ground, and that Christianity must finally prevail throughout all Japan. . . . Now, when Buddhism and Christianity are in conflict for the ascendency, this indifference of the Japanese people to the difference of sects is a great disadvantage to Buddhism. That they should worship Jesus Christ with the same mind as they do *Inari* or *Miōjin* is not at all inconsistent in their estimation or contrary to their custom."—Fukuzawa, of Tokio.

"How long halt ye between two opinions? If the Lord be God, follow him: but if Baal, then follow him."—Elijah.

"Do men gather grapes of thorns or figs of thistles?"—Jesus.

"Doth a fountain send forth at the same place sweet water and bitter?"—James.

"What concord hath Christ with Belial?"—Paul.

CHAPTER VII

RIYŌBU, OR MIXED BUDDHISM

Syncretism in Religion

Two centuries and a half of Buddhism in Japan, showed the leaders and teachers of the Indian faith that complete victory over the whole nation was yet very far off. The court had indeed been invaded and won. Even the Mikado, the ecclesiastical head of Shintō, and the incarnation and vicar of the heavenly gods, had not only embraced Buddhism, but in many instances had shorn the hair and taken the vows of the monk. Yet the people clung tenaciously to their old traditions, customs and worship; for their gods were like themselves and indeed were of themselves, since Shintō is only a transfiguration of Japanese life. In the Japanese of those days we can trace the same traits which we behold in the modern son of Nippon, especially his intense patriotism and his warlike tendencies. To convert these people to the peaceful dogmas of Siddartha and to make them good Buddhists, something more than teaching and ritual was necessary. It was indispensable that there should be complete substitution, all along the ruts and paths of national habit, and especially that the names of the gods and the festivals should be Buddhaized.

Popular customs are nearly immortal and ineradicable. Though wars may come, dynasties rise and fall, and convulsions in nature take place, yet the people's manners and amusements are very slow in changing. If, in the history of Christianity, the European missionaries found it necessary in order to make conquest of our pagan forefathers, to baptize and re-name without radically changing old notions and habits, so did it seem equally indispensable that in Japan there should be some system of reconciliation of the old and the new, some theological revolution, which should either fulfil, absorb, or destroy Shintō.

In the histories of religions in Western Asia, Northern Africa and Europe, we are familiar with efforts at syncretism. We have seen how Philo attempted to unite Hebrew righteousness and Greek beauty, and to harmonize Moses and Plato. We know of Euhemerus, who thought he read in the old mythologies not only the outlines of real history, but the hieroglyphics of legend and tradition, truth and revelation.[1] Students of Church history are well aware that this principle of interpretation was followed only too generously by Tertullian, Clement of Alexandria, Lactantius, Chrysostom and others of the Church Fathers. Indeed, it would be hard to find in any of the great religions of the world an utter absence of syncretism, or the union of apparently hostile religious ideas. In the Thousand and One Nights, we have an example in popular literature. We see that the ancient men of India, Persia and pre-Mohammedan Arabia now act and talk as orthodox Mussulmans. In matters pertaining to art and furniture, the statue of Jupiter in Rome serves for St. Peter, and in Japan that of the Virgin and child for the Buddha and his mother.[2]

What, however, chiefly concerns the critic and student of religions is to inquire how far the process has been natural, and the efforts of those who have brought about the union have been honest, and their motives pure. The Bible pages bear witness, that Israelites too often tried to make the same fountain give forth sweet waters and bitter, and to grow thistles and grapes on the same stem, by uniting the cults of Jehovah and the Baalim. King Solomon's enterprises in the same direction are more creditable to him as a politician than as a worshipper.[3] In the history of Christianity one cannot commend the efforts either of the Gnostics or the neo-Platonists, nor always justify the mediæval missionaries in their methods. Nor can we accurately describe as successful the ingenuity of Vossius, the Dutch theologian, who, following the scheme of Euhemerus, discovered the Old Testament patriarchs in the disguise of the gods of Paganism. Nor, even though Germany be the land of learning, can the clear-headed scholar agree with some of her rationalists, who are often busy in the same field of industry, setting forth wild criticism as " science."

The Kami and the Buddhas.

In Japan, to solve the problem of reconciliation between the ancient traditions of the divine ancestors and the dogmas of the Indian cult, it was necessary that some master spirit, profoundly learned in the two Ways, of the Kami and of the Buddhas, should be bold, and also as it seems, crafty and unscrupulous. To convert a line of theocratic emperors, whose authority was derived from their alleged divine origin and sacerdotal

13

character, into patrons and propagandists of Buddhism, and to transform indigenous Shintō gods into Buddhas elect, or Buddhas to come, or Buddhas in a former state of existence, were tasks that might appall the most prodigious intellect, and even strain the capacities of what one might imagine to be the universal religion for all mankind.

Yet from such a task continental Buddhism had not shrunk before and did not shrink then, nor indeed from it do the insular Japanese sects shrink now. Indeed, Buddhism is quite ready to adopt, absorb and swallow up Japanese Christianity. With all encompassing tentacles, and with colossal powers of digestion and assimilation, Northern Buddhism had drawn into itself a large part of the Brahminism out of which it originally sprang,[1] reversing the old myth of Chronos by swallowing its parents. It had gathered in, pretty much all that was in the heavens above and the earth beneath and the waters that were under the earth, in Nepal, Tibet, China and Korea. Thoroughly exercised and disciplined, it was ready to devour and digest all that the imagination of Japan had conceived.

We must remember that, at the opening of the ninth century, the Buddhism rampant in China and indeed throughout Chinese Asia, was the Tantra system of Yoga-chara.[5] This compound of polytheism and pantheism, with its sensuous paradise, its goddess of mercy and its pantheon of every sort of worshipable beings, was also equipped with a system of philosophy by which Buddhism could be adapted to almost every yearning of human nature in its lowest or its highest form, and by which things apparently contradictory could be reconciled. Furthermore—and this is not

the least important thing to consider when the work to
be done is for the ordinary man as an individual and
for the common people in the mass—it had also a tremendous apparatus for touching the imagination and
captivating the fancy of the unthinking and the uneducated.

For example, consider the equipment of the Buddhist priests of the ninth century in the matter of art
alone. Shintō knows next to nothing of art,[6] and indeed one might almost say that it knows little of civilization. It is like ultra-Puritanic Protestantism and
Iconoclasm. Buddhism, on the contrary, is the mother
of art, and art is her ever-busy child and handmaid.
The temples of the Kami were bald and bare. The
Kojiki told nothing of life hereafter, and kept silence
on a hundred points at which human curiosity is sure
to be active, and at which the Yoga system was vol-
uble. Buddhism came with a set of visible symbols
which should attract the eye and fire the imagination,
and within ethical limits, the passions also. It was a
mixed and variegated system,—a resultant of many
forces.[7] It came with the thought of India, the art-
influence of Greece, the philosophy of Persia, the speculations of the Gnostics and, in all probability, with
ideas borrowed indirectly from Nestorian or other
forms of Christianity; and thus furnished, it entered
Japan.

The Mission of Art.

Thus far the insular kingdom had known only the
monochrome sketches of the Chinese painters, which
could have a meaning for the educated few alone. The
composite Tantra dogmas fed the fancy and stimulated

the imagination, filling them with pictures of life, past, present and future. " The sketch was replaced by the illumination." Whole schools of artists, imported from China and Korea, multiplied their works and attracted the untrained senses of the people, by filling the temples with a blaze of glory. " This result was sought by a gorgeous but studied play of gold and color, and a lavish richness of mounting and accessories, that appear strangely at variance with the begging bowl and patched garments of primitive Buddhism." [8] The change in the Japanese temple was as though the gray clouds had been kissed by the sun and made to laugh rainbows. The country of the Fertile Plain of Sweet Flags was transformed. It suddenly became the land wherein gods grew not singly but in whole forests. Like the Shulamite, when introduced among the jewelled ladies of Solomon's harem, so stood the boor amid the sheen and gold of the new temples.

"Gold was the one thing essential to the Buddhist altarpiece, and sometimes, when applied on a black ground, was the only material used. In all cases it was employed with an unsparing hand. It appeared in uniform masses, as in the body of the Buddha or in the golden lakes of the Western Paradise ; in minute diapers upon brocades and clothing, in circlets and undulating rays, to form the glory surrounding the head of Amitaba ; in raised bosses and rings upon the armlets or necklets of the Bodhisattvas and Devas, and in a hundred other manners. The pigments chosen to harmonize with this display were necessarily body colors of the most pronounced hues, and were untoned by any trace of chiaroscuro. Such materials as these would surely try the average artist, but the Oriental painter knew how to dispose them without risk of crudity or gaudiness, and the precious metal, however lavishly applied, was distributed over the picture with a judgment that would make it difficult to alter or remove any part without detriment to the beauty of the work."⁹

In our day, Japanese art has won its own place in the world's temple of beauty. Even those familiar with the master-pieces of Europe do not hesitate to award to the artists of Nippon a meed of praise which, within certain limits, is justly applied to them equally with the masters of the Italian, the Dutch, the Flemish, or the French schools. It serves our purpose simply to point out that art was a powerful factor in the religious conquest of the Japanese for the new doctrines of the Yoga system, which in Japan is called Riyōbu, or Mixed Buddhism.

We say Mixed Buddhism rather than Riyōbu Shintō, for Shintō was less corrupted than swallowed up, while Buddhism suffered one more degree of mixture and added one more chapter of decay. It increased in its visible body, while in its mind it became less and less the religion of Buddha and more and more a thing with the old Shintō heart still in it, making a strange growth in the eyes of the continental believers. To the Northern and Southern was now added an Eastern or Japanese Buddhism.

Who was the wonder-worker that annexed the Land of the Gods to Buddhadom and re-read the Kojiki as a sutra, and all Japanese history and traditions as only a chapter of the incarnations of Buddha?

Kōbō the Wonder Worker.

The Philo and Euhemerus of Japan was the priest Kukai, who was born in the province of Sanuki, in the year 774. He is better known by his posthumous title

Kōbō Daishi, or the Great Teacher who promulgates
the Law. By this name we shall call him. About his
birth, life and death, have multiplied the usual swad-
dling bands of Japanese legend and tradition,[10] and to
his tomb at the temple on Mount Kō-ya, the Campo
Santo of Japanese Buddhism, still gather innumerable
pilgrims. The "hall of ten thousand lamps," each
flame emblematic of the Wisdom that saves, is not, indeed, in these days lighted annually as of old ; but the
vulgar yet believe that the great master still lives in
his mausoleum, in a state of profoundly silent meditation. Into the hall of bones near by, covering a deep
pit, the teeth and "Adam's apple " of the cremated
bodies of believers are thrown by their relatives, though
the pit is cleared out every three years. The devotees
believe that by thus disposing of the teeth and
" Adam's apple," they obtain the same spiritual privi-
leges as if they were actually entombed there, that is,
of being born again into the heaven of the Bodhisattva
or the Pure Land of Absolute Bliss, by virtue of the
mystic formulas repeated by the great master in his
lifetime.

Let us sketch the life of Kōbō,

First named Toto-mono, or Treasure, by his parents,
who sent him to Kiōtō to be educated for the priesthood, the youth spent four years in the study of the
Chinese classics. Dissatisfied with the teachings of
Confucius, he became a disciple of a famous Buddhist
priest, named Iwabuchi (Rock-edge or throne). Soon
taking upon himself the vows of the monk, he was first
named Kukai, meaning " space and sea," or heaven
and earth.[11] He overcame the dragons that assaulted
him, by prayers, by spitting at them the rays of the

evening star which had flown from heaven into his mouth and by repeating the mystic formulas called Dharani.[12] Annoyed by hobgoblins with whom he was obliged to converse, he got rid of them by surrounding himself with a consecrated imaginary enclosure into which they were unable to enter against his will.

We mention these legends only to call the attention to the fact that they are but copies of those already accepted in China at that time, and are the logical and natural fruit of the Tantra school at which we have glanced. In 804, Kōbō was appointed to visit the Middle Kingdom as a government student. By means of his clever pen and calligraphic skill he won his way into the Chinese capital. He became the favored disciple of a priest who taught him the mystic doctrines of the Yoga. Having acquired the whole of the system, and equipped himself with a large library of Buddhist doctrinal works and still more with every sort of ecclesiastical furniture and religious goods, he returned to Japan.

Multitudes of wonders are reported about Kōbō, all of which show the growth of the Tantra school. It is certain that his erudition was immense, and that he was probably the most learned man of Japan in that age, and possibly of any other age. Besides being a Japanese Ezra in multiplying writings, he is credited with the invention of the hira-gana, or running script, and if correctly so, he deserves on this account alone an immortal honor equal to that of Cadmus or Sequoia. The kana [13] is a syllabary of forty-seven letters, which by diacritical marks, may be increased to seventy. The kata-kana is the square or print form, the hira-kana is the round or "grass" character for writing. Though not as valuable as a true phonetic alphabet, such as the Koreans and the Cherokees possess, the *i-ro-ha*, or kana script, even though a syllabary and not an alphabet, was a wonderful aid to popular writing and instruction.

Evidently the idea of the i-ro-ha, or Japanese A B C, was derived from the Sanskrit alphabet, or, what some modern Anglo-Indian has called the Deva-Nagari or the god-alphabet. There is no evidence, however, to show that Kōbō did more than arrange in order forty-seven of the easiest Chinese signs then used, in such a manner that they conveyed in a few lines of doggerel the sense of a passage from a sutra in which the mortality of man and the emptiness of all things are taught, and the doctrine of Nirvana is suggested.[14] Hokusai, the artist, in a sketch which embodies the popular idea of this bonze's immense industry, represents him copying the shastras and sutras. Kōbō is on a seat before a large upright sheet of paper. He holds a brush-pen in his mouth, and one in each of his hands and feet, all moving at once.[15] Favorite portions of the Buddhist scriptures were indeed so rapidly multiplied in Japan in the ninth century, as to suggest the idea, that, even in this early age, block printing had been imported from China, whence also afterward, in all probability, it was exported into Europe before the days of Guttenberg and Coster.[16] The popular imagination, however, was more easily moved on seeing five brushes kept at work and all at once by the muscles in the fingers, toes and mouth of one man. Yet, "had his life lasted six hundred years instead of sixty, he could hardly have graven all the images, scaled all the mountain peaks, confounded all the sceptics, wrought all the miracles and performed all the other feats with which he is popularly credited.[17]

Kōbō's Irenicon.

Kōbō indeed was both the Philo and Euhemerus of Japan, plus a large amount of priestly cunning and what his enemies insist was dishonesty and forgery. Soon after his return from China, he went to the temples of Isé,[18] the most holy place of Shintō.[19] Taking a reverent attitude before the chief shrine, that of Toko Uké Bimé no Kami or Abundant-Food-Lady-God, or the deified Earth as the producer of food and the upholder of all things upon its surface, the suppliant waited patiently while fasting and praying.

In this, Kōbō did but follow out the ordinary Shintō plan for securing god-possession and obtaining revelation ; that is, by starving both the stomach and the brain.[20] After a week's waiting he obtained the vision. The Food-possessing Goddess revealed to him the yoke (or Yoga) by which he could harness the native and the imported gods to the chariot of victorious Buddhism. She manifested herself to him and delivered the revelation on which his system is founded, and which, briefly stated, is as follows :

All the Shintō deities are avatars or incarnations of Buddha. They were manifestations to the Japanese, before Gautama had become the enlightened one, or the jewel in the lotus, and before the holy wheel of the law or the sacred shastras and sutras had reached the island empire. Furthermore, provision was made for the future gods and deified holy ones, who were to proceed from the loins of the Mikado, or other Japanese fathers, according to the saying of Buddha which is thus recorded in a Japanese popular work :

"Life has a limited span, and naught may avail to extend it. This is manifested by the impermanence of human beings, but yet, whenever necessary, I will hereafter make my appearance from time to time as a god (Kami), a sage (Confucian teacher), or a Buddha (Hotoké)." [21]

In a word, the Shintō goddess talked as orthodox (Yoga) Buddhism as the ancient characters of the Indian, Persian and pre-Islam-Arabic stories in the Arabian Nights now talk the purest Mohammedanism.[22] According to the words put into Gautama's mouth at the time of his death, the Buddha was already to reappear in the particular form and in all the forms, acceptable to Shintōists, Confucianists, or Buddhists of whatever sect.

Descending from the shrine of vision and revelation, with a complete scheme of reconciliation, with correlated catalogues of Shintō and Buddhist gods, with liturgies, with lists of old popular festivals newly named, with the apparatus of art to captivate the senses, Kōbō forthwith baptized each native Shintō deity with a new Chinese-Buddhistic name. For every Shintō festival he arranged a corresponding Buddhist's saints' day or gala time. Then, training up a band of disciples, he sent them forth proclaiming the new irenicon.

The Hindu Yoga Becomes Japanese Riyōbu.

It was just the time for this brilliant and able ecclesiastic to succeed. The power and personal influence of the Mikado were weakening, the court swarmed with monks, the rising military classes were already safely under the control of the shavelings, and the pen of learning had everywhere proved itself mightier than the sword and muscle. Kōbō's particular dialectic weapons were those of the Yoga-chara, or in Japanese, the Shingon Shu, or Sect of the True Word.[23] He, like his Chinese master, taught that we can attain the state of the Enlightened or Buddha, while in the present physical body which was born of our parents.

This branch of Buddhism is said to have been founded in India about A.D. 200, by a saint who made the discovery of an iron pagoda inhabited by the holy one, Vagrasattva, who communicated the exact doctrine to those who have handed it down through the Hindoo and Chinese patriarchs. The books or scriptures of this sect are in three sutras; yet the essential point in them is the Mandala or the circle of the Two Parts, or in Japanese Riyōbu. Introduced into China, A.D. 720, it is known as the Yoga-chara school.

Kōbō finding a Chinese worm, made a Japanese dragon, able to swallow a national religion. In the act of deglutition and the long process of the digestion of Shintō, Japanese Buddhism became something different from every other form of the faith in Asia. Noted above all previous developments of Buddhism for its pantheistic tendencies, the Shingon sect could recognize in any Shintō god, demi-god, hero, or being, the avatar in a previous stage of existence of some Buddhist being of corresponding grade.

For example,[24] Amatérasŭ or Ten-Shō-Dai-Jin, the sun-goddess, becomes Dai Nichi Niōrai or Amida, whose colossal effigies stand in the bronze images Dai Butsu at Nara, Kiōto and Kamakura.

Ojin, the god of war, became Hachiman Dai Bosatsu, or the great Bodhisattva of the Eight Banners. Adopted as their patron by the fighting Genji or Minamoto warriors of mediæval times, the Buddhists could not well afford to have this popular deity outside their pantheon.

For each of the thirty days of the month, a Bodhisattva, or in Japanese pronunciation Bosatsu, was appointed. Each of these Bodhisattvas became a Dai Miō Jin or Great Enlightened Spirit, and was represented as an avatar in Japan of Buddha in the previous ages, when the Japanese were not yet prepared to receive the holy law of Buddhism.

Where there were not enough Dai Miō Jin already existing in native traditions to fill out the number required by the new scheme, new titles were invented. One of these was Ten-jin, Heavenly being or spirit. The famous statesman and scholar of the tenth century, Sugawara Michizané, was posthumously named Tenjin, and is even to this day worshipped by many children of Japan as he was formerly for a thousand years by nearly all of them, as the divine patron of letters. Kompira, Benten and other popular deities, often considered as properly belonging to Shintō, "are evidently the offspring of Buddhist priestly ingenuity."[25] Out of the eight millions or so of native gods, several hundred were catalogued under the general term Gon-gen, or temporary manifestations of Buddha. In this list are to be found not only the heroes of local tradition, but even deified forces of nature, such as wind and fire. The custom of making gods of great men after their death, thus begun on a large scale by Kōbō, has gone on for centuries. Iyéyasŭ, the political unifier of

Japan, shines as a star of the first magnitude in the heavens of the Riyōbu system, under the name of Tō-shō-gū, or Great Light of the East. The common people speak of him as Gon-gen Sama, the latter word being an honorary form of address for all beings from a baby to a Bosatsu.

In this way, Kōbō arranged a sort of clearing-house or joint-stock company in which the Bodhisattvas, kami and other miscellaneous beings, in either the native or foreign religion, were mutually interchangeable. In a large sense, this feat of priestly dexterity was but the repetition in history, of that of Asanga with the Brahmanism and Buddhism of India three centuries before. It was this Asanga who wrote the Yoga-chara Bhumi. The succession of syncretists in India, China and Japan is Asanga, Hiukiō and Kōbō.

The Happy Family of Riyōbu.

Nevertheless this attempt at making a happy family and ploughing with an ox and ass in the same yoke, has not been an unqualified success. It will sometimes happen that one god escapes the classification made by the Buddhists and slips into the fold of Shintō, or *vice versa ;* while again the label-makers and pasters— as numerous in scholastic Buddhism as in sectarian Christendom—have hard work to make the labels stick. A popular Gon-gen or Dai-Miō-jin, whose name and re-nown has for centuries attracted crowds of pilgrims, and yielded fat revenues as regularly as the autumn harvests, is not readily surrendered by the old Buddh-ist proprietors, however cleverly or craftily the bonzes may yield outward conformity to governmental edicts.

On the other hand, the efforts, both archæological and practical, which have been made in recent years by fiercely zealous Shintōists, savor of the smartness of New Japan more than they suggest either sincerity or edification. It often requires the finest tact on the part of both the strenuous Buddhists and the stalwart purists of Shintō, to extricate the various gods out of the mixture and mess of Riyōbu Shintō, and to keep them from jostling each other.

This reclaiming and kidnapping of gods and transferring them from one camp to another, has been especially active since 1870, when, under government auspices, the Riyōbu temples were purged of all Buddhist idols, furniture and influences. The term Dai Miō Jin, or Great Illustrious Spirit, is no longer officially permitted to be used of the old kami or gods of Shintō, who were known to have existed before the days of Kōbō. In some cases these gods have lost much of the esteem in which they were held for centuries. Especially is this true of the infamous rebel of the tenth century, Masakado.²⁶ On the entrance into Yedo of the Imperial army, in 1868, his idol was torn from its shrine and hacked to pieces by the patriots. His place as a deity (Kanda Dai Miō Jin, or Great Illustrious Spirit of Kanda) was taken by another deified being, a brother to the aboriginal earth-god who, in the ages of the Kami, "resigned his throne in favor of the Mikado's ancestors when they descended from Heaven." The apotheosis of the rebel Masakado had been resorted to by the Buddhist canonizers because the unquiet spirit of the dead man troubled the people. This method of laying a ghost by making a god of him, was for centuries a favorite one in Japanese Buddhism. Indeed, a large part of the practical and parochial duties of the bonzes consists in quieting the restless spirits of the departed.

All Japanese popular religion of the past has been intensely local and patriotic. The ancient idea that Nippon was the first country created and the centre of the world, has persisted through the ages, modifying every imported religion. Hence the noticeable fact in Japanese Buddhism, of the comparative degradation of the Hindu deities and the exaltation of those which were native to the soil.

The normal Japanese, be he priest or lay brother, theologian or statesman, is nothing if not patriotic. Even the Chinese gods and goddesses which, clothed in Indian drapery and still preserving their Aryan features, were imported to Japan, could not hold their own in competition with the popularity of the indigenous inhabitants of the Japanese pantheon. The normal Japanese eye does not see the ideals of beauty in the human face and form in common with the Aryan vision. Benten or Kuanon, with the features and drapery of the homelike beauties of Yamato or Adzuma, have ever been more lovely to the admiring eye of the Japanese sailor and farmer, than the Aryan features of the idols imported from India. So also, the worshipper to whom the lovely scenery of Japan was fresh from the hands of the kami who were so much like himself, turned naturally in preference, to the " gods many " of his own land.

Succeeding centuries only made it worse for the imported devas or gods, while the kami, or the gods sprung from the soil created by Izanami and Izanagi steadily rose in honor.

Degradation of the Foreign Deities.

For example, the Indian saint Dharma is reputed to
have come to the Dragon-fly Country long before the
advent of Buddhism, but the people were not ready for
him or his teachings, and therefore he returned to
India. So at least declares the book entitled San Kai
Ri [27] (Mountain, Sea and Earth), which is a re-reading
and explanation of Japanese mythology and tradition as
recorded in the Kojiki, by a Kiōtō priest of the Shin
Shu Sect. Of this Dharma, it is said, that he outdid
the Roman Regulus who suffered involuntary loss of
his eyelids at the hands of the Carthaginians. Dharma cut off his own eyelids, because he could not keep
awake.[28] Throwing the offending flesh upon the ground,
he saw the tea-plant arise to help holy men to keep
vigil. Daruma, as the Japanese spell his name, has a
temple in central Japan. It is related that when Shōtoku, the first patron of Buddhism, was one day walk-
ing abroad he found a poor man dying of hunger, who
refused to answer any questions or give his name.
Shōtoku ordered food to be given him, and wrapped
his own mantle round him. Next day the beggar died,
and the prince charitably had him buried on the spot.
Shortly afterward it was observed that the mantle was
lying neatly folded up, on the tomb, which on examination proved to be empty. The supposed dying beggar was no other than the Indian Saint Dharma, and a
pagoda was built over the grave, in which images of
the priest and saint were enshrined.[29] Yet, alas, to-day
Daruma the Hindoo and foreigner, despite his avatar,
his humility, his vigils and his self-mutilation, has

been degraded to be the shop-sign of the tobacconists. Besides being ruthlessly caricatured, he is usually pictured with a scowl, his lidless eyes as wide open as those upon a Chinese junk-prow or an Egyptian coffinlid. Often even, he has a pipe in his mouth—a comical anachronism, suggestive to the smoker of the dark ages that knew no tobacco, before nicotine made the whole world of savage and of civilized kin. Legless dolls and snow-men are named after this foreigner, whose name is associated almost entirely with what is ludicrous.

On Kōbō's expounding his scheme to the Mikado, the emperor was so pleased with his servant's ingenuity, that he gave it the name of Riyōbu[30] Shintō ; that is, the two-fold divine doctrine, double way of the gods, or amalgamated theology. Henceforth the Japanese could enter Nirvana or Paradise through a two-leaved gate. As for the people, they also were pleased, as they usually are when change or reform does not mean abolition of the old festivals, or of the washings, sousings, and fun at the tombs of their ancestors in the graveyards, or the merry-makings, or the pilgrimages,[31] which are usually only other names for social recreation, and often for sensual debauch. The Yoga had become a *kubiki*, for Shintō and Buddhism were now harnessed together, not indeed as true yoke-fellows, but yet joined as inseparably as two oxen making the same furrow.

Many a miya now became a tera. At first in many edifices, the rites of Shintō and Buddhism were alternately performed. The Buddhist symbols might be in the front, and the Shintōist in the rear of the sacred hall, or *vice versa*, with a bamboo curtain be-

14

tween ; but gradually the two blended. Instead of austere simplicity, the Shintō interior contained a museum of idols.

Image carvers had now plenty to do in making, out of camphor or *hinoki* wood, effigies of such of the eight million or so of kamis as were given places in the new and enlarged pantheon. The multiplication was always on the side of Buddhism. Soon, also, the architecture was altered from the type of the primitive hut, to that of the low Chinese temple with great sweeping roof, re-curved eaves, many-columned auditorium and imposing gateway, with lacquer, paint, gilding and ceilings, on which, in blazing gold and color, were depicted the emblems of the Buddhist paradise. Many of these still remain even after the national purgation of 1870, just as the Christian inscriptions survive in the marble palimpsests of Mahometan mosques, converted from basilicas, at Damascus or Constantinople. The torii was no longer raised in plain hinoki wood, but was now constructed of hewn stone, rounded or polished. Sometimes it was even of bronze with gilded crests and Sanskrit monograms, surmounted, it may be, with tablets of painted or stained wood, on which were Chinese letters glittering with gold. This departure from the primitive idea of using only the natural trunks of trees, "somewhat on the principle of Exodus, 20:25,"[32] was a radical one in the ninth century. The elongated barrels with iron hoops, or the riveted boiler-plate and stove-pipe pattern, in this era of Meiji is a still more radical and even scandalous innovation.

Shintō Buried in Buddhism.

So complete was the victory of Riyōbuism, that for nearly a thousand years Shintō as a religion, except in a few isolated spots, ceased from sight and sank to a mere mythology or to the shadow of a mythology. The very knowledge even of the ancient traditions was lost in the Buddhaized forms in which the old stories[33] were cast, or in the omnipresent ritual of the Buddhist tera.

Yet, after all, it is a question as to which suffered most, Buddhism or Shintō. Who can tell which was the base and which was the true metal in the alloy that was formed? The San Kai Ri shows how superstitions manifold became imbedded in Buddhism. It was not alone through the Shingon sect, which Kōbō introduced, that this Yoga or union came. In the other great sect called the Tendai, and in the later sects, more especially in that of Nichiren, the same principle of absorption was followed. These sects also adopted many elements derived from the god-way and thus became Shintōized. Indeed, it seems certain that that vast development of Japanese Buddhism, peculiar to Japan and unknown to the rest of the Buddhist world, scouted by the Southern Buddhists as dreadful heresy, and rousing the indignation of students of early Buddhism, like Max Müller and Professor Whitney, is largely owing to this attempted digestion of Japanese mythology. The anaconda may indeed be able, by reason of its marvellously flexible jaws and its abundant activity of salivary glands, to swallow the calf, and even the ox; but sometimes the serpent is killed by its own voracity, or at least made helpless before the destroying hunter. When sweet potatoes and pumpkins are planted in the same hill, and the cooked product comes on the table, it is hard to tell whether it is tuber or hollow fruit, subterranean or superficial growth, that we are eating. So in Riyōbu, whether it be most *imo* or *kabocha* is a fair question. If the Buddhism in Japan did but add a chapter of decay and degradation to the religion of the Light of Asia, is not this owing to the act of Kōbō—justified indeed by those who imitated his example, yet hardly to be called honest? A stroke of ecclesiastical dexterity, it may have been, but scarcely a lawful example or an illustrious and commendable specimen of syncretism in religion.

Many students have asked what is the peculiar, the characteristic difference between the Buddhism of Japan and the other Buddhisms of the Asian continent. If there be one cause, leading all others, we incline to believe it is because Japanese Buddhism is not the Buddhism of Gautama, but is so largely Riyōbu or Mixed. Yet in the alloy, which ingredient has preserved most of its qualities? Is Japanese Buddhism really Shintōized Buddhism, or Buddhaized Shintō? Which is the parasite and which the parasitized? Is the hermit crab Shintō, and the shell Buddhism, or *vice versa?* About as many corrupt elements from Shintō entered into the various Buddhist sects as Buddhism gave to Shintō.

This process of Shintōizing Buddhism or of Buddhaizing Shintō—that is, of combining Shintō or purely Japanese ideas and practices with the systems imported from India, went on for five centuries. The old native habits and mental characteristics were not eradicated or profoundly modified; they were rather safely preserved in so-called Buddhism, not indeed as dead flies in amber but as live creatures, fattening on a body, which, every year, while keeping outward form and name, was being emptied of its normal and typical life. It is no gain to pure water to add either microbes or the food which nourishes them.

Buddhism Writes New Chapters of Decay.

Phenomenally, the victory was that of Buddhism. The mustard-seed has indeed become a great tree, lodging every fowl of heaven, clean and unclean; but potentially and in reality, the leavening power, as now seen, seems to have been that of Shintō. Or, to change metaphor, since the hermit crab and the shell were separated by law only one generation ago, in 1870, we shall soon, before many generations, discern clearly which has the life and which has only the shell.[34]

There are but few literary monuments [35] of Riyōbuism, and it has left few or no marks in the native chronicles, misnamed history, which utterly omit or ignore so many things interesting to the student and humanist.[36] Yet to this mixture or amalgamation of Buddhism with Shintō, more probably than to any other direct influence, may also be ascribed that striking alteration in the system of Chinese ethics or Confucianism which differentiates the Japanese form from that prevalent in China. That is, instead of filial piety, the relation of parent and child, occupying the first place, loyalty, the relation of lord and retainer, master and servant, became supreme. Although Buddhism made the Mikado first a King (Tennō) or Son of

Heaven (Ten-Shi), and then a monk (Hō-ō), and after his death a Hotoké or Buddhist deity, it caused him early to abdicate from actual life. Buddhism is thus directly responsible for the habitual Japanese resignation from active life almost as soon as it is entered, by men in all classes. Buddhism started all along and down through the lines of Japanese society the idea of early retirement from duty ; so that men were considered old at forty, and *hors concours* before forty-five.[37] Life was condemned as vanity of vanities before it was mature, and old age a friend that nobody wished to meet,[38] although Japanese old age is but European prime. In a measure, Buddhism is thus responsible for the paralysis of Japanese civilization, which, like oft-tapped maple-trees, began to die at the top. This was in accordance with its theories and its literature. In the Bible there is, possibly, one book which is pessimistic in tone, Ecclesiastes. In the bulky and dropsical canon of Buddhism there is a whole library of despondency and despair.

Nevertheless, the ethical element held its own in the Japanese mind ; and against the pessimism and puerility of Buddhism and the religious emptiness of Shintō, the bond of Japanese society was sought in the idea of loyalty. While then, as we repeat, everything that comes to the Japanese mind suffers as it were " a sea change, into something new and strange," is it not fair to say that the change made by Kōbō was at the expense of Buddhism as a system, and that the thing that suffered reversion was the exotic rather than the native plant ? For, in the emergence of this new idea of loyalty as supreme, Shintō and not Buddhism was the dictator.

Even more after Kōbō's death than during his life, Japan improved upon her imported faith, and rapidly developed new sects of all degrees of reputableness and disreputableness. Had Kōbō lived on through the centuries, as the boors still believe,[39] he could not have stopped, had he so desired, the workings of the leaven he had brought from China. From the sixth to the twelfth century, was the missionary age of Japanese Buddhism. Then followed two centuries of amazing development of doctrine. Novelties in religion blossomed, fruited and became monuments as permanent as the age-enduring forests Hakoné, or Nikkō. Gautama himself, were he to return to "red earth" again, could not recognize his own cult in Japan.

In China to-day Buddhism is in a bad state. One writer calls it, "The emasculated descendant that now occupies the land with its drone of priests and its temples, in which scarce a worthy disciple of the learned patriarchs of ancient days is to be found. Received with open arms, persecuted, patronized, smiled upon, tolerated, it with the last phase of its existence, has reached, not the halcyon days of peace and rest, but its final stage, foreshadowing its decay from rottenness and corruption."[40] So also, in a like report, agree many witnesses. The common people of China are to-day Taoists rather than Buddhists.[41]

If this be the position in China, something not very far from it is found in Japan to-day. Whatever may be the Buddhism of the few learned scholars, who have imbibed the critical and scientific spirit of Christendom, and whatever be the professions and representations of its earnest adherents and partisans, it is certain that popular Buddhism is both ethically and vitally in a low state. In outward array the system is still imposing. There are yet, it may be, millions of stone statues and whole forests of wayside effigies, outdoors and unroofed — irreverently called by the Japanese themselves, " wet gods." Hosts upon hosts of lacquered and gilded images in wood, sheltered under the temple tiles or shingles, still attract worshippers. Despite shiploads of copper Buddhas exported as old metal to Europe and America, and thousands of tons of gods and imps melted into coin or cannon, there are myriads of metal reminders of those fruits of a religion that once educated and satisfied ; but these are, in the main, no longer to the natives instruments of inspiration or compellers to enthusiasm. In this time of practical charity, they are poor substitutes for those hospitals and orphan asylums which were practically unknown in Japan until the advent of Christianity.

Kōbō's smart example has been followed only too well by the people in every part of the country. One has but to read the stacks of books of local history to see what an amazing proportion of legends, ideas, superstitions and revelations rests on dreams ; how incredibly numerous are the apparitions ; how often the floating images of Buddha are found on the water ; how frequently flowers have rained out of the sky ; how many times the idols have spoken or shot forth their dazzling rays—in a word ; how often art and artifices have become alleged and accepted reality. Unfortunately, the characteristics of this literature and undergrowth of idol lore are monotony and lack of originality ; for nearly all are copies of Kōbō's model. His cartoon has been constantly before the busy weavers of legend.

It may indeed be said, and said truly, that in its multiplication of sects and in its growth of legend and superstition, Buddhism has but followed every known religion, including traditional Christianity itself. Yet popular Buddhism has reached a point which shows, that, instead of having a self-purgative and self-reforming power, it is apparently still treading in the steps of the degradation which Kōbō began.

The Seven Gods of Good Fortune.

We repeat it, Riyōbu Buddhism is Japanese Buddhism with vengeance. It is to-day suffering from the effect of its own sins. Its *ingwa* is manifest. Take, for example, the little group of divinities known as the Seven Gods of Good Fortune, which forms a popular appendage to Japanese Buddhism and which are a direct and logical growth of the work done by Kōbō, as shown in his Riyōbu system. Not from foreign writers and their fancies, nor even from the books which profess to describe these divinities, do we get such an idea of their real meaning and of their influence with the people, as we do by observation of every-day practice, and a study of the idols themselves and of Japanese folk-lore, popular romance, local history and guide-books. These familiar divinities, indeed, at the present day owe their vitality rather to the artists than the priests, and, it may be, have received, together with some rather rude handling, nearly the whole of their extended popularity and influence from their lay supporters. The Seven Happy Gods of Fortune form nominally a Buddhist assemblage, and their effigies on the kami-dana or god-shelf, found in nearly every Jap-

anese house, are universally visible. The child in
Japan is rocked to sleep by the soothing sound of the
lullaby, which is often a prayer to these gods. Even
though it may be with laughing and merriment, that,
in their name the evil gods and imps are exorcised
annually on New Year's eve, with showers of beans
which are supposed to be as disagreeable to the Buddhist demons "as drops of holy water to the Devil,"
yet few households are complete without one or more
of the images or the pictures of these favorite deities.

The separate elements of this conglomerate, so
typical of Japanese religion, are from no fewer than
four different sources : Brahmanism, Buddhism, Taoism and Shintōism. "Thus, Bishamon is the Buddhist *Vâis'ramana* [42] and the Brahmanic Kuvera ; Benten is Sarasvatî, the wife of Brahmâ ; Daikoku is an
extremely popularized form of Mahakala, the black-
faced Temple Guardian ; Hotéi has Taoist attributes,
but is regarded as an incarnation of Mâitreyâ, the
Buddhist Messiah ; Fuku-roku-jiu is of purely Taoist
origin, and is perhaps a personification of Lao-Tsze
himself ; Ju-rō-jin is almost certainly a duplicate of
Fuku-roku-jiu ; and, lastly, Ebisu, as the son of Izanagi and Izanami, is a contribution from the Shintō
hero-worship." [43] If Riyōbu Buddhism be two-fold,
here is a texture or amalgam that is *shi-bu*, four-fold.
Let us watch lest *go-bu*, with Christianity mixed in, be
the next result of the process. To play the Japanese
game of go-ban, with Christianity as the fifth counter,
and Jesus as a Palestinian avatar of some Dhyani
Buddha, crafty priests in Japan are even now planning.

This illustration of the Seven Gods of Happiness,
whose local characters, functions and relations have

been developed especially within the last three or four hundred years, is but one of many that could be adduced, showing what proceeded on a larger scale. The Riyōbu process made it almost impossible for the average native to draw the line between history and mythology. It destroyed the boundary lines, as Pantheism invariably does, between fact and fiction, truth and falsehood. The Japanese mind, by a natural, possibly by a racial, tendency, falls easily into Pantheism, which may be called the destroyer of boundaries and the maker of chaos and ooze. Pretty much all early Japanese "history" is ooze; yet there are grave and learned men, even in the Constitutional Japan of the Méiji era—masters in their arts and professions, graduates of technical and philosophical courses—who solemnly talk about their "first emperor ascending the throne, B.C. 660," and to whom the dragon-born, early Mikados, and their fellow-tribesmen, seen through the exaggerated mists of the Kojiki, are divine personages.

The Gon-gen in the Processions.

While living in Japan between 1870 and 1874, the writer used to enjoy watching and studying the long processions which celebrated the foundation of temples, national or local festivals, or the completion of some great public enterprise, such as the railway between Tōkio and Yokohama. In rich costume, decoration, and representation most of the cultus-objects were marvels of art and skill. Besides the gala dresses and uniforms, the fantastic decorations and personal adornments, the dances which represented the comedies and tragedies of the gods and the striking scenes in the

Kojiki, there were colossal images of Kami, Bodhisatt-vas, Gon-gen, Dai Miō Jin, and of imps, oni, mythical animal forms and imaginary monsters.[44] More inter-esting than anything else, however, were the male and female figures, set high upon triumphal cars having many tiers, and arrayed in characteristic primeval, ancient, mediæval, or early modern dress. Some were of scowling, others of benign visage. In some years, everyone of the eight hundred and eight streets of Yedo sent its contribution of men, money, decora-tions, or vehicles.

As seen by four kinds of spectators, the average ig-norant native, the Shintōist, the learned Buddhist, and the critical historical scholar, these effigies represented three different characters or creations. Especially were those divine personages called Gon-gen worth the study of the foreign observer.

(1) The common boor or streetman saluted, for ex-ample, this or that Dai Miō Jin, as the great illustrious spirit or god of a particular district. To this spirit and image he prayed; in his honor he made offerings; his wrath he feared; and his smile he hoped to win, for the Gon-gen was a divine being.

(2) To the Shintōist, who hated Buddhism and the Riyōbu Shintō which had overlaid his ancestral faith, and who scorned and tabooed this Chinese term Dai Miō Jin, this or that image represented a divine ances-tor whose name had in it many Japanese syllables, with no defiling Chinese sounds, and who was the Kami or patron deity of this or that neighborhood.

(3) To the Buddhist, this or that personage, in his lifetime, in the early ages of Japanese history, had been an avatar of Buddha who had appeared in human

flesh and brought blessings to the people and neighborhood; yet the people of the early ages being un-
prepared to receive his doctrine or revelation, he had
not then revealed or preached it; but now, as for a
thousand years since the time of the illustrious and
saintly Kōbō, he had his right name and received his
just honors and worship as an avatar of the eternal
Buddha. So, although Buddhist and Shintōist might
quarrel as to his title, and divide, even to anger, on
minor points, they would both agree in letting the common people take their pleasure, enjoy the festivals and
merriment, and preserve their reverence and worship.

(4) Still another spectator studied with critical interest the swaying figure high in air. With a taste for
archæology, he admired the accuracy of the drapery
and associations. He was amused, it may be, with occasional anachronisms as to garments or equipments.
He knew that the original of this personage had been
nothing more than a human being, who might indeed
have been conspicuous as a brave soldier in war, or as
a skilful physician who helped to stop the plague, or as
a civilizer who imported new food or improved agriculture.

In a word, had this subject of the ancient Mikado
lived in modern Christendom, he might be honored
through the government, patent office, privy council,
the admiralty, the university, or the academy, as the case
or worth might be. He might shine in a plastic representation by the sculptor or artist, or be known in
the popular literature; but he would never receive religious worship, or aught beyond honor and praise. In
this swamping of history in legend and of fact in dogma,
we behold the fruit of Kōbō's work, Riyōbu Buddhism.

Kōbō's Work Undone.

Buddhism calls itself the jewel in the lotus. Japanese poetry asks of the dewdrop "why, having the heart of the lotus for its home, does it pretend to be a gem?" For a thousand years Riyōbu Buddhism was received as a pure brilliant of the first water, and then the scholarship of the Shintō revivalists of the eighteenth century exposed the fraudulent nature of the unrelated parts and declared that the jewel called Riyōbu was but a craftsman's doublet and should be split apart. Only a splinter of diamond, they declared, crowned a mass of paste. Indignation made learning hot, and in 1870 the cement was liquefied in civil war. The doublet was rent asunder by imperial decree, as when a lapidist melts the mastic that holds in deception adamant and glass, while real diamond stands all fire short of the hydro-oxygen flame. The Riyōbu temples were purged of all Buddhist symbols, furniture, equipment and personnel, and were made again to assume their august and austere simplicity. In the eyes of the purely æsthetic critic, this national purgation was Puritanical iconoclasm; in those of the priests, cast out to earn rice elsewise and elsewhere, it was outrage, which in individual instances called for reprisal in blood, fire and assassination; to the Shintōist, it was an exhibition of the righteous judgment of the long-insulted gods; in the ken of the critical student, it seems very much like historic and poetic justice.

In our day and time, Riyōbu Buddhism furnishes us with a warning, for, looked at from a purely human point of view, what happened to Shintō may possibly

happen to Japanese Christianity. The successors of
those who, in the ninth century, did not scruple to
Buddhaize Shintō, and in later times, even our own, to
Shintōize Buddhism while holding to Buddha's name
and all the revenue possible, will Buddhaize Christianity if they have power and opportunity; and signs
are not wanting to show that this is upon their pro-
gramme.

The water of stagnant Buddhism is still a swarming
mass, which needs cleansing to purity by a knowledge
of one God who is Light and Love. Without such
knowledge, the manifold changes in Buddhism will but
form fresh chapters of degradation and decay. Holding
such knowledge, Christianity may pass through endless changes, for this is her capability by Divine power
and the authorization of her Founder. The new
Buddhism of our day is endeavoring to save itself
through reformation and progress. In doing so, the
danger of the destruction of the system is great, for
thus far change has meant decay.

NORTHERN BUDDHISM IN ITS DOCTRINAL
EVOLUTIONS

"To the millions of China, Corea, and Japan, creator and creation are new and strange terms."—J. H. De Forest.

"The Law of our Lord, the Buddha, is not a natural science or a religion, but a doctrine of enlightenment; and the object of it is to give rest to the restless, to point out the Master (the Inmost Man) to those that are blind and do not perceive their Original State."

"The Saddharma Pundarika Sutra teaches us how to obtain that desirable knowledge of the mind as it is in itself [universal wisdom]. . . . Mind is the One Reality, and all scriptures are the micrographic photographs of its images. He that fully grasps the Divine Body of Sakyamuni, holds ever, even without the written Sutra, the inner Saddharma Pundarika in his hand. He ever reads it mentally, even though he would never read it orally. He is unified with it, though he has no thought about it. He is the true keeper of the Sutra."—Zitsuzen Ashitsu of the Tendai sect.

"It [Buddhism] is idealistic. Everything is as we think it. The world is my idea. . . . Beyond our faith is naught. Hold the Buddhist to his creed and insist that such logic destroys itself, and he triumphs smilingly, 'Self-destructive! Of course it is. All logic is. That is the centre of my philosophy.'"

"It [Buddhism] denounces all desire and offers salvation as the reward of the murder of our affections, hopes, and aspirations. It is possible where conscious existence is believed to be the chief of evils."—George William Knox.

"Swallowing the device of the priests, the people well satisfied, dance their prayers."—Japanese Proverb.

"The wisdom that is from above is. . . . without variance, without hypocrisy."—James.

"The mystery of God, even Christ in whom are all the treasures of wisdom and knowledge."—Paul.

CHAPTER VIII

Chronological Outline

IN sketching the history of the doctrinal developments of Buddhism in Japan, we note that the system, greatly corrupted from its original simplicity, was in 552 A.D. already a millennium old. Several distinct phases of the much-altered faith of Gautama, were introduced into the islands at various times between the sixth and the ninth century. From these and from others of native origin have sprung the larger Japanese sects. Even as late as the seventeenth century, novelties in Buddhism were imported from China, and the exotics took root in Japanese soil; but then, with a single exception, only to grow as curiosities in the garden, rather than as the great forests, which had already sprung from imported and native specimens.

We may divide the period of the doctrinal development of Buddhism in Japan into four epochs:

I. The first, from 552 to 805 A.D., will cover the first six sects, which had for their centre of propagation, Nara, the southern capital.

II. Then follows Riyōbu Buddhism, from the ninth to the twelfth centuries.

III. This was succeeded by another explosion of

doctrine wholly and peculiarly Japanese, and by a wide missionary propagation.

IV. From the sixteenth to the nineteenth century, there is little that is doctrinally noticeable, until our own time, when the new Buddhism of to-day claims at least a passing notice.

The Japanese writers of ecclesiastical history classify in three groups the twelve great sects as the first six, the two mediæval, and the four modern sects.

In this lecture we shall merely summarize the characteristics of the first five sects which existed before the opening of the ninth century but which are not formally extant at the present time, and treat more fully the purely Japanese developments. The first three sects may be grouped under the head of the Hinayana, or Smaller Vehicle, as Southern or primitive orthodox Buddhism is usually called.

Most of the early sects, as will be seen, were founded upon some particular sutra, or upon selections or collections of sutras. They correspond to some extent with the manifold sects of Christendom, and yet this illustration or reference must not be misleading. It is not as though a new Christian sect, for example, were in A.D. 500 to be formed wholly on the gospel of Luke, or the book of the Revelation ; nor as though a new sect should now arise in Norway or Tennessee because of a special emphasis laid on a combination of the epistle to the Corinthians and the book of Daniel. It is rather as though distinct names and organizations should be founded upon the writings of Tertullian, of Augustine, of Luther, or of Calvin, and that such sects should accept the literary work of these scholars not only as commentaries but as Holy Scripture itself.

The Buddhist body of scriptures has several times been imported and printed in Japan, but has never been translated into the vernacular. The canon [1] is not made up simply of writings purporting to be the words of Buddha or of the apostles who were his immediate companions or followers. On the contrary, the canon, as received in Japan, is made up of books, written for the most part many centuries after the last of the contemporaries of Gautama had passed away. Not a few of these writings are the products of the Chinese intellect. Some books held by particular sects as holy scripture were composed in Japan itself, the very books themselves being worshipped. Nevertheless those who are apparently farthest away from primitive Buddhism, claim to understand Buddha most clearly.

The Standard Doctrinal Work.

One of the most famous of books, honored especially by several of the later and larger sects in Japan, and probably the most widely read and most generally studied book of the canon, is the Saddharma Pundarika. [2] Professor Kern, who has translated this very rhetorical work into English, thinks it existed at or some time before 250 A.D., and that in its most ancient form it dates some centuries earlier, possibly as early as the opening of the Christian era. It has now twenty-seven chapters, and may be called the typical scripture of Northern Buddhism. It is overflowingly full of those sensuous images and descriptions of the Paradise, in which the imagination of the Japanese Buddhist so revels, and in it both rhetoric and mathematics run wild. Of this book, "the cream of the revealed doc-

trine," we shall hear often again. It is the standard of
orthodoxy in Japanese Buddhism, the real genius of
which is monastic asceticism in morals and philosophical scepticism in religion.

In most of the other sutras the burden of thought
is ontology. Doctrinally, Buddhism seems to be less
a religion than a system of philosophy. Hundreds of
volumes in the canon concern themselves almost wholly
with ontological speculations. The Japanese mind,[3]
as described by those who have studied most acutely
and profoundly its manifestations in language and literature, is essentially averse to speculation. Yet the
first forms of Buddhism presented to the Japanese,
were highly metaphysical. The history of thought in
Japan, shows that these abstractions of dogma were
not congenial to the islanders. The new faith won its
way among the people by its outward sensuous attrac-
tions, and by appeals to the imagination, the fancy and
the emotions; though the men of culture were led captive by reasoning which they could not answer, even if
they could comprehend it. Though these early forms
of dogma and philosophy no longer survive in Japan,
having been eclipsed by more concrete and sensuous
arguments, yet it is necessary to state them in order to
show : first, what Buddhism really is ; second, doctrinal development in the farthest East; and, third,
the peculiarities of the Japanese mind.

In this task, we are happy to be able to rely upon
native witness and confession.[4] The foreigner may
easily misrepresent, even when sincerely inclined to
utter only the truth. Each religion, in its theory at
least, must be judged by its ideals, and not by its failures. Its truth must be stated by its own professors.

In the "History of The Twelve Japanese Sects," by Bunyiu Nanjio, M.A. Oxon., and in "Le Bouddhisme Japonais," by Ryauon Fujishima, we have the untrammelled utterances, of nine living lights of the religion of Shaka as it is held and taught in Dai Nippon. The former scholar is a master of texts, and the latter of philosophy, each editor excelling in his own department; and the two books complement each other in value.

Buddhism, being a logical growth out of Brahmanism, used the old sacred language of India and inherited its vocabulary. In the Tripitaka, that is, the three book-baskets or boxes, we have the term for canon of scripture, in the complete collection of which are *sutra*, *vinaya* and *abidharma*. We shall see, also, that while Gautama shut out the gods, his speculative followers who claimed to be his successors, opened the doors and allowed them to troop in again. The democracy of the congregation became a hierarchy and the empty swept and garnished house, a pantheon.

A sutra, from the root *siv*, to sew, means a thread or string, and in the old Veda religion referred to household rites or practices and the moral conduct of life; but in Buddhist phraseology it means a body of doctrine. A shaster or shastra, from the Sanskrit root *ças*, to govern, relates to discipline. Of these shastras and sutras we must frequently speak. In India and China some of these sutras are exponents, of schools of thought or opinion, or of views or methods of looking at things, rather than of organizations. In Japan these schools of philosophy, in certain instances, become sects with a formal history.

In China of the present day, according to a Japanese

traveller and author, "the Chinese Buddhists seem
. . . . to unite all different sects, so as to make one
harmonious sect." The chief divisions are those of the
blue robe, who are allied with the Lamaism of Tibet and
whose doctrine is largely "esoteric," and those of the
yellow robe, who accept the three fundamentals of principle, teaching and discipline. Dhyana or contemplation is their principle ; the Kégon or Avatamsaka sutra
and the Hokké or Saddharma Pundarika sutra, etc.,
form the basis of their teaching ; and the Vinaya of the
Four Divisions (Dharmagupta) is their discipline. On
the contrary, in Japan there are vastly greater diver-
sities of sect, principle, teaching and discipline.

Buddhism as a System of Metaphysics.

The date of the birth of the Buddha in India, accepted by the Japanese scholars is B.C. 1027—the day
and month being also given with suspicious accuracy.
About nine centuries after Gautama had attained Nirvana, there were eighteen schools of the Hinayana or
the doctrine of the Smaller Vehicle. Then a shastra
or institute of Buddhist ontology in nine chapters, was
composed, the title of which in English, is, Book of the
Treasury of Metaphysics. It had such a powerful influence that it was called an intelligence-creating, or as
we say, an epoch-making book.

This Ku-sha shastra, from the Sanskrit *kosa*, a store,
is eclectic, and contains nine chapters embodying the
views of one of the schools, with selections from those
of others. It was translated in A.D. 563, into Chinese
by a Hindu scholar ; but about a hundred years later
the famous pilgrim, whom the Japanese call Gen-jō, but

who is known in Europe as Hiouen Thsang,[5] made a better translation, while his disciples added commentaries.

In A.D. 658, two Japanese priests[6] made the sea-journey westward into China, as Gen-jō had before made the land pilgrimage into India, and became pupils of the famous pilgrim. After long study they returned, bringing the Chinese translation of this shastra into Japan. They did not form an independent sect; but the doctrines of this shastra, being eclectic, were studied by all Japanese Buddhist sects. This Ku-sha scripture is still read in Japan as a general institute of ontology, especially by advanced students who wish to get a general idea of the doctrines. It is full of technical terms, and is well named The Store-house of Metaphysics.

The Ku-sha teaches control of the passions, and the government of thought. The burden of its philosophy is materialism; that is, the non-existence of self and the existence of the matter which composes self, or, as the Japanese writer says: "The reason why all things are so minutely explained in this shastra is to drive away the idea of self, and to show the truth in order to make living beings reach Nirvana." Among the numerous categories, to express which many technical terms are necessary, are those of "forms," eleven in number, including the five senses and the six objects of sense; the six kinds of knowledge; the forty-six mental qualities, grouped under six heads; and the fourteen conceptions separated from the mind; thus making in all seventy-two compounded things and three immaterial things. These latter are "conscious cessation of existence," "unconscious cessation of existence," and "space."

The Reverend Shuzan Emura, of the Shin-shu sect of Japan, after specifying these seventy-five Dharmas, or things compounded and things immaterial, says :[7] " The former include all things that proceed from a cause. This cause is Karma, to which everything existing is due, Space and Nirvana alone excepted. Again, of the three immaterial things the last two are not subjects to be understood by the wisdom not free from frailty. Therefore the 'conscious cessation of existence' is considered as being the goal of all effort to him who longs for deliverance from misery."

In a word, this one of the many Buddhisms of Asia is vastly less a religion, in any real sense of the word, than a system of metaphysics. However, the doctrine to be mastered is graded in three Yanas or Vehicles ; for there are now, as in the days of Shaka, three classes of being, graded according to their ability or power to understand " the truth." These are :

(I.) The Sho-mon or lowest of the disciples of Shaka, or hearers who meditate on the cause and effect of everything. If acute in understanding, they become free from confusion after three births; but if they are dull, they pass sixty kalpas [8] or æons before they attain to the state of enlightenment.

(II.) The Engaku or Pratyeka Buddhas, that is, " singly enlightened," or beings in the middle state, who must extract the seeds or causes of actions, and must meditate on the twelve chains of causation, or understand the non-eternity of the world, while gazing upon the falling flowers or leaves. They attain enlightenment after four births or a hundred kalpas, according to their ability.

(III.) The Bodhisattvas or Buddhas-elect, who practise the six perfections (perfect practice of alms-giving, morality, patience, energy, meditation and wisdom) as preliminaries to Nirvana, which they reach only after countless kalpas.

These three grades of pupils in the mysteries of Buddha doctrine, are said to have been ordered by Shaka himself, because understanding human beings so thoroughly, he knew that one person could not comprehend two ways or vehicles (Yana) at once. People were taught therefore to practise anyone of the three vehicles at pleasure.

We shall see how the later radical and democratic Japanese Buddhism swept away this gradation, and declaring but the one vehicle (éka), opened the kingdom to all believers.

The second of the early Japanese schools of thought, is the Jō-jitsu,[9] or the sect founded chiefly upon the shastra which means The Book of the Perfection of the Truth, containing selections from and explanations of the true meaning of the Tripitaka. This shastra was the work of a Hindu whose name means Lion-armor, and who lived about nine centuries after Gautama. Not satisfied with the narrow views of his teacher, who may have been of the Dharmagupta school (of the four Disciplines), he made selections of the best and broadest interpretations then current in the several different schools of the Smaller Vehicle. The book is eclectic, and attempts to unite all that was best in each of the Hinayana schools ; but certain Chinese teachers consider that its explanations are applicable to the Great Vehicle also. Translated into Chinese in 406 A.D., the commentaries upon it soon numbered hundreds, and it was widely expounded and lectured upon.

Commentaries upon this shastra were also written in Korean by Dō-zō. From the peninsula it was introduced into Japan. This Jō-jitsu doctrine was studied by prince Shōtoku, and promulgated as a division of the school called San-Ron. The students of the Jō-jitsu school never formed in Japan a distinct organization.

The burden of the teachings of this school is pure nihilism, or the non-existence of both self and of matter. There is an utter absence of substantiality in all things. Life itself is a prolonged dream. The objects about us are mere delusive shadows or mirage, the product of the imagination alone. The past and the future are without reality, but the present state of things only stands as if it were real. That is to say: the true state of things is constantly changing, yet it seems as if the state of things were existing, even as does a circle of fire seen when a rope watch is turned round very quickly.

Japanese Pilgrims to China.

The Ris-shu or Vinaya sect is one of purely Chinese origin, and was founded, or rather re-founded, by the Chinese priest Dōsen, who lived on Mount Shunan early in the seventh century, and claimed to be only re-proclaiming the rules given by Gautama himself. He was well acquainted with the Tripitaka and especially versed in the Vinaya or rules of discipline. His purpose was to unite the teachings of both the Greater and the Lesser Vehicle in a sutra whose burden should be one of ethics and not of dogma.

The founder of this sect was greatly honored by the Chinese Emperor. Furthermore, he was honored in vision by the holy Pindola or Binzura,[10] who praised the founder as the best man that had promulgated the discipline since Buddha himself. In later centuries, successors of the founder compiled commentaries and reproclaimed the teachings of this sect.

In A.D. 724 two Japanese priests went over to China, and having mastered the Ris-shu doctrine, received permission to propagate it in Japan. With eighty-two Chinese priests they returned a few years later, having attempted, it is said, the journey five times and spent twelve years on the sea. On their return, they received an imperial invitation to live in the great monastery at Nara, and soon their teachings exerted a powerful influence on the court. The emperor, empress and four hundred persons of note were received into the Buddhist communion by a Chinese priest of the Ris-shu school in the middle of the eighth century. The Mikado Shōmu resigned his throne and took the vow and robes of a monk, becoming Hō-ō or cloistered emperor. Under imperial direction a great bronze image of the Vairokana Buddha, or Perfection of Morality, was erected, and terraces, towers, images and all the paraphernalia of the new kind of Buddhism were prepared. Even the earth was embroidered, as it were, with sutras and shastras. Symbolical landscape gardening, which, in its mounds and paths, variously shaped stones and lanterns, artificial cascades and streamlets, teaches the holy geography as well as the allegories and hidden truths of Buddhism, made the city of Nara beautiful to the eyes of faith as well as of sight.

This sect, with its excellence in morality and benevolence, proved itself a beautifier of human life, of society and of the earth itself. Its work was an irenicon. It occupied itself exclusively with the higher ethics, the higher meditations and the higher knowledge. Interdicting what was evil and prescribing what was good, its precepts varied in number and rigor according to the status of the disciple, lay or clerical. It is by the observance of the *sila*, or grades of moral perfection, that one becomes a Buddha. Besides making so powerful a conquest at the southern capital, this sect was the one which centuries afterward built the first Buddhist temple in Yedo. Being ordinary human mortals, however, both monk and layman occasionally illustrated the difference between profession and practice.

These three schools or sects, Ku-sha, Jō-jitsu, and Ris-shu, may be grouped under the Hinayana or Smaller Vehicle, with more or less affiliation with Southern Buddhism ; the others now to be described were wholly of the Northern division.

The Hossō-shu, or the Dharma-lakshana sect, as described by the Rev. Dai-ryo Takashi of the Shin-gon sect, is the school which studies the nature of Dharmas or things. The three worlds of desire, form and formlessness, consist in thought only ; and there is nothing outside thought. Nine centuries after Gautama, Maitreya,[11] or the Buddha of kindness, came down from the heaven of the Bodhisattva to the lecture-hall in the kingdom in central India at the request of the Buddhas elect, and discoursed five shastras. After that two Buddhist fathers who were brothers, composed many more shastras and cleared up the meaning of the Mahayana. In 629 A.D., in his twenty-ninth year, the famous Chinese pilgrim, Gen-jō (Hiouen-thsang), studied these shastras and sciences,

and returning to China in 645 A.D., began his great work
of translation, at which he continued for nineteen years.
One of his disciples was the author of a hundred commentaries on sutras and shastras. The doctrines of
Gen-jō and his disciples were at four different times,
from 653 to 712 A.D., imported into Japan, and named,
after the monasteries in which they were promulgated,
the Northern and Southern Transmission.

The Middle Path.

The burden of the teachings of this sect is subjective idealism. They embrace principles enjoining complete indifference to mundane affairs, and, in fact,
thorough personal nullification and the ignoring of all
actions by its disciples. In these teachings, thought
only, is real. As we have already seen with the Ku-
sha teaching, human beings are of three classes, divided according to intellect, into higher, middle and
lower, for whom the systems of teachings are necessarily of as many kinds. The order of progress with
those who give themselves to the study of the Hossō
tenets, is,[12] first, they know only the existence of things,
then the emptiness of them, and finally they enter the
middle path of " true emptiness and wonderful existence."

From the first, such discipline is long and painful,
and ultimate victory scarcely comes to the ordinary
being. The disciple, by training in thought, by destroying passions and practices, by meditating on the
only knowledge, must pass through three kalpas or
æons. Constantly meditating, and destroying the two
obstacles of passion and cognizable things, the dis-

ciple then obtains four kinds of wisdom and truly attains perfect enlightenment or Pari-Nirvana.

The San-ron Shu, as the Three-Shastra sect calls itself, is the sect of the Teachings of Buddha's whole life.[13] Other sects are founded upon single sutras, a fact which makes the student liable to narrowness of opinion. The San-ron gives greater breadth of view and catholicity of opinion. The doctrines of the Greater Vehicle are the principal teachings of Gautama, and these are thoroughly explained in the three shastras used by this sect, which, it is claimed, contain Buddha's own words. The meanings of the titles of the three favorite sutras, are, The Middle Book, The Hundred, and The Book of Twelve Gates. Other books of the canon are also studied and valued by this sect, but all of them are apt to be perused from a particular point of view; *i.e.*, that of Pyrronism or infinite negation.

There are two lines of the transmission of this doctrine, both of them through China, though the introduction to Japan was made from Korea, in 625 A.D. Not to dwell upon the detail of history, the burden of this sect's teaching, is, infinite negation or absolute nihilism. Truth is the inconceivable state, or, in the words of the Japanese writer: " The truth is nothing but the state where thoughts come to an end; the right meditation is to perceive this truth. He who has obtained this meditation is called Buddha. This is the doctrine of the San-ron sect."

This sect, by its teachings of the Middle Path, seems to furnish a bridge from the Hinayana or Southern school, to the Mahayana or Northern school of Buddhism. Part of its work, as set forth by the

Rev. Kō-chō Ogurusu, of the Shin sect, is to defend the authenticity, genuineness and canonicity of the books which form the Northern body of scriptures.

In these two sects Hos-sō and San-ron, called those of Middle Path, and much alike in principle and teaching, the whole end and aim of mental discipline, is nihilism—in the one case subjective, and in the other absolute, the end and goal being nothing—this view into the nature of things being considered the right one.

Is it any wonder that such teachings could in the long run satisfy neither the trained intellects nor the unthinking common people of Japan? Is it far from the truth to suspect that, even when accepted by the Japanese courtiers and nobles, they were received, only too often, in a Platonic, not to say a Pickwickian, sense? The Japanese is too polite to say "no" if he can possibly say "yes," even when he does not mean it; while the common people all over the world, as between metaphysics and polytheism, choose the latter. Is it any wonder that, along with this propagation of Nihilism as taught in the cloisters and the court, history informs us of many scandals and much immorality between the women of the court and the Buddhist monks?

Such dogmas were not able to live in organized forms, after the next importations of Buddhism which came in, not partly but wholly, under the name of the Mahayana or Great Vehicle, or Northern Buddhism. By the new philosophy, more concrete and able to appeal more closely to the average man, these five schools, which, in their discussions, dealt almost wholly with *noumena*, were absorbed. As matter of fact, none of

16

them is now in existence, nor can we trace them, speaking broadly, beyond the tenth century. Here and there, indeed, may be a temple bearing the name of one of the sects, or grades of doctrine, and occasionally an eccentric individual who "witnesses" to the old metaphysics; but these are but fossils or historical relics, and are generally regarded as such.

Against such baldness of philosophy not only might the cultivated Japanese intellect revolt and react, but as yet the common people of Japan, despite the modern priestly boast of the care of the imperial rulers for what the bonzes still love to call "the people's religion," were but slightly touched by the Indian faith.

The Great Vehicle.

The Kégon-Shu or Avatamsaka-sutra sect, is founded on a certain teaching which Gautama is said to have promulgated in nine assemblies held at seven different places during the second week of his enlightenment. This sutra exists in no fewer than six texts, around each of which has gathered some interesting mythology. The first two texts were held in memory and not committed to palm leaves; the second pair are secretly preserved in the dragon palace of Riu-gu [14] under the sea, and are not kept by the men of this world. The fifth text of 100,000 verses, was obtained by a Bodhisattva from the palace of the dragon king of the world under the sea and transmitted to men in India. The sixth is the abridged text.

It concerns us to notice that the shorter texts were translated into Chinese in the fourth century, and that later, other translations were made—36,000 verses of

the fifth text, 45,000 verses of the sixth text, etc.
When the doctrine of the sect had been perfected by
the fifth patriarch and he lectured on the sutra, rays of
white light came from his mouth, and there rained wonderful heavenly flowers. In A.D. 736 a Chinese Vinaya
teacher or instructor in Buddhist discipline, named
Dō-sen, first brought the Kégon scriptures to Japan.
Four years later a Korean priest gave lectures on them
in the Golden-Bell Hall of the Great Eastern Monastery at Nara. He completed his task of expounding
the sixty volumes in three years. Henceforth, lectur-
ing on this sutra became one of the yearly services of
the Eastern Great Monastery.

"The Ké-gon sutra is the original book of Buddha's
teachings of his whole life. All his teachings therefore sprang from this sutra. If we attribute all the
branches to the origin, we may say that there is no
teaching of Buddha for his whole life except this
sutra." [15] The title of the book, when literally translated, is Great - square - wide - Buddha - flower - adorn-
ment-teaching — a title sufficiently indicative of its
rhetoric. The age of hard or bold thinking was giving
way to flowery diction, and the Law was to be made
easy through fine writing.

The burden of doctrine is the unconditioned or realistic, pantheism. Nature absolute, or Buddha-tathata,
is the essence of all things. Essence and form were in
their origin combined and identical. Fire and water,
though phenomenally different, are from the point of
view of Buddha-tathata absolutely identical. Matter
and thought are one — that is Buddha-tathata. In
teaching, especially the young, it must be remembered
that the mind resembles a fair page upon which the

artist might trace a design, especial care being needed to prevent the impression of evil thoughts, in order to accomplish which one must completely and always direct the mind to Buddha.[16] One notable sentence in the text is, "when one first raises his thoughts toward the perfect knowledge, he at once becomes fully enlightened."

In some parts of the metaphysical discussions of this sect we are reminded of European mediæval scholasticism, especially of that discussion as to how many angels could dance on the point of a cambric needle without jostling each other. It says, "Even at the point of one grain of dust, of immeasurable and unlimited worlds, there are innumerable Buddhas, who are constantly preaching the Ké-gon kiō (sutra) throughout the three states of existence, past, present and future, so that the preaching is not at all to be collected."[17]

A New Chinese Sect.

In its formal organization the Ten-dai sect is of Chinese origin. It is named after Tien Tai,[18] a mountain in China about fifty miles south of Ningpo, on which the book which forms the basis of its tenets was composed by Chi-sha, now canonized as a Dai Shi or Great teacher. Its special doctrine of completion and suddenness was, however, transmitted directly from Shaka to Vairokana and thence to Maitreya, so that the apostolical succession of its orthodoxy cannot be questioned.

The metaphysics of this sect are thought to be the most profound of the Greater Vehicle, combining into a system the two opposite ideas of being and not being.

The teachers encourage all men, whether quick or slow in understanding, to exercise the principle of "completion" and "suddenness," together with four doctrinal divisions, one or all of which are taught to men according to their ability. The object of the doctrine is to make men get an excellent understanding, practise good discipline and attain to the great fruit of Enlightenment or Buddha-hood.

Out of compassion, Gautama appeared in the world and preached the truth in several forms, according to the circumstances of time and place. There are four doctrinal divisions of "completion," "secrecy," "meditation," and "moral precept," which are the means of knowing the principle of "completion." From Gautama Vairokana and Maitreya the doctrine passed through more than twenty Buddhas elect, and arrived in China on the twentieth day of the twelfth month, A.D. 401. The delivery to disciples was secret, and the term used for this esoteric transmission means "handed over within the tower."

In A.D. 805, two Japanese pilgrims went to China, and received orthodox training. With twenty others, they brought the Ten-dai doctrines into Japan. During this century, other Japanese disciples of the same sect crossed the seas to study at Mount Tien Tai. On coming back to Japan they propagated the various shades of doctrine, so that this main sect has many branches. It was chiefly through these pilgrims from the West that the Sanskrit letters, writing and literature were imported. In our day, evidences of Sanskrit learning, long since neglected and forgotten, are seen chiefly in the graveyards and in charms and amulets.

Although the philosophical doctrines of Ten-dai are

much the same as those of the Ké-gon sect, being based on pantheistic realism, and teaching that the Buddha-tathata or Nature absolute is the essence of all things, yet the Ten-dai school has striking and peculiar features of its own. Instead of taking some particular book or books in the canon, shastra, or sutra, selection or collection, as a basis, the Chinese monk Chi-sha first mastered, and then digested the whole canon. Then selecting certain doctrines for emphasis he supported them by a wide range of quotation, professing to give the gist of the pure teachings of Gautama rather than those of his disciples. In practice, however, the Saddharma Pundarika is the book most honored by this sect; the other sutras being employed mainly as commentary. Furthermore, this sect makes as strenuous a claim for the true apostolical succession from the Founder, as do the other sects.

The teachers of Ten-dai doctrine must fully estimate character and ability in their pupils, and so apportion instruction. In this respect and in not a few others, they are like the disciples of Loyola, and have properly been called the Jesuits of Buddhism. They are ascetics, and teach that spiritual insight is possible only through prolonged thought. Their purpose is to recognize the Buddha, in all the forms he has assumed in order to save mankind. Nevertheless, the highest truths are incomprehensible except to those who have already attained to Buddha-hood.[19] In contrast to the Nichirenites, who give an emotional and ultra-concrete interpretation and expression to the great sutra Hokké Kiō, the Ten-dai teachers are excessively philosophical and intellectual.

In its history the Ten-dai sect has followed out its

logic. Being realistic in pantheism, it reverences not only Gautama the historic Buddha, but also, large numbers of the Hindu deities, the group of idols called Jizō, the god Fudo, and Kuannon the god or goddess of mercy, under his or her protean forms. In its early history this sect welcomed to its pantheon the Shintō gods, who, according to the scheme of Riyōbu Shintō, were declared to be avatars or manifestations of Buddha. The three sub-sects still differ in their worship of the avatars selected as supreme deities, but their philosophy enables them to sweep in the Buddhas of every age and clime, name and nation. Many other personifications are found honored in the Ten-dai temples. At the gateways may usually be seen the colossal painted and hideous images of the two Devas or kings (Ni-O). These worthies are none other than Indra and Brahma of the old Vedic mythology.

Space and time—which seem never to fail the Buddhists in their literature—would fail us to describe this sect in full, or to show in detail its teachings, wherein are wonderful resemblances to European ideas and facts—in philosophy, to Hegel and Spinoza and in history, to Jesuitism. Nor can we stay to point out the many instances in which, invading the domain of politics, the Ten-dai abbots with their armies of monks, having made their monasteries military arsenals and issuing forth clad in armor as infantry and cavalry, have turned the scale of battle or dictated policies to emperors. Like the Prætorian guard of Rome or the clerical militia in Spain, these men of keen intellect have left their marks deep upon the social and political history of the country in which they dwelt. They have understood thoroughly the art of practising religion for the sake of revenue. To secure their ends, priests have made partnerships with other sects; in order to hold Shintō shrines, they have married to secure heirs and make office hereditary; and finally in the Purification of 1870, when the Riyōbu system was blown to the winds by the Japanese Government, not a few priests of this sect became laymen, in order to keep both office and emolument in the purified Shintō shrines.

The Sect of the True Word.

It is probable that the conquest and obliteration of Shintō might have been accomplished by some priest or priests of the Ten-dai sect, had such a genius as Kōbō been found in its household; but this great achievement was reserved for the man who introduced into Japan the Shin-gon Shu, or Sect of the True Word. The term *gon* is the equivalent of Mantra,[30] a Sanskrit term meaning word, but in later use referring to the mystic salutations addressed to the Buddhist gods. " The doctrine of this sect is a great secret law. It teaches us that we can attain to the state of the ' Great Enlightened,' that is the state of ' Buddha,' while in the present physical body, which was born of our parents (and which consists of six elements,[21] Earth, Water, Fire, Wind, Ether, and Knowledge), if we follow the three great secret laws, regarding Body, Speech, and Thought." [22]

The history of the transmission of the doctrine from the greatest of the spirit-bodied Buddhas to the historic founder, Vagrabodhi, is carefully given. The latter was a man very learned in regard to many doctrines of Buddhism and other religions, and was es-

pecially well acquainted with the deepest meaning of
the doctrine of this sect, which he taught in India for
a considerable time. The doctrine is recorded in several sutras, yet the essential point is nothing but the
Mandala, or circle of the two parts, or, in Japanese,
Riyōbu.

The great preacher, Vagrabodhi, in 720 A.D., came
with his disciples to the capital of China, and translated the sacred books, seventy-seven in number. This
doctrine is the well-known Yoga-chara, which has been
well set forth by Doctor Edkins in his scholarly volume
on Chinese Buddhism. As "yoga" becomes in plain
English "yoke," and as "mantra" is from the same
root as "man" and "mind," we have no difficulty in
recognizing the original meaning of these terms ; the
one in its nobler significance referring to union with
Buddha or Gnosis, and the other to the thought taking
lofty expression or being debased to hocus-pocus in
charm or amulet. Like the history of so many Sanskrit words as now uttered in every-day English speech,
the story of the word mantra forms a picture of mental
processes and apparently of the degradation of thought,
or, as some will doubtless say, of the decay of religion.
The term mantra meant first, a thought ; then thought
expressed ; then a Vedic hymn or text ; next a spell or
charm. Such have been the later associations, in India,
China and Japan with the term mantra.

The burden of the philosophy of the Shin-gon,
looked at from one point of view, is mysticism, and
from another, pantheism. One of the forms of Buddha
is the principle of everything. There are ten stages
of thought, and there are two parts, "lengthwise" and
"crosswise" or exoteric and esoteric. Other doctrines

of Buddhism represent the first, or exoteric stage, and those of the Shin-gon or true word, the second, or esoteric. The primordial principle is identical with that of Maha-Vairokana, one of the forms [23] of Buddha. The body, the word and the thought are the three mysteries, which being found in all beings, animate and inanimate, are to be fully understood only by Buddhas, and not by ordinary men.

To show the actual method of intellectual procedure in order to reach Buddha-hood, many categories, tables and diagrams are necessary; but the crowning tenet, most far reaching in its practical influence, is the teaching that it is possible to reach the state of Buddha-hood in this present body.

As discipline for the attainment of excellence along the path marked out in the " Mantra sect," there are three mystic rites : (1) worshipping the Buddha with the hand in certain positions called signs ; (2) repeating Dharani, or mystic formulas ; (3) contemplation.

Kōbō himself and all those who imitated him, practised fasting in order to clear the spiritual eyesight. The thinking - chairs, so conspicuous in many old monasteries, though warmed at intervals through the ages by the living bodies of men absorbed in contemplation, are rarely much worn by the sitters, because almost absolute cessation of motion characterizes the long and hard thinkers of the Shin-gon philosophers. The idols in the Shin-gon temples represent many a saint and disciple, who, by perseverance in what a critic of Buddhism calls "mind-murder," and the use of mystic finger twistings and magic formulas, has won either the Nirvana or the penultimate stage of the Bodhisattva.

In the sermons and discourses of Shin-gon, the subtle points of an argument are seized and elaborated. These are mystical on the one side, and pantheistic on the other. It is easily seen how Buddha, being in Japanese gods as well as men, and no being without Buddha, the way is made clear for that kind of a marriage between Buddhism and Shintō, in which the two become one, and that one, as to revenue and advantage, Buddhism.

Truth Made Apparent by One's Own Thought.

The Japanese of to-day often speak of these seven religious bodies which we have enumerated and described, as " the old sects," because much of the philosophy, and many of the forms and prayers, are common to all, or, more accurately speaking, are popularly supposed to be; while the priests, being celibates, refrain from saké, flesh and fish, and from all intimate relations with women. Yet, although these sects are considered to be more or less conformable to the canon of the Greater Vehicle, and while the last three certainly introduce many of its characteristic features—one sect teaching that Buddha-hood could be obtained even in the present body of flesh and blood—yet the idea of Paradise had not been exploited or emphasized. This new gospel was to be introduced into Japan by the Jō-dō Shu or Sect of the Pure Land.

Before detailing the features of Jō-dō, we call attention to the fact that in Japan the propagation of the old sects was accompanied by an excessive use of idols, images, pictures, sutras, shastras and all the furniture thought necessary in a Buddhist temple. The course of thought and action in the Orient is in many respects similar to that in the Occident. In western lands, with the ebb and flow of religious sentiment, the iconolater has been followed by the iconoclast, and the over-crowded cathedrals have been purged by the hammer and fire of the Protestant and Puritan. So in Japan we find analogous, though not exactly similar, reactions. The rise and prosperity of the believers in the Zen dogmas, which in their early history used sparingly the eikon, idol and sutra, give some indication of protest against too much use of externals in religion. May we call them the Quakers of Japanese Buddhism? Cer-tainly, theirs was a movement in the direction of sim-plicity.

The introduction of the Zen, or contemplative sect, did, in a sense, both precede and follow that of Shin-gon. The word Zen is a shortened form of the term Zenna, which is a transliteration into Chinese of the Sanskrit word Dhyana, or contemplation. It teaches that the truth is not in tradition or in books, but in one's self. Emphasis is laid on introspection rather than on language. "Look carefully within and there you will find the Buddha," is its chief tenet. In the Zen monasteries, the chair of contemplation is, or ought to be, always in use.

The Zen Shu movement may be said to have arisen out of a reaction against the multiplication of idols. It indicated a return to simpler forms of worship and conduct. Let us inquire how this was.

It may be said that Buddhism, especially Northern Buddhism, is a vast, complicated system. It has a literature and a sacred canon which one can think of only in connection with long trains of camels to carry,

or freight trains to transport, or ships a good deal
bigger than the Mayflower to import. Its multitudinous rules and systems of discipline appall the spirit
and weary the flesh even to enumerate them ; so that,
from one point of view, the making of new sects is a
necessity. These are labor-saving inventions. They
are attempts to reduce the great bulk of scriptures to
manageable proportions. They seek to find, as it were,
the mother-liquor of the great ocean, so as to express
the truth in a crystal. Hence the endeavors to sim-
plify, to condense ; here, by a selection of sutras,
rather than the whole collection ; there, by emphasis
on a single feature and a determination to put the
whole thing in a form which can be grasped, either by
the elect few or by the people at large.

The Zen sect did this in a more rational way than
that set forth as orthodox by later priestcraft, which
taught that to the believer who simply turned round
the revolving library containing the canon, the merit of
having read it all would be imputed. The rin-zō[24]
found near the large temples,—the cunning invention
of a Chinese priest in the sixth century,—soon became
popular in Japan. The great wooden book-case turning on a pivot contains 6,771 volumes, that being the
number of canonical volumes enumerated in China and
Japan.

The Zen sect teaches that, besides all the doctrines
of the Greater and the Lesser Vehicles, whether hidden or apparent, there is one distinct line of transmission of a secret doctrine which is not subject to any
utterance at all. According to their tenet of contemplation, one is to see directly the key to the thought of
Buddha by his own thought, thus freeing himself from

the multitude of different doctrines—the number of which is said to be eighty-four thousand. In fact, Zen Shu or "Dhyana sect" teaches the short method of making truth apparent by one's own thought, apart from the writings.

The story of the transmission of the true Zen doctrine is this:

" When the blessed Shaka was at the assembly on Vulture's Peak, there came the heavenly king, who offered the Buddha a golden-colored flower and asked him to preach the law. The Blessed One simply took the flower and held it in his hand, but said no word. No one in the whole assembly could tell what he meant. The venerable Mahahasyapa alone smiled. Then the Blessed One said to him, ' I have the wonderful thought of Nirvana, the eye of the Right Law, which I shall now give to you.' [25] Thus was ushered in the doctrine of thought transmitted by thought."

After twenty-eight patriarchs 'had taught the doctrine of contemplation, the last came into China in A.D. 520, and tried to teach the Emperor the secret key of Buddha's thought. This missionary Bodhidharma was the third son of a king of the Kashis, in Southern India, and the historic original of the tobacconist's shop-sign in Japan, who is known as Daruma. The imperial Chinaman was not yet able to understand the secret key of Buddha's thought. So the Hindu missionary went to the monastery on Mount Su, where in meditation, he sat down cross-legged with his face to a wall, for nine years, by which time, says the legend, his legs had rotted off and he looked like a snow-image. During that period, people did not know him, and called him simply the Wall-gazing Brahmana. Afterward he had a number of disciples, but they had different views that are called the transmissions of the skin, flesh, or bone of the teacher. Only one of them got the whole body of his teachings. Two great sects were formed : the Northern, which was undivided, and the Southern, which branched off into five houses and seven schools. The Northern Sect was introduced into Japan by a Chinese priest in 729 A.D., while the Southern was not brought over until the twelfth century. In both it is taught that perfect tranquillity of body and mind is essential to salvation. The doctrine is the most sublime one, of thought transmitted by thought being entirely independent of any letters or words. Another name for them is, "The Sect whose Mind Assimilates with Buddha," direct from whom it claims to have received its articles of faith.

Too often this idea of Buddhaship, consisting of absolute freedom from matter and thought, means practically mind-murder, and the emptiness of idle reverie.

Contrasting modern reality with their ancient ideal, it must be confessed that in practice there is not a little letter worship and a good deal of pedantry ; for, in all the teachings of abstract principles by the different sects, there are endless puns or plays upon words in the renderings of Chinese characters. This arises from that antithesis of extreme poverty in sounds with amazing luxuriance in written expression, which characterizes both the Chinese and Japanese languages.

In the temples we find that the later deities introduced into the Buddhist pantheon are here also welcome, and that the triads or groups of three precious ones, the "Buddhist trinity," so-called,[26] are surrounded by gods of Chinese or Japanese origin. The Zen sect, according to its professions and early history, ought to be indifferent to worldly honors and emoluments, and indeed many of its devotees are. Its history, however, shows how poorly mortals live up to their principles and practise what they preach. Furthermore, these professors of peace and of the joys of the inner life in the Sō-tō or sub-sect have made the twenty-fifth and twenty-sixth years of Meiji, or A.D. 1893 and 1894, famous and themselves infamous by their long-continued and scandalous intestine quarrels. Of the three sub-sects, those called Rin-zai and Sō-tō, take their names from Chinese monks of the ninth century; while the third, O-baku, founded in Japan in the seventeenth century, is one of the latest importations of Chinese Buddhistic thought in the Land of the Rising Sun.

Japanese authors usually classify the first six denominations at which we have glanced, some of which are phases of thought rather than organizations, as "the ancient sects." Ten-dai and Shin-gon are "the mediæval sects." The remaining four, of which we shall now treat, and which are more particularly Japanese in spirit and development, are "the modern sects."

THE BUDDHISM OF THE JAPANESE

> " A drop of spray cast by the infinite
> I hung an instant there, and threw my ray
> To make the rainbow. A microcosm I
> Reflecting all. Then back I fell again,
> And though I perished not, I was no more."—
>
> The Pantheist's Epitaph.

" Buddhism is essentially a religion of compromise."

" Where Christianity has One Lord, Buddhism has a dozen."

" I think I may safely challenge the Buddhist priesthood to give a plain historical account of the Life of Amida, Kwannon, Dainichi, or any other Mahāyāna Buddha, without being in serious danger of forfeiting my stakes."

" Christianity openly puts this Absolute Unconditioned Essence in the forefront of its teaching. In Buddhism this absolute existence is only put forward when the logic of circumstances compels its teachers to have recourse to it."—A. Lloyd, in The Higher Buddhism in the Light of the Nicene creed.

" Now these six characters, ' Na-mu-A-mi-da-Butsu,' Zend-ō has explained as follows : ' Namu ' means [our] following His behest—and also [His] uttering the Prayer and bestowing [merit] upon us. ' Amida Butsu ' is the practice of this, consequently by this means a certainty of salvation is attained."

" By reason of the conferring on us sentient creatures of this great goodness and great merit through the utterance of the Prayer, and the bestowal [by Amida] the evil Karma and [effect of the] passions, accumulated through the long Kalpas, since when there was no beginning, are in a moment annihilated, and, in consequence, those passions and evil Karma of ours all disappearing, we live already in the condition of the steadfast, who do not return [to revolve in the cycle of Birth and Death]."—Rennyo of the Shin sect, †1473.

" In the beginning was the Word, and the Word was with God, and the Word was God."—John.

" The Father of lights, with whom there is no variableness, neither shadow of turning."—James.

CHAPTER IX

THE BUDDHISM OF THE JAPANESE

The Western Paradise

WE cannot take space to show how, or how much, or whether at all, Buddhism was affected by Christianity, though it probably was. Suffice it to say that the Jō-dō Shu, or Sect of the Pure Land, was the first of the many denominations in Buddhism which definitely and clearly set forth that especial peculiarity of Northern Buddhism, the Western Paradise. The school of thought which issued in Jō-dō Shu was founded by the Hindoo, Memio. In A.D. 252 an Indian scholar, learned in the Tripitaka, came to China, and translated one of the great sutras, called Amitayus. This sutra gives a history of Tathagata Amitabha,[1] from the first spiritual impulses which led him to the attainment of Buddha-hood in remote Kalpas down to the present time, when he dwells in the Western World, called the Happy, where he receives all living beings from every direction, helping them to turn away from confusion and to become enlightened.[2] The apocalyptic twentieth chapter of the Hokké Kiō is a glorification of the transcendent power of the Tathagatas, expressed in flamboyant oriental rhetoric.

We have before called attention to the fact that, with the multiplication of sutras or the Sacred Canon and the vast increase of the apparatus of Buddhism as well as of the hardships of brain and body to be undergone in order to be a Buddhist, it was absolutely necessary that some labor-saving system should be devised by which the burden could be borne. Now, as a matter of fact, all sects claim to found their doctrine on Buddha or his work. According to the teaching of certain sects, the means of salvation are to be found in the study of the whole canon, and in the practice of asceticism and meditation. On the contrary, the new lights of Buddhism who came as missionaries into China, protested against this expenditure of so much mental and physical energy. One of the first Chinese propagators of the Jō-dō doctrine declared that it was impossible, owing to the decay of religion in his own age, for anyone to be saved in this way by his own efforts. Hence, instead of the noble eight-fold path of primitive Buddhism, or of the complicated system of the later Buddhistic Phariseeism of India, he substituted for the difficult road to Nirvana, a simple faith in the all-saving power of Amida. In one of the sutras it is taught, that if a man keeps in his memory the name of Amida one day, or seven days, the Buddha together with Buddhas elect, will meet him at the moment of his death, in order to let him be born in the Pure Land, and that this matter has been equally approved by all other Buddhas of ten different directions.

One of the sutras, translated in China during the fifth century, contains the teaching of Buddha, which he delivered to the wife of the King of Magadha, who on account of the wickedness of her son was feeling weary of this world. He showed her how she might be born into the Pure Land. Three paths of good ac-

tions were pointed out. Toward the end of the particular sutra which he advised her to read and recite,
Buddha says : " Let not one's voice cease, but ten times
complete the thought, and repeat the formula of the
adoration of Amida." "This practice," adds the Japanese exegete and historian, "is the most excellent
of all."

How well this latter teaching is practised may be
demonstrated when one goes into a Buddhist temple
of the Jō-dō sect in Japan, and hears the constant refrain,—murmured by the score or more of listeners to the
sermon, or swelling like the roar of the ocean's waves,
on festival days, when thousands sit on the mats beneath the fretted roof to enjoy the exposition of doctrine—" Namu Amida Butsu "—" Glory to the Eternal
Buddha ! " [3]

The apostolical succession or transmission through
the patriarchs and apostles of India and China, is well
known and clearly stated, withal duly accredited and
embellished with signs and wonders, in the historical
literature of the Jō-dō sect. In Buddhism, as in
Christianity, the questions relating to True Churchism,
High Churchism, the succession of the apostles, teachers and rulers, and the validity of this or that method
of ordination, form a large part of the literature of controversy. Nevertheless, as in the case of many a Christian sect which calls itself the only true church, the
date of the organization of Jō-dō was centuries later
than that of the Founder and apostles of the original
faith. Five hundred years after Zen-dō (A.D. 600-650),
the great propagator of the Jō-dō philosophy, Hō-nen,
the founder of the Jō-dō sect, was born ; and this phase
of organized Buddhism, like that of Shin Shu and

Nichirer Shu, may be classed under the head of Eastern or Japanese Buddhism.

When only nine years of age, the boy afterward called Hō-nen, was converted by his father's dying words. He went to school in his native province, but his priest-teacher foreseeing his greatness, sent him to the monastery of Hiyéizan, near Kiōto. The boy's letter of introduction contained only these words : "I send you an image of the Bodhisattva, (Mon-ju) Manjusri." The boy shaved his head and received the precepts of the Ten-dai sect, but in his eighteenth year, waiving the prospect of obtaining the headship of the great denomination, he built a hut in the Black Ravine and there five times read through the five thousand volumes [4] of the Tripitaka. He did this for the purpose of finding out, for the ordinary and ignorant people of the present day, how to escape from misery. He studied Zen-dō's commentary, and repeated his examination eight times. At last, he noticed a passage in it beginning with the words, "Chiefly remember or repeat the name of Amida with a whole and undivided heart." Then he at once understood the thought of Zen-dō, who taught in his work that whoever at any time practises to remember Buddha, or calls his name even but once, will gain the right effect of going to be born in the Pure Land after death. This Japanese student then abandoned all sorts of practices which he had hitherto followed for years, and began to repeat the name of Amida Buddha sixty thousand times a day. This event occurred in A.D. 1175.

Hō-nen, Founder of the Pure Land Sect.

This path-finder to the Pure Land, who developed a special doctrine of salvation, is best known by his post-humous title of Hō-nen. During his lifetime he was very famous and became the spiritual preceptor of three Mikados. After his death his biography was compiled in forty - eight volumes by imperial order, and later, three other emperors copied or republished it. In the history of Japan this sect has been one of the most influential, especially with the imperial and shōgunal families. In Kiōto the magnificent temples and monasteries of Chiōn-in, and in Tōkiō Zō-jō-ji, are the chief seats of the two principal divisions of this sect. The gorgeous mausoleums,—well known to every foreign tourist,—at Shiba and Uyéno in Tōkiō, and the clustered and matchless splendors of Nikkō, belong to this sect, which has been under the patronage of the illustrious line of the Tokugawa,[5] while its temples and shrines are numbered by many thousands.

The doctrine of the Jō dō, or the Pure Land Sect, is easily discerned. One of Buddha's disciples said, that in the teachings of the Master there are two divisions or vehicles. In the Maha - yana also there are two gates; the Holy path, and the Pure Land. The Smaller Vehicle is the doctrine by which the immedi-ate disciples of Buddha and those for five hundred years succeeding, practised the various virtues and dis-cipline. The gateway of the Maha-yana is also the doctrine, by which in addition to the trainings men-tioned, there are also understood the three virtues of spiritual body, wisdom and deliverance. The man who is able successfully to complete this course of discipline and practice is no ordinary person, but is supposed to possess merit produced from good actions performed in a former state of existence. The doctrine by which man may do so, is called the gate of the Holy Path.

During the fifteen hundred years after Buddha there were from time to time, such personages in the world, who attained the end of the Holy Path; but in these latter days people are more insincere, covetous and contentious, and the discipline is too hard for degenerate times and men. The three trainings already spoken of are the correct causes of deliverance; but if people think them as useless as last year's almanac, when can they complete their deliverance? Hō-nen, deeply meditating on this, shut up the gate of the Holy Path and opened that of the Pure Land; for in the former the effective deliverance is expected in this world by the three trainings of morality, thought and learning, but in the latter the great fruit of going to be born in the Pure Land after death, is expected through the sole practice of repeating Buddha's name.

Moreover, it is not easy to accomplish the cause and effect of the Holy Path, but both those of the doctrine of the Pure Land are very easy to be completed. The difference is like that between travelling by land and travelling by water.[6] The doctrines preached by the Buddha are eighty-four thousand in number; that is to say, he taught one kind of people one system, that of the Holy Path, and another kind that of the Pure Land. The Pure Land doctrine of Hō-nen was derived from the sutra preached by the great teacher Shaka.

This simple doctrine of "land travel to Paradise" was one which the people of Japan could easily understand, and it became amazingly popular. Salvation along this route is a case of being "carried to the skies on flowery beds of ease, while others sought to win the prize and sailed through bloody seas."

Largely through the influence of Jō-dō Shu and of those sects most closely allied to it, the technical terms, peculiar phraseology and vocabulary of Buddhism became part of the daily speech of the Japanese. When one studies their language he finds that it is a complicated organism, including within itself several distinct systems. Just as the human body harmonizes within itself such vastly differing organized functions as the osseous, digestive, respiratory, etc., so, embedded in what is called the Japanese language, there are, also, a Chinese vocabulary, a polite vernacular, one system of expression for superiors, another for inferiors, etc. Last of all, there is, besides a peculiar system of pronunciation taught by the priests, a Buddhist language, which suggests a firmament of starry and a prairie of flowery metaphors, with intermediate deeps of space full of figurative expressions.

In our own mother tongue we have something similar. The dialect of Canaan, the importations of Judaism, the irruptions of Hebraic idioms, phrases and names into Puritanism, and the ejaculations of the camp-meeting, which vein and color our English speech, may give some idea of the variegated strains which make up the Japanese language. Further, the peculiar nomenclature of the Fifth Monarchy men, is fully paralleled in the personal names of priests and even of laymen in Japan.

Characteristics of the Jō-dō Sect.

Hō-nen teaches that the solution of abstract questions and doctrinal controversies is not needed as means of grace to promote the work of salvation. Whether the priests and their followers were learned and devout, or the contrary, mattered little as regards the final result, as all that is necessary is the continual repetition of the prayer to Amida.

It may be added that his followers practise the master's precepts with emphasis. Their incessant pounding upon wooden fish-drums and bladder-shaped bells during their public exercises, is as noisy as a frontier camp-meeting. The rosary is a notable feature in the private devotions of the Buddhists, but the Jō-dō sect makes especial use of the double rosary, which was invented with the idea of being manipulated by the left hand only ; this gave freedom to the right hand, " facilitating a happy combination of spiritual and secular duty." At funerals of believers a particular ceremony was exclusively practised by this sect, at which the friends of the deceased sat in a circle facing the priest, making as many repetitions as possible.⁷

In Mohammedan countries, blind men, who cannot look down into the surrounding gardens or house tops at the pretty women in or on them, but who have clear and penetrating voices, are often chosen as muezzins to utter the call to prayer from the minarets. On much the same principle, in Old Japan, Jō-dō priests, blind to metaphysics, but handsome, elegantly dressed and with fine delivery, went about the streets singing and intoning prayers, rich presents being made to them, especially by the ladies. The Jō-dō people cultivate art and æsthetic ornamentation to a notable degree. They also understand the art of fictitious and sensational miracle-mongering. It is said that Zen-dō, the famous Chinese founder of this Chinese sect, when writing his commentary, prayed for a wonderful exhibition of supernatural power. Thereupon, a being arrayed as a priest of dignified presence gave him instruction on the division of the text in his first volume. Hence Zen-dō treats his own work as if it were the work of Buddha, and says that no one is allowed either to add or to take away even a word or sentence of the book.

The Pure Land is the western world where Amida lives. It is perfectly pure and free from faults. Those who wish to go thither will certainly be re-born there, but otherwise they will not. This world, on the contrary, is the effect of the action of all beings, so that even those who do not wish to be born here are nevertheless obliged to come. This world is called the Path of Pain, because it is full of all sorts of pains, such as birth, old age, disease, death, etc. This is therefore a world not to be attached to, but to be estranged and separated from. One who is disgusted with this world, and who is filled with desire for that world, will after death be born there. Not to doubt about these words of Buddha, even in the slightest degree, is called deep faith ; but if one entertains the least doubts he will not be born there. Hence the saying : " In the great sea of the law of Buddha, faith is the only means to enter."

Salvation Through the Merits of Another.

In this absolute trust in the all-saving power of Amida as compared with the ways promulgated before, we see the emergence of the Buddhist doctrine of justification by faith, the simplification of theology, and a revolt against Buddhist scholasticism. The Japanese technical term, "*tariki*," or relying upon the strength of another, renouncing all idea of *ji-riki* or self-power,[8] is the substance of the Jō-dō doctrine; but the expanded term *ta-riki chiu no ji-riki*, or "self-effort depending on another," while expressing the whole dogma, is rather scornfully applied to the Jō-dōists by the men of the Shin sect. The invocation of Amida is a meritorious act of the believer, much repetition being the substance of this combination of personal and vicarious work.

Hō-nen, after making his discovery, believing it possible for all mankind eventually to attain to perfect Buddhaship, left, as we have seen, the Ten-dai sect, which represented particularism and laid emphasis on the idea of the elect. Hō-nen taught Buddhist universalism. Belief and repetition of prayer secure birth into the Pure Land after the death of the body, and then the soul moves onward toward the perfection of Buddha-hood.

The Japanese were delighted to have among them a genius who could thus Japanize Buddhism, and Jō-dō doctrine went forth conquering and to conquer. From the twelfth century, the tendency of Japanese Buddhism is in the direction of universalism and democracy. In later developments of Jō-dō, the pantheistic tendencies are emphasized and the syncretistic powers are enlarged. While mysticism is a striking feature of the sect and the attainment of truth is by the grace of Amida, yet the native Kami of Japan are logically accepted as avatars of Buddha. History had little or no rights in the case; philosophy was dictator, and that philosophy was Hō-nen's. Those later Chinese deities made by personifying attributes or abstract ideas, which sprang up after the introduction of Buddhism into China, are also welcomed into the temples of this sect. That the common people really believe that they themselves may attain Buddha-hood at death, and enter the Pure Land, is shown in the fact that their ordinary expression for the dead saint is Hotoké—a general term for all the gods that were once human. Some popular proverbs indicate this in a form that easily lends itself to irreverence and merriment.

The whole tendency of Japanese Buddhism and its full momentum were now toward the development of doctrine even to startling proportions. Instead of the ancient path of asceticism and virtue with agnosticism and atheism, we see the means of salvation put now, and perhaps too easily, within the control of all. The pathway to Paradise was made not only exceedingly plain, but also extremely easy, perhaps even ridiculously so; while the door was open for an outburst of new and local doctrines unknown to India, or even to China. The rampant vigor with which Japanese Buddhism began to absorb everything in heaven, earth and sea, which it could make a worshipable object or cause to stand as a Kami or deity to the mind, will be seen as we proceed. The native proverb, instead of

being an irreverent joke, stands for an actual truth—
"Even a sardine's head may become an object of worship."

"Reformed" Buddhism.

We now look at what foreigners call "Reformed" Buddhism, which some even imagine has been borrowed from Protestant Christianity—notwithstanding that it is centuries older than the Reformation in Europe.

The Shin Shu or True Sect, though really founded on the Jō-dō doctrines, is separate from the sect of the Pure Land. Yet, besides being called the Shin Shu, it is also spoken of as the Jō-dō Shin Shu or the True Sect of the Pure Land. It is the extreme form of the Protestantism of Buddhism. It lays emphasis on the idea of salvation wholly through the merits of another, but it also paints in richer tints the sensuous delights of the Western Paradise. As the term Pure Land is antithetical to that of the Holy Path, so the word Shin, or True, expresses the contrary of what are termed the "temporary expedients."

While some say that we should practise good works, bring our stock of merits to maturity, and be born in the Pure Land, others say that we need only repeat the name of Amida in order to be born in the Pure Land, by the merit produced from such repetition. These doctrines concerning repetitions, however, are all considered but "temporary expedients." So also is the rigid classification, so prominent in "the old sects," of all beings or pupils into three grades. As in Islam or Calvinism, all believers stand on a level. To Shinran the Radical, the practices even of Jō-dō seemed

complicated and difficult, and all that appeared necessary to him was faith in the desire of Amida to bless
and save. To Shinran,[9] faith was the sole saving act.
To rely upon the power of the Original Prayer of
Amitabha Buddha with the whole heart and give up
all idea of *ji-riki* or self-power, is called the truth. This
truth is the doctrine of this sect of Shin.[10] In a word,
not synergism, not faith *and* works, but faith only is
the teaching of Shin Shu.

Shinran, the founder of this sect in Japan, was born
A.D. 1173 and died in the year 1262. He was very
naturally one who had been first educated in the Jō-dō
sect, then the ruling one at the imperial court in Kiōto.
Shall we call him a Japanese Luther, because of his
insistence on salvation by faith only? He is popularly believed to have been descended from one of the
Shintō gods, being on his father's side the twenty-first
in the line of generation. On his mother's side he
was of the lineage of the Minamoto or Genji, a clan
sprung from Mikados and famous during centuries for
its victorious warriors. Hō-nen was his teacher, and
like his teacher, Shinran studied at the great monastery near Kiōto, learning first the doctrine of the Ten-
dai, and then, at the age of twenty-nine, receiving from
Hō-nen the tenets of the Jō-dō sect. Shortly after, at
thirty years of age, he began to promulgate his doctrines. Then he took a step as new to Buddhism, as
was Luther's union with Katharine von Bora, to the
ecclesiasticism of his time. He married a lady of the
imperial court, named **Tamayori**, who was the daughter of the Kuambaku or premier.

Shinran thus taught by example, if not formally and
by written precept, that marriage was honorable, and

that celibacy was an invention of the priests not warranted by primitive Buddhism. Penance, fasting, prescribed diet, pilgrimages, isolation from society whether as hermits or in the cloister, and generally amulets and charms, are all tabooed by this sect. Monasteries imposing life-vows are unknown within its pale. Family life takes the place of monkish seclusion. Devout prayer, purity, earnestness of life and trust in Buddha himself as the only worker of perfect righteousness, are insisted upon. Morality is taught to be more important than orthodoxy.

In practice, the Shin sect even more than the Jō-dō, teaches that it is faith in Buddha which accomplishes the salvation of the believer. Instead of waiting for death in order to come under the protection of Amida, the faithful soul is at once received into the care of the Boundlessly Compassionate. In a word, the Shin sect believes in instantaneous conversion and sanctification. Between the Roman and the Reformed soteriology of Christendom, was Melancthonism or the coöperate union of the divine and the human will. So, the old Buddhism prior to Shinran taught a phase of synergism, or the union of faith and works. Shinran, in his "Reformed" Buddhism, taught the simplicity of faith.

So also in regard to the sacred writings, Shinran opposed the San-ron school and the three-grade idea. The scriptures of other sects are in Sanskrit and Chinese, which only the learned are able to read. The special writings of Shinran are in the vernacular. Three of the sutras, also, have been translated into Japanese and expressed in the kana script. Singleness of purpose characterized this sect, which was often called Monto, or followers of the gate, in reference to its unity of organization, and the opening of the way to all by Shinran and the doctrine taught by him. Yet, lest the gate might seem too broad, the Shin teachers insist that morality is as important as faith, and indeed the proof of it. The high priests of Shin Shu have ever held a high position and wielded vast influence in the religious development of the people. While the temples of other sects are built in sequestered places among the hills, those of Shin Shu are erected in the heart of cities, on the main streets, and at the centres of population,—the priests using every means within their power to induce the people to come to them. The altars are on an imposing scale of magnificence and gorgeous detail. No Roman Catholic church or cathedral can outshine the splendor of these temples, in which the way to the Western Paradise is made so clear and plain. Another name for the sect is Ikko.

After the death of Shinran, his youngest daughter and one of his grandsons erected a monastery near his tomb in the eastern suburbs of Kiōto, to which the Mikado gave the title of Hon-guanji, or Monastery of the Original Vow. This was in allusion to the vow made by Amida, that he would not accept Buddhaship except under the condition that salvation be made attainable for all who should sincerely desire to be born into his kingdom, and signify their desire by invoking his name ten times.[11] It is upon the passage in the sutra where this vow is recorded, that the doctrine of the sect is based. Its central idea is that man is to be saved by faith in the mercy of the boundlessly compassionate Amida, and not by works or vain repetitions. Within our own time, on November 28, 1876,

18

the present reigning Mikado bestowed upon Shinran the posthumous title Ken - shin Dai - shi, or Great Teacher of the Revelation of Truth.

The Protestants of Japanese Buddhism.

This is the sect which, being called "Reformed" Buddhism [12] and resembling Protestantism in so many points, both large and minute, foreigners think has been borrowed or imitated from European Protestantism.[13] As matter of fact, the foundation principles of Shin-Shu are at least six hundred years old. They are perfectly clear in the writings of the founder,[14] as well as in those of his successor Renniō,[15] who wrote the Ofumi or sacred writings, now daily read by the disciples of this denomination. With the characteristic object of reaching the masses, they are written, as we have shown, not in the mixed Chinese and Japanese characters, but in the common script, or kana, which all the people of both sexes can read. Within the last two decades the Shin educators have been the first to organize their schools of learning on the models of those in Christendom, so that their young men might be trained to resist Shintō or Christianity, or to measure the truth in either. Their new temples also show European influence in architecture and furniture. Liberty of thought and action, and incoercible desire to be free from governmental, traditional, ultra-ecclesiastical, or Shintō influence—in a word, protestantism in its pure sense, is characteristic of the great sect founded by Shinran.

Indeed the Shin sect, which sprang out of the Jō-dō, maintains that it alone professes the true teaching of

Hō-nen, and that the Jō-dō sect has wandered from the original doctrines of its founder. Whereas the Jō-dō or Pure Land sect believes that Amida will come to meet the soul of the believer on its separation from the body, in order to conduct it to Paradise, the Shin or True Sect of the Pure Land believes in immediate salvation and sanctification. It preaches that as soon as a man believes in Amida he is taken by him under his merciful protection. Some might denominate these people the Methodists of Buddhism.

One good point in their Protestantism is their teaching that morality is of equal importance with faith. To them Buddha-hood means the perfection and unlimitedness of wisdom and compassion. " Therefore," writes one, " knowing the inability of our own power we should believe simply in the vicarious Power of the Original Prayer. If we do so, we are in correspondence with the wisdom of the Buddha and share his great compassion, just as the water of rivers becomes salt as soon as it enters the sea. For this reason this is called the faith in the Other Power."

To their everlasting honor, also, the Shin believers have probably led all other Japanese Buddhists in caring for the Eta, even as they probably excel in preaching the true spiritual democracy of all believers, yes, even of women.[16] "According to the earlier and general view of Buddhism, women are condemned, in virtue of the pollution of their nature, to look forward to rebirth in other forms. By no possibility can they, in their existence as women, reach the higher grades of holiness which lead to Nirvana. According to the Shin Shu system, on the other hand, a believing woman may hope to attain the goal of the Buddhist at the

close of her present life." [17] This doctrine seems to be
founded on that passage in the eleventh chapter of the
Saddharma Pundarika, in which the daughter of Sāgara,
the Nāga-king, loses her sex as female and reappears as
a Bodhisattva of male sex.[18]

The Shin sect is the largest in Japan, having more
than twice as many temples as any four of the great
sects, and five thousand more than the So-dō or sub-
sect of Jō-dō, which is the next largest; or, over nine-
teen thousand in all. It is also supposed to be one of
the richest and most powerful of all the Japanese sects.
In reality, however, it possesses no fixed property, and
is dependent entirely upon the voluntary contributions
of its adherents. To-day, it is probably the most active
of them all in education, learning and missionary
operations in Yezo, China and Korea.

Interesting as is the development of the Jō-dō and
Shin sects, which became popular largely through
their promulgation of dogmas founded on the Western Paradise, we must not forget that both of them
preached a new Buddha—not the real figure in history,
but an unhistoric and unreal phantom, the creation
and dream of the speculator and visionary. Amida,
the personification of boundless light, is one of the
luxuriant growths of a sickly scholasticism—a hollow
abstraction without life or reality. Amidaism is utterly
repudiated by many Japanese Buddhists, who give no
place to his idol on their altars, and reject utterly the
teaching as to Paradise and salvation through the
merits of another.

Yet these two special developments by natives,
though embodying tendencies of the Japanese mind,
did not reach the limit to which Northern Buddhism

was to go in those almost incredible lengths, which prompted Professor Whitney [19] to call it "the high-faluting school," and which we have seen in our own time under the cultivation of western admirers.

The Nichiren Sect.

The Japanese mind runs to pantheism as naturally as an unpruned grape-vine runs to fibre and leaves.

When Nichiren, the ultra-patriotic and ultra-democratic bonze, saw the light in A.D. 1222, he was destined to bring religion not only down to man, but even down to the beasts and to the mud. He founded the Saddharma-Pundarika sect, now called Nichiren Shu.

Born at Kominato, near the mouth of Yedo Bay, he became a neophite in the Shin-gon sect at the age of twelve, and was admitted into the priesthood when but fifteen years old. Then he adopted his name, which means Sun-lotus, because, according to a typical dream very common in Korea and Japan, his mother thought that she had conceived by the sun entering her body. Through a miracle, he acquired a thorough knowledge of the whole Buddhist canon, in the course of which he met with words, which he converted into that formula which is constantly in the mouth of the members of the Nichiren sect, Namu-myō-ho-ren-gé-kyō—"O, the Sutra of the Lotus of the Wonderful Law." [20] His history, full of amazing activity and of romantic adventure, is surrounded by a perfect sunrise splendor, or, shall we say, sunset gorgeousness, of mythology and fable. The scenes of his life are mostly laid in the region of the modern Tōkiō, and to the cultivated traveller, its story lends fascinating charms to the landscape in the region of Yedo Bay. Nichiren was a fiery patriot, and ultra-democratic in his sympathies. He was a radical believer in "Japan for the Japanese." He was an ecclesiastical *Soshi*. He felt that the developments of Buddhism already made, were not sufficiently comprehensive, or fully suited to the common people. So, in A.D. 1282, he founded a new sect which gradually included within its pantheon all possible Buddhas, and canonized pretty nearly all the saints, righteous men and favorite heroes known to Dai Nippon. Nichiren first made Japan the centre of the universe, and then brought religion down to the lowest. He considered that the period in which he lived was the latter day of the law, and that all creatures ought to share in the merit of Buddha-hood. Only the original Buddha is the real moon in the sky, but all Buddhas of the subordinate states are like the images of the moon, reflected upon the waters. All these different Buddhas, be they gods or men, beasts, birds or snakes, are to be honored. Indeed, they are both honored and worshipped in the Nichiren pantheon. Besides the historic Buddha, this sect, which is the most idolatrous of all, admits as objects of its reverence such personages as Nichiren, the founder; Kato Kiyomasa, the general who led the army of invasion in Korea and was the persecutor of the Christians; and Shichimen— a word which means seven points of the compass or seven faces. This Shichimen is the being that appeared to Nichiren as a beautiful woman, but disappeared from his sight in the form of a snake, twenty feet long, covered with golden scales and armed with iron teeth. It is now deified under the name meaning the Great God of the Seven Faces, and is identified with the Hindoo deity Siva.

Another idol usually seen in the Nichiren temples is Mioken. Under this name the pole star is worshipped, usually in the form of a Buddha with a wheel of a Buddha elect. Standing on a tortoise, with a sword in his right hand, and with the left hand half open—a gesture which symbolizes the male and female principles in the physical world, and the intelligence and the law in the spiritual world—Mioken is a striking figure. Indeed, the list of glorified animals reminds us somewhat of the ancient beast-worship of Egypt. In the Nichiren hierology, it is as though the symbolical figures in the Book of Revelation had been deified and worshipped. It is evident that all the creatures in that Buddhist chamber of imagery, the Hokké Kiō, that could possibly be made into gods have received apotheosis. The very book itself is also worshipped, for the Nichirenites are extreme believers in verbal inspiration, and pay divine honors to each jot and tittle of the sutra, which to them is a god. They adore also the triad of the three precious ones, the Buddha, the Rule or Discipline, and the Organization; or, Being, Law, and Church. The hideous idol, Fudo, "Eleven-faced," "Horse-headed," "Thousand-handed," or girt in a robe of fiery flame, is believed by Buddhists to represent Avalokitesvara; but, in recent times he has been recognized, detected and recaptured by the Shintōists as Kotohira. The goddess Kishi, and that miscellaneous assortment or group known as the Seven Patrons of Happiness, which form a sort of encyclopædia or museum of curiosities derived from the cults of India, China and Japan, are also components

of the amazing menagerie and pantheon of this sect,
in which scholasticism run mad, and emotional kindness to animals become maudlin, join hands.

The Ultra-realism of Northern Buddhism.

Like most of the other Japanese sects, the Nichirenites claim that their principles are contained in the
Hok-ké-kiō, which is considered the consummate white
flower of Buddhist doctrine and literature. This is the
Japanese name for that famous sutra, the Saddharma
Pundarika, so often mentioned in these chapters but
a thousand - fold more so in Japanese literature.
The Ten-dai and the Nichiren sects are allied, in that
both lay supreme emphasis upon this sutra; but the
former interprets it with an intellectual, and the latter
with an emotional emphasis. Philosophically, the
two bodies have much in common. Outwardly they
are very far apart. One has but to read their favorite
scripture, to see the norm upon which the gorgeous art
of Japan has been developed. Probably no single
book in the voluminous canon of the Greater Vehicle
gives one so masterful a key to Japanese Buddhism.
Its pages are crowded with sensuous descriptions of
all that is attractive to both the reason and the understanding. Its descriptions of Paradise are those which
would suit also the realistic Mussulman. Its rhetoric
and visions seem to be those of some oriental De
Quincey, who, out of the dreams of an opium-eater, has
made the law-book of a religion. Translated into matter-of-fact Chinese, none better than Nichiren knew
how to present its realism to his people.

In its ethical standards, which are two, this sect, like

most others, prescribes one course of life for the monk, which is difficult, and another for the laity, which is easy. The central dogma is that every part of the universe, including not only gods and men, but animals, plants and the very mud itself, is capable, by successive transmigrations, of attaining to Buddhaship. In one sense, Nichirenism is the transfiguration of atheistic evolution. In its teachings there are also two forms : the one, largely in symbol, is intended to attract followers; the other, the pure truth, is employed to convert the obstinately ignorant, against their wills. As in the history of the papal organization in Europe, a materialistic interpretation has been given to the canons of dogma and discipline.

Contrary to the doctrine of those sects which teach the attainment of salvation solely through the aid of Amida, or Another, the Nichirenites insist that it is necessary for man to work out his own salvation, by observing the law, by self-examination, by reflecting on the blessings vouchsafed to the members of this elect and orthodox sect and by constant prayer. They consider themselves as in the only true church, and their succession to the priesthood, the only valid one. The strict Nichiren churchmen will not have the Shintō gods in their household shrines, nor will they intermarry among the sects. The Nichirenites are also very fond of controversy, and their language in speaking of other creeds and sects is not that characteristic of the gentle Buddha. The people of this sect are much given to the belief in demoniacal possession, and a considerable part of the duty and revenue-yielding business of the Nichiren priests consists in exorcising the foxes, badgers and other demons, which have possessed subjects who are generally women at certain stages of illness or convalescence. The phenomena and pathology of these disorders seem to be allied to those of hysteria and hypnotism.

This popular sect also makes greatest use of charms, spells and amulets, lays great store on pilgrimages, and is very fond of noise-making instruments whether prayer-books or the wooden bells or drums which are prominent features in their temples and revival meetings. In one sense it is the Salvation Army of Buddhism, being especially powerful in what strikes the eye and ear. The Nichirenites have been well called the Ranters of Buddhism. Their revival meetings make Bedlam seem silent, and reduce to gentle murmurs the camp-meeting excesses with which we are familiar in our own country. They are the most sectarian of all sects. Their vocabulary of Billingsgate and the ribaldry employed by them even against their Buddhist brethren, cast into the shade those of Christian sectarians in their fiercest controversies. "A thousand years in the lowest of the hells is the atonement prescribed by the Nichirenites for the priests of all other sects." When the Parliament of Religions was called in Chicago, the successors of Nichiren, with their characteristic high-church modesty, promptly sent letters to America, warning the world against all other Japanese Buddhists, and denouncing especially those coming to speak in the Parliament, as misrepresenting the true doctrines of Buddha.

Doctrinal Culmination.

When the work of Nichiren had been completed, and his realistic pantheism had been able to include within its great receiver and processes of Buddha-making, everything from gods to mud, the circle of doctrine was complete. Kōbō's leaven had now every possible lump in which to do its work. All grades of men in Japan, from the most devout and intellectual to the most ranting and fanatical, could choose their sect. Yet it may be that Buddhism in Nichiren's day was in danger of stagnation and formalism, and needed the revival which this fiery bonze gave it; for, undoubtedly, along with zeal even to bigotry, came fresh life and power to the religion. This invigoration was followed by the mighty missionary labors of the last half of the thirteenth century, which carried Buddhism out to the northern frontier and into Yezo. Although, from time to time minor sects were formed either limiting or developing further the principles of the larger parent sects, and although, even as late as the seventeenth century, a new subsect, the Obaku of Zen Shu, was imported from China, yet no further doctrinal developments of importance took place; not even in presence of or after sixteenth century Christianity and seventeenth century Confucianism.

The fourteenth and fifteenth centuries form the golden age of Japanese Buddhism.

In the sixteenth century, the feudal system had split into fragments and the normal state of the country was that of civil war. Sect was arrayed against sect, and the Shin bonzes, especially, formed a great military body in fortified monasteries.

In the first half of the sixteenth century, came the tremendous onslaught of Portuguese Christianity. Then followed the militarism and bloody persecutions of Nobunaga.

In clashing with the new Confucianism of the seventeenth century, Buddhism utterly weakened as an intellectual power. Though through the favor of the Yedo shōguns it recovered lands and wealth, girded itself anew as the spy, persecutor and professed extirpator of Christianity, and maintained its popularity with the common people, it was, during the eighteenth century, among the educated Japanese, as good as dead. Modern Confucianism and the revival of Chinese learning, resulted in eighteenth century scepticism and in nineteenth century agnosticism.

The New Buddhism.

In our day and time, Japanese Buddhism, in the presence of aggressive Christianity, is out of harmony with the times, and the needs of forty-one millions of awakened and inquiring people; and there are deep searchings of heart. Politically disestablished and its landed possessions sequestrated by the government, it has had, since 1868, a history, first of depression and then of temporary revival. Now, amid much mechanical and external activity, the employment of the press, the organization of charity, of summer schools of " theology," and of young men's and other associations copied from the Christians, it is endeavoring to keep New Japan within its pale and to dictate the future. It seeks to utilize the old bottles for the new vintage.

There is, however, a movement discernible which may be called the New Buddhism, and has not only new wine but new wineskins. It is democratic, optimistic, empirical or practical; it welcomes women and children; it is hospitable to science and every form of truth. It is catholic in spirit and has little if any of the venom of the old Buddhist controvertists. It is represented by earnest writers who look to natural and spiritual means, rather than to external and mechanical methods. As a whole, we may say that Japanese Buddhism is still strong to-day in its grip upon the people. Though unquestionably moribund, its death will be delayed. Despite its apparent interest in, and harmony with, contemporaneous statements of science, it does not hold the men of thought, or those who long for the spiritual purification and moral elevation of Japan.

Are the Japanese eager for reform? Do they possess that quality of emotion in which a tormenting sense of sin, and a burning desire for self-surrender to holiness, are ever manifest?

Frankly and modestly, we give our opinion. We think not. The average Japanese man has not come to that self-consciousness, that searching of heart, that self-seeing of sin in the light of a Holy God's countenance which the gospel compels. Yet this is exactly what the Japanese need. Only Christ's gospel can give it.

The average man of culture in Dai Nippon has to-day no religion. He is waiting for one. What shall be the issue, in the contest between a faith that knows no personal God, no Creator, no atonement, no gospel of salvation from sin, and the gospel which bids man seek and know the great First Cause, as Father and Friend, and proclaims that this Infinite Friend seeks man to bless him, to bestow upon him pardon and holiness and to give him earthly happiness and endless life? Between one religion which teaches personality in God and in man, and another which offers only a quagmire of impersonality wherein a personal god and an individual soul exist only as the jack-lights of the marsh, mere phosphorescent gleams of decay, who can fail to choose? Of the two faiths, which shall be victor?

JAPANESE BUDDHISM IN ITS MISSIONARY
DEVELOPMENT

"The heart of my country, the power of my country, the light of my country, is Buddhism."—Yatsubuchi, of Japan.

"Buddhism was the teacher under whose instruction the Japanese nation grew up."—Chamberlain.

"Buddhism was the civilizer. It came with the freshness of religious zeal, and religious zeal was a novelty. It came as the bearer of civilization and enlightenment."

"Buddhism has had a fair field in Japan, and its outcome has not been elevating. Its influence has been æsthetic and not ethical. It added culture and art to Japan, as it brought with itself the civilization of continental Asia. It gave the arts, and more, it added the artistic atmosphere. . . . Reality disappears. 'This fleeting borrowed world' is all mysterious, a dream ; moonlight is in place of the clear hot sun . . . It has so fitted itself to its surroundings that it seems indigenous."—George William Knox.

"The Japanese . . . are indebted to Buddhism for their present civilization and culture, their great susceptibility to the beauties of nature, and the high perfection of several branches of artistic industry."—Rein.

"We speak of *God*, and the Japanese mind is filled with idols. We mention *sin*, and he thinks of eating flesh or the killing of insects. The word *holiness* reminds him of crowds of pilgrims flocking to some famous shrine, or of some anchorite sitting lost in religious abstraction till his legs rot off. He has much error to unlearn before he can take in the truth."— R. E. McAlpine.

> " There in a life of study, prayer, and thought,
> Kenshin became a saintly priest—not wide
> In intellect nor broad in sympathies,
> For such things come not from the ascetic life ;
> But narrow, strong, and deep, and like the stream
> That rushes fervid through the narrow path
> Between the rocks at Nikkō—so he grasped,
> Heart, soul, and strength, the holy Buddha's Law
> With no room left for doubt, or sympathy
> For other views."—Kenshin's Vision.

"For from the rising of the sun even unto the going down of the same, my name is great among the Gentiles ; and in every place incense is offered unto my name, and a pure offering, for my name is great among the Gentiles, saith the LORD of hosts."—Malachi.

CHAPTER X.

Missionary Buddhism the Measure of Japan's Civilization

BROADLY speaking, the history of Japanese Buddhism in its missionary development is the history of Japan. Before Buddhism came, Japan was pre-historic. We know the country and people through very scanty notices in the Chinese annals, by pale reflections cast by myths, legends and poems, and from the relics cast up by the spade and plough. Chinese civilization had filtered in, though how much or how little we cannot tell definitely; but since the coming of the Buddhist missionaries in the sixth century, the landscape and the drama of human life lie before us in clear detail. Speaking broadly again, it may be said that almost from the time of its arrival, Buddhism became on its active side the real religion of Japan—at least, if the word "religion" be used in a higher sense than that connoted by either Shintō or Confucianism. Though as a nation the Japanese of the Méiji era are grossly forgetful of this fact, yet, as Professor Chamberlain says,[1] "All education was for centuries in Buddhist hands. Buddhism introduced art; introduced medicine; created the folk-lore of the country; created its dramatic poetry; deeply influenced politics, and every

19

sphere of social and intellectual activity; in a word, Buddhism was the teacher under whose instruction the Japanese nation grew up."

For many centuries all Japanese, except here and there a stern Shintōist, or an exceptionally dogmatic Confucian, have acknowledged these patent facts, and from the emperor to the eta, glorified in them. It was not until modern Confucian philosophy entered the Mikado's empire in the seventeenth century, that hostile criticism and polemic tenets denounced Buddhism, and declared it only fit for savages. This bitter denunciation of Buddhism at the lips and hands of Japanese who had become Chinese in mind, was all the more inappropriate, because Buddhism had for over a thousand years acted as the real purveyor and disperser of the Confucian ethics and culture in Japan. Such denunciation came with no better grace from the Yedo Confucianists than from the Shintō revivalists, like Motoōri, who, while execrating everything Chinese, failed to remember or impress upon his countrymen the fact, that almost all which constituted Japanese civilization had been imported from the Middle Kingdom.

Buddhism, in its purely doctrinal development, seems to be rather a system of metaphysics than a true religion, being a conglomeration, or rather perhaps an agglomeration, of all sorts of theories relating to the universe and its contents. Its doctrinal and metaphysical side, however, is to be carefully distinguished from its popular and external features, for in its missionary development Buddhism may be called a system of national improvement. The history of its propagation, in the land farthest east from its cradle, is not only the outline of the history of Japanese civilization, but is nearly the whole of it.

Pre-Buddhistic Japan.

It is not perhaps difficult to reconstruct in imagination the landscape of Japan in pre-Buddhistic days. Certainly we may, with some accuracy, draw a contrast between the appearance of the face of the earth then and now. Supposing that there were as many as a million or two of souls in the Japanese Archipelago of the sixth century—the same area which in the nineteenth century contains over forty-one millions—we can imagine only here and there patches of cultivated fields, or terraced gullies. There were no roads except paths or trails. The horse was probably yet a curiosity to the aborigines, though well known to the sons of the gods. Sheep and goats then, as now, were unknown. The cow and the ox were in the land, but not numerous.[2] In architecture there was probably little but the primeval hut. Tools were of the rudest description; yet it is evident that the primitive Japanese were able to work iron and apply it to many uses. There were other metals, though the tell-tale etymology of their names in Japanese metallurgy, as in so many other lines of industry and articles of daily use, points to a Chinese origin. It is the almost incredible fact that the Japanese man or woman wore on the person neither gold nor silver jewelry. In later times, decoration was added to the sword hilt and pins were thrust in the hair.

Possibly a prejudice against metal touching the skin, such as exists in Korea, may account for this absence of jewelry, though silver was not discovered until A.D.

675, or gold until A.D. 749. The primitive Japanese, however, did wear ornaments of ground and polished stone, and these so numerously as to compel contrast with the severer tastes of later ages. Some ot these magatama—curved jewels or perforated cylinders— were made of very hard stone which requires skill to drill, cut and polish. Among the substances used was jade, a mineral found only in Cathay.[3] Indeed, we cannot follow the lines of industry and manufactures, of personal adornment and household decoration, of scientific terms and expressions, of literary, intellectual and religious experiment, without continually finding that the Japanese borrowed from Chinese storehouses. Possibly their debt began at the time of the alleged conquest of Korea[4] in the third century.

In Japanese life, as it existed before the introduction of Buddhism, there was, with barbaric simplicity, a measure of culture somewhat indeed above the level of savagery, but probably very little that could be appraised beyond that of the Iroquois Indians in the days of their Confederacy. For though granting that there were many interesting features of art, industry, erudition and civilization which have been lost to the historic memory, and that the research of scholars may hereafter discover many things now in oblivion ; yet, on the other hand, it is certain that much of what has long been supposed to be of primitive Japanese origin, and existent before the eighth century, has been more or less infused or enriched with Chinese elements, or has been imported directly from India, or Persia,[5] or has crystallized into shape from the mixture of things Buddhistic and primitive Japanese.

Apart from all speculation, we know that in the train

of the first missionaries came artisans, and instructors in every line of human industry and achievement, and that the importation of the inventions and appliances of " the West "—the West then being Korea and China, and the " Far West," India—was proportionately as general, as far-reaching, as sensational, as electric in its effects upon the Japanese minds, as, in our day, has been the introduction of the modern civilization of Europe and the United States.[6]

The Purveyors of Civilization.

The Buddhist missionaries, in their first " enthusiasm of humanity," were not satisfied to bring in their train, art, medicine, science and improvements of all sorts, but they themselves, being often learned and practical men, became personal leaders in the work of civilizing the country. In travelling up and down the empire to propagate their tenets, they found out the necessity of better roads, and accordingly, they were largely instrumental in having them made. They dug wells, established ferries and built bridges.[7] They opened lines of communication ; they stimulated traffic and the exchange of merchandise ; they created the commerce between Japan and China ; and they acted as peacemakers and mediators in the wars between the Japanese and Koreans. For centuries they had the monopoly of high learning. In the dark middle ages when civil war ruled, they were the only scholars, clerks, diplomatists, mediators and peacemakers.

Japanese diet became something new under the direction of the priests. The bonzes taught the wickedness of slaughtering domestic animals, and indeed, the wrong of putting any living thing to death, so that kindness to animals has become a national trait. To this day it may be said that Japanese boys and men are, at least within the limits of their light, more tender and careful with all living creatures than are those of Christendom.[8] The bonzes improved the daily fare of the people, by introducing from Korea and China articles of food hitherto unknown. They brought over new seeds and varieties of vegetables and trees. Furthermore, necessity being the mother of invention, not a few of the shorn brethren made up for the prohibition of fish and flesh, by becoming expert cooks. They so exercised their talents in the culinary art that their results on the table are proverbial. Especially did they cultivate mushrooms, which in taste and nourishment are good substitutes for fish.

The bonzes were lovers of beauty and of symbolism. They planted the lotus, and the monastery ponds became seats of splendor, and delights to the eye. Their teachings, metaphysical and mystical, poetical and historical, scientific and literary, created, it may be said, the Japanese garden, which to the refined imagination contains far more than meets the eye of the alien.[9] Indeed, the oriental imitations in earth, stone, water and verdure, have a language and suggestion far beyond what the usual parterres and walks, borders and lines, fountains and statuary of a western garden teach. It may be said that our " language of flowers " is more luxuriant and eloquent than theirs ; yet theirs is very rich also, besides being more subtle in suggestion. The bonzes instilled doctrine, not only by sermons, books and the emblems and furniture of the temples, but they also taught dogma and ethics by the flower-ponds and plots, by the artificial landscape, and by outdoor symbolism of all kinds. To Buddhism our thanks are due, for the innumerable miniature conti-nents, ranges of mountains, geographical outlines and other horticultural allusions to their holy lands and spiritual history, seen beside so many houses, temples and monasteries in Japan. In their floral art, no peo-ple excels the Japanese in making leaf and bloom teach history, religion, philosophy, æsthetics and patrio-tism.

Not only around the human habitation,[10] but within it, the new religion brought a marvellous change. In-stead of the hut, the dwelling-house grew to spacious and comfortable proportions, every part of the Japan-ese house to-day showing to the cultured student, especially to one familiar with the ancient poetry, the lines of its origin and development, and in the larger dwellings expressing a wealth of suggestion and mean-ing. The oratory and the kami-dana or shelf holding the gods, became features in the humblest dwelling. Among the well-to-do there were of course the gilded ancestral tablets and the worship of progenitors, in special rooms, with imposing ritual and equipment, with which Buddhism did not interfere; but on the shelf over the door of nearly every house in the land, along with the emblems of the kami, stood images representing the avatars of Buddha.[11] There, the light ever burned, and there, offerings of food and drink were thrice daily made. Though the family worship might vary in its length and variety of ceremony, yet even in the home where no regular system was followed, the burning lights and the stated offering made, called the mind up to thoughts higher than the mere level of providing for daily wants. The visitation of the priests in time of sorrow, or of joy, or for friendly converse, made religion sweetly human.[12]

Outwardly the Buddhist architecture made a profound change in the landscape. With a settled religion requiring gorgeous ceremonial, the chanting of liturgies by large bodies of priests and the formation of monasteries as centres of literary and religious activity, there were required stability and permanence in the imperial court itself. While, therefore, the humble village temples arose all over the country, there were early erected, in the place where the court and emperor dwelt, impressive religious edifices.[13] The custom of migration ceased, and a fixed spot selected as the capital, remained such for a number of generations, until finally Héian-jō or the place of peace, later called Kiōto, became the "Blossom Capital" and the Sacred City for a thousand years. At Nara, where flourished the first six sects introduced from Korea, were built vast monasteries, temples and images, and thence the influence of civilization and art radiated. From the first, forgetting its primitive democracy and purely moral claims, Buddhism lusted for power in the State. As early as A.D. 624, various grades were assigned to the priesthood by the government.[14] The sects eagerly sought and laid great stress upon imperial favor. To this day they keenly enjoy the canonization of their great teachers by letters patent from the Throne.

Ministers of Art.

On the establishment of the imperial capital, at Kiōto, toward the end of the eighth century, we find still further development and enlargement of those latent artistic impulses with which the Heavenly Father endowed his Japanese child. That capacity for beauty, both in appreciation and expression, which in our day makes the land of dainty decoration the resort of all those who would study oriental art in unique fulness and decorative art in its only living school—a school founded on the harmonious marriage of the people and the nature of the country—is discernible from quite early ages. The people seem to have responded gladly to the calls for gifts and labor. The direction from which it is supposed all evils are likely to come is the northeast; this special point of the compass being in pan-Asian spiritual geography the focus of all malign influences. Accordingly, the Mikado Kwammu, in A.D. 788, built on the highest mountain called Hiyéi a superb temple and monastery, giving it in charge of the Ten-dai sect, that there should ever be a bulwark against the evil that might otherwise swoop upon the city. Here, as on castellated walls, should stand the watchman, who, by the recitation of the sacred liturgies, would keep watch and ward. In course of time this great mountain became a city of three thousand edifices and ten thousand monks, from which the droning of litanies and the chanting of prayers ascended daily, and where the chief industries were, the counting of beads on rosaries and the burning of incense before the altars. This was in the long bright day of a prosperity which has been nourished by vast sums obtained from the government and nobles. One notes the contrast at the end of our century, when " disestablished " as a religion and its bonzes reduced to beggary, Hiyéi-san is used as the site of a Summer School of Christian Theology.

Along with the blossoming of the lotus in every part of the empire, bloomed the grander flowers of sculpture, of painting and of temple architecture. It was because of the carpenter's craft in building temples that he won his name of Dai-ku, or the great workman. The artificers of the sunny islands cultivated an ambition, not only to equal but to excel, their continental brethren of the saw and hammer. Yet the carpenter was only the leader of great hosts of artisans that were encouraged, of craftsmen that were educated and of industries that were called into being by the spread of Buddhism.[15] It was not enough that village temples and town monasteries should be built, under an impulse that meant volumes for the development of the country. The ambitious leaders chose sightly spots on mountains whence were lovely vistas of scenery, on which to erect temples and monasteries, while it seemed to be their further ambition to allow no mountain peak to be inaccessible. With armies of workmen, supported by the contributions of the faithful who had been aroused to enthusiasm by the preaching of the bonzes, great swaths were cut in the forest ; abundant timber was felled ; rocky plateaus were levelled ; and elegant monastic edifices were reared, soon to be filled with eager students, and young men in training for the priesthood.

Whether the pilgrimage [16] be of Shintō or of Buddhist origin, or simply a contrivance of human nature to break the monotony of life, we need not discuss. It is certain that if the custom be indigenous, the imported faith adopted, absorbed and enlarged it. The peregrinations made to the great temples and to the mountain tops, being meritorious performances, soon filled the roads with more or less devout travellers. In thus finding vent for their piety, the pilgrims mingled sanctification with recreation, enjoying healthful holidays, and creating trade with varied business, commercial and commissarial activities, while enlarging also their ideas and learning something of geography. Thus, in the course of time, it has come to pass that Japan is a country of which almost every square mile is known, while it is well threaded with paths, banded with roads, and supplied to a remarkable extent with handy volumes of description and of local history.[17] Her people being well educated in their own lore and local traditions, possessed also a voluminous literature of guidebooks and cyclopedias of information. The devotees were, withal, well instructed and versed in a code of politeness and courtesy, as pilgrimage and travel became settled habits of a life. As a further result, the national tongue became remarkably homogeneous. Broadly speaking, it may be said that the Japanese language, unlike the Chinese in this as it is in almost every other point, has very little dialectic variation.[18] Except in some few remote eddies lying outside the general currents, there is a uniform national speech. This is largely owing to that annual movement of pilgrims in the summer months especially, habitual during many centuries.

Buddhism coming to Japan by means of the Great Vehicle, or with the features of the Northern development, was the fertile mother of art. In the exterior equipment of the temple, instead of the Shintō thatch, the tera or Buddhist edifice called for tiles on its

sweeping roof, with ornamental terra-cotta at the end
of its imposing roof-ridge, or for sheets of copper soon
to be made verdant, then sombre and then sable by
age and atmosphere. Outwardly the edifice required
the application of paint and lacquer in rich tints, its
recurved roof-edges gladly welcoming the crest and
monogram of the feudal prince, and its railings and
stairways accepting willingly the bronze caps and
ornaments. In front of its main edifice was the imposing gateway with proportions almost as massive as
the temple itself, with prodigal wealth of curiously
fitted and richly carved, painted and gilded supports
and morticings, with all the fancies and adornments
of the carpenter's art, and having as its frontlet and
blazon the splendidly gilt name, style or title. Often
these were impressive to eye and mind, to an extent
which the terse Chinese or curt monosyllables could
scarcely suggest to an alien.[19] The number, forms and
positions of the various parts of the temple easily lent
themselves to the expression of the elaborate symbolism of the India faith.

Resemblances between Buddhism and Christianity.

Within the sacred edifice everything to strike the
senses was lavishly displayed. The passion of the
East, as opposed to Greek simplicity, is for decoration ;
yet in Japan, decorative art, though sometimes bursting
out in wild profusion or running to unbridled lengths,
was in the main a regulated mass of splendor in which
harmony ruled. Differing though the Buddhist sects
do in their temple furniture and altar decorations, they
are, most of them, so elaborately full in their equip-

ment as to suggest repeatedly the similarity between the Roman Catholic organization, altars, vestments and ritual, and those of Buddhism, and remarks on this point seem almost commonplace. Almost everything in Roman Catholicism is found in Buddhism,[20] and one may even say, *vice versa*, at least in things exterior. We take the liberty of transcribing here a passage from the chapter entitled "Christianity and Foreigners" in The Mikado's Empire, written twenty years ago.

"Furthermore, the transition from the religion of India to that of Rome was extremely easy. The very idols of Buddha served, after a little alteration with the chisel, for images of Christ. The Buddhist saints were easily transformed into the Twelve Apostles. The Cross took the place of the *torii*. It was emblazoned on the helmets and banners of the warriors, and embroidered on their breasts. The Japanese soldiers went forth to battle like Christian crusaders. In the roadside shrine Kuanon, the Goddess of Mercy, made way for the Virgin, the mother of God. Buddhism was beaten with its own weapons. Its own artillery was turned against it. Nearly all the Christian churches were native temples, sprinkled and purified. The same bell, whose boom had so often quivered the air announcing the orisons and matins of paganism, was again blessed and sprinkled, and called the same hearers to mass and confession ; the same lavatory that fronted the temple served for holy water or baptismal font ; the same censer that swung before Amida could be refilled to waft Christian incense ; the new convert could use unchanged his old beads, bells, candles, incense, and all the paraphernalia of his old faith in celebration of the new.

"Almost everything that is distinctive in the Roman form of Christianity is to be found in Buddhism : images, pictures, lights, altars, incense, vestments, masses, beads, wayside shrines, monasteries, nunneries, celibacy, fastings, vigils, retreats, pilgrimages, mendicant vows, shorn heads, orders, habits, uniforms, nuns, convents, purgatory, saintly and priestly intercession, indulgences, works of supererogation, pope, archbishops, abbots, abbesses, monks, neophytes, relics and relic-worship, exclusive burial-ground, etc., etc., etc." [21]

Nevertheless, these resemblances are almost wholly superficial, and have little or nothing to do with genuine religion. Such matters are of æsthetic and of commercial, rather than of spiritual, interest. They concern priestcraft and vulgar superstition rather than truth and righteousness. "In point of dogma a whole world of thought separates Buddhism from every form of Christianity. Knowledge, enlightenment, is the condition of Buddhistic grace, not faith. Self-perfectionment is the means of salvation, not the vicarious sufferings of a Redeemer. Not eternal life is the end and active participation in unceasing prayer and praise, but absorption into Nirvana (Jap. Nehan), practical annihilation." [22] At certain points, the metaphysic of Buddhism is so closely like that of Christian theology, that a connection on reciprocal exchange of ideas is not only possible but probable. In their highest thinking,[23] the sincere Christian and Buddhist approach each other in their search after truth.

The key-word of Buddhism is Ingwa, which means law or fate, the chain of cause and effect in which man is found, atheistic "evolution applied to ethics," the grinding machinery of a universe in which is no Creator-Father, no love, pity or heart. If the cry of the human spirit has compelled the makers of Buddhist theology to furnish a goddess of mercy, it is but one subordinate being among many. If a boundlessly compassionate Amida is thought out, it is an imaginary being. The symbol of Buddhism is the wheel of the law, which revolves as mercilessly as ceaselessly.[24]

The key-word of Christianity is love, and its message is grace. Its symbol is the cross, and its sacrament the supper, in token of the infinite love of the Father who wrote his revelation in a human life. The resemblances between the religions of Gautama and of Jesus, are purely superficial. They appear to the outward man. The inward man cannot, even from Darien peaks of observation or in his scrutiny *de profundis*, discover any vital or historical connection between the two faiths, Christianity and Buddhism. In his theology the Christian says God is all; but the Buddhist says All is god. Buddhism says destroy the passions: Christianity says control them. The Buddhist's watchword is Nirvana. The Christian's is Eternal Life in Christ Jesus.[25]

The Temples and Their Symbolism.

In the vast airy halls of a Buddhist temple one will often see columns made of whole tree-trunks, sheeted with gold and supporting massive ceilings which are empanelled and gorgeous with every hue and tint known to the palette. Besides the coloring, carving and gilding, the rich symbolism strikes the eye and touches the imagination. It is a pleasing study for one familiar with the background and world of Buddhism, to note their revelation and expression in art, as well as to discern what the varying sects accept or reject. There is the lotus, in leaf, bud, flower and calyx;[26] the diamond in every form, real and imaginary, with the vagra or emblem of conquest; while on the altars, beside the central image, be it that of Shaka or of Amida, are Bodhisattvas or Buddhas by brevet, beings in every state of existence, as well as deities of many names and forms. Abstract ideas and attributes are expressed in the art language not only of Japan, Korea and China, but also in that of India and even of Persia and Greece,[27] until one wonders how an Aryan religion, like Buddhism, could have so conquered and unified the many nations of Chinese Asia. He wonders, indeed, until he remembers how it has itself been transformed and changed in popular substance, from lofty metaphysics and ethics into pantheism for the shorn, and into polytheism for the unshorn.

Looking at early Japanese pictures with the eye of the historian, as well as of the connoisseur of art, one will see that the first real school of Japanese art was Buddhistic. The modern school of pictorial art, named from the monkish phrase, Ukioyé—pictures of the Passing World—is indeed very interesting to the western student, because it seems to be more in touch with the human nature of the whole world, as distinct from what is local, Chinese, or sectarian. Yet, casting a glance back of the mediæval Kano, Chinese and Yamato-Tosa styles, he finds that Buddhism gave Japan her first examples of and stimulus to pictorial art.[28] He sees further that instead of the monochrome of Chinese exotic art, or the first rude attempts of the native pencil, Buddhism began Japanese sculpture, carving and nearly every other form of plastic or pictorial representation, in which are all the elements of Northern Buddhism, as so lavishly represented, for example, in that great sutra which is the book, *par excellence*, of Japanese Buddhism, the Saddharma Pundarika.

Turning from text to art, we behold the golden lakes of joy, the mountain of gems, the floating female angels with their marvellous drapery and lovely faces, the gentle benignity of the goddesses of mercy, the rays of light and the glory streaming from face and head of the holy ones, the splendors of costume, the varied beauties of the lotus, the hosts of ministering intelligences, the luxuriant symbolism, the purple clouds, the wheel of the law, the swastika[29] or double cross, and the vagra,[30] or diamond trefoil. All that color, perfume, sensuous delights, art and luxury can suggest, are here, together with all the various orders of beings that inhabit the Buddhist universe; and these are set forth in their fulness and detail. In the six conditions of sentient existence are devas or gods, men, asuras or monsters, pretas or demons, beasts, and beings in hell. In portraying these, the artists and sculptors do not always slavishly follow tradition or uniformity. The critical eye notes nearly as much genius, wit and variety as in the mediæval cathedral architecture of Europe. Probably the most popular groups of idols are those of the seven or the thirty-three Kuannon, of the six Jizo[31] or compassionate helpers, and of the sixteen or the five hundred Rakan[32] or circles of primitive disciples of Gautama. The angelic beings and sweetly singing birds of Paradise are also favorite subjects of the artists.

One who has lived alongside the great temples ; who knows the daily routine and sees what powerful engines of popular instruction they are; who has been present at the great festivals and looked upon the mighty kitchens and refectories in operation ; and who has gone in and out among their monasteries and examined their records, their genealogies and their relics, can see how powerfully Buddhism has moulded the whole life of the people through long ages. The village temple is often the epitome and repository of the social life of the people now living, and of the story of their ancestors for generations upon generations past. It is the historico-genealogical society, the museum, the repository of documents and trophies, the place of national thanksgiving and praise, of public sorrow and farewell, a place of rendezvous and separation, the starting-point of procession, and the centre of festival and joy ; and thus it is linked with the life of the people.

In other respects, also, the temple is like the old village cathedral of mediæval Europe. It is in many sects the centre of popular pleasure of all sorts, both reputable and disreputable. Not only shops and bazaars, fairs and markets, games and sports, cluster around it, but also curiosities and works of popular art, the relics of war, and the trophies of travel and adventure. Except that Buddhism—outside of India—never had the unity of European Christianity, the Buddhist temple is the mirror and encyclopædia both of history and of contemporary life. As fame and renown are necessary for the glory of the place or the structure, favorite gods, or rather their idols, are frequently carried about on " starring " tours. At the opening to public view of some famous image or relic, a great festival or revival called Kai-chō is held, which becomes a scene of trade and merry-making like that of the mediæval fair or kermis in Europe. The far-oriental is able as skilfully as his western confrère, to mix business and religion and to suppose that gain is godliness. Further, the manufacture of legend becomes a thriving industry ; while the not-infrequent sensation of a popular miracle is manipulated by the bonzes—for priestcraft in all ages and climes is akin throughout the world. It is no wonder that some honest Japanese, incensed at the shams utilized by the religious, has struck out like coin the proverb that rings true—"Good doctrine needs no miracle."

The Bell and the Cemetery.

The Buddhist missionaries, and especially the founders of temples, thoroughly understood the power of natural beauty to humble, inspire and soothe the soul of man. The instinctive love of the Japanese people for fine scenery, was made an ally of faith. The sites for temples were chosen with reference to their imposing surroundings or impressive vistas. Whether as spark-arresters and protectives against fire, or to compel reverent awe, the loftiest evergreen trees are planted around the sacred structure. These "trees of Jehovah" are compellers to reverence. The alien's hat comes off instinctively—though it may be less convenient to shed boots than sandals—as he enters the sacred structure.

The great tongueless bell is another striking accessory to the temple services. Near at hand stands the belfry out of which boom forth tidings of the hours. In the flow of time and years, the note of the bell becomes more significant, and in old age solemn, making in the lapse of centuries an educating power in seriousness. "As sad as a temple bell" is the coinage of popular speech. Many of the inscriptions, though with less of sunny hope and joy than even Christian grave-stones bear, are yet mournfully beautiful.[33] They preach Buddhism in its reality. Whereas, the general associations of the Christian spire and belfry, apart from the note of time, are those of joy, invitation and good news, those of the tongueless and log-struck bells of Buddhism are sombre and saddening. " As merry as a marriage bell," could never be said of the boom from a Buddhist temple, even though it pour waves of sound through sunny leagues. There is a vast difference between the peal and play of the chimes of Europe and the liquid melody which floods the landscape of Chinese Asia. The one music, high in air, seems ever to tell of faith, triumph and aspiration ; the other in minor notes, from bells hung low on yokes, perpetually echoes the pessimism of despair, the folly of living and the joy that anticipates its end.

Above all, the temple holds and governs the cemetery,[34] as well as the cradle ; while from it emanate influences that enwrap and surround the villager, from birth to death. Since the outlawry of Christianity, and especially since the division of the empire into Buddhist parishes, the bonzes have had the oversight of birth, death, marriage and divorce. Particularly tenacious, in common with priestcraft all over the world, is their clutch upon what they call " consecrated ground." In a large sense Japan is still, what China has always been, a country governed by the graveyard. These cities of the dead are usually kept in attractive order and made beautiful with flowers in memoriam. The study of epitaphs and mortuary architecture, though not without elements bordering on the ludicrous, is enjoyed by the thoughtful student.[35]

In every community the inhabitants are enrolled at birth at the local temple, whose priests are the authorized religious teachers, and are always expected to take charge of the funerals of those whose names are thus enrolled. So long as an individual remains in the region of the family temple, the tie which binds him to it is exceedingly difficult to break ; but if he moves away he is no longer bound by this tie. This explains the fact, so often observed by missionaries, that the membership of Christian churches is made up almost entirely of people who have come from other localities. In the city of Osaka, for instance, it is a very rare thing to find a native Osakan in any of the churches. The same is true in all parts of the country. So long as a Japanese remains in the neighborhood of his family temple it is almost impossible to get him to break the temple tie and join a Christian church ; but when he moves to another place he is free to do as he likes.[36]

This statement of a resident in modern Japan will long remain true for a large part of the empire.

Political and Military Influences.

A volume might be written and devoted to Japanese Buddhism as a political power ; for, having quickly obtained intellectual possession of the court and emperor, it dictated the policies of the rulers. In A.D. 624, it was recognized as a state religion, and the hierarchy of priests was officially established. At this date there were 46 temples and monasteries, with 816 monks and 569 nuns. As early as the eighth century, beginning with Shōmu, who reigned A.D. 724–728, and who with his daughter, afterward the female Mikado, became a disciple of Shaka, the habit of the emperors becoming monks, shaving their heads and retiring from public life, came in vogue and lasted until near the nineteenth century. By this means the bonzes were soon enabled to call Buddhism " the people's religion," and to secure the resources of the national treasury as an aid to their temple and monastery building, and for the erection of those images and wayside shrines on which so many millions of dollars have been lavished. In addition to this subsidized propaganda, the Buddhist confessor was too often able, by means of the wife, concubine, or other female member of the household, imperial or noble, to dictate the imperial policy in accordance with monkish or priestly ideas. Ugéno Dō-kiō, a monk, is believed to have aspired to the throne. Being made premier by the Empress Kō-ken, whose passion for him is the scandal of history, he made no scruple of extending the power as well as the influence of the Buddhist hierarchy.

Buddhism had also a distinct influence on the military history of the country,[37] and this was greatest during the civil wars of the rival Mikados (1336–1392), when the whole country was a camp and two lines of nominees claimed to be descendants of the sun-goddess. Japan's only foreign wars have been in the neighboring peninsula of Korea, and thither the bonzes went with the armies in the expeditions of the early centuries, and in that great invasion of 1592–1597, which has left a scar even to this day on the Korean mind. At home, Buddhist priests only too gladly accompanied the imperial armies of conquest and occupation. During centuries of activity in the southwest and in the far east and extreme north, the military brought the outlying portions of the empire, throughout the whole archipelago, under the sway of the Yamato tribe and the Mikado's dominion. The shorn clerks not only lived in camp, ministered to the sick and shrived the dying soldier, but wrote texts for the banners, furnished the amulets and war cries, and were ever assistant and valuable in keeping up the temper and morals of the armies.[38] No sooner was the campaign over and peace had become the order of the day, than the enthusiastic missionaries began to preach and to teach in the pacified region. They set up the shrines, anon started the school and built the temple ; usually, indeed, with the aid of the law and the government, acting as agents of a politico-ecclesiastical establishment, yet with energy and consecration.

In later feudal days, when the soldier classes obtained the upper hand, overawed the court and Mikado and gradually supplanted the civil authority, introducing feudalism and martial law, the bonzes often represented the popular and democratic side. Protesting against arbitrary government, they came into collision with the warrior rulers, so as to be exposed to imprisonment and the sword. Yet even as refugees and as men to whom the old seats of activity no longer offered success or comfort, they went off into the distant and outlying provinces, preaching the old tenets and the new fashions in theology. Thus again they won hosts of converts, built monasteries, opened fresh paths and were purveyors of civilization.

The feudal ages in Japan bred the same type of militant priest known in Europe—the military bishop and the soldier monk. So far from Japan's being the "Land of Great Peace," and Buddhism's being necessarily gentle and non-resistant, we find in the chequered history of the island empire many a bloody battle between the monks on horseback and in armor.[39] Rival sectarians kept the country disquieted for years. Between themselves and their favored laymen, and the enemy, consisting of the rival forces, lay and clerical, in like array, many a bloody battle was fought.

The writer lived for one year in Echizen, which, in the fifteenth century, was the battle-ground for over fifty years, of warring monks. The abbot of the Monastery of the Original Vow, of the Shin sect in Kiōto, had built before the main edifice a two-storied gate, which was expected to throw into the shade every other gateway in Japan, and especially to humble the pride of the monks of the Tendai sect, in Hiyéizan. The monks of the mountain, swarming down into the capital city, attacked the gate and monastery of the Shin sect and burned the former to ashes. The abbot thus driven off by fire, fled northward, and, joined by a powerful body of adherents, made himself possessor of the rich provinces of Kaga and Echizen, holding this region for half a century, until able to rebuild the mighty fortress-monasteries near Kiōto and at Osaka.

These strongholds of the fighting Shin priests had become so powerful as arsenals and military headquarters, that in 1570, Nobunaga, skilful general as he was, and backed by sixty thousand men, was unsuccessful in his attempt to reduce them. For ten years, the war between Nobunaga and the Shin sectarians kept the country in disorder. It finally ended in the conflagration of the great religious fortress at Osaka, and the retreat of the monks to another part of the country. By their treachery and incendiarism, the shavelings prevented the soldiers from enjoying the prizes.

To detail the whole history of the fighting monks would be tedious. They have had a foothold for many centuries and even to the present time, in every province except that of Satsuma. There, because they treacherously aided the great Hidéyoshi to subdue the province, the fiery clansmen, never during Tokugawa days, permitted a Buddhist priest to come.[40]

Literature and Education.

In its literary and scholastic development, Japanese Buddhism on its popular educational side deserves great praise. Although the Buddhist canon [41] was never translated into the vernacular,[42] and while the library of native Buddhism, in the way of commentary or general literature, reflects no special credit upon the priests, yet the historian must award them high honor, because of the part taken by them as educators and schoolmasters.[43] Education in ancient and mediæval times was, among the laymen, confined almost wholly to the imperial court, and was considered chiefly to be, either as an adjunct to polite accomplishments, or as valuable especially in preparing young men for political office.[44] From the first introduction of letters until well into the nineteenth century, there was no special provision for education made by the government, except that, in modern and recent times in the castle towns of the Daimiōs, there were schools of Chinese learning for the Samurai. Private schools and school-masters [45] were also creditably numerous. In original literature, poetry, fiction and history, as well as in the humbler works of compilation, in the making of text-books and in descriptive lore, the pens of many priests have been busy.[46] The earliest biography written in Japan was of Shōtoku, the great lay patron of Buddhism. In the ages of war the monastery was the ark of preservation amid a flood of desolation.

The temple schools were early established, and in the course of centuries became at times almost coextensive with the empire. Besides the training of the neophytes in the Chinese language and the vernacular, there were connected with thousands of temples, schools in which the children, not only of the well-to-do, but largely of the people, were taught the rudiments of education, chiefly reading and writing. Most of the libraries of the country were those in monasteries. Although it is not probable that Kōbō invented the Kana or common script, yet it is reasonably certain that the bonzes [47] were the chief instrument in the diffusion and popularization of that simple system of writing, which made it possible to carry literature down into the homes of the merchant and peasant, and enabled even women and children to beguile the tedium of their lives. Thus the people expanded their thoughts through the medium of the written, and later of the printed, page. [48] Until modern centuries, when the school of painters, which culminated in Hokŭsai and his contemporaries, brought a love of art down to the lowest classes of the people, the only teacher of pictorial and sculptural art for the multitude, was Buddhism. So strong is this popular delight in things artistic that probably, to this passion as much as to the religious instinct, we owe many of the wayside shrines and images, the symbolical and beautifully prepared landscapes, and those stone stairways which slope upward toward the shrines on the hill-tops. In Japan, art is not a foreign language; it is vernacular.

Thus, while we gladly point out how Buddhism, along the paths of exploration, commerce, invention, sociology, military and political influence, education and literature, not only propagated religion, but civilized Japan,[49] it is but in the interest of fairness and truth that we point out that wherein the great system was deficient. If we make comparison with Christendom and the religion of Jesus, it is less with the purpose of the polemic who must perhaps necessarily disparage, and more with the idea of making contrast between what we have seen in Japan and what we have enjoyed as commonplace in the United States and Europe.

Things Which Buddhism Left Undone.

In the thirteen hundred years of the life of Buddhism in Japan, what are the fruits, and what are the failures? Despite its incessant and multifarious activities, one looks in vain for the hospital, the orphan asylum, the home for elderly men or women or aged couples, or the asylum for the insane, and much less, for that vast and complicated system of organized charities, which, even amid our material greed of gain, make cities like New York, or London, or Chicago, so beautiful from the point of view of humanity. Buddhism did indeed teach kindness to animals, making even the dog, though ownerless and outcast, in a sense sacred. Because of his faith in the doctrine of the transmigration of souls, the toiling laborer will keep his wheels or his feet from harming the cat or dog or chicken in the road, even though it be at risk and trouble and with added labor to himself. The pious will buy the live birds or eels from the old woman who sits on the bridge, in order to give them life and liberty again in air or water. The sacred rice is for sale at the temples, not only to feed but to fatten the holy pigeons.

Yet, while all this care is lavished on animals, the human being suffers.[50] Buddhism is kind to the brute, and cruel to man. Until the influx of western ideas in recent years, the hospital and the orphanage did not exist in Japan, despite the gentleness and tenderness of Shaka, who, with all his merits, deserted his wife and babe in order to enlighten mankind.[51] If Buddhism is not directly responsible for the existence of that class of Japanese pariahs called *hi-nin*, or not-human, the name and the idea are borrowed from the sutras ; while the execration of all who prepare or sell the flesh of animals is persistently taught in the sacred books. These unfortunate bearers of the human image, during twelve hundred years and until the fiat of the present illustrious emperor made them citizens, were not reckoned in the census, nor was the land on which they dwelt measured. The imperial edict which finally elevated the Eta to citizenship, was suggested by one whose life, though known to men as that of a Confucian, was probably hid with Christ, Yokoi Héishiro.[52] The emperor Mutsuhito, 123d of the line of Japan, born on the day when Perry was on the Mississippi and ready to sail, placed over these outcast people in 1871, the protecting ægis of the law.[53] Until that time, the people in this unfortunate class, numbering probably a million, or, as some say, three millions, were compelled to live outside of the limits of human habitation, having no rights which society or the law was bound to respect. They were given food or drink only when benevolence might be roused ; but the donor would never again touch the vessel in which the offering was made. The Eta,[54] though in individual cases becoming measurably rich, rotted and starved, and were made the filth and off-scouring of the earth, because they were the butchers, the skinners, the leather workers, and thus handled dead animals, being made also the executioners and buriers of the dead. After a quarter of a century the citizens, whose ancestry is not forgotten, suffer social ostracism even more than do the freed slaves of our country, though between them and the other Japanese there is no color line, but only the streak of difference which Buddhism created and has maintained. Nevertheless, let it be said to the eternal honor of Shin Shu and of some of the minor sects, that they were always kind and helpful to the Eta.

Furthermore it would be hard to discover Buddhist missionary activities among the Ainos, or benefits conferred upon them by the disciples of Gautama. One would suppose that the Buddhists, professing to be believers in spiritual democracy, would be equally active among all sorts and conditions of men; but they have not been so. Even in the days when the regions of the Ébisu or barbarians (Yezo) extended far southward upon the main island, the missionary bonze was conspicuous by his absence among these people. It would seem as though the popular notion that the Ainos are the offspring of dogs, had been fed by prejudices inculcated by Buddhism. It has been reserved for Christian aliens to reduce the language of these simple savages to writing, and to express in it for their spiritual benefit the ideas and literature of a religion higher than their own, as well as to erect church edifices and build hospitals.

The Attitude Toward Woman.

In its attitude toward woman, which is perhaps one of the crucial tests of a religion as well as of a civilization, Buddhism has somewhat to be praised and much to be blamed for. It is probable that the Japanese woman owes more to Buddhism than to Confucianism, though relatively her position was highest under Shintō. In Japan the women are the freest in Asia, and probably the best treated among any Asiatic nation, but this is not because of Gautama's teaching.[55] Very early in its history Japanese Buddhism welcomed womanhood to its fraternity and order,[56] yet the Japanese *ama, bikuni,* or nun, never became a sister of mercy, or reached, even within a measurable distance, the dignity of the Christian lady in the nunnery. In European history the abbess is a notable figure. She is hardly heard of beyond the Japanese nunnery, even by the native scholar—except in fiction.

So far as we can see, the religion founded by one who deserted his wife and babe did nothing to check concubinage or polygamy. It simply allowed these things, or ameliorated their ancient barbaric conditions through the law of kindness. Nevertheless, it brought education and culture within the family as well as within the court. It would be an interesting question to discuss how far the age of classic vernacular prose or the early mediæval literature of romance, which is almost wholly the creation of woman, [57] is due to Buddhism, or how far the credit belongs, by induction or reaction, to the Chinese movement in favor of learning. Certainly, the faith of India touches and feeds the imagination far more than does that of China. Certainly also, the animating spirit of most of the popular literature is due to Buddhistic culture. The Shin sect, which permits the marriage of the priests and preaches the salvation of woman, probably leads all others in according honor to her as well as in elevating her social position.

Buddhism, like Roman Catholicism, and as compared to Confucianism which is protestant and masculine, is feminine in its type. In Japan the place of the holy Virgin Mary is taken by Kuannon, the goddess of mercy ; and her shrine is one of the most popular of all. Much the same may be said of Benten, the queen of the heaven and mistress of the seas. The angels of Buddhism are always feminine, and, as in the unscriptural and pagan conception of Christian angels, have wings.[58] So also in the legends of Gautama, in the Buddhist lives of the saints, and in legendary lore as well as in glyptic and pictorial art, the female being transfigured in loveliness is a striking figure. Nevertheless, after all is summed up that can possibly be said in favor of Buddhism, the position it accords to woman is not only immeasurably beneath that given by Christianity, but is below that conceded by Shintō, which knows not only goddesses and heroines, but also priestesses and empresses.[59]

According to the popular ethical view as photographed in language, literature and art, jealousy is always represented by a female demon. Indeed, most of the tempters, devils, and transformations of humanity into malign beings, whether pretas, asuras, oni, foxes, badgers, or cats, are females. As the Chinese ideographs associate all things weak or vile with women, so the tell-tale words of Japanese daily speech are but reflections of the dogmas coined in the Buddhist mint. In Japanese, chastity means not moral cleanliness without regard to sex, but only womanly duties. For, while the man is allowed a loose foot, the woman is expected not only to be absolutely spotless, but also never to show any jealousy, however wide the husband may roam, or however numerous may be the concubines in his family. In a word, there is the double standard of morals, not only of priest and laity, but of man and woman. The position of the Japanese woman even of to-day, despite that eagerness once shown to educate her—an eagerness which soon cooled in the government schools, but which keeps an even pulse in the Christian home and college—is still relatively one of degradation as compared with that of her sister in Christendom. For this, the mid-Asian religion is not wholly responsible, yet it is largely so.

Influence on the Japanese Character.

In regard to the influence of Buddhism upon the morals and character of the Japanese, there is much to be said in praise, and much also in criticism. It has aided powerfully to educate the people in habits of gentleness and courtesy, but instead of aspiration and expectancy of improvement, it has given to them that spirit of hopeless resignation which is so characteristic of the Japanese masses. Buddhism has so dominated common popular literature, daily life and speech, that all their mental procedure and their utterance is cast in the moulds of Buddhist doctrine. The fatalism of the Moslem world expressed in the idea of Kismet, has its analogue in the Japanese Ingwa, or "cause and effect,"—the notion of an evolution which is atheistic, but viewed from the ethical side. This idea of Ingwa is the key to most Japanese novels as well as dramas of real life.[60] While Buddhism continually preaches this doctrine of Karma or Ingwa,[61] the law of cause and effect, as being sufficient to explain all things, it shows its insufficiency and emptiness by leaving out the great First Cause of all. In a word, Buddhism is law, but not gospel. It deals much with man, but not with man's relations with his Creator, whom it utterly ignores. Christianity comes not to destroy its ethics, beautiful as they are, nor to ignore its metaphysics ; but to fulfil, to give a higher truth, and to reveal a larger Universe and One who fills it all—not only law, but a Law-giver.

21

A CENTURY OF ROMAN CHRISTIANITY

" *Sicut cadaver.*"

" Et fiet unum ovile et unus pastor."—Vulgate, John x. 16.

" He (Xavier) has been the moon of that ' Society of Jesus ' of which Ignatius Loyola was the guiding sun."—S. W. Duffield.

> " My God I love Thee ; not because I hope for Heaven thereby,
> Nor yet because, who love Thee not, must die eternally.
> So would I love Thee, dearest Lord, and in Thy praise will sing ;
> Solely because thou art my God, and my eternal King."
>
> —Hymn attributed to Francis Xavier.

> " Half hidden, stretching in a lengthened line
> In front of China, which its guide shall be,
> Japan abounds in mines of silver fine,
> And shall enlighten'd be by holy faith divine."
>
> —Camoens.

" The people of this Iland of Iapon are good of nature, curteous aboue measure, and valiant in warre ; their iustice is seuerely executed without any partialitie vpon transgressors of the law. They are gouerned in great ciuilitie. I meane, not a land better gouerned in the world by ciuill policie. The people be verie superstitious in their religion, and are of diuers opinions."—Will Adams, October 22, 1611.

" A critical history of Japan remains to be written . . . We should know next to nothing of what may be termed the Catholic episode of the sixteenth and seventeenth centuries, had we access to none but the official Japanese sources. How can we trust those sources when they deal with times yet more remote ? "—Chamberlain.

" The annals of the primitive Church furnish no instances of sacrifice or heroic constancy, in the Coliseum or the Roman arenas, that were not paralleled on the dry river-beds or execution-grounds of Japan."

" They . . . rest from their labors ; and their works do follow them."—Revelation.

CHAPTER XI

A CENTURY OF ROMAN CHRISTIANITY

Darkest Japan

THE story of the first introduction and propagation of Roman Christianity in Japan, during the sixteenth and seventeenth centuries, has been told by many writers, both old and new, and in many languages. Recent research upon the soil,[1] both natives and foreigners making contributions, has illustrated the subject afresh. Relics and memorials found in various churches, monasteries and palaces, on both sides of the Pacific and the Atlantic, have cast new light upon the fascinating theme. Both Christian and non-Christian Japanese of to-day, in their travels in the Philippines, China, Formosa, Mexico, Spain, Portugal and Italy, being keenly alert for memorials of their countrymen, have met with interesting trovers. The descendants of the Japanese martyrs and confessors now recognize their own ancestors, in the picture galleries of Italian nobles, and in Christian churches see lettered tombs bearing familiar names, or in western museums discern far-eastern works of art brought over as presents or curiosities, centuries ago.

Roughly speaking, Japanese Christianity lasted phenomenally nearly a century, or more exactly from 1542 to 1637. During this time, embassies or missions crossed the seas not only of Chinese and Peninsular Asia, circumnavigating Africa and thus reaching Europe, but also sailed across the Pacific, and visited papal Christendom by way of Mexico and the Atlantic Ocean.

This century of Southern Christianity and of commerce with Europe enabled Japan, which had previously been almost unheard of, except through the vague accounts of Marco Polo and the semi-mythical stories by way of China, to leave a conspicuous mark, first upon the countries of southern Europe, and later upon Holland and England. As in European literature Cathay became China, and Zipango or Xipangu was recognized as Japan, so also the curiosities, the artistic fabrics, the strange things from the ends of the earth, soon became familiar in Europe. Besides the traffic in mercantile commodities, there were exchanges of words. The languages of Europe were enriched by Japanese terms, such as soy, moxa, goban, japan (lacquer or varnish), etc., while the tongue of Nippon received an infusion of new terms,[2] and a notable list of inventions was imported from Europe.

We shall merely outline, with critical commentary, the facts of history which have been so often told, but which in our day have received luminous illustration. We shall endeavor to treat the general phenomena, causes and results of Christianity in Japan in the same judicial spirit with which we have considered Buddhism.

Whatever be the theological or political opinions of the observer who looks into the history of Japan at about the year 1540, he will acknowledge that this point of time was a very dark moment in her known history. Columbus, who was familiar with the descriptions of Marco Polo, steered his caravels westward with the idea of finding Xipangu, with its abundance of gold and precious gems ; but the Genoese did not and could not know the real state of affairs existing in Dai Nippon at this time. Let us glance at this.

The duarchy of Throne and Camp, with the Mikado in Kiōto and the Shōgun at Kamakura, with the elaborate feudalism under it, had fallen into decay. The whole country was split up into a thousand warring fragments. To these convulsions of society, in which only the priest and the soldier were in comfort, while the mass of the people were little better than serfs, must be added the frequent violent earthquakes, drought and failure of crops, with famine and pestilence. There was little in religion to uplift and cheer. Shintō had sunk into the shadow of a myth. Buddhism had become outwardly a system of political gambling rather than the ordered expression of faith. Large numbers of the priests were like the mercenaries of Italy, who sold their influence and even their swords or those of their followers, to the highest bidder. Besides being themselves luxurious and dissolute, their monasteries were fortresses, in which only the great political gamblers, and not the oppressed people, found comfort and help. Millions of once fertile acres had been abandoned or left waste. The destruction of libraries, books and records is something awful to contemplate ; and "the times of Ashikaga" make a wilderness for the scapegoat of chronology. Kiōto, the sacred capital, had been again and again plundered and burnt. Those who might be tempted to live in the city amid the ruins, ran the risk of fire, murder, or starvation. Kamakura, once the Shō-gun's seat of authority, was a level waste of ashes.

Even China, Annam and Korea suffered from the practical dissolution of society in the island empire; for Japanese pirates ravaged their coasts to steal, burn and kill. Even as for centuries in Europe, Christian churches echoed with that prayer in the litanies: "From the fury of the Norsemen, good Lord, deliver us," so, along large parts of the deserted coasts of Chinese Asia, the wretched inhabitants besought their gods to avenge them against the "Wojen." To this day in parts of Honan in China, mothers frighten their children and warn them to sleep by the fearful words "The Japanese are coming."

First Coming of Europeans.

This time, then, was that of darkest Japan. Yet the people who lived in darkness saw great light, and to them that dwelt in the shadow of death, light sprang up.

When Pope Alexander VI. bisected the known world, assigning the western half, including America to Spain, and the eastern half, including Asia and its outlying archipelagos to the Portuguese, the latter sailed and fought their way around Africa to India, and past the golden Chersonese. In 1542, exactly fifty years after the discovery of America, Dai Nippon was reached. Mendez Pinto, on a Chinese pirate junk which had been driven by a storm away from her companions, set foot upon an island called Tanégashima. This name among the country folks is still synonymous with guns and pistols, for Pinto introduced fire-arms and powder.[3]

During six months spent by the "mendacious" Pinto on the island, the imitative people made no fewer than six hundred match-locks or arquebuses. Clearing twelve hundred per cent. on their cargo, the three Portuguese loaded with presents, returned to China. Their countrymen quickly flocked to this new market, and soon the beginnings of regular trade with Portugal were inaugurated. On the other hand, Japanese began to be found as far west as India. To Malacca, while Francis Xavier was laboring there, came a refugee Japanese, named Anjiro. The disciple of Loyola, and this child of the Land of the Rising Sun met. Xavier, ever restless and ready for a new field, was fired with the idea of converting Japan. Anjiro, after learning Portuguese and becoming a Christian, was baptized with the name of Paul. The heroic missionary of the cross and keys then sailed with his Japanese companion, and in 1549 landed at Kagoshima,[4] the capital of Satsuma. As there was no central government then existing in Japan, the entrance of the foreigners, both lay and clerical, was unnoticed.

Having no skill in the learning of languages, and never able to master one foreign tongue completely, Xavier began work with the aid of an interpreter. The jealousy of the daimiō, because his rivals had been supplied with fire-arms by the Portuguese merchants, and the plots and warnings of those Buddhist priests (who were later crushed by the Satsuma clansmen as traitors), compelled Xavier to leave this province. He went first to Hirado,[5] next to Nagatō, and then to Bungo, where he was well received. Preaching and teaching through his Japanese interpreter, he formed Christian congregations, especially at Yamaguchi.[6]

Thus, within a year, the great apostle to the Indies had seen the quick sprouting of the seed which he had planted. His ambition was now to go to the imperial capital, Kiōto, and there advocate the claims of Christ, of Mary and of the Pope.

Thus far, however, Xavier had seen only a few seaports of comparatively successful daimiōs. Though he had heard of the unsettled state of the country because of the long-continued intestine strife, he evidently expected to find the capital a splendid city. Despite the armed bands of roving robbers and soldiers, he reached Kiōto safely, only to find streets covered with ruins, rubbish and unburied corpses, and a general situation of wretchedness. He was unable to obtain audience of either the Shōgun or the Mikado. Even in those parts of the city where he tried to preach, he could obtain no hearers in this time of war and confusion. So after two weeks he turned his face again southward to Bungo, where he labored for a few months ; but in less than two years from his landing in Japan, this noble but restless missionary left the country, to attempt the spiritual conquest of China. One year later, December 2, 1551, he died on the island of Shanshan, or Sancian, in the Canton River, a few miles west of Macao.

Christianity Flourishes.

Nevertheless, Xavier's inspiring example was like a shining star that attracted scores of missionaries. There being in this time of political anarchy and religious paralysis none to oppose them, their zeal, within five years, bore surprising fruits. They wrote home that there were seven churches in the region around Kiōto, while a score or more of Christian congregations had been gathered in the southwest. In 1581 there were two hundred churches and one hundred and fifty thousand native Christians. Two daimiōs had confessed their faith, and in the Mikado's minister, Nobunaga (1534–1582), the foreign priests found a powerful supporter.[7] This hater and scourge of the Buddhist priesthood openly welcomed and patronized the Christians, and gave them eligible sites on which to build dwellings and churches. In every possible way he employed the new force, which he found pliantly political, as well as intellectually and morally a choice weapon for humbling the bonzes, whom he hated as serpents. The Buddhist church militant had become an army with banners and fortresses. Nobunaga made it the aim of his life to destroy the military power of the hierarchy, and to humble the priests for all time. He hoped at least to extract the fangs of what he believed to be a politico-religious monster, which menaced the life of the nation. Unfortunately, he was assassinated in 1582. To this day the memory of Nobunaga is execrated by the Buddhists. They have deified Kato Kiyomasa and Iyéyasŭ, the persecutors of the Christians. To Nobunaga they give the title of Bakadono, or Lord Fool.

In 1583, an embassy of four young noblemen was despatched by the Christian daimiōs of Kiushiu, the second largest island in the empire, to the Pope to declare themselves spiritual—though as some of their countrymen suspected, political—vassals of the Holy See. It was in the three provinces of Bungo, Omura and Arima, that Christianity was most firmly rooted.

After an absence of eight years, in 1590, the envoys
from the oriental to the occidental ends of the earth,
returned to Nagasaki, accompanied by seventeen more
Jesuit fathers—an important addition to the many
Portuguese "religious" of that order already in Japan.

Yet, although there was to be still much missionary
activity, though printing presses had been brought
from Europe for the proper diffusion of Christian literature in the Romanized colloquial,[8] though there
were yet to be built more church edifices and monasteries, and Christian schools to be established, a sad
change was nigh. Much seed which was yet to grow
in secret had been planted,—like the exotic flowers
which even yet blossom and shed their perfume in certain districts of Japan, and which the traveller from
Christendom instantly recognizes, though the Portuguese Christian church or monastery centuries ago disappeared in fire, or fell to the earth and disappeared.
Though there were to be yet wonderful flashes of
Christian success, and the missionaries were to travel
over Japan even up to the end of the main island and
accompany the Japanese army to Korea ; yet it may be
said that with the death of Nobunaga at the hands of
the traitor Akéchi, we see the high-water mark of the
flood-tide of Japanese Christianity. "Akéchi reigned
three days," but after him were to arise a ruler and central government jealous and hostile. After this flood
was to come slowly but surely the ebb-tide, until it
should leave, outwardly at least, all things as before.

The Jesuit fathers, with instant sensitiveness, felt
the loss of their champion and protector, Nobunaga.
The rebel and assassin, Akéchi, ambitious to imitate
and excel his master, promised the Christians to do

more for them even than Nobunaga had done, provided they would induce the daimiō Takayama to join forces with his. It is the record of their own friendly historian, and not of an enemy, that they, led by the Jesuit father Organtin, attempted this persuasion. To the honor of the Christian Japanese Takayama, he refused.⁹ On the contrary, he marched his little army of a thousand men to Kiōto, and, though opposed to a force of eight thousand, held the capital city until Hidéyoshi, the loyal general of the Mikado, reached the court city and dispersed the assassin's band. Hidéyoshi soon made himself familiar with the whole story, and his keen eye took in the situation.

This "man on horseback," master of the situation and moulder of the destinies of Japan, Hidéyoshi (1536–1598), was afterward known as the Taikō, or Retired Regent. The rarity of the title makes it applicable in common speech to this one person. Greater than his dead master, Nobunaga, and ingenious in the arts of war and peace, Hidéyoshi compelled the warring daimiōs, even the proud lord of Satsuma,¹⁰ to yield to his power, until the civil minister of the emperor, reverently bowing, could say: "All under Heaven, Peace." Now, Japan had once more a central government, intensely jealous and despotic, and with it the new religion must sooner or later reckon. Religion apart from politics was unknown in the Land of the Gods.

Yet, in order to employ the vast bodies of armed men hitherto accustomed to the trade of war, and withal jealous of China and hostile to Korea, Hidéyoshi planned the invasion of the little peninsular kingdom by these veterans whose swords were restless in their scabbards. After months of preparation, he despatched an army in two great divisions, one under the Christian general Konishi, and one under the Buddhist general Kato. After a brilliant campaign of eighteen days, the rivals, taking different routes, met in the Korean capital. In the masterly campaign which followed, the Japanese armies penetrated almost to the extreme northern boundary of the kingdom. Then China came to the rescue and the Japanese were driven southward.

During the six or seven years of war, while the invaders crossed swords with the natives and their Chinese allies, and devastated Korea to an extent from which she has never recovered, there were Jesuit missionaries attending the Japanese armies. It is not possible or even probable, however, that any seeds of Christianity were at this time left in the peninsula. Korean Christianity sprang up nearly two centuries later, wind-wafted from China.[11]

During the war there was always more or less of jealousy, mostly military and personal, between Konishi and Kato, which however was aggravated by the priests on either side. Kato, being then and afterward a fierce champion of the Buddhists, glorified in his orthodoxy, which was that of the Nichiren sect. He went into battle with a banneret full of texts, stuck in his back and flying behind him. His example was copied by hundreds of his officers and soldiers. On their flags and guidons was inscribed the famous apostrophe of the Nichiren sect, so often heard in their services and revivals to-day (Namu miyō ho ren gé kiō), and borrowed from the Saddharma Pundarika: "Glory be to the salvation-bringing Lotus of the True Law."

The Hostility of Hidéyoshi.

Konishi, on the other hand, was less numerously and perhaps less influentially backed by, and made the champion of, the European brethren; and as all the negotiations between the invaders and the allied Koreans and Chinese had to be conducted in the Chinese script, the alien fathers were, as secretaries and interpreters, less useful than the native Japanese bonzes. Yet this jealousy and hostility in the camps of the invaders proved to be only correlative to the state of things in Japan. Even supposing the statistics in round numbers, reported at that time, to be exaggerated, and that there were not as many as the alleged two hundred thousand Christians, yet there were, besides scores of thousands of confessing believers among the common people, daimiōs, military leaders, court officers and many persons of culture and influence. Nevertheless, the predominating influence at the Kioto court was that of Buddhism; and as the cult that winks at polygamy was less opposed to Hidéyoshi's sensualism and amazing vanity, the illustrious upstart was easily made hostile to the alien faith. According to the accounts of the Jesuits, he took umbrage because a Portuguese captain would not please him by risking his ship in coming out of deep water and nearer land, and because there were Christian maidens of Arima who scorned to yield to his degrading proposals. Some time after these episodes, an edict appeared, commanding every Jesuit to quit the country within twenty days. There were at this time sixty-five foreign missionaries in the country.

Then began a series of persecutions, which, however, were carried on spasmodically and locally, but not
universally or with system. Bitter in some places,
they were neutralized or the law became a dead letter,
in other parts of the realm. It is estimated that ten
thousand new converts were made in the single year,
1589, that is, the second year after the issue of the
edict, and again in the next year, 1590. It might even
be reasonable to suppose that, had the work been conducted wisely and without the too open defiance of the
letter of the law, the awful sequel which history knows,
might not have been.

Let us remember that the Duke of Alva, the tool of
Philip II., failing to crush the Dutch Republic had
conquered Portugal for his master. The two kingdoms
of the Iberian peninsula were now united under one
crown. Spain longed for trade with Japan, and while
her merchants hoped to displace their Portuguese
rivals, the Spanish Franciscans not scrupling to wear
a political cloak and thus override the Pope's bull of
world-partition, determined to get a foothold alongside of the Jesuits. So, in 1593 a Spanish envoy of
the governor of the Philippine Islands came to Kiôto,
bringing four Spanish Franciscan priests, who were
allowed to build houses in Kiôto, but only on the express understanding that this was because of their
coming as envoys of a friendly power, and with the
explicitly specified condition that they were not to
preach, either publicly or privately. Almost immediately violating their pledge and the hospitality
granted them, these Spaniards, wearing the vestments
of their order, openly preached in the streets. Besides exciting discord among the Christian congrega-

tions founded by the Jesuits, they were violent in their language.

Hidéyoshi, to gratify his own mood and test his power as the actual ruler for a shadowy emperor, seized nine preachers while they were building churches at Kiōto and Osaka. They were led to the execution-ground in exactly the same fashion as felons, and executed by crucifixion, at Nagasaki, February 5, 1597. Three Portuguese Jesuits, six Spanish Franciscans and seventeen native Christians were stretched on bamboo crosses, and their bodies from thigh to shoulder were transfixed with spears. They met their doom uncomplainingly.

In the eye of the Japanese law, these men were put to death, not as Christians, but as law-breakers and as dangerous political conspirators. The suspicions of Hidéyoshi were further confirmed by a Spanish sea-captain, who showed him a map of the world on which were marked the vast dominions of the King of Spain; the Spaniard informing the Japanese, in answer to his shrewd question, that these great conquests had been made by the king's soldiers following up the priests, the work being finished by the native and foreign allies.

The Political Character of Roman Christianity.

The Roman Catholic "Histoire del' Église Chrétienne" shows the political character of the missionary movement in Japan, a character almost inextricably associated with the papal and other political Chistianity of the times, when State and Church were united in all the countries of Europe, both Catholic and Protestant. Even republican Holland, leader of toleration and

22

forerunner of the modern Christian spirit, permitted, indeed, the Roman Catholics to worship in private houses or in sacred edifices not outwardly resembling churches, but prohibited all public processions and ceremonies, because religion and politics at that time were as Siamese twins. Only the Anabaptists held the primitive Christian and the American doctrine of the separation of politics from ecclesiasticism. Except in the country ruled by William the Silent, all magistrates meddled with men's consciences.[12]

In 1597, Hidéyoshi died, and the missionaries took heart again. The Christian soldiers returning by thousands from Korea, declared themselves in favor of Hidéyori, son of the dead Taikō. Encouraged by those in power, and by the rising star Iyéyasŭ (1542–1616), the fathers renewed their work and the number of converts increased.

Though peace reigned, the political situation was one of the greatest uncertainty, and with two hundred thousand soldiers gathered around Kiōto, under scores of ambitious leaders, it was hard to keep the sword in the sheath. Soon the line of cleavage found Iyéyasŭ and his northern captains on one side, and most of the Christian leaders and southern daimiōs on the other. In October, 1600, with seventy-five thousand men, the future unifier of Japan stood on the ever-memorable field of Sékigahara. The opposing army, led largely by Christian commanders, left their fortress to meet the one whom they considered a usurper, in the open field. In the battle which ensued, probably the most decisive ever fought on the soil of Japan, ten thousand men lost their lives. The leading Christian generals, beaten, but refusing out of principle because they were Christians, to take their own lives by *hara-kiri*, knelt willingly at the common blood-pit and had their heads stricken off by the executioner.

Then began a new era in the history of the empire, and then were laid by Iyéyasŭ the foundation-lines upon which the Japan best known to Europe has existed for nearly three centuries. The creation of a central executive government strong enough to rule the whole empire, and hold down even the southern and southwestern daimiōs, made it still worse for the converts of the European teachers, because in the Land of the Gods government is ever intensely pagan.

In adjusting the feudal relations of his vassals in Kiushiu, Iyéyasŭ made great changes, and thus the political status of the Christians was profoundly altered. The new daimiōs, carrying out the policy of their predecessors who had been taught by the Jesuits, but reversing its direction, began to persecute their Christian subjects, and to compel them to renounce their faith. One of the leading opposers of the Christians and their most cruel persecutor, was Kato, the zealous Nichirenite. Like Brandt, the famous Iroquois Indian, who, in the Mohawk Valley is execrated as a bloodthirsty brute, and on the Canadian side is honored with a marble statue and considered not only as the translator of the prayer-book but also as a saint ; even also as Claverhouse, who, in Scotland is looked upon as a murderous demon, but in England as a conscientious and loyal patriot ; so Kato, the *vir ter execrandus* of the Jesuits, is worshipped in his shrine at the Nichiren temple at Ikégami, near Tōkiō,[13] and is praised by native historians as learned, brave and true.

The Christians of Kiushiu, in a few cases, actually

took up arms against their new rulers and oppressors, though it was a new thing under the Japanese sun for peasantry to oppose not only civil servants of the law, but veterans in armor. Iyéyasŭ, now having time to give his attention wholly to matters of government and to examine the new forces that had entered Japanese life, followed Hidéyoshi in the suspicion that, under the cover of the western religion, there lurked political designs. He thought he saw confirmation of his theories, because the foreigners still secretly or openly paid court to Hidéyori, and at the same time freely disbursed gifts and gold as well as comfort to the persecuted. Resolving to crush the spirit of independence in the converts and to intimidate the foreign emissaries, Iyéyasŭ with steel and blood put down every outbreak, and at last, in 1606, issued his edict [14] prohibiting Christianity.

The Quarrels of the Christians.

About the same time, Protestant influences began to work against the papal emissaries. The new forces from the triumphant Dutch republic, which having successfully defied Spain for a whole generation had reached Japan even before the Great Truce, were opposed to the Spaniards and to the influence of both Jesuits and Franciscans. Hollanders at Lisbon, obtaining from the Spanish archives charts and geographical information, had boldly sailed out into the Eastern seas, and carried the orange white and blue flag to the ends of the earth, even to Nippon. Between Prince Maurice, son of William the Silent, and the envoys of Iyéyasŭ, there was made a league of commerce as well as of peace and friendship. Will Adams,[15] the English pilot of the Dutch ships, by his information given to Iyéyasŭ, also helped much to destroy the Jesuits influ- ence and to hurt their cause, while both the Dutch and English were ever busy in disseminating both correct information and polemic exaggeration, forging letters and delivering up to death by fire the *padres* when cap- tured at sea.

In general, however, it may be said that while Chris- tian converts and the priests were roughly handled in the South, yet there was considerable missionary ac- tivity and success in the North. Converts were made and Christian congregations were gathered in regions remote from Kiôto and Yedo, which latter place, like St. Petersburg in the West, was being made into a large city. Even outlying islands, such as Sado, had their churches and congregations.

The Anti-Christian Policy of the Tokugawas.

The quarrels between the Franciscans and Jesuits,[16] however, were probably more harmful to Christianity than were the whispers of the Protestant Englishmen or Hollanders. In 1610, the wrath of the government was especially aroused against the *bateren,* as the people called the *padres,* by their open and persistent viola- tion of Japanese law. In 1611, from Sado, to which island thousands of Christian exiles had been sent to work the mines, Iyéyasŭ believed he had obtained documentary proof in the Japanese language, of what he had long suspected—the existence of a plot on the part of the native converts and the foreign emissaries to reduce Japan to the position of a subject state.[17] Putting forth strenuous measures to root out utterly what he believed to be a pestilential breeder of sedition and war, the Yedo Shōgun advanced step by step to that great proclamation of January 27, 1614,[18] in which the foreign priests were branded as triple enemies—of the country, of the Kami, and of the Buddhas. This proclamation wound up with the charge that the Christian band had come to Japan to change the government of the country, and to usurp possession of it. Whether or not he really had sufficient written proof of conspiracy against the nation's sovereignty, it is certain that in this state paper, Iyéyasŭ shrewdly touched the springs of Japanese patriotism. Not desiring, however, to shed blood or provoke war, he tried transportation. Three hundred persons, namely, twenty-two Franciscans, Dominicans and Augustines, one hundred and seventeen foreign Jesuits, and nearly two hundred native priests and catechists, were arrested, sent to Nagasaki, and thence shipped like bundles of combustibles to Macao.

Yet, as many of the foreign and native Christian teachers hid themselves in the country and as others who had been banished returned secretly and continued the work of propaganda, the crisis had not yet come. Some of the Jesuit priests, even, were still hoping that Hidéyori would mount to power ; but in 1615, Iyéyasŭ, finding a pretext for war,[19] called out a powerful army and laid siege to the great castle of Osaka, the most imposing fortress in the country. In the brief war which ensued, it is said by the Jesuit fathers, that one hundred thousand men perished. On June 9, 1615, the castle was captured and the citadel burned. After thousands of Hidéyori's followers had committed *hara-kiri*, and his own body had been

burned into ashes, the Christian cause was irretrievably ruined.

Hidétada, the successor of Iyéyasŭ in Yedo, who ruled
from 1605 to 1622, seeing that his father's peaceful
methods had failed in extirpating the alien politico-religious doctrine, now pronounced sentence of death on
every foreigner, priest, or catechist found in the country. The story of the persecutions and horrible sufferings that ensued is told in the voluminous literature
which may be gathered from every country in Europe;[20]
though from the Japanese side " The Catholic martyr-
ology of Japan is still an untouched field for a [native]
historian." [21] All the church edifices which the last
storm had left standing were demolished, and temples
and pagodas were erected upon their ruins. In 1617,
foreign commerce was restricted to Hirado and Nagasaki. In 1621, Japanese were forbidden ever to leave
the country. In 1624, all ships having a capacity of
over twenty-five hundred bushels were burned, and no
craft, except those of the size of ordinary junks, were
allowed to be built.

The Books of the Inferno Opened.

For years, at intervals and in places, the books of
the Inferno were opened, and the tortures devised by
the native pagans and Buddhists equalled in their
horror those which Dante imagines, until finally, in
1636, even Japanese human nature, accustomed for
ages to subordination and submission, could stand it
no longer. Then a man named Nirado Shiro raised
the banner of the Virgin and called on all Christians
and others to follow him. Probably as many as thirty

thousand men, women and children, but without a single foreigner, lay or clerical, among them, gathered from parts of Kiushiu. After burning Shintō and Buddhist temples, they fortified an old abandoned castle at Shimabara, resolving to die rather than submit. Against an army of veterans, led by skilled commanders, the fortress held out during four months. At last, after a bloody assault, it was taken, and men, women and children were slaughtered.[22] Thousands suffered death at the point of the spear and sword; many were thrown into the sea; and others were cast into boiling hot springs, emblems of the eight Buddhist Hells.

All efforts were now put forth to uproot not only Christianity but also everything of foreign planting. The Portuguese were banished and the death penalty declared against all who should return. The ai no ko, or half-breed children, were collected and shipped by hundreds to Macao. All persons adopting or harboring Eurasians were to be banished, and their relatives punished. The Christian cause now became like the doomed city of Babylon or like the site of Nineveh, which, buried in the sand and covered with the desolation and silence of centuries, became lost to the memory of the world, so that even the very record of scripture was the jest of the infidel, until the spade of Layard brought them again to resurrection. So, Japanese Christianity, having vanished in blood, was supposed to have no existence, thus furnishing Mr. Lecky with arguments to prove the extirpative power of persecution.[23]

Yet in 1859, on the opening of the country by treaty, the Roman Catholic fathers at Nagasaki found to their surprise that they were re-opening the old mines, and that their work was in historic continuity with that of their predecessors. The blood of the martyrs had been the seed of the church. Amid much ignorance and darkness, there were thousands of people who, through the Virgin, worshipped God; who talked of Jesus, and of the Holy Spirit; and who refused to worship at the pagan shrines.[24]

Summary of Roman Christianity in Japan.

Let us now strive impartially to appraise the Christianity of this era, and inquire what it found, what it attempted to do, what it did not strive to attain, what was the character of its propagators, what was the mark it made upon the country and upon the mind of the people, and whether it left any permanent influence.

The gospel net which had gathered all sorts of fish in Europe brought a varied quality of spoil to Japan. Among the Portuguese missionaries, beginning with Xavier, there are many noble and beautiful characters, who exemplified in their motives, acts, lives and sufferings some of the noblest traits of both natural and redeemed humanity. In their praise, both the pagan and the Christian, as well as critics biased by their prepossessions in favor either of the Reformed or the Roman phase of the faith, can unite.

The character of the native converts is, in many instances, to be commended, and shows the direct truth of Christianity in fields of life and endeavor, in ethics and in conceptions, far superior to those which the Japanese religious systems have produced. In the teaching that there should be but one standard of morality for man and woman, and that the male as well as the female should be pure ; in the condemnation of polygamy and licentiousness ; in the branding of suicide as both wicked and cowardly ; in the condemnation of slavery ; and in the training of men and women to lofty ideals of character, the Christian teachers far excelled their Buddhist or Confucian rivals.

The benefits which Japan received through the coming of the Christian missionaries, as distinct and separate from those brought by commerce and the merchants, are not to be ignored. While many things of value and influence for material improvement, and many beneficent details and elements of civilization were undoubtedly imported by traders, yet it was the priests and itinerant missionaries who diffused the knowledge of the importance of these things and taught their use throughout the country. Although in the reaction of hatred and bitterness, and in the minute, universal and long-continued suppression by the government, most of this advantage was destroyed, yet some things remained to influence thought and speech, and to leave a mark not only on the language, but also on the procedure of daily life. One can trace notable modifications of Japanese life from this period, lasting through the centuries and even until the present time.

Christianity, in the sixteenth century, came to Japan only in its papal or Roman Catholic form. While in it was infused much of the power and spirit of Loyola and Xavier, yet the impartial critic must confess that this form was military, oppressive and political.[25] Nevertheless, though it was impure and saturated with

the false principles, the vices and the embodied superstitions of corrupt southern Europe, yet, such as it
was, Portuguese Christianity confronted the worst
condition of affairs, morally, intellectually and materi-
ally, which Japan has known in historic times. Defective as the critic must pronounce the system of religion imported from Europe, it was immeasurably
superior to anything that the Japanese had hitherto
known.

It must be said, also, that Portuguese Christianity
in Japan tried to do something more than the mere
obtaining of adherents or the nominal conversion of
the people.[26] It attempted to purify and exalt their
life, to make society better, to improve the relations
between rulers and ruled; but it did not attempt to do
what it ought to have done. It ignored great duties
and problems, while it imitated too fully, not only
the example of the kings of this world in Europe
but also of the rulers in Japan. In the presence
of soldier-like Buddhist priests, who had made war
their calling, it would have been better if the Christian
missionaries had avoided their bad example, and followed only in the footsteps of the Prince of Peace; but
they did not. On the contrary, they brought with
them the spirit of the Inquisition then in full blast in
Spain and Portugal, and the machinery with which
they had been familiar for the reclamation of native
and Dutch "heretics." Xavier, while at Goa, had even
invoked the secular arm to set up the Inquisition in
India, and doubtless he and his followers would have
put up this infernal enginery in Japan if they could
have done so. They had stamped and crushed out
"heresy" in their own country, by a system of hellish

tortures which in its horrible details is almost inde-
scribable. The rusty relics now in the museums of
Europe, but once used in church discipline, can be
fully appreciated only by a physician or an anatomist.
In Japan, with the spirit of Alva and Philip II., these
believers in the righteousness of the Inquisition attacked violently the character of native bonzes, and in-
cited their converts to insult the gods, destroy the
Buddhist images, and burn or desecrate the old shrines.
They persuaded the daimiōs, when these lords had become Christians, to compel their subjects to embrace
their religion on pain of exile or banishment. Whole
districts were ordered to become Christian. The bonzes
were exiled or killed, and fire and sword as well as
preaching, were employed as means of conversion. In
ready imitation of the Buddhists, fictitious ·miracles
were frequently got up to utilize the credulity of the
superstitious in furthering the faith — all of which
is related not by hostile critics, but by admiring historians and by sympathizing eye-witnesses.[29]

The most prominent feature of the Roman Catholicism of Japan, was its political animus and complexion.
In writings of this era, Japanese historians treat of the
Christian missionary movement less as something religious, and more as that which influenced government
and politics, rather than society on its moral side. So
also, the impartial historian must consider that on the
whole, despite the individual instances of holy lives
and unselfish purposes, the work of the Portuguese
and Spanish friars and "fathers" was, in the main, an
attempt to bring Japan more or less directly within
the power of the Pope or of those rulers called
Most Catholic Majesties, Christian Kings, etc., even as

they had already brought Mexico, South America and large portions of India under the same control. The words of Jesus before the Roman procurator had not been apprehended : — "My kingdom is not of this world."

TWO CENTURIES OF SILENCE

" The frog in the well knows not the great ocean."

—Sanskrit and Japanese **Proverb.**

" When the blind lead the blind, both fall into the ditch."

—Japanese **Proverb.**

"The little island of Déshima, well and prophetically signifying Fore-Island, was Japan's window, through which she looked at the whole Occident . . . We are under obligation to Holland for the arts of engineering, mining, pharmacy, astronomy, and medicine . . . ' Rangaku' (*i.e.*, Dutch learning) passed almost as a synonym for medicine." [1615-1868].— Inazo Nitobé.

" The great peace, of which we are so proud, was more like the stillness of stagnant pools than the calm surface of a clear lake."—Mitsukuri.

" The ancestral policy of self-contentment must be done away with. If it was adopted by your forefathers, because it was wise in their time, why not adopt a new policy if it is sure to prove wise in your time."—Sakuma Shozan, wrote in 1841, assassinated 1864.

" And slowly floating onward go
Those Black Ships, wave-tossed to and fro."

—Japanese Ballad of the Black Ship, 1845.

" The next day was Sunday (July 10th), and, as usual, divine service was held on board the ships, and, in accordance with proper reverence for the day, no communication was held with the Japanese authorities." —Perry's Narrative.

" Praise God, from whom all blessings flow,
Praise Him, all creatures here below,
Praise Him above, ye heavenly host,
Praise Father, Son, and Holy Ghost."

—Sung on U. S. S. S. Mississippi, in Yedo Bay, July 10, 1853.

" I refuse to see anyone on Sunday, I am resolved to set an example of a proper observance of the Sabbath . . . I will try to make it what I believe it was intended to be—a day of rest."—Townsend Harris's Diary, Sunday, August 31, 1856.

" I have called thee by thy name. I have surnamed thee, though thou hast not known me. I am the LORD, and there is none else; besides me there is no God."—Isaiah.

" I saw underneath the altar the souls of them that had been slain for the word of God, and for the testimony which they held."—John.

" That they should seek God, if haply they might feel after him, though he is not far from each one of us."—Paul.

" Other sheep have I which are not of this fold: them also I must bring, and they shall hear my voice; and they shall become one flock, one shepherd."—Jesus.

CHAPTER XII

The Japanese Shut In

SINCERELY regretting that we cannot pass more favorable judgments upon the Christianity of the seventeenth century in Japan, let us look into the two centuries of silence, and see what was the story between the paling of the Christian record in 1637, and the glowing of the palimpsest in 1859, when the new era begins.

The policy of the Japanese rulers, after the supposed utter extirpation of Christianity, was the double one of exclusion and inclusion. A deliberate attempt, long persisted in and for centuries apparently successful, was made to insulate Japan from the shock of change. The purpose was to draw a whole nation and people away from the currents and movements of humanity, and to stereotype national thought and custom. This was carried out in two ways: first, by exclusion, and then by inclusion. All foreign influences were shut off, or reduced to a minimum. The whole western world, especially Christendom, was put under ban.

Even the apparent exception made in favor of the Dutch was with the motive of making isolation more complete, and of securing the perfect safety which that

23

isolation was expected to bring. For, having built, not indeed with brick and mortar, but by means of edict and law, both open and secret, a great wall of exclusion more powerful than that of China's, it was necessary that there should be a port-hole, for both sally and exit, and a slit for vigilant scrutiny of any attempt to force seclusion or violate the frontier. Hence, the Hollanders were allowed to have a small place of residence in front of a large city and at the head of a land-locked harbor. There, the foreigners being isolated and under strict guard, the government could have, as it were, a nerve which touched the distant nations, and could also, as with a telescope, sweep the horizon for signs of danger.

So, in 1640, the Hollanders were ordered to evacuate Hirado, and occupy the little "outer island" called Déshima, in front of the city of Nagasaki, and connected therewith by a bridge. Any ships entering this hill-girdled harbor, it was believed, could be easily managed by the military resources possessed by the government. Vessels were allowed yearly to bring the news from abroad and exchange the products of Japan for those of Europe. The English, who had in 1617 opened a trade and conducted a factory for some years,[1] were unable to compete with the Γ itch, and about 1624, after having lost in the venture forty thousand pounds sterling, withdrew entirely from the Japanese trade. The Dutch were thus left without a rival from Christendom.

Japan ceased her former trade and communications with the Philippine Islands, Annam, Siam, the Spice Islands and India,[2] and began to restrict trade and communication with Korea and China. The Koreans, who were considered as vassals, or semi-vassals, came to Japan to present their congratulations on the accession of each new Shōgun; and some small trade was done at Fusan under the superintendence of the daimiō of Tsushima. Even this relation with Korea was rather one of watchfulness. It sprang from the pride of a victor rather than from any desire to maintain relations with the rest of the world. As for China, the communication with her was astonishingly little, only a few junks crossing yearly between Nankin and Nagasaki; so that, with the exception of one slit in their tower of observation, the Japanese became well isolated from the human family.

This system of exclusion was accompanied by an equally vigorous policy of inclusiveness. It was deliberately determined to keep the people from going abroad, either in their bodies or minds. All seaworthy ships were destroyed. Under pain of imprisonment and death, all natives were forbidden to go to a foreign country, except in the rare cases of urgent government service. By settled precedents it was soon made to be understood that those who were blown out to sea or carried away in stress of weather, need not come back; if they did, they must return only on Chinese and Korean vessels, and even then would be grudgingly allowed to land. It was given out, both at home and to the world, that no shipwrecked sailors or waifs would be welcomed when brought on foreign vessels.

This inclusive policy directed against physical exportation, was still more stringently carried out when applied to imports affecting the minds of the Japanese. The "government deliberately attempted to establish a society impervious to foreign ideas from without, and fostered within by all sorts of artificial legislation. This isolation affected every depấrtment of private and public life. Methods of education were cast in a definite mould ; even matters of dress and household architecture were strictly regulated by the State, and industries were restricted or forced into specified channels, thus retarding economic developments." [3]

Starving of the Mind.

In the science of keeping life within stunted limits and artificial boundaries, the Japanese genius excels. It has been well said that " the Japanese mind is great in little things and little in great things." To cut the tap-root of a pine-shoot, and, by regulating the allowance of earth and water, to raise a pine-tree which when fifty years old shall be no higher than a silver dollar, has been the proud ambition of many an artist in botany. In like manner, the Tokugawa Shōguns (1604–1868) determined to so limit the supply of mental food, that the mind of Japan should be of those correctly dwarfed proportions of puniness, so admired by lovers of artificiality and unconscious caricature. Philosophy was selected as a chief tool among the engines of oppression, and as the main influence in stunting the intellect. All thought must be orthodox according to the standards of Confucianism, as expounded by Chu Hi. Anything like originality in poetry, learning or philosophy must be hooted down. Art must follow Chinese, Buddhist and Japanese traditions. Any violation of this order would mean ostracism. All learning must be in the Chinese and Japanese languages—the former mis - pronounced and in

sound bearing as much resemblance to Pekingise speech
as "Pennsylvania Dutch" does to the language of Ber-
lin. Everything like thinking and study must be with
a view of sustaining and maintaining the established
order of things. The tree of education, instead of
being a lofty or wide-spreading cryptomeria, must be
the measured nursling of the teacup. If that trio of
emblems, so admired by the natives, the bamboo, pine
and plum, could produce glossy leaves, ever-green
needles and fragrant blooms within a space of four
cubic inches, so the law, the literature and the art of
Japan must display their normal limit of fresh fragrance, of youthful vigor and of venerable age, endur-
ing for aye, within the vessel of Japanese inclusion so
carefully limited by the Yedo authorities.

Such a policy, reminds one of the Amherst agricultural experiment in which bands of iron were strapped
around a much-afflicted squash, in order to test vital
potency. It recalls the pretty little story of Picciola,
in which a tender plant must grow between the inter-
stices of the bricks in a prison yard. Besides the
potent bonds of the only orthodox Confucian philosophy which was allowed and the legally recognized religions, there was gradually formed a marvellous system of legislation, that turned the whole nation into a
secret society in which spies and hypocrites flourished
like fungus on a dead log. Besides the unwritten code
of private law,[4] that is, the local and general customs
founded on immemorial usage, there was that peculiar
legal system framed by Iyéyasŭ, bequeathed as a
legacy and for over two hundred years practically the
supreme law of the land.

What this law was, it was exceedingly difficult, if not

utterly impossible, for the aliens dwelling in the country at Nagasaki ever to find out. Keenly intellectual, as many of the physicians, superintendents and elect members of the Dutch trading company were, they seem never to have been able to get hold of what has been called "The Testament of Iyéyasŭ." [5] This consisted of one hundred laws or regulations, based on a home-spun sort of Confucianism, intended to be orthodoxy "unbroken for ages eternal."

To a man of western mode of thinking, the most astonishing thing is that this law was esoteric. [6] The people knew of it only by its irresistible force, and by the constant pressure or the rare easing of its iron hand. Those who executed the law were drilled in its routine from childhood, and this routine became second nature. Only a few copies of the original instrument were known, and these were kept with a secrecy which to the people became a sacred mystery guarded by a long avenue of awe.

The Dutchmen at Déshima.

The Dutchmen who lived at Déshima for two centuries and a half, and the foreigners who first landed at the treaty ports in 1859, on inquiring about the methods of the Japanese Government, the laws and their administration, found that everything was veiled behind a vague embodiment of something which was called "the Law." What that law was, by whom enacted, and under what sanctions enforced, no one could tell; though all seemed to stand in awe of it as something of superhuman efficiency. Its mysteriousness was only equalled by the abject submission which it received. Foreign diplomatists, on trying to deal with the seat and source of authority, instead of seeing the real head of power, played, as it were, a game of chess against a mysterious hand stretched out from behind a curtain. Morally, the whole tendency of such a dual system of exclusion and of inclusion was to make a nation of liars, foster confirmed habits of deceit, and create a code of politeness vitiated by insincerity.

With such repression of the natural powers of humanity, it was but in accordance with the nature of things that licentiousness should run riot, that on the fringes of society there should be the outcast and the pariah, and that the social waste of humanity by prostitution, by murder, by criminal execution under a code that prescribed the death penalty for hundreds of offences, should be enormous. It is natural also that in such a state of society population [7] should be kept down within necessary limits, not only by famine, by the restraints of feudalism, by legalized murder in the form of vendetta, by a system of prostitution that made and still makes Japan infamous, by child murder, by lack of encouragement given to feeble or malformed children to live, and by various devices known to those who were ingenious in keeping up so artificial a state of society.

That there were many who tried to break through this wall, from both the inside and the outside, and to force the frontiers of exclusion and inclusion, is not to be wondered at. Externally, there were bold spirits from Christendom who burned to know the secrets of the mysterious land. Some even yearned to wear the ruby crown. The wonderful story of past Christian triumphs deeply stirred the heart of more than one fiery spirit, and so we find various attempts made by the clerical brethren of southern Europe to enter the country. Bound by their promises, the Dutch captains could not introduce these emissaries of a banned religion within the borders ; yet there are several notable instances of Roman Catholic " religious " [8] getting themselves left by shipmasters on the shores of Japan. The lion's den of reality was Yedo. Like the lion's den of fable, the footprints all led one way, and where these led the bones of the victims soon lay.

Besides these men with religious motives, the ships of the West came with offers of trade and threats of invasion. These were English, French, Russian and American, and the story of the frequent episodes has been told by Hildreth, Aston,[9] Nitobé, and others. There is also a considerable body of native literature which gives the inside view of these efforts to force the seclusion of the hermit nation, and coax or compel the Japanese to be more sociable and more human. All were in vain until the peaceful armada, under the flag of thirty-one stars, led by Matthew Calbraith Perry,[10] broke the long seclusion of this Thorn-rose of the Pacific, and the unarmed diplomacy of Townsend Harris,[11] brought Japan into the brotherhood of commercial and Christian nations.

Within the isolating walls and the barred gates the story of the seekers after God is a thrilling one. The intellect of choice spirits, beating like caged eagles the bars of their prisons, yearned for more light and life. " Though an eagle be starving," says the Japanese proverb, " it will not eat grain ; " and so, while the mass of the people and even the erudite, were content with ground food—even the chopped straw and husks of

materialistic Confucianism and decayed Buddhism—
there were noble souls who soared upward to exercise
their God-given powers, and to seek nourishment fitted
for that human spirit which goeth upward and not
downward, and which, ever in restless discontent, seeks
the Infinite.

Protests of Inquiring Spirits.

There is no stronger proof of the true humanity and
the innate god-likeness of the Japanese, of their wor-
thiness to hold and their inherent power to win a high
place among the nations of the earth, than this longing
of a few elect ones for the best that earth could give
and Heaven bestow. We find men in travail of spirit,
groping after God if haply they might find Him, following the ways of the Spirit along lines different, and
in pathways remote, from those laid down by Confucius
and his materialistic commentators, or by Buddha and
his parodists or caricaturists. The story of the philosophers, who mutinied against the iron clamps and
governmentally nourished system of the Séido College
expounders, is yet to be fully told.[12] It behooves some
Japanese scholar to tell it.

How earnest truth-seeking Japanese protested and
rebelled against the economic fallacies, against the political despotism, against the abominable usurpations,
against the false strategies and against the inherent
immoralities of the Tokugawa system, has of late years
been set forth with tantalizing suggestiveness, but
only in fragments, by the native historians. Heart-
rending is the narrative of these men who studied,
who taught, who examined, who sifted the mountains
of chaff in the native literature and writings, who made

long journeys on foot all over the country, who furtively travelled in Korea and China, who boarded
Dutch and Russian vessels, who secretly read forbidden books, who tried to improve their country and
their people. These men saw that their country was
falling behind not only the nations of the West, but, as
it seemed to them, even the nations of the East. They
felt that radical changes were necessary in order to reform the awful poverty, disease, licentiousness, national
weakness, decay of bodily powers, and the creeping paralysis of the Samurai intellect and spirit. How they
were ostracized, persecuted, put under ban, hound-
ed by the spies, thrown into prison; how they died
of starvation or of disease; how they were beheaded, crucified, or compelled to commit *hara-kiri ;* how
their books were purged by the censors, or put under
ban or destroyed,[13] and their maps, writings and plates
burned, has not yet been told. It is a story that, when
fully narrated, will make a volume of extraordinary interest. It is a story which both Christian and human
interests challenge some native author to tell.

During all this time, but especially during the first
half of the nineteenth century, there was one steady
goal to which the aspiring student ever kept his faith,
and to which his feet tended. There was one place of
pilgrimage, toward which the sons of the morning
moved, and which, despite the spy and the informer
and the vigilance of governors, fed their spirits, and
whence they carried the sacred fire, or bore the seed
whose harvest we now see. That goal of the pilgrim
band was Nagasaki, and the place where the light
burned and the sacred flames were kindled was Déshima. The men who helped to make true patriots, dar-

ing thinkers, inquirers after truth, bringers in of a better time, yes, and even Christians and preachers of the good news of God, were these Dutchmen of Déshima.

A Handful of Salt in a Stagnant Mass.

The Nagasaki Hollanders were not immaculate saints, neither were they sooty devils. They did not profess to be Christian missionaries. On the other hand, they were men not devoid of conscience nor of sympathy with aspiring and struggling men in a hermit nation, eager for light and truth. The Dutchman during the time of hermit Japan, as we see him in the literature of men who were hostile in faith and covetous rivals in trade, is a repulsive figure. He seems to be a brutal wretch, seeking only gain, and willing to sell conscience, humanity and his religion, for pelf. In reality, he was an ordinary European, probably no better, certainly no worse, than his age or the average man of his country or of his continent. Further, among this average dozen of exiles in the interest of commerce, science or culture, there were frequently honorable men far above the average European, and shining examples of Christianity and humanity. Even in his submission to the laws of the country, the Dutchman did no more, no less, but exactly as the daimios,[14] who like himself were subject to the humiliations imposed by the rulers in Yedo.

It was the Dutch, who, for two hundred years supplied the culture of Europe to Japan, introduced Western science, furnished almost the only intellectual stimulant, and were the sole teachers of medicine and science.[15] They trained up hundreds of Japanese to be physicians who practised rational medicine and surgery. They filled with needed courage the hearts of men, who, secretly practising dissection of the bodies of criminals, demonstrated the falsity of Chinese ideas of anatomy. It was Dutch science which exploded and drove out of Japan that Chinese system of medicine, by means of which so many millions have, during the long ages, been slowly tortured to death.

The Déshima Dutchman was a kindly adviser, helper, guide and friend, the one means of communication with the world, a handful of salt in the stagnant mass. Long before the United States, or Commodore Perry, the Hollanders advised the Yedo government in favor of international intercourse. The Dutch language, nearest in structure and vocabulary to the English, even richer in the descriptive energy of its terms, and saturated withal with Christian truth, was studied by eager young men. These speakers of an impersonal language which in psychological development was scarcely above the grade of childhood, were exercised in a tongue that stands second to none in Europe for purity, vigor, personality and philosophical power. The Japanese students of Dutch held a golden key which opened the treasures of modern thought and of the world's literature. The minds of thinking Japanese were thus made plastic for the reception of the ideas of Christianity. Best of all, though forbidden by their contracts to import Bibles into Japan, the Dutchmen, by means of works of reference, pointed more than one inquiring spirit to the information by which the historic Christ became known. The books which they imported, the information which they gave, the stimulus which they imparted, were as seeds planted within masonry-covered earth, that were to upheave and overthrow the fabric of exclusion and inclusion reared by the Tokugawa Shōguns.

Time and space fail us to tell how eager spirits not only groped after God, but sought the living Christ—though often this meant to them imprisonment, suicide enforced by the law, or decapitation. Yet over all Japan, long before the broad pennant of Perry was mirrored on the waters of Yedo Bay, there were here and there masses of leavened opinion, spots of kindled light, and fields upon which the tender green sprouts of new ideas could be detected. To-day, as inquiry among the oldest of the Christian leaders and scores of volumes of modern biography shows, the most earnest and faithful among the preachers, teachers and soldiers in the Christian army, were led into their new world of ideas through Dutch culture. The fact is revealed in repeated instances, that, through father, grandfather, uncle, or other relative—some pilgrim to the Dutch at Nagasaki—came their first knowledge, their initial promptings, the environment or atmosphere, which made them all sensitive and ready to receive the Christian truth when it came in its full form from the living missionary and the vital word of God. Some one has well said that the languages of modern Europe are nothing more than Christianity expressed with differing pronunciation and vocabulary. To him who will receive it, the mastery of any one of the languages of Christendom, is, in a large sense, a revelation of God in Christ Jesus.

Seekers after God.

Pathetic, even to the compulsion of tears, is the story of these seekers after God. We, who to-day are surrounded by every motive and inducement to Christian living and by every means and appliance for the practice of the Christian life, may well consider for a moment the struggle of earnest souls to find out God. Think of this one who finds a Latin Bible cast up on the shore from some broken ship, and bearing it secretly in his bosom to the Hollander, gains light as to the meaning of its message. Think of the nobleman, Watanabé Oboru,[16] who, by means of the Japanese interpreter of Dutch, Takano Choyéi, is thrilled with the story of Jesus of Nazareth who helped and healed and spake as no other man spake, teaching with an authority above that of the masters Confucius or Buddha. Think of the daimiō of Mito,[17] who, proud in lineage, learned and scholarly, and surrounded by a host of educated men, is yet unsatisfied with what the wise of his own country could give him, and gathers around him the relics unearthed from the old persecutions. From a picture of the Virgin, a fragment of a litany, or it may be a part of a breviary, he tries to make out what Christianity is.

Think of Yokoi Héishiro,[18] learned in Confucius and his commentators, who seeks better light, sends to China for a Chinese translation of the New Testament, and in his lectures on the Confucian ethics, to the delight and yet to the surprise of his hearers who hear grander truth than they are able to find in text or commentary, really preaches Christ, and prophesies that

the time will come when the walls of isolation being
levelled, the brightest intellects of Japan will welcome
this same Jesus and His doctrine. Think of him again,
when unable to purify the Augean stables of Yedo's
moral corruption, because the time was at hand for
other cleansing agencies, he retires to his home, content awhile with his books and flowers. Again, see
him summoned to the capital, to sit at Kiōto—like
aged Franklin among the young statesmen of the Constitution in Philadelphia—with the Mikado's youthful
advisers in the new government of 1868. Think of
him pleading for the elevation of the pariah Eta, accursed and outcast through Buddhism, to humanity
and citizenship. Then hear him urge eloquently the
right of personal belief, and argue for toleration under
the law, of opinions, which the Japanese then stigmatized as " evil " and devilish, but which we, and many
of them now, call sound and Christian. Finally, behold him at night in the public streets, assaulted by
assassins, and given quick death by their bullet and
blades. See his gray head lying severed from his
body and in its own gore, the wretched murderers
thinking they have stayed the advancing tide of Christianity ; but at home there dwells a little son destined
in God's providence to become an earnest Christian
and one of the brilliant leaders of the native Christianity of Japan in our day.

The Buddhist Inquisitors.

During the nation's period of Thorn-rose-like seclusion, the three religions recognized by the law were
Buddhism, Shintō and Confucianism. Christianity

was the outlawed sect. All over the country, on the high-roads, at the bridges, and in the villages, towns and cities, the fundamental laws of the country were written on wooden tablets called kosatsŭ. These, framed and roofed for protection from the weather, but easily before the eyes of every man, woman and child, and written in a style and language understood of all, denounced the Christian religion as an accursed "sect," and offered gold to the spy and informer ; [19] while once a year every Samurai was required to swear on the true faith of a gentleman that he had nothing to do with Christianity. From the seventeenth century, the country having been divided into parishes, the inquisition was under the charge of the Buddhist priests who penetrated into the house and family and guarded the graveyards, so that neither earth nor fire should embrace the carcass of a Christian, nor his dust or ashes defile the ancestral graveyards. Twice—in 1686 and in 1711—were the rewards increased and the Buddhist bloodhounds of Japan's Inquisition set on fresh trails. On one occasion, at Osaka, in 1839,[20] a rebellion broke out which was believed, though without evidence, to have been instigated in some way by men with Christian ideas, and was certainly led by Oshio, the bitter opponent of Buddhism, of Tokugawa, and of the prevalent Confucianism. Possibly, the uprising was aided by refugees from Korea. Those implicated were, after speedy trial, crucified or beheaded. In the southern part of the country the ceremony of Ébumi or trampling on the cross,[21] was long performed. Thousands of people were made to pass through a wicket, beneath which and on the ground lay a copper plate engraved with the image of the Christ and the cross. In this way it was hoped to utterly eradicate the very memory of Christianity, which, to the common people, had become the synonym for sorcery.

But besides the seeking after God by earnest souls and the protest of philosophers, there was, amid the prevailing immorality and the agnosticism and scepticism bred by decayed Buddhism and the materialistic philosophy based on Confucius, some earnest struggles for the purification of morals and the spiritual improvement of the people.

The Shingaku Movement.

One of the most remarkable of the movements to this end was that of the Shingaku or New Learning. A class of practical moralists, to offset the prevailing tendency of the age to much speculation and because Buddhism did so little for the people, tried to make the doctrines of Confucius a living force among the great mass of people. This movement, though Confucian in its chief tone and color, was eclectic and intended to combine all that was best in the Chinese system with what could be utilized from Shintō and Buddhism. With the preaching was combined a good deal of active benevolence. Especially in the time of famine, was care for humanity shown. The effect upon the people was noticeable, followers multiplied rapidly, and it is said that even the government in many instances made them, the Shingaku preachers, the distributors of rice and alms for the needy. Some of the preachers became famous and counted among their followers many men of influence. The literary side of the movement [22] has been brought to the attention

24

of English readers through Mr. Mitford's translation of three sermons from the volume entitled Shingaku Dōwa. Other discourses have been from time to time rendered into English, those by Shibata, entitled The Sermons of the Dove-like Venerable Master, being especially famous.

This movement, interesting as it was, came to an end when the country began to be convulsed by the approaching entrance of foreigners, through the Perry treaty; but it serves to show, what we believe to be the truth, that the moral rottenness as well as the physical decay of the Japanese people reached their acme just previous to the apparition of the American fleet in 1853.

The story of nineteenth century Reformed Christianity in Japan does not begin with Perry, or with Harris, or with the arrival of Christian missionaries in 1859; for it has a subterranean and interior history, as we have hinted; while that of the Roman form and order is a story of unbroken continuity, though the life of the tunnel is now that of the sunny road. The parable of the leaven is first illustrated and then that of the mustard-seed. Before Christianity was phenomenal, it was potent. Let us now look from the interior to the outside.

On Perry's flag-ship, the Mississippi, the Bible lay open, a sermon was preached, and the hymn " Before Jehovah's Awful Throne " was sung, waking the echoes of the Japan hills. The Christian day of rest was honored on this American squadron. In the treaty signed in 1854, though it was made, indeed, with use of the name of God and terms of Christian chronology, there was nothing upon which to base, either by right or privilege, the residence of missionaries in the country. Townsend Harris, the American Consul-General, who hoisted his flag and began his hermit life at Shimoda, in September, 1855, had as his only companion a Dutch secretary, Mr. Heusken, who was later, in Yedo, to be assassinated by ronins.

Without ship or soldier, overcoming craft and guile, and winning his way by simple honesty and persever-ence, Mr. Harris obtained audience [23] of " the Tycoon " in Yedo, and later from the Shōgun's daring minister Ii, the signature to a treaty which guaranteed to Americans the rights of residence, trade and com-merce. Thus Americans were enabled to land as cit-izens, and pursue their avocation as religious teachers. As the government of the United States of America knows nothing of the religion of American citizens abroad, it protects all missionaries who are law-abid-ing citizens, without regard to creed.[24]

Japan Once More Missionary Soil.

The first missionaries were on the ground as soon as the ports were open. Though surrounded by spies and always in danger of assassination and incendiarism, they began their work of mastering the language. To do this without trained teachers or apparatus of dic-tionary and grammar, was then an appalling task. The medical missionary began healing the swarms of human sufferers, syphilitic, consumptive, and those scourged by small-pox, cholera and hereditary and acute diseases of all sorts. The patience, kindness and persistency of these Christian men literally turned the edge of the sword, disarmed the assassin, made the spies' occupation useless, shamed away the suspicious, and conquered the nearly invincible prejudices of the government. Despite the awful under-tow in the immorality of the sailor, the adventurer and the gain-greedy foreigner, the tide of Christianity began steadily to rise. Notwithstanding the outbursts of the flames of persecution, the torture and imprisonment of Christian captives and exiles, and the slow worrying to death of the missionary's native teachers, inquirers came and converts were made. In 1868, after revolution and restoration, the old order changed, and duarchy and feudalism passed away. Quick to seize the opportunity, Dr. J. C. Hepburn, healer of bodies and souls of men, presented a Bible to the Emperor, and the gift was accepted.

No sooner had the new government been established in safety, and the name of Yedo, the city of the Bay-door, been changed into that of Tōkiō, the Eastern Capital, than an embassy [25] of seventy persons started on its course round the world. At its head were three cabinet ministers of the new government and the court noble, Iwakura, of immemorial lineage, in whose veins ran the blood of the men called gods. Across the Pacific to the United States they went, having their initial audience of the President of the Republic that knows no state church, and whose Christianity had compelled both the return of the shipwrecked Japanese and the freedom of the slave.

This embassy had been suggested and its course planned by a Christian missionary, who found that of the seventy persons, one-half had been his pupils. [26]

The Imperial Embassy Round the World.

The purpose of these envoys was, first of all, to ask of the nations of Christendom equal rights, to get removed the odious extra-territoriality clause in the treaties, to have the right to govern aliens on their soil, and to regulate their own tariff.[27] Secondarily, its members went to study the secrets of power and the resources of civilization in the West, to initiate the liberal education of their women by leaving in American schools a little company of maidens, to enlarge the system of education for their own country, and to send abroad with approval others of their young men who, for a decade past had, in spite of every ban and obstacle, been furtively leaving the country for study beyond the seas.

In the lands of Christendom, the eyes of ambassadors, ministers, secretaries and students were opened. They saw themselves as others saw them. They compared their own land and nation, mediæval in spirit and backward in resources, and their people untrained as children, with the modern power, the restless ambition, the stern purpose, the intense life of the western nations, with their mighty fleets and armaments, their inventions and machinery, their economic and social theories and forces, their provision for the poor, the sick, and the aged, the peerless family life in the Christian home. They found, further yet, free churches divorced from politics and independent of the state; that the leading force of the world was Christianity, that persecution was barbarous, and that toleration was the law of the future, and largely the condition of the present. It took but a few whispers over the telegraphic wire, and the anti-Christian edicts disappeared from public view like snow-flakes melting on the river. The right arm of persecution was broken.[28]

The story of the Book of Acts of the modern apostles in Japan is told, first in the teaching of inquirers, preaching to handfuls, the gathering of tiny companies, the translation of the Gospel, and then prayer and waiting for the descent of the Holy Spirit. A study of the Book of the Acts of the Apostles, followed in order to find out how the Christian Church began. On the 10th day of March, in the year of our Lord and of the era of Meiji (Enlightened Peace) the fifth, 1872, at Yokohama, in the little stone chapel built on part of Commodore Perry's treaty ground, was formed the first Reformed or Protestant Christian Church in Japan.[29]

At this point our task is ended. We cannot even glance at the native Christian churches of the Roman, Reformed, or Greek order, or attempt to appraise the work of the foreign missionaries. He has read these pages in vain, however, who does not see how well, under Providence, the Japanese have been trained for higher forms of faith.

The armies of Japan are upon Chinese soil, while we pen our closing lines. The last chains of purely local and ethnic dogma are being snapped asunder. May the sons of Dai Nippon, as they win new horizons of truth, see more clearly and welcome more loyally that Prince of Peace whose kingdom is not of this world.

May the age of political conquest end, and the era of the self-reformation of the Asian nations, through the gospel of Jesus Christ, be ushered in.

NOTES, AUTHORITIES, AND ILLUSTRA-
TIONS

NOTES, AUTHORITIES, AND ILLUSTRATIONS

THE few abbreviations used in these pages stand for well-known works: T. A. S. J., for Transactions of the Asiatic Society of Japan; Kojiki, for Supplement to Volume X., T. A. S. J., Introduction, Translation, Notes, Map, etc., by Professor Basil Hall Chamberlain; T. J., for Things Japanese (2d ed.), by Professor B. H. Chamberlain; S. and H., for Satow and Hawes's Hand-book for Japan, now continued in new editions (4th, 1894), by Professor B. H. Chamberlain; C. R. M., for Mayers's Chinese Reader's Manual; M. E., The Mikado's Empire (7th ed.); B. N., for Mr. Bunyiu Nanjio's A Short History of the Twelve Japanese Buddhist Sects, Tōkiō, 1887.

CHAPTER I

PRIMITIVE FAITH : RELIGION BEFORE BOOKS

[1] The late Professor Samuel Finley Breese Morse, LL. D., who applied the principles of electro-magnetism to telegraphy, was the son of the Rev. Jedediah Morse, D.D., the celebrated theologian, geographer, and gazetteer. In memory of his father, Professor Morse founded this lectureship in Union Theological Seminary, New York, on "The Relation of the Bible

to the Sciences," May 20, 1865, by the gift of ten thousand dollars.

[2] An American Missionary in Japan, p. 209, by Rev. M. L. Gordon, M.D., Boston, 1892.

[3] Lucretia Coffin Mott.

[4] " I remember once making a calculation in Hong Kong, and making out my baptisms to have amounted to about six hundred. . . . I believe with you that the study of comparative religion is important for all missionaries. Still more important, it seems to me, is it that missionaries should make themselves thoroughly proficient in the languages and literature of the people to whom they are sent."—Dr. Legge's Letter to the Author, November 27, 1893.

[5] The Religions of China, p. 240, by James Legge, New York, 1881.

[6] The Autocrat of the Breakfast Table, p. 22, Boston editions of 1859 and 1879.

[7] One of the many names of Japan is that of the Country Ruled by a Slender Sword, in allusion to the clumsy weapons employed by the Chinese and Koreans. See, for the shortening and lightening of the modern Japanese sword (*katana*) as compared with the long and heavy (*ken*) of the " Divine " (*kami*) or uncivilized age, "The Sword of Japan; Its History and Traditions," T. A. S. J., Vol. II., p. 58.

[8] The course of lectures on The Religions of Chinese Asia (which included most of the matter in this book), given by the author in Bangor Theological Seminary, Bangor, Me., in April, 1894, was upon the Bond foundation, founded by alumni and named after the chief donor, Rev. Elias Bond, D.D., of Kohala, long an active missionary in Hawaii.

[9] This is the contention of Professor Kumi, late of the Imperial University of Japan ; see chapter on Shintō.

[10] In illustration, comical or pitiful, the common people in Satsuma believe that the spirit of the great Saigo Takamori, leader of the rebellion of 1877, " has taken up its abode in the planet Mars," while the spirits of his followers entered into a new race of frogs that attack man and fight until killed.—Mounsey's The Satsuma Rebellion, p. 217. So, also, the *Heiké-gani*, or crabs at Shimonoséki, represent the transmigration of the souls of the Heiké clan, nearly exterminated in 1184 A.D., while the " Hōjō bugs " are the avatars of the execrated rulers of Kamakura (1219–1333 A.D.). —Japan in History, Folk-lore, and Art, Boston, 1892, pp. 115, 133.

[11] The Future of Religion in Japan. A paper read at the Parliament of Religions by Nobuta Kishimoto.

[12] " The Ainos, though they deify all the chief objects of nature, such as the sun, the sea, fire, wild beasts, etc., often talk of a Creator, *Kotan kara kamui*, literally the God who made the World. At the fact of creation they stop short. . . . One gathers that the creative act was performed not directly, but through intermediaries, who were apparently animals." —Chamberlain's Aino Studies, p. 12. See also on the Aino term " Kamui," by Professor B. H. Chamberlain and Rev. J. Batchelor, T. A. S. J., Vol. XVI.

[13] See Unbeaten Tracks in Japan, by Isabella Bird (Bishop), Vol. II. ; The Ainu of Japan, by Rev. John Batchelor ; B. Douglas Howard's Life With Trans-Siberian Savages ; Ripley Hitchcock's Report, Smithsonian Institute, Washington. Professor B. H. Cham-

berlain's invaluable "Aino Studies," Tōkiō, 1887, makes scholarly comparison of the Japanese and Aino language, mythology, and geographical nomenclature.

[14] M. E., The Mythical Zoölogy of Japan, pp. 477–488. C. R. M., *passim.*

[15] See the valuable article entitled Demoniacal Possession, T. J., p. 106, and the author's Japanese Fox Myths, *Lippincott's Magazine*, 1873.

[16] See the Aino animal stories and evidences of beast worship in Chamberlain's Aino Studies. For this element in Japanese life, see the Kojiki, and the author's Japanese Fairy World.

[17] The proprietor of a paper-mill in Massachusetts, who had bought a cargo of rags, consisting mostly of farmers' cast off clothes, brought to the author a bundle of scraps of paper which he had found in this cheap blue - dyed cotton wearing apparel. Besides money accounts and personal matters, there were numerous temple amulets and priests' certificates. See also B. H. Chamberlain's Notes on Some Minor Japanese Religious Practices, *Journal of the Anthropological Institute*, May, 1893.

[18] M. E., p. 440.

[19] See the Lecture on Buddhism in its Doctrinal Development.—The Nichiren Sect.

[20] The phallus was formerly a common emblem in all parts of Japan, Hondo, Kiushiu, Shikoku, and the other islands. Bayard Taylor noticed it in the Riu Kiu (Loo Choo) Islands; Perry's Expedition to Japan, p. 196; Bayard Taylor's Expedition in Lew Chew; M. E., p. 33, note; Rein's Japan, p. 432; Diary of Richard Cocks, Vol. I., p. 283. The native guide-books and gazetteers do not allude to the subject.

Although the author of this volume has collected considerable data from personal observations and the testimony of personal friends concerning the vanishing nature-worship of the Japanese, he has, in the text, scarcely more than glanced at the subject. In a work of this sort, intended both for the general reader as well as for the scientific student of religion, it has been thought best to be content with a few simple references to what was once widely prevalent in the Japanese archipelago.

Probably the most thorough study of Japanese phallicism yet made by any foreign scholar is that of Edmund Buckley, A.M., Ph.D., of the Chicago University, Lecturer on Shintō, the Ethnic Faith of Japan, and on the Science of Religion. Dr. Buckley spent six years in central and southwestern Japan, most of the time as instructor in the Doshisha University, Kiōto. He will publish the results of his personal observations and studies in a monograph on phallicism, which will be on sale at Chicago University, in which the Buckley collection illustrating Shintō-worship has been deposited.

[21] Mr. Takahashi Gorō, in his Shintō Shin-ron, or New Discussion of Shinto, accepts the derivation of the word *kami* from *kabé*, mould, mildew, which, on its appearance, excites wonder. For Hirata's discussion, see T. A. S. J., Vol. III., Appendix, p. 48. In a striking paper on the Early Gods of Japan, in a recent number of the Philosophical Magazine, published in Tōkiō, a Japanese writer, Mr. Kenjirō Hiradé, states also that the term kami does not necessarily denote a spiritual being, but is only a relative term meaning above or high, but this respect toward something high or above

has created many imaginary deities as well as those having a human history. See also T. A. S. J., Vol. XXII., Part I., p. 55, note.

[22] " There remains something of the Shintō heart after twelve hundred years of foreign creeds and dress. The worship of the marvellous continues. . . . Exaggerated force is most impressive. . . . So the ancient gods, heroes, and wonders are worshipped still. The simple countryfolk clap their hands, bow their heads, mumble their prayers, and offer the fraction of a cent to the first European-built house they see."—Philosophy in Japan, Past and Present, by Dr. George Wm. Knox.

[23] M. E., p. 474. Honda the Samurai, pp. 256–267.

[24] Kojiki, pp. 127, 136, 213, 217.

[25] See S. and H., pp. 39, 76.

" The appearance of anything unusual at a particular spot is held to be a sure sign of the presence of divinity. Near the spot where I live in Ko-ishi-kawa, Tōkiō, is a small Miya, built at the foot of a very old tree, that stands isolated on the edge of a rice-field. The spot looks somewhat insignificant, but upon inquiring why a shrine has been placed there, I was told that a white snake had been found at the foot of the old tree." . . .

" As it is, the religion of the Japanese consists in the belief that the productive ethereal spirit, being expanded through the whole universe, every part is in some degree impregnated with it ; and therefore, every part is in some measure the seat of the Deity." —Legendre's Progressive Japan, p. 258.

[26] De Verflauwing der Grenzen, by Dr. Abraham

Kuyper, Amsterdam, 1892; translated by Rev. T. Hendrik de Vries, in the Methodist Review, New York, July–Sept., 1893.

CHAPTER II

SHINTŌ: MYTHS AND RITUAL

[1] The scholar who has made profound researches in all departments of Japanese learning, but especially in the literature of Shintō, is Mr. Ernest Satow, now the British Minister at Tangier. He received the degree of B.A. from the London University. After several years' study and experience in China, Mr. Satow came to Japan in 1861 as student-interpreter to the British Legation, receiving his first drill under Rev. S. R. Brown, D.D., author of A Grammar of Colloquial Japanese. To ceaseless industry, this scholar, to whom the world is so much indebted for knowledge of Japan, has added philosophic insight. Besides unearthing documents whose existence was unsuspected, he has cleared the way for investigators and comparative students by practically removing the barriers reared by archaic speech and writing. His papers in the T. A. S. J., on The Shintō Shrines at Isé, the Revival of Pure Shintō, and Ancient Japanese Rituals, together with his Hand-book for Japan, form the best collection of materials for the study of the original and later forms of Shintō.

[2] The scholar who above all others has, with rare acumen united to laborious and prolonged toil, illuminated the subject of Japan's chronology and early his-

tory is Mr. W. G. Aston of the British Civil Service. He studied at the Queen's University, Ireland, receiving the degree of M.A. He was appointed student-interpreter in Japan, August 6, 1864. He is the author of a Grammar of the Written Japanese Language, and has been a student of the comparative history and speech and writing of China, Korea, and Japan, during the past thirty years. See his valuable papers in the T. A. S. J., and the learned societies in Great Britain. In his paper on Early Japanese History, T. A. S. J., Vol. XVI., pp. 39–75, he recapitulates the result of his researches, in which he is, in the main, supported by critical native scholars, and by the late William Bramsen, in his Japanese Chronological Tables, Tōkiō, 1880. He considers A.D. 461 as the first trustworthy date in the Japanese annals. We quote from his paper, Early Japanese History, T. A. S. J., Vol. XVI., p. 73.

1. The earliest date of the accepted Japanese Chronology, the accuracy of which is confirmed by external evidence, is A.D. 461.

2. Japanese History, properly so called, can hardly be said to exist previous to A.D. 500. (A cursory examination leads me to think that the annals of the sixth century must also be received with caution.)

3. Korean History and Chronology are more trustworthy than those of Japan during the period previous to that date.

4. While there was an Empress of Japan in the third century A.D., the statement that she conquered Korea is highly improbable.

5. Chinese learning was introduced into Japan from Korea 120 years later than the date given in Japanese History.

6. The main fact of Japan having a predominant influence in some parts of Korea during the fifth century is confirmed by the Korean and Chinese chronicles, which, however, show that the Japanese accounts are very inaccurate in matters of detail.

[3] Basil Hall Chamberlain, who has done the world of learning such signal service by his works on the Japanese language, and especially by his translation, with critical introduction and commentary, of the Kojiki, is an English gentleman, born at Southsea, Hampshire, England, on the 18th day of October, 1830. His mother was a daughter of the well-known traveller and author, Captain Basil Hall, R.N., and his father an Admiral in the British Navy. He was educated for Oxford, but instead of entering, for reasons of health, he spent a number of years in western and southern Europe, acquiring a knowledge of various languages and literatures. His coming to Japan (in May, 1873) was rather the result of an accident—a long sea voyage and a trial of the Japanese climate having been recommended. The country and the field of study suited the invalid well. After teaching for a time in the Naval College the Japanese honored themselves and this scholar by making him, in April, 1886, Professor of Philology at the Imperial University. His works, The Classical Poetry of the Japanese, his various grammars and hand-books for the acquisition of the language, his Hand-book for Japan, his Aino Studies, Things Japanese, papers in the T. A. S. J. and his translation of the Kojiki are all of a high order of value. They are marked by candor, fairness, insight, and a mastery of difficult themes that makes his readers his constant debtors.

25

[4] " If the term ' Altaic ' be held to include Korean and Japanese, then Japanese assumes prime importance as being by far the oldest living representative of that great linguistic group, its literature antedating by many centuries the most ancient productions of the Manchus, Mongols, Turks, Hungarians, or Finns." —Chamberlain, Simplified Grammar, Introd., p. vi.

[5] Corea, the Hermit Nation, pp. 13–14 ; Mr. Pom K. Soh's paper on Education in Korea ; Report of U. S. Commissioner of Education, 1890–91.

[6] T. A. S. J., Vol. XVI., p. 74; Bramsen's Chronological Tables, Introd., p. 34 ; T. J., p. 32.

[7] The Middle Kingdom, Vol. I., p. 531.

[8] " The frog in the well knows not the great ocean." This proverb, so freely quoted throughout Chinese Asia, and in recent years so much applied to themselves by the Japanese, is of Hindu origin and is found in the Sanskrit.

[9] This is shown with literary skill and power in a modern popular work, the title of which, Dai Nippon Kai-biyaku Yurai-iki, which, very freely indeed, may be translated Instances of Divine Interposition in Behalf of Great Japan. A copy of this work was presented to the writer by the late daimiō of Echizen, and was read with interest as containing the common people's ideas about their country and history. It was published in Yedo in 1856, while Japan was still excited over the visits of the American and European fleets. On the basis of the information furnished in this work General Le Gendre wrote his influential book, Progressive Japan, in which a number of quotations from the *Kai-biyaku* may be read.

[10] In the Kojiki, pp. 101–104, we have the poetical

account of the abdication of the lord of Idzumo in favor of the Yamato conqueror, on condition that the latter should build a temple and have him honored among the gods. One of the rituals contains the congratulatory address of the chieftains of Idzumo, on their surrender to "the first Mikado, Jimmu Tennō." See also T. J., p. 206.

[11] "The praying for Harvest, or Toshigoi no Matsuri, was celebrated on the 4th day of the 2d month of each year, at the capital in the Jin-Gi-Kuan or office for the Worship of the Shintō gods, and in the provinces by the chiefs of the local administrations. At the Jin-Gi-Kuan there were assembled the ministers of state, the functionaries of that office, the priests and priestesses of 573 temples, containing 737 shrines, which were kept up at the expense of the Mikado's treasury, while the governors of the provinces superintended in the districts under their administration the performance of rites in honor of 2,395 other shrines. It would not be easy to state the exact number of deities to whom these 3,132 shrines were dedicated. A glance over the list in the 9th and 10th books of the Yengishiki shows at once that there were many gods who were worshipped in more than half-a-dozen different localities at the same time; but exact calculation is impossible, because in many cases only the names of the temples are given, and we are left quite in the dark as to the individuality of the gods to whom they were sacred. Besides these 3,132 shrines, which are distinguished as Shikidai, that is contained in the catalogue of the Yengishiki, there were a large number of enumerated shrines in temples scattered all over the country, in every village or ham-

let, of which it was impossible to take any account,
just as at the present day there are temples of Hachiman, Kompira, Tenjin sama, San-no sama- and Sen-
gen sama, as they are popularly called, wherever
twenty or thirty houses are collected together. The
shrines are classed as great and small, the respective
numbers being 492 and 2,640, the distinction being
twofold, firstly in the proportionately larger quantity
of offerings made at the great shrines, and secondly
that the offerings in the one case were arranged upon
tables or altars, while in the other they were placed
on mats spread upon the earth. In the Yengishiki the
amounts and nature of the offerings are stated with
great minuteness, but it will be sufficient if the kinds
of articles offered are alone mentioned here. It will
be seen, by comparison with the text of the norito,
that they had varied somewhat since the date when
the ritual was composed. The offerings to a greater
shrine consisted of coarse woven silk (*ashiginu*), thin
silk of five different colors, a kind of stuff called *shi-
dori* or *shidzu*, which is supposed by some to have
been a striped silk, cloth of broussonetia bark or
hemp, and a small quantity of the raw materials of
which the cloth was made, models of swords, a pair of
tables or altars (called *yo-kura-oki* and *ya-kura-oki*), a
shield or mantlet, a spear-head, a bow, a quiver, a
pair of stag's horns, a hoe, a few measures of saké or
rice-beer, some haliotis and bonito, two measures of
kitali (supposed to be salt roe), various kinds of edi-
ble seaweed, a measure of salt, a saké jar, and a few
feet of matting for packing. To each of the temples
of Watarai in Isé was presented in addition a horse ;
to the temple of the Harvest god Mitoshi no kami, a

white horse, cock, and pig, and a horse to each of nine-teen others.

" During the fortnight which preceded the celebration of the service, two smiths and their journeymen, and two carpenters, together with eight inbe [or hereditary priests] were employed in preparing the apparatus and getting ready the offerings. It was usual to employ for the Praying for Harvest members of this tribe who held office in the Jin-Gi-Kuan, but if the number could not be made up in that office, it was supplied from other departments of state. To the tribe of quiver-makers was intrusted the special duty of weaving the quivers of wistaria tendrils. The service began at twenty minutes to seven in the morning, by our reckoning of time. After the governor of the province of Yamashiro had ascertained that everything was in readiness, the officials of the Jin-Gi-Kuan arranged the offerings on the tables and below them, according to the rank of the shrines for which they were intended. The large court of the Jin-Gi-Kuan where the service was held, called the Sai-in, measured 230 feet by 370. At one end were the offices and on the west side were the shrines of the eight Protective Deities in a row, surrounded by a fence, to the interior of which three sacred archways (torii) gave access. In the centre of the court a temporary shed was erected for the occasion, in which the tables or altars were placed. The final preparations being now complete, the ministers of state, the virgin priestesses and priests of the temples to which offerings were sent by the Mikado, entered in succession, and took the places severally assigned to them. The horses which formed a part of the offerings were next brought in from the

Mikado's stable, and all the congregation drew near, while the reader recited or read the norito. This reader was a member of the priestly family or tribe of Nakatomi, who traced their descent back to Amenokoyané, one of the principal advisers attached to the sun-goddess's grandchild when he first descended on earth. It is a remarkable evidence of the persistence of certain ideas, that up to the year 1868 the nominal prime-minister of the Mikado, after he came of age, and the regent during his minority, if he had succeeded young to the throne, always belonged to this tribe, which changed its name from Nakatomi to Fujiwara in the seventh century, and was subsequently split up into the Five Setsuké or governing families. At the end of each section the priests all responded ' O! ' which was no doubt the equivalent of ' Yes ' in use in those days. As soon as he had finished, the Nakatomi retired, and the offerings were distributed to the priests for conveyance and presentation to the gods to whose service they were attached. But a special messenger was despatched with the offerings destined to the temples at Watarai. This formality having been completed, the President of the Jin-Gi-Kuan gave the signal for breaking up the assembly."—Ancient Japanese Rituals, T. A. S. J., Vol. VII., pp. 104–107.

[12] S. and H., p. 461

[13] Consult Chamberlain's literal translations of the name in the Kojiki, and p. lxv. of his Introduction.

[14] The parallel between the Hebrew and Japanese accounts of light and darkness, day and night, before the sun, has been noticed by several writers. See the comments of Hirata, a modern Shintō expounder.— T. A. S. J., Vol. III., Appendix, p. 72.

[15] Westminster Review, July, 1878, p. 19.

CHAPTER III

"THE KOJIKI" AND ITS TEACHINGS

[1] Kojiki, pp. 9–13 ; T. A. S. J., Vol. III., Appendix, p. 20.

[2] M. E., p. 43 ; McClintock and Strong's Cyclopedia, Art. Shintō; in T. A. S. J., Vol. III., Appendix, is to be found Mr. Satow's digest of the commentaries of the modern Shintō revivalists; in Mr. Chamberlain's translation of the Kojiki, the text with abundant notes. See also Mr. Twan-Lin's Account of Japan up to A.D. 1200, by E. H. Parker. T. A. S. J., Vol. XXII., Part I.

[3] " The various abstractions which figure at the commencement of the ' Records ' (Kojiki) and of the ' Chronicles ' (Nihongi) were probably later growths, and perhaps indeed were inventions of individual priests."—Kojiki, Introd., p. lxv. See also T. A. S. J., Vol. XXII., Part I, p. 56. " Thus, not only is this part of the Kojiki pure twaddle, but it is not even consistent twaddle."

[4] Kojiki, Section IX.

[5] Dr. Joseph Edkins, D.D., author of Chinese Buddhism, who believes that the primeval religious history of men is recoverable, says in Early Spread of Religious Ideas, Especially in the Far East, p. 29, " In Japan Amatérasŭ, . . . in fact, as I suppose, Mithras written in Japanese, though the Japanese themselves are not aware of this etymology." Compare Kojiki, Introduction, pp. lxv.–lxvii.

[6] Kojiki, p. xlii.

[7] T. A. S. J., Vol. III., Appendix, p. 67.

[8] E. Satow, Revival of Pure Shintō, pp. 67–68.

[9] This curious agreement between the Japanese and other ethnic traditions in locating " Paradise," the origin of the human family and of civilization, at the North Pole, has not escaped the attention of Dr. W. F. Warren, President of Boston University, who makes extended reference to it in his interesting and sugges- tive book, Paradise Found : The Cradle of the Human Race at the North Pole; A Study of the Prehistoric World, Boston, 1885.

[10] The pure Japanese numerals equal in number the fingers ; with the borrowed Chinese terms vast amounts can be expressed.

[11] This custom was later revived, T. A. S. J., pp. 28, 31. Mitford's Tales of Old Japan, Vol. II., p. 57 ; M. E., pp. 156, 238.

[12] See in Japanese Fairy World, "How the Sun-Goddess was enticed out of her Cave." For the nar- rative see Kojiki, pp. 54–59; T. A. S. J., Vol. II., 128–133.

[13] See Choméi and Wordsworth, A Literary Par- allel, by J. M. Dixon, T. A. S. J., Vol. XX., pp. 193– 205 ; Anthologie Japonaise, by Leon de Rosny ; Chamberlain's Classical Poetry of the Japanese ; Suyématsŭ's Genji Monogatari, London, 1882.

[14] Oftentimes in studying the ancient rituals, those who imagine that the word Kami should be in all cases translated gods, will be surprised to see what puerility, bathos, or grandiloquence, comes out of an attempt to express a very simple, it may be humiliating, experience.

[15] Mythology and Religious Worship of the Japan-

ese, Westminster Review, July, 1878 ; Ancient Japanese Rituals, T. A. S. J., Vols. VII., IX. ; Esoteric Shintō, by Percival Lowell, T. A. S. J., Vol. XXI.

[16] Compare Sections IX. and XXIII. of the Kojiki.

[17] This indeed seems to be the substance of the modern official expositions of Shintō and the recent Rescripts of the Emperor, as well as of much popular literature, including the manifestoes or confessions found on the persons of men who have " consecrated " themselves as " the instruments of Heaven for punishing the wicked," *i.e.,* assassinating obnoxious statesmen. See The Ancient Religion, M. E., pp. 96–100 ; The Japan Mail, *passim.*

[18] Revival of Pure Shintō, pp. 25–38.

[19] Japanese Homes, by E. S. Morse, pp. 228–233, note, p. 332.

[20] Chamberlain's Aino Studies, p. 12.

[21] Geological Survey of Japan, by Benj. S. Lyman, 1878–9.

[22] The Shell Mounds of Omori ; and The Tokio Times, Jan. 18, 1879, by Edward S. Morse ; Japanese Fairy World, pp. 178, 191, 196.

[23] Kojiki, pp. 60–63.

[24] S. and H., pp. 58, 337, etc.

[25] This study in comparative religion by a Japanese, which cost the learned author his professorship in the Téi-Koku Dai Gaku or Imperial University (lit. Theocratic Country Great Learning Place), has had a tendency to chill the ardor of native investigators. His paper was first published in the Historical Magazine of the University, but the wide publicity and popular excitement followed only after republication, with comments by Mr. Taguchi, in the Kéizai Zasshi (Econo-

mical Journal). The Shintōists denounced Professor Kumi for "making our ancient religion a branch of Christianity," and demanded and secured his "retirement" by the Government. See Japan Mail, April 2, 1892, p. 440.

²⁶ T. A. S. J., Vol. XXI., p. 282.

²⁷ Kojiki, p. xxviii.

²⁸ For the use of salt in modern "Esoteric" Shintō, both in purification and for employment as of salamandrine, see T. A. S. J., pp. 125, 128.

²⁹ In the official census of 1893, nine Shintō sects are named, each of which has its own Kwancho or Presiding Head, recognized by the government. The sectarian peculiarities of Shintō have been made the subject of study by very few foreigners. Mr. Satow names the following:

The Yui-itsu sect was founded by Yoshida Kané-tomo. His signature appears as the end of a ten-volume edition, issued A.D. 1503, of the liturgies extracted from the Yengishiki or Book of Ceremonial Law, first published in the era of Yengi (or En-gi), A.D. 901–922. He is supposed to be the one who added the *kana*, or common vernacular script letters, to the Chinese text and thus made the norito accessible to the people. The little pocket prayer-books, folded in an accordeon-like manner, are very cheap and popular. The sect is regarded as heretical by strict Shintōists, as the system Yuwiitsu consists "mainly of a Buddhist superstructure on a Shintō foundation." Yoshida applied the tenets of the Shingon or True Word sect of Buddhists to the understanding and practice of the ancient god-way.

The Suiga sect teaches a system which is a combination of Yuwiitsu and of the modern philosophical form of Confucianism as elaborated by Chu Hi, and known in Japan as the Téj-shu philosophy. The founder was Yamazaki Ansai, who was born in 1618 and died in 1682. By combining the forms of the Yoshida sect, which is based on the Buddhism of the Shingon sect, with the materialistic philosophy of Chu Hi, he adapted the old god-way to what he deemed modern needs.

In the Déguchi sect, the ancient belief is explained by the Chinese Book of Changes (or Divination). Déguchi Nobuyoshi, the founder, was god-warden or *kannushi* of the Géiku or Outer Palace Temple at Isé. He promulgated his views about the year 1660, basing them upon the book called Éki by the Japanese and Yi-king by the Chinese. This Yi-king, which Professor Terrien de Lacouperie declares is only a very ancient book of pronunciation of comparative Accadian and Chinese Syllabaries, has been the cause of incredible waste of labor, time, and brains in China —enough to have diked the Yellow River or drained the swamps of the Empire. It is the chief basis of Chinese superstition, and the greatest literary barrier to the advance of civilization. It has also made much mischief in Japan. Déguchi explained the myths of the age of the gods by divination or éki, based on the Chinese books. As late as 1893 there was published in Tōkiō a work in Japanese, with good translation into English, on Scientific Morality, or the practical guidance of life by means of divination—The Takashima Ékidan (or Monograph on the Éki of Mr. Takashima), by S. Sugiura.

The Jikko sect, according to its representative at

the World's Parliament of Religions at Chicago, is
"the practical." It lays stress less upon speculation
and ritual, and more upon the realization of the best
teachings of Shintō. It was founded by Haségawa
Kakugiō, who was born at Nagasaki in 1541. Living
in a cave in Fuji-yama, "he received inspiration
through the miraculous power of the mountain." It
believes in one absolute Deity, often mentioned in the
Kojiki, which, self-originated, took the embodiment
of two deities, one with the male nature and the other
female, though these two deities are nothing but forms
of the one substance and unite again in the absolute
deity. These gave birth to the Japanese Archipelago,
the sun and moon, the mountains and streams, the
divine ancestors, etc. According to the teachings of
this sect, the peerless mountain, Fuji, ought to be reverenced as the sacred abode of the divine lord, and as
"the brains of the whole globe." The believer must
make Fuji the example and emblem of his thought and
action. He must be plain and simple, as the form of
the mountain, making his body and mind pure and
serene, as Fuji itself. The present world with all its
practical works must be respected more than the
future world. We must pray for the long life of the
country, lead a life of temperance and diligence, co-
operating with one another in doing good.

Statistics of Shintōism.

From the official Résumé Statistique de l'Empire
du Japon, 1894. In 1891 there were nine administrative heads of sects; 75,877 preachers, priests, and
shrine-keepers, with 1,158 male and 228 female stu-

dents. There were 163 national temples of superior rank and 136,652 shrines or temples in cities and prefectures; a total of 193,153, served by 14,700 persons of the grade of priests. Most of the expenses, apart from endowments and local contributions, are included in the first item of the annual Treasury Budget, " Civil List, Appanage and Shintō Temples."

CHAPTER IV

THE CHINESE ETHICAL SYSTEM IN JAPAN

[1] " He was fond of saying that Princeton had never originated a new idea; but this meant no more than that Princeton was the advocate of historical Calvinism in opposition to the modified and provincial Calvinism of a later day."—Francis L. Patton, in Schaff-Herzog Encyclopædia, Article on Charles Hodge.

[2] We use Dr. James Legge's spelling, by whom these classics have been translated into English. See Sacred Books of the East, edited by Max Müller.

[3] The Canon or Four Classics has a somewhat varied literary history of transmission, collection, and redaction, as well as of exposition, and of criticism, both "lower" and " higher." As arranged under the Han Dynasty (B.C. 206–A.D. 23) it consisteα of—I. The Commentary of Tso Kiuming (a disciple who expounded Confucius's book, The Annals of State of Lu); II. The Commentary of Kuh-liang upon the same work of Confucius; III. The Old Text of the Book of History; IV. The Odes, collected by Mao Chang, to whom is ascribed the text of the Odes as handed down to

the present day. The generally accepted arrangement is that made by the mediæval schoolmen of the Sung Dynasty (A.D. 960–1341), Cheng Teh Sio and Chu Hi, in the twelfth century : I. The Great Learning ; II. The Doctrine of the Mean ; III. Conversations of Confucius ; IV. The Sayings of Mencius.—C. R. M., pp. 306–309.

[4] See criticisms of Confucius as an author, in Legge's Religions of China, pp. 144, 145.

[5] Religions of China, by James Legge, p. 140.

[6] See Article China, by the author, Cyclopædia of Political Science, Chicago, 1881.

[7] This subject is critically discussed by Messrs. Satow, Chamberlain, and others in their writings on Shintō and Japanese history. On Japanese chronology, see Japanese Chronological Tables, by William Bramsen, Tōkiō, 1880, and Dr. David Murray's Japan (p. 95), in the series Story of the Nations, New York.

[8] The absurd claim made by some Shintōists that the Japanese possessed an original native alphabet called the Shingi (god-letters) before the entrance of the Chinese or Buddhist learning in Japan, is refuted by Aston, Japanese Grammar, p. 1 ; T. A. S. J., Vol. III., Appendix, p. 77. Mr. Satow shows " their unmistakable identity with the Corean alphabet."

[9] For the life, work, and tombs of the Chinese scholars who fled to Japan on the fall of the Ming Dynasty, see M. E., p. 298 ; and Professor E. W. Clement's paper on The Tokugawa Princes of Mito, T. A. S. J., Vol. XVIII., and his letters in The Japan Mail.

[10] " We have consecrated ourselves as the instruments of Heaven for punishing the wicked man,"—from the document submitted to the Yedo authorities, by the

assassins of Ii Kamon no Kami, in Yedo, March 23, 1861, and signed by seventeen men of the band. For numerous other instances, see the voluminous literature of the Forty-seven Ronins, and the Meiji political literature (1868–1893), political and historical documents, assassins' confessions, etc., contained in that thesarus of valuable documents, The Japan Mail ; Kinsé Shiriaku, or Brief History of Japan, 1853–1869, Yokohama, 1873, and Nihon Guaishi, translated by Mr. Ernest Satow ; Adams's History of Japan ; T. A. S. J., Vol. XX., p. 145 ; Life and Letters of Yokoi, Héishiro ; Life of Sir Harry Parkes, London, 1893, etc., for proof of this assertion.

[11] For proof of this, as to vocabulary, see Professor B. H. Chamberlain's Grammars and other philological works; Mr. J. H. Gubbins's Dictionary of Chinese-Japanese Words, with Introduction, three vols., Tōkiō, 1892 ; and for change in structure, Rev. C. Munzinger, on The Psychology of the Japanese Language in the Transactions of the German Asiatic Society of Japan. See also Mental Characteristics of the Japanese, T. A. S. J., Vol. XIX., pp. 17–37.

[12] See The Ghost of Sakura, in Mitford's Tales of Old Japan, Vol. II., p. 17.

[13] M. E., 277–280. See an able analysis of Japanese feudal society, by M. F. Dickins, Life of Sir Harry Parkes, pp. 8–13 ; M. E., pp. 277–283.

[14] This subject is discussed in Professor Chamberlain's works ; Mr. Percival Lowell's The Soul of the Far East; Dr. M. L. Gordon's An American Missionary in Japan; Dr. J. H. De Forest's The Influence of Pantheism, in The Japan Evangelist, 1894.

[15] T. A. S. J., Vol. XVII., p. 96.

[16] The Forty Seven-Ronins, Tales of Old Japan, Vol. I. ; Chiushiugura, by F. V. Dickens ; The Loyal Ronins, by Edward Greey ; Chiushiugura, translated by Enouyé.

[17] See Dr. J. H. De Forest's article in the Andover Review, May, June, 1893, p. 309. For details and instances, see the Japanese histories, novels, and dramas ; M. E. ; Rein's Japan ; S. and H. ; T. A. S. J., etc. Life of Sir Harry Parkes, p. 11 *et passim.*

[18] M. E., pp. 180–192, 419. For the origin and meaning of hara-kiri, see T. J., pp. 199–201 ; Mitford's Tales of Old Japan, Vol. I., Appendix ; Adams's History of Japan, story of Shimadzŭ Séiji.

[19] M. E., p. 133.

[20] For light upon the status of the Japanese family, see F. O. Adams's History of Japan, Vol. II., p. 334 ; Kinsé Shiriaku, p. 137 ; Naomi Tamura, The Japanese Bride, New York, 1893 ; E. H. House, Yoné Santo, A Child of Japan, Chicago, 1888 ; Japanese Girls and Women, by Miss A. M. Bacon, Boston, 1891 ; T. J., Article Woman, and in Index, Adoption, Children, etc. ; M. E., 1st ed., p. 585 ; Marriage in Japan, T. A. S. J., Vol. XIII., p. 114 ; and papers in the German Asiatic Society of Japan.

[21] See Mr. F. W. Eastlake's papers in the Popular Science Monthly.

[22] See Life of Sir Harry Parkes, Vol. II., pp. 181–182. " It is to be feared, however, that this reform [of the Yoshiwara system], like many others in Japan, never got beyond paper, for Mr. Norman in his recent book, The Real Japan [Chap. XII.], describes a scarcely modified system in full vigor." See also Japanese Girls and Women, pp. 289–292.

[23] See Pung Kwang Yu's paper, read at the Parliament of Religions in Chicago, and The Chinese as Painted by Themselves, by Colonel Tcheng - Ki-Tong, New York and London, 1885. Dr. W. A. P. Martin's scholarly book, The Chinese, New York, 1881, in the chapter Remarks on the Ethical Philosophy of the Chinese, gives in English and Chinese a Chart of Chinese Ethics in which the whole scheme of philosophy, ethics, and self-culture is set forth.

[24] See an exceedingly clear, able, and accurate article on The Ethics of Confucius as Seen in Japan, by the veteran scholar, Rev. J. H. De Forest, The Andover Review, May, June, 1893. He is the authority for the statements concerning non-attendance (in Old Japan) of the husband at the wife's, and older brother at younger brother's funeral.

[25] A Japanese translation of Mrs. Caudle's Curtain Lectures, in a Tōkiō morning newspaper "met with instant and universal approval," showing that Douglas Jerrold's world-famous character has her counterpart in Japan, where, as a Japanese proverb declares, "the tongue three inches long can kill a man six feet high." Sir Edwin Arnold and Mr. E. H. House, in various writings, have idealized the admirable traits of the Japanese woman. See also Mr. Lafcadio Hearn's Glimpses of Unfamiliar Japan, Boston, 1894; and papers (The Eternal Feminine, etc.), in the Atlantic Monthly.

[26] Summary of the Japanese Penal Codes, T. A. S. J., Vol. V., Part II. ; The Penal Code of Japan, and The Code of Criminal Procedure of Japan, Yokohama.

[27] See T. A. S. J., Vol. XIII., p. 114; the Chapter on Marriage and Divorce, in Japanese Girls and Women,

pp. 57–84. The following figures are from the Résumé Statistique de l'Empire du Japon, published annually by the Imperial Government:

	MARRIAGES.		DIVORCES.	
	Number.	Per 1,000 Persons.	Number.	Per 1,000 Persons.
1887....	334,149	8.55	110,859	2.84
1888....	330,246	8.34	109,175	2.76
1889....	340,445	8.50	107,458	2.68
1890....	325,141	8.04	197,088	2.70
1891....	352,651	8.00	112,411	2.76
1892....	348,489	8.48	113,498	2.76

[28] This was strikingly brought out in the hundreds of English compositions (written by students of the Imperial University, 1872–74, describing the home or individual life of students), examined and read by the author.

[29] Homo sum : humani nil a me alienum puto— Héauton Tomoroumenos, Act —, Scene 1, line 25, where Chremes inquires about his neighbor's affairs. For the golden rule of Jesus and the silver rule of Confucius, see Doolittle's Social Life of the Chinese.

[30] "What you do not want done to yourselves, do not do to others." Legge, The Religions of China, p. 137 ; Doolittle's Social Life of the Chinese ; The Testament of Iyéyasŭ, Cap. LXXI., translated by J. C. Lowder, Yokohama, 1874.

[31] Die politische Bedeutung der amerikanischer Expedition nach Japan, 1852, by Tetsutaro Yoshida, Heidelberg, 1893 ; The United States and Japan (p. 39), by Inazo Nitobé, Baltimore, 1891 ; Matthew Calbraith Perry, Chap. XXVIII. ; T. J., Article Perry ; Life and Letters of S. Wells Williams, New York, 1889.

[32] See Life of Matthew Calbraith Perry, pp. 363, 364.

[33] Lee's Jerusalem Illustrated, p. 88.

CHAPTER V

CONFUCIANISM IN ITS PHILOSOPHICAL FORM

[1] See On the Early History of Printing in Japan, by E. M. Satow, T. A. S. J., Vol. X., pp. 1–83, 252–259 ; The Jesuit Mission Press in Japan, by E. M. Satow (privately printed, 1888), and Review of this monograph by Professor B. H. Chamberlain, T. A. S. J., Vol. XVII., pp. 91–100.

[2] The Tokugawa Princes of Mito, by Ernest W. Clement, T. A. S. J., Vol. XVIII., pp. 1–24, and Letters in The Japan Mail, 1889.

[3] Effect of Buddhism on the Philosophy of the Sung Dynasty, p. 318, Chinese Buddhism, by Rev. J. Edkins, Boston, 1880.

[4] C. R. M., p. 200 ; The Middle Kingdom, by S. Wells Williams, Vol. II., p. 174.

[5] C. R. M., p. 34. He was the boy-hero, who smashed with a stone the precious water-vase in order to save from drowning a playmate who had tumbled in, so often represented in Chinese popular art.

[6] C. R. M., pp. 25–26 ; The Middle Kingdom, Vol. I., pp. 113, 540, 652–654, 677.

[7] This decade in Chinese history was astonishingly like that of the United States from 1884 to 1894, in which the economical theories advocated in certain

journals, in the books Progress and Poverty, Looking Backward, and by the Populists, have been so widely read and discussed, and the attempts made to put them into practice. The Chinese theorist of the eleventh century, Wang Ngan-shih was "a poet and author of rare genius."—C. R. M., p. 244.

[8] John xxi. 25.

[9] This is the opinion of no less capable judges than Dr. George Wm. Knox and Professor Basil Hall Chamberlain.

[10] The United States and Japan, pp. 25–27 ; Life of Takano Choyéi by Kato Sakayé, Tōkiō, 1888.

[11] Note on Japanese Schools of Philosophy, by T. Haga, and papers by Dr. G. W. Knox, Dr. T. Inoué, T. A. S. J., Vol. XX., Part I.

[12] A religion, surely, with men like Yokoi Héishiro.

[13] See pp. 110–113.

[14] *Kinno*—loyalty to the Emperor ; T. A. S. J., Vol. XX., p. 147.

[15] " Originally recognizing the existence of a Supreme personal Deity, it [Confucianism] has degenerated into a pantheistic medley, and renders worship to an impersonal *anima mundi* under the leading forms of visible nature."—Dr. W. A. P. Martin's The Chinese, p. 108.

[16] Ki, Ri, and Ten, Dr. George Wm. Knox, T. A. S. J., Vol. XX., pp. 155–177.

[17] T. J., p. 94.

[18] T. A. S. J., Vol. XX., p. 156.

[19] Matthew Calbraith Perry, p. 373 ; Japanese Life of Yoshida Shoin, by Tokutomi, Tōkiō, 1894 ; Life of Sir Harry Parkes, Vol. II., p. 83.

[20] " The Chinese accept Confucius in every detail,

both as taught by Confucius and by his disciples. . . .
The Japanese recognize both religions [Buddhism and
Confucianism] equally, but Confucianism in Japan has
a direct bearing upon everything relating to human
affairs, especially the extreme loyalty of the people to
the emperor, while the Koreans consider it more useful in social matters than in any other department of
life, and hardly consider its precepts in their business
and mercantile relations."

"Although Confucianism is counted a religion, it is
really a system of sociology. . . . Confucius was a
moralist and statesman, and his disciples are moralists
and economists."—Education in Korea, by Mr. Pom
K Soh, of the Korean Embassy to the United States ;
Report of U. S. Commissioner of Education, 1890–91,
Vol. I., pp. 345–346.

[21] In Bakin, who is the great teacher of the Japanese
by means of fiction, this is the idea always inculcated.

CHAPTER VI

THE BUDDHISM OF NORTHERN ASIA

[1] See his Introduction to the Saddharma Pundarika,
Sacred Books of the East, and his Buddhismus.

[2] Origin and Growth of Religion as Illustrated by
Buddhism ; Non-Christian Religious Systems—Buddhism.

[3] The sketch of Indian thought here following is
digested from material obtained from various works on
Buddhism and from the Histories of India. See the

excellent monograph of Romesh Chunder Dutt, in Epochs of Indian History, London and New York, 1893 ; and Outlines of The Mahayana, as Taught by Buddha ("for circulation among the members of the Parliament of Religions," and distributed in Chicago), Tōkiō, 1893.

[4] Dyaus-Pitar, afterward ζεὺς πατήρ. See Century Dictionary, Jupiter.

[5] Yoga is the root form of our word yoke, which at once suggests the union of two in one. See Yoga, in The Century Dictionary.

[6] Dutt's History of India.

[7] The differences between the simple primitive narrative of Gautama's experiences in attaining Buddhahood, and the richly embroidered story current in later ages, may be seen by reading, first, Atkinson's Prince Sidartha, the Japanese Buddha, and then Arnold's Light of Asia. See also S. and H., Introduction, pp. 70–84, etc. Atkinson's book is refreshing reading after the expurgation and sublimation of the same theme in Sir Edwin Arnold's Light of Asia.

[8] Romesh Chunder Dutt's Ancient India, p. 100.

[9] Origin and Growth of Religion by T. Rhys Davids, p. 28.

[10] Job i. 6, Hebrew.

[11] Origin and Growth of Religion, p. 29.

[12] "Buddhism so far from tracing 'all things' to 'matter' as their original, denies the reality of matter, but it nowwhere denies the reality of existence."—The Phœnix, Vol. I., p. 156.

[13] See A Year among the Persians, by Edward G. Browne, London, 1893.

[14] Dutt's History of India, pp. 153–156. See also

Mozoomdar's The Spirit of God, p. 305. "Buddhism, though for a long time it supplanted the parent system, was the fulfilment of the prophecy of universal peace, which Hinduism had made ; and when, in its turn, it was outgrown by the instincts of the Aryans, it had to leave India indeed forever, but it contributed quite as much to Indian religion as it had ever borrowed."

[15] Korean Repository, Vol. I., pp. 101, 131, 153 ; Siebold's Nippon, Archiv; Report of the U. S. Commissioner of Education, 1890–91, Vol. I., p. 346 ; Dallet's Histoire de l'Église de Corée, Vol. I., Introd., p. cxlv. ; Corea, the Hermit Nation, p. 331.

[16] See Brian H. Hodgson's The Literature and History of the Buddhists, in Journal of the Asiatic Society of Bengal, which is epitomized in The Phœnix, Vol. I. ; Beal's Buddhism in China, Chap. II. ; T. Rhys Davids's Buddhism, etc. To Brian Houghton Hodgson, (of whose death at the ripe age of ninety-three years we read in Luzac's Oriental List) more than to any one writer, are we indebted for our knowledge of Northern or Mahayana Buddhism.

[17] See the very accurate, clear, and full definitions and explanations in The Century Dictionary.

[18] This subject is fully discussed by Professor T. Rhys Davids in his compact Manual of Buddhism.

[19] See Century Dictionary.

[20] Jap. Mon-ju. One of the most famous images of this Bodhisattva is at Zenkô-ji, Nagano. See Kern's Saddharma Pundarika, p. 8, and the many references to Manjusri in the Index. That Manjusri was the legendary civilizer of Nepaul seems probable from the following extract from Brian Hodgson :

"The Swayambhu Purana relates in substance as follows: That formerly the valley of Nepaul was of circular form, and full of very deep water, and that the mountains confining it were clothed with the densest forests, giving shelter to numberless birds and beasts. Countless waterfowl rejoiced in the waters. . . .

". . . Vipasyi, having thrice circumambulated the lake, seated himself in the N. W. (Váyubona) side of it, and, having repeated several mantras over the root of a lotos, he threw it into the water, exclaiming, ' What time this root shall produce a flower, then, from out of the flower, Swayambhu, the Lord of Agnishtha Bhuvana, shall be revealed in the form of flame ; and then shall the lake become a cultivated and populous country.' Having repeated these words, Vipasyi departed. Long after the date of this prophecy, it was fulfilled according to the letter. . . .

". . . When the lake was dessicated (by the sword of Manjusri says the myth—probably earthquake) Karkotaka had a fine tank built for him to dwell in ; and there he is still worshipped, also in the cave-temple appendant to the great Buddhist shrine of Swayambhu Nath. . . .

". . . The Bodhisatwa above alluded to is Manju Sri, whose native place is very far off, towards the north, and is called Pancha Sirsha Parvata (which is situated in Maha China Des). After the coming of Viswabhu Buddha to Naga Vasa, Manju Sri, meditating upon what was passing in the world, discovered by means of his divine science that Swayambhu-jyotirupa, that is, the self-existent, in the form of flame, was revealed out of a lotos in the lake of Naga Vasa. Again, he reflected within himself : ' Let me behold that sacred spot, and

my name will long be celebrated in the world ; ' and
on the instant, collecting together his disciples, com-
prising a multitude of the peasantry of the land, and a
Raja named Dharmakar, he assumed the form of Vis-
wakarma, and with his two Devis (wives) and the persons above-mentioned, set out upon the long journey
from Sirsha Parvata to Naga Vasa. There having arrived, and having made puja to the self-existent, he
began to circumambulate the lake, beseeching all the
while the aid of Swayambhu in prayer. In the second
circuit, when he had reached the central barrier mountain to the south, he became satisfied that that was the
best place whereat to draw off the waters of the lake.
Immediately he struck the mountain with his scimitar,
when the sundered rock gave passage to the waters,
and the bottom of the lake became dry. He then descended from the mountain, and began to walk about
the valley in all directions."—The Phœnix, Vol. II.,
pp. 147–148.

[21] Jap. Kwannon, god or goddess of mercy, in his
or her manifold forms, Thousand-handed, Eleven-faced,
Horse-headed, Holy, etc.

[22] Or, The Lotus of the Good Law, a mystical name
for the cosmos. " The good law is made plain by flowers of rhetoric." See Bernouf and Kern's translations,
and Edkin's Chinese Buddhism, pp. 43, 214. Translations of this work, so influential in Japanese Buddhism,
exist in French, German, and English. See Sacred
Books of the East, Vol. XXI., by Professor H. Kern,
of Leyden University. In the Introduction, p. xxxix.,
the translator discusses age, authorship, editions, etc.
Bunyiu Nanjio's Short History of the Twelve Jap-
ananese Buddhist Sects, pp. 132–134. Beal in his

Catena of Buddhist Scriptures, pp. 389–396, has translated Chapter XXIV.

[23] At the great Zenkōji, a temple of the Tendai sect, at Nagano, Japan, dedicated to three Buddhist divinities, one of whom is Kwannon (Avalokitesvara), the rafters of the vast main hall are said to number 69,384, in reference to the number of Chinese characters contained in the translation of the Saddharma Pundarika.

[24] " The third (collection of the Tripitaka) was . . . made by Manjusri and Maitreya. This is the collection of the Mahāyāna books. Though it is as clear or bright as the sun at midday yet the men of the Hinayana are not ashamed of their inability to know them and speak evil of them instead, just as the Confucianists call Buddhism a law of barbarians, without reading the Buddhist books at all."—B. N., p. 51.

[25] See the writings of Brian Hodgson, J. Edkins, E. J. Eitel, S. Beal, T. Rhys Davids, Bunyiu Nanjio, etc.

[26] See Chapter VIII. in T. Rhys Davids's Buddhism, a book of great scholarship and marvellous condensation.

[27] Davids's Buddhism, p. 206. Other illustrations of the growth of the dogmas of this school of Buddhism we select from Brian Hodgson's writings.

1. The line of division between God and man, and between gods and man, was removed by Buddhism.

" Genuine Buddhism never seems to contemplate any measures of acceptance with the deity; but, overleaping the barrier between finite and infinite mind, urges its followers to aspire by their own efforts to that divine perfectibility of which it teaches that man is capable, and by attaining which man becomes God—and thus is explained both the quiescence of the imaginary celestial, and the plenary omnipotence of the real Manushi Buddhas—thus, too, we must account for the fact that genuine Buddhism has no priesthood ; the saint despises the priest ; the saint scorns the aid of mediators, whether on earth or in heaven ; ' conquer (exclaims the adept or Buddha to the novice or Bodhi-Sattwa)—conquer the importunities of the body, urge your mind to the meditation of abstraction, and you shall, in time, discover the great secret (Sunyata) of nature : know this, and you become, on the instant, whatever priests have feigned of Godhead—you become identified with Prajna, the sum of all the power and all the wisdom which sustain and govern the world, and which, as they are manifested out of matter, must belong solely to matter; not indeed in the gross and palpable state of pravritti, but in the archetypal and pure state of nirvritti. Put off, therefore, the vile, pravrittika necessities of the body, and the no less vile affections of the mind (Tapas) ; urge your thought into pure abstraction (Dhyana), and then, as assuredly you can, so assuredly you shall, attain to the wisdom of a Buddha (Bodhijnana), and become associated with the eternal unity and rest of nirvritti.' "—The Phœnix, Vol. I., p. 194.

2. A specimen of "esoteric" and "exoteric" Buddhism ; — the Buddha Tathagata.

" And as the wisdom of man is, in its origin, but an effluence of the Supreme wisdom (*Prajná*) of nature, so is it perfected by a refluence to its source, but without loss of individuality ; whence Prajna is feigned in the exoteric system to be both the mother and the wife of all the Buddhas, '*janani sarva Buddhánám*,' and '*Jina-*

sundarí; ' for the efflux is typified by a birth, and the reflux by a marriage.

"The Buddha is the adept in the wisdom of Buddhism (*Bodhijnána*) whose first duty, so long as he remains on earth, is to communicate his wisdom to those who are willing to receive it. These willing learners are the 'Bodhisattwas,' so called from their hearts being inclined to the wisdom of Buddhism, and 'Sanghas,' from their companionship with one another, and with their Buddha or teacher, in the *Viháras* or cœnobitical establishments."

"And such is the esoteric interpretation of the third (and inferior) member of the Prájniki Triad. The Bodhisattwa or Sangha continues to be such until he has surmounted the very last grade of that vast and laborious ascent by which he is instructed that he can 'scale the heavens,' and pluck immortal wisdom from its resplendent source : which achievement performed, he becomes a Buddha, that is, an Omniscient Being, and a *Tathágata*—a title implying the accomplishment of that gradual increase in wisdom by which man becomes immortal or ceases to be subject to transmigration."—The Phœnix, Vol. I., pp. 194, 195.

3. Is God all, or is all God ?

"What that grand secret, that ultimate truth, that single reality, is, whether all is God, or God is all, seems to be the sole *propositum* of the oriental philosophic religionists, who have all alike sought to discover it by taking the high *priori* road. That God is all, appears to be the prevalent dogmatic determination of the Brahmanists ; that all is God, the preferential but sceptical solution of the *Buddhists ;* and, in a large view, I believe it would be difficult to indicate any further essential difference between their theoretic systems, both, as I conceive, the unquestionable growth of the Indian soil, and both founded upon transcendental speculation, conducted in the very same style and manner."—The Phœnix, Vol. II., p. 45.

4. Buddha, Dharma, and Sangha.

" In a philosophical light, the precedence of Buddha or of Dharma indicates the theistic or atheistic school. With the former, Buddha is intellectual essence, the efficient cause of all, and underived. Dharma is material essence, the plastic cause, and underived, a coequal biunity with Buddha; or else the plastic cause, as before, but dependent and derived from Buddha. Sangha is derived from, and compounded of, Buddha, and Dharma, is their collective energy in the state of action; the immediate operative cause of creation, its type or its agent. With the latter or atheistic schools, Dharma is *Diva natura*, matter as the sole entity, invested with intrinsic activity and intelligence, the efficient and material cause of all.

" Buddha is derivative from Dharma, is the active and intelligent force of nature, first put off from it and then operating upon it. Sangha is the *result* of that operation; is embryotic creation, the type and sum of all specific forms, which are spontaneously evolved from the union of Buddha with Dharma."—The Phœnix, Vol. II., p. 12.

5. The mantra or sacred sentence best known in the Buddhadom and abroad.

" *Amitábha* is the fourth *Dhyani* or celestial *Buddha*: *Padma-pani* his *Æon* and executive minister. *Padma-pani* is the *præsens Divus* and creator of the *exist-*

ing system of worlds. Hence his identification with the third member of the *Triad*. He is figured as a graceful youth, erect, and bearing in either hand a *lotos* and a jewel. The last circumstance explains the meaning of the celebrated *Shadakshari Mantra*, or six-lettered invocation of him, viz., *Om ! Manipadme hom !* of which so many corrupt versions and more corrupt interpretations have appeared from Chinese, Tibetan, Mongolian, and other sources. The *mantra* in question is one of three, addressed to the several members of the *Triad*. 1. *Om sarva vidye hom.* 2. *Om Prajnaye hom.* 3. *Om mani-padme hom.* 1. The mystic triform Deity is in the all-wise (Buddha). 2. The mystic triform Deity is in Prajna (Dharma). 3. The mystic triform Deity is in him of the jewel and lotos (Sangha). But the præsens Divus, whether he be Augustus or *Padma-pani*, is everything with the many. Hence the notoriety of this *mantra*, whilst the others are hardly ever heard of, and have thus remained unknown to our travellers."—The Phœnix, Vol. II., p. 64.

[28] " Nine centuries after Buddha, Maitreya (Miroku or Ji-shi) came down from the Tushita heaven to the lecture-hall in the kingdom of Ayodhya (A-ya-sha) in Central India, at the request of the Bodhisattva Asamga (Mu-jaku) and discoursed five Sastras, 1, Yoga-karya-bhumi-sastra (Yu-ga-shi-ji-ron), etc. . . . After that, the two great Sastra teachers, Asanga and Vasubandhu (Se-shin), who were brothers, composed many Sastras (Ron) and cleared up the meaning of the Mahayana" (or Greater Vehicle, canon of Northern Buddhism).—B. N., p. 32.

[29] Buddhism, T. Rhys Davids, pp. 206–211.

[30] Prayer-wheels in Japan are used by the Tendai and Shingon sects, but without written prayers attached, and rather as an illustration of the doctrine of cause and effect (ingwa) ; the prayers being usually offered to Jizo the merciful.—S. and H., p. 29 ; T. J., p. 360.

[31] For this see Edkins's Chinese Buddhism ; Eitel's Three Lectures, and Hand - book ; Rev. S. Beal's Buddhism, and A Catena of Buddhist Scriptures from the Chinese ; The Romantic Legend of Sakya Buddha, from the Chinese ; Texts from the Buddhist canon commonly known as the Dhammapeda ; Notes on Buddhist Words and Phrases, the Chrysanthemum, Vol. I. ; The Phœnix, Vols. I.–III.

See, also, a spirited sketch of Ancient Japan, by Frederick Victor Dickins, in the Life of Sir Harry Parkes, Vol. II., pp. 4–14.

[32] S. and H., pp. 289, 293 ; Chamberlain's Hand-book for Japan, p. 220 ; Summer's Notes on Osaka, T. A. S. J., Vol. VII., p. 382 ; Buddhism, and Traditions Concerning its Introduction into Japan, T. A. S. J., Vol. XIV., p. 78.

[33] S. and H., p. 344.

[34] T. J., p. 73.

[35] Vairokana is the first or chief of the five personifications of Wisdom, and in Japan the idol is especially noticeable in the temples of the Tendai sect.— "The Action of Vairokana, or the great doctrine of the highest vehicle of the secret union," etc., B. N., p. 75.

[36] S. and H., p. 390 ; B. N., p. 29.

[37] "Hinduism stands for philosophic spirituality and emotion, Buddhism for ethics and humanity, Chris-

tianity for fulness of God's incarnation in man, while Mohammedanism is the champion of uncompromising monotheism."—F. P. C. Mozoomdar's The Spirit of God, Boston, 1894, p. 305.

CHAPTER VII

RIYŌBU, OR MIXED BUDDHISM

[1] Is not something similar frankly attempted in Rev. Dr. Joseph Edkins's The Early Spread of Religious Ideas in the Far East (London, 1893) ?

[2] M. E., p. 252; Honda the Samurai, pp. 193–194.

[3] See The Lily Among Thorns, A Study of the Biblical Drama Entitled the Song of Songs (Boston 1890), in which this subject is glanced at.

[4] See The Religion of Nepaul, Buddhist Philosophy, and the writings of Brian Hodgson in The Phœnix, Vols. I., II., III.

[5] See Century Dictionary, Yoga; Edkins's Chinese Buddhism, pp. 169–174; T. Rhys Davids's Buddhism, pp. 206–211; Index of B. N., under Vagrasattwa; S. and H., pp. 85–87.

[6] T. J., p. 226; Kojiki, Introduction.

[7] See in the Journal of the Royal Asiatic Society, 1893, a very valuable paper by Mr. L. A. Waddell, on The Northern Buddhist Mythology, epitomized in the Japan Mail, May 5, 1894.

[8] See Catalogue of Chinese and Japanese Paintings in the British Museum, and The Pictorial Arts of Japan, by William Anderson, M.D.

[9] Anderson's Catalogue, p. 24.

[10] S. and H., p. 415; Chamberlain's Hand-book for Japan ; T. J. ; M. E., p. 162, etc.

[11] The names of Buddhist priests and monks are usually different from those of the laity, being taken from events in the life of Gautama, or his original disciples, passages in the sacred classics, etc.   Among some personal acquaintances in the Japanese priesthood were such names as Lift-the-Kettle, Take-Hold-of-the-Dipper, Drivelling-Drunkard, etc.   In the raciness, oddity, literalness, realism, and close connection of their names with the scriptures of their system, the Buddhists quite equal the British Puritans.

[12] Kern's Saddharma-Pundarika, pp. 311, 314; Davids's Buddhism p. 208 ; The Phœnix, Vol. I., p. 169 ; S. and H., p. 502 ; Du Bose's Dragon, Demon, and Image, p. 407 ; Fuso Mimi Bukuro, p. 134 ; Hough's Corean Collections, Washington, 1893, p. 480, plate xxviii.

[13] Japan in History, Folk-lore and Art, pp. 86, 80–88 ; A Japanese Grammar, by J. J. Hoffman, p. 10 ; T. J., pp. 465–470.

[14] This is the essence of Buddhism, and was for centuries repeated and learned by heart throughout the empire :

> " Love and enjoyment disappear,
>   What in our world endureth here ?
> E'en should this day in oblivion be rolled,
> 'Twas only a vision that leaves me cold."

[15] This legend suggests the mediæval Jewish story, that Ezra, the scribe, could write with five pens at once ; Hearn's Glimpses of Unfamiliar Japan, pp. 29–33.

27

[16] Brave Little Holland, and What She Taught Us, p. 124.

[17] T. J., pp. 75, 342 ; Chamberlain's Hand-book for Japan, p. 41 ; M. E., p. 162.

[18] T. A. S. J., Vol. II., p. 101 ; S. and H., p. 176.

[19] It was for lifting with his walking-stick the curtain hanging before the shrine of this Kami that Arinori Mori, formerly H.I.J.M. Minister at Washington and London, was assassinated by a Shintō fanatic, February 11, 1889 ; T. J., p. 229 ; see Percival Lowell's paper in the Atlantic Monthly.

[20] See Mr. P. Lowell's Esoteric Shintō, T. A. S. J., Vol. XXI., pp. 165–167, and his "Occult Japan."

[21] S. and H., Japan, p. 83.

[22] See the Author's Introduction to the Arabian Nights' Entertainments, Boston, 1891.

[23] B. N., Index and pp. 78–103 ; Edkins's Chinese Buddhism, p. 169.

[24] Satow's or Chamberlain's Guide-books furnish hundreds of other instances, and describe temples in which the renamed kami are worshipped.

[25] S. and H., p. 70.

[26] M. E., pp. 187, 188 ; S. and H., pp. 11, 12.

[27] San Kai Ri (Mountain, Sea, and Land). This work, recommended to me by a learned Buddhist priest in Fukui, I had translated and read to me by a Buddhist of the Shin Shu sect. In like manner, even Christian writers in Japan have occasionally endeavored to rationalize the legends of Shintō, see Kojiki, p. liii., where Mr. T. Goro's Shintō Shin-ron is referred to. I have to thank my friend Mr. R. Watanabé, of Cornell University, for reading to me Mr. Takahashi's interesting but unconvincing monographs on Shintō and Buddhism.

[28] T. J., p. 402 ; Some Chinese Ghosts, by Lafcadio Hearn, p. 129.

[29] S. and H., Japan, p. 397 ; Classical Poetry of the Japanese, p. 201, note.

[30] The Japanese word Ryō means both, and is applied to the eyes, ears, feet, things correspondent or in pairs, etc. ; *bu* is a term for a set, kind, group, etc.

[31] Rein, p. 432 ; T. A. S. J., Vol. XXI., pp. 241–270 ; T. J., p. 339.

[32] The Chrysanthemum, Vol. I., p. 401.

[33] Even the Takétori Monogatari (The Bamboo Cutter's Daughter), the oldest and the best of the Japanese classic romances is (at least in the text and form now extant) a warp of native ideas with a woof of Buddhist notions.

[34] Mr. Percival Lowell argues, in Esoteric Shintō, T. A. S. J., Vol. XXI., that besides the habit of pilgrimages, fire-walking, and god-possession, other practices supposed to be Buddhistic are of Shintō origin.

[35] The native literature illustrating Riyōbuism is not extensive. Mr. Ernest Satow in the American Cyclopædia (Japan : Literature) mentions several volumes. The Tenchi Réiki Noko, in eighteen books contains a mixture of Buddhism and Shintō, and is ascribed by some to Shōtoku and by others to Kōbō, but now literary critics ascribe these, as well as the books Jimbetsuki and Tenshoki, to be modern forgeries by Buddhist priests. The Kogoshiui, written in A.D. 807, professes to preserve fragments of ancient tradition not recorded in the earlier books, but the main object is that which lies at the basis of a vast mass of Japanese literature, namely, to prove the author's own descent from the gods. The Yuiitsu Shintō Miyoho Yoshiu,

in two volumes, is designed to prove that Shintō and Buddhism are identical in their essence. Indeed, almost all the treatises on Shintō before the seventeenth century maintained this view. Certain books like the Shintō Shu, for centuries popular, and well received even by scholars, are now condemned on account of their confusion of the two religions. One of the most interesting works which we have found is the San Kai Ri, to which reference has been made.

[36] T. J., p. 224.

[37] " Human life is but fifty years," Japanese Proverb ; M. E., p. 107.

[38] Chamberlain's Classical Poetry of the Japanese, p. 130.

[39] S. and H., p. 416.

[40] Things Chinese, by J. Dyer Ball, p. 70 ; see also Edkins and Eitel.

[41] The Japan Weekly Mail of April 28, 1893, translating and condensing an article from the Bukkyō, a Buddhist newspaper, gives the results of a Japanese Buddhist student's tour through China—" Taoism prevails everywhere. . . . Buddhism has decayed and is almost dead."

[42] Vaisramana is a Deva who guarded, praised, fed with heavenly food, and answered the questions of the Chinese Dō-sen (608–907 A.D.) who founded the Risshu or Vinaya sect.—B. N., p. 25.

[43] Anderson, Catalogue, pp. 29–45.

[44] Some of these are pictured in Aimé Humbert's Japon Illustré, and from the same pictures reproduced by electro-plates which, from Paris, have transmigrated for a whole generation through the cheaper books on Japan, in every European language.

CHAPTER VIII

NORTHERN BUDDHISM IN ITS DOCTRINAL EVOLUTIONS

[1] On the Buddhist canon, see the writings of Beal, Spence Hardy, T. Rhys Davids, Bunyiu Nanjio, etc.

[2] Edkins's Chinese Buddhism, pp. 43, 108, 214; Classical Poetry of the Japanese, p. 173.

[3] See T. A. S. J., Vol. XIX., Part I., pp. 17–37; The Soul of the Far East; and the writings of Chamberlain, Aston, Dickins, Munzinger, etc.

[4] Much of the information as to history and doctrine contained in this chapter has been condensed from Mr. Bunyiu Nanjio's A Short History of the Twelve Japanese Buddhist Sects, translated out of the Japanese into English. This author, besides visiting the old seats of the faith in China, studied Sanskrit at Oxford with Professor Max Müller, and catalogued in English the Tripitaka or Buddhist canon of China and Japan, sent to England by the ambassador Iwakura. The nine reverend gentlemen who wrote the chapters and introduction of the Short History are Messrs. Kō-chō Ogurusu, and Shu-Zan Emura of the Shin sect; Rev. Messrs. Shō-hen Uéda, and Dai-ryo Takashi, of the Shin-gon Sect; Rev. Messrs. Gyō-kai Fukuda, Kenkō Tsuji, Renjō Akamatsu, and Zé-jun Kobayashi of the Jō-dō, Zen, Shin, and Nichiren sects, respectively. Though execrably printed, and the English only tolerable, the work is invaluable to the student of Japanese Buddhism. It has a historical introduction and a Sanskrit-Chinese Index, 1 vol., pp. 172, Tokio, 1887. Substantially the same work, translated into French,

is Le Bouddhisme Japonais, by Ryauon Fujishima, Paris, 1889. Satow and Hawes's Hand-book for Japan has brief but valuable notes in the Introduction, and, like Chamberlain's continuation of the same work, is a storehouse of illustrative matter. Edkins's and Eitel's works on Chinese Buddhism have been very helpful.

[5] M. Abel Remusat published a translation of a Chinese Pilgrim's travels in 1836; M. Stanislais Julien completed his volume on Hiouen Thsang in 1858; and in 1884 Rev. Samuel Beal issued his Travels of Fah-Hian and Sung-Yun, Buddhist Pilgrims from China to India (400 A.D. and 518 A.D.). The latter work contains a map.

[6] B. N., p. 3.

[7] B. N., p. 11.

[8] Three hundred and twenty million years. See Century Dictionary.

[9] See the paper of Rev. Shō-hen Uéda of the Shingon sect, in B. N., pp. 20-31; and R. Fujishima's Le Bouddhisme Japonais, pp. xvi., xvii., from which most of the information here given has been derived.

[10] M. E., p. 383 ; S. and H., pp. 23, 30.

The image of Binzuru is found in many Japanese temples to-day, a famous one being at Asakusa, in Tōkiō. He is the supposed healer of all diseases. The image becomes entirely rubbed smooth by devotees, to the extinguishment of all features, lines, and outlines.

[11] Davids's Buddhism, pp. 180, 200 ; S. and H., pp. (87) 389, 416.

[12] B. N., pp. 32-43.

[13] B. N., pp. 44-56.

[14] Japanese Fairy World, p. 282 ; Anderson's Catalogue, pp. 103–7.

[15] B. N., p. 62.

[16] Pfoundes, Fuso Mimi Bukuro, p. 102.

[17] B. N., p. 58. See also The Monist for January, 1894, p. 168.

[18] " Tien Tai, a spot abounding in Buddhist antiquities, the earliest, and except Puto the largest and richest seat of that religion in eastern China. As a monastic establishment it dates from the fourth century." —Edkins's Chinese Buddhism, pp. 137–142.

[19] S. and H., p. 87. See the paper read at the Parliament of Religions by the Zen bonze Ashitsu of Hiyéisan, the poem of Right Reverend Shaku Soyen, and the paper on The Fundamental Teachings of Buddhism, in The Monist for January, 1894 ; Japan As We Saw It, p. 297.

[20] See Century Dictionary, *mantra.*

[21] See Chapter XX. Ideas and Symbols in Japan : in History, Folk-lore, and Art. Buddhist tombs (go-rin) consist of a cube (earth), sphere (water), pyramid (fire), crescent (wind), and flame-shaped stone (ether), forming the go-rin or five-blossom tomb, typifying the five elements.

[22] B. N., p. 78.

[23] To put this dogma into intelligible English is, as Mr. Satow says, more difficult than to comprehend the whole doctrine, hard as that may be. " Dai Nichi Niyorai (Vairokana) is explained to be the collectivity of all sentient beings, acting through the mediums of Kwan-non, Ji-zō, Mon-ju, Shaka, and other influences which are popularly believed to be self-existent deities." In the diagram called the eight-leaf enclosure,

by which the mysteries of Shingon are explained, Maha-Vairokana is in the centre, and on the eight petals are such names as Amitabha, Manjusri, Maitreya, and Avalokitesvara; in a word, all are purely speculative beings, phantoms of the brain, the mushrooms of decayed Brahmanism, and the mould of primitive Buddhism disintegrated by scholasticism.

[24] S. and H., p. 31.

[25] B. N., p. 115.

[26] Here let me add that in my studies of oriental and ancient religion, I have never found one real Trinity, though triads, or tri-murti, are common. None of these when carefully analyzed yield the Christian idea of the Trinity.

CHAPTER IX

THE BUDDHISM OF THE JAPANESE

[1] Tathagata is one of the titles of the Buddha, meaning " thus come," *i.e.*, He comes bringing human nature as it truly is, with perfect knowledge and high intelligence, and thus manifests himself. Amitabha is the Sanskrit of Amida, or the deification of boundless light.

[2] B. N., p. 104.

[3] Literally, I yield to, or I adore the Boundless or the Immeasurable Buddha.

[4] A Chinese or Japanese volume is much smaller than the average printed volume in Europe.

[5] Legacy of Iyéyasŭ, Section xxviii. Doctrinally, this famous document, written probably long after

Iyéyasŭ's death and canonization as a *gongen*, is a mixture or *Riyōbu* of Confucianism and Buddhism.

[6] At first glance a forcible illustration, since the Japanese proverb declares that " A sea-voyage is an inch of hell." And yet the original saying of Ryū-ju, now proverbial in Buddhadom, referred to the ease of sailing over the water, compared with the difficulty of surmounting the obstacles of land travel in countries not yet famous for good roads. See B. N., p. 111.

[7] Fuso Mimi Bukuro, p. 108 ; Descriptive Notes on the Rosaries as used by the different Sects of Buddhists in Japan, T. A. S. J., Vol. IX., pp. 173–182.

[8] B. N., p. 122.

[9] S. and H., p. 361.

[10] S. and H., pp. [90–92] ; Unbeaten Tracks in Japan, Vol. II., pp. 242–253.

[11] These three sutras are those most in favor with the Jō-dō sect also, they are described, B. N., 104–106, and their tenets are referred to on pp. 260, 261.

[12] For modern statements of Shin tenets and practices, see E. J. Reed's Japan, Vol. I., pp. 84–86 ; The Chrysanthemum, April, 1881, pp. 109–115 ; Unbeaten Tracks in Japan, Vol. II., 242–246 ; B. N., 122–131. Edkins's Religion in China, p. 153. The Chrysanthemum, April, 1881, p. 115.

[13] S. and H., p. 361 ; B. N., pp. 105, 106. Toward the end of the Amitayus-dhyana sutra, Buddha says : " Let not one's voice cease, but ten times complete the thought, and repeat Namo'mitābhāya Buddhāya (Namu Amida Butsu) or adoration to Amitbāha Buddha."

[14] M. E., pp. 164–166.

[15] Schaff's Encyclopædia, Article, Buddhism.

[16] On the Tenets of the Shin Shiu, or "True Sect" of Buddhists, T. A. S. J., Vol. XIV., p. 1.

[17] The Gobunsho, or Ofumi, of Rennyō Shōnin, T. A. S. J., Vol. XVII., pp. 101–143.

[18] At the gorgeous services in honor of the founder of the great Higashi Hongwanji Western Temple of the Original Vow at Asakusa, Tōkiō, November 21 to 28, annually, the women attend wearing a head-dress called "horn-hider," which seems to have been named in allusion to a Buddhist text which says: "A woman's exterior is that of a saint, but her heart is that of a demon."—Chamberlain's Hand-book for Japan, p. 82; T. A. S. J., Vol. XVII., pp. 106, 141; Sacred Books of the East, Vol. XXI., pp. 251–254.

[19] Review of Buddhist Texts from Japan, The Nation, No. 875, April 6, 1882. "The *Mahāyāna* or Great Vehicle (we might fairly render it 'highfalutin') school. . . . Filled as these countries [Tibet, China, Japan] are with Buddhist monasteries, and priests, and nominal adherents, and abounding in voluminous translations of the Sanskrit Buddhistic literature, little understood and wellnigh unintelligible (for neither country has had the independence and mental force to produce a literature of its own, or to add anything but a chapter of decay to the history of this religion). . . . ."

[20] M. E., pp. 164, 165; B. N., pp. 132–147; Mitford's Tales of Old Japan, Vol. II., pp. 125–134.

[21] See article Demoniacal Possessions, T. J., 106–113; T. A. S. J., Vol. XXI., Esoteric Shintō; Occult Japan.

CHAPTER X

JAPANESE BUDDHISM IN ITS MISSIONARY DEVELOP-
MENT

[1] T. J., p. 71. Further illustrations of this statement
may be found in his Classical Poetry of the Japanese,
especially in the Selection and Appendices of this
book; also in T. R. H. McClatchie's Japanese Plays
(Versified), London, 1890.

[2] See Introduction to the Kojiki, pp. xxxii.–xxxiv., and
in Bakin's novel illustrating popular Buddhist beliefs,
translated by Edward Greey, A Captive of Love, Boston, 1886.

[3] See jade in Century Dictionary; " Magatama, so
far as I am aware, do not ever appear to have been
found in shell heaps" (of the aboriginal Ainos),
Milne's Notes on Stone Implements, T. A. S. J., Vol.
VIII., p. 71.

[4] Concerning this legendary, and possibly mythical,
episode, which has so powerfully influenced Japanese
imagination and politics, see T. A. S. J., Vol. XVI.,
Part I., pp. 39–75 ; M. E., pp. 75–85.

[5] See Corea, the Hermit Nation, pp. 1, 2 ; Persian Elements in Japanese Legends, T. A. S. J., Vol. XVI.,
Part I, pp. 1–10 ; Journal of the Royal Asiatic Society,
January, 1894. Rein's book, The Industries of Japan,
points out, as far as known, the material debt to India.
Some Japanese words like *beni-gari* (Bengal) or rouge
show at once their origin. The mosaic of stories in the
Takétori Monogatari, an allegory in exquisite literary
form, illustrating the Buddhist dogma of Ingwa, or law

of cause and effect, and written early in the ninth century, is made up of Chinese-Indian elements. See F. V. Dickins's translation and notes in Journal of the Royal Oriental Society, Vol. XIX., N. S. India was the far off land of gems, wonders, infallible drugs, roots, etc.; Japanese Fairy World, p. 137.

⁶ M. E., Chap. VIII. ; Klaproth's Annales des Empereurs du Japon (a translation of Nippon O Dai Ichi Ran) ; Rein's Japan, p. 224.

⁷ See Klaproth's Annales, *passim*. S. and H. p. [85]. Bridges are often symbolical of events, classic passages in the shastras and sutras, or are antetypes of Paradisaical structures. The ordinary native *hashi* is not remarkable as a triumph of the carpenter's art, though some of the Japanese books mention and describe in detail some structures that are believed to be astonishing.

⁸ Often amusingly illustrated, M. E., p. 390. A translation into Japanese of Göethe's Reynard the Fox is among the popular works of the day. " Strange to say, however, the Japanese lose much of the exquisite humor of this satire in their sympathy with the woes of the maltreated wolf."—The Japan Mail. This sympathy with animals grows directly out of the doctrine of metempsychosis. The relationship between man and ape is founded upon the pantheistic identity of being. " We mention sin," says a missionary now in Japan, " and he [the average auditor] thinks of eating flesh, or the killing of insects." Many of the sutras read like tracts and diatribes of vegetarians.

⁹ See The Art of Landscape Gardening in Japan, T. A. S. J., Vol. XIV. ; Theory of Japanese Flower Arrangements, by J. Conder, T. A. S. J., Vol. XVII. ; T. J., p. 168 ; M. E., p. 437 ; T. J., p. 163.

[10] *The* book, by excellence, on the Japanese house, is Japanese Homes and Their Surroundings, by E. S. Morse. See also Constructive Art in Japan, T. A. S. J., Vol. II., p. 57, III., p. 20 ; Feudal Mansions of Yedo, Vol. VII., p. 157.

[11] See Hearn's Glimpses of Unfamiliar Japan, pp. 385, 416, and *passim.*

[12] For pathetic pictures of Japanese daily life, see Our Neighborhood, by the late Dr. T. A. Purcell, Yokohama, 1874 ; A Japanese Boy, by Himself (S. Shigémi), New Haven, 1889 ; Lafcadio Hearn's Glimpses of Unfamiliar Japan, Boston, 1894.

[13] Klaproth's Annales, and S. and H. *passim.*

[14] See Pfoundes's Fuso Mimi Bukuro, p. 130, for a list of grades from Ho-ō or cloistered emperor, Miya or sons of emperors, chief priests of sects, etc., down to priests in charge of inferior temples. This Budget of Notes, pp. 99–144, contains much valuable information, and was one of the first publications in English which shed light upon the peculiarities of Japanese Buddhism.

[15] Isaiah xl. 19, 20, and xli. 6, 7, read to the dweller in Japan like the notes of a reporter taken yesterday.

[16] T. J., p. 339 ; Notes on Some Minor Japanese Religious Practices, *Journal of the Anthropological Institute,* May, 1893 ; Lowell's Esoteric Shintō, T. A. S. J., Vol. XXI. ; Satow's The Shintō Temples of Isé, T. A. S. J., Vol. II., p. 113.

[17] M. E. p. 45 ; American Cyclopædia, Japan, Literature—History, Travels, Diaries, etc.

[18] That is, no dialects like those which separate the people of China. The ordinary folks of Satsuma and Suruga, for example, however, would find it difficult to

understand each other if only the local speech were used. Men from the extremes of the Empire use the Tōkiō standard language in communicating with each other.

[19] For some names of Buddhist temples in Shimoda see Perry's Narrative, pp. 470–474, described by Dr. S. Wells Williams ; S. and H. *passim.*

[20] The Abbé Huc in his Travels in Tartary was one of the first to note this fact. I have not noticed in my reading that the Jesuit missionaries in Japan in the seventeenth century call attention to the matter. See also the writings of Arthur Lillie, voluminous but unconvincing, Buddha and Early Buddhism, and Buddhism and Christianity, London, 1893.

[21] M. E., p. 252.

[22] T. J., p. 70.

[23] See The Higher Buddhism in the Light of the Nicene Creed, Tōkiō, 1894, by Rev. A. Lloyd.

[24] " I preach with ever the same voice, taking enlightenment as my text. For this is equal for all ; no partiality is in it, neither hatred nor affection. . . . I am inexorable, bear no love or hatred towards anyone, and proclaim the law to all creatures without distinction, to the one as well as to the other."—Saddharma Pundarika.

[25] Unbeaten Tracks in Japan, Vol. II., p. 247.

[26] For the symbolism of the lotus see M. E., p. 437 ; Unbeaten Tracks in Japan, Vol. I., p. 299 ; M. E. index ; and Saddharma Pundarika, Kern's translation, p. 76, note :

" Here the Buddha is represented as a wise and benevolent father ; he is the heavenly father, Brahma. As such he was represented as sitting on a 'lotus-seat.'

How common this representation was in India, at least in the sixth century of our era, appears from Varâha-mihira's Brihat-Samhita, Ch. 58, 44, where the following rule is laid down for the Buddha idols : ' Buddha shall be (represented) sitting on a lotus-seat, like the father of the world.' "

[27] See The Northern Buddhist Mythology in *Journal of the Royal Asiatic Society*, January, 1894.

[28] See The Pictorial Arts of Japan, and Descriptive and Historical Catalogue, William Anderson, pp. 13–94.

[29] See fylfot in Century Dictionary.

[30] The word *vagra*, diamond, is a constituent in scores of names of sutras, especially those whose contents are metaphysical in their nature. The Vajrasan, Diamond Throne or Thunderbolt seat, was the name applied to the most sacred part of the great temple reared by Asoka on the site of the bodhi tree, under which Gautama received enlightenment. " The adamantine truths of Buddha struck like a thunderbolt upon the superstitions of his age." " The word vagra has the two senses of hardness and utility. In the former sense it is understood to be compared to the secret truth which is always in existence and not to be broken. In the latter sense it implies the power of the enlightened, that destroys the obstacles of passions."—B. N., p. 88. " As held in the arms of Kwannon and other images in the temples," the vagra or " diamond club " (is that) with which the foes of the Buddhist Church are to be crushed.—S. and H., p. 444. Each of the gateway gods Ni-ō (two Kings, Indra and Brahma) " bears in his hand the tokko (Sanskrit *vagra*), an ornament originally designed to represent a dia-

mond club, and now used by priests and exorcists, as a religious sceptre symbolizing the irresistible power of prayer, meditation, and incantation."—Chamberlain's Hand-book for Japan, p. 31.

[31] Jizō is the compassionate helper of all in trouble, especially of travellers, of mothers, and of children. His Sanskrit name is Kshiugarbha. His idol is one of the most common in Japan. It is usually necklaced with baby's bibs, often by the score, while the pedestal is heaped with small stones placed there by sorrowing mothers.—S. and H., p. 29, 394 ; Chamberlain's Handbook of Japan, 29, 101. Hearn's Japan, p. 34, and *passim*.

[32] Sanskrit *arhat* or *arhan*, meaning worthy or deserving, *i.e.*, holy man, the highest rank of Buddhist saintship. See Century Dictionary.

[33] M. E., p. 201. The long inscription on the bell in Wellesley College, which summons the student-maidens to their hourly tasks has been translated by the author and Dr. K. Kurahara and is as follows :

1. A prose preface or historical statement.

2. Two stanzas of Chinese poetry, in four-syllable lines, of four verses each, with an apostrophe in two four-syllable lines.

3. The chronology.

4. The names of the composer and calligraphist, and of the bronze-founder.

The characters in vertical lines are read from top to bottom, the order of the columns being from right to left. There are in all 117 characters.

The first tablet reads :

Lotus-Lily Temple (of) Law-Grove Mountain ; Bell-inscription (and) Preface.

" Although there had been of old a bell hung in the Temple of the Lotus-Lily, yet being of small dimensions its note was quickly exhausted, and no volume of melody followed (after having been struck). Whereupon, for the purpose of improving upon this state of affairs, we made a subscription, and collected coin to obtain a new bell. All believers in the doctrine, gods as well as devils, contributed freely. Thus the enterprise was soon consummated, and this inscription prepared, to wit :

" ' The most exalted Buddha having pitiful compassion upon the people, would, by means of this bell, instead of words, awaken them from earthly illusions, and reveal the darkness of this world.

" ' Many of the living hearkening to its voice, and making confession, are freed from the bondage of their sins, and forever released from their disquieting desires.

" ' How great is (Buddha's) merit ! Who can utter it ? Without measure, boundless !'

" Eleventh year of the Era of the Foundation of Literature (and of the male element) Wood (and of the zodiac sign) Dog ; Autumn, seventh month, fifteenth day (A.D. August 30, 1814).

" Composition and penmanship by Kaméda Koyésen. Cast by the artist Sugiwara Kuninobu."

(The poem in unrhymed metre.)

Buddha in compassion tender
With this bell, instead of words,
Wakens souls from life's illusions,
Lightens this world's darkness **drear**.

Many souls its sweet tones heeding,
From their chains of sin are freed ;

All the mind's unrest is soothéd,
Sinful yearnings are repressed.

Oh how potent is his merit,
Without bounds in all the worlds !

[34] Fuso Mimi Bukuro, p. 129.

[35] M. E., pp. 287–290, 513–514 ; Perry's Narrative, pp. 471, 472 ; Our Neighborhood, pp. 119–124. The following epitaphs are gathered from various sources :

" This stone marks the remains of the believer who never grows old."

" The believing woman Yu-ning, Happy was the day of her departure."

" Multitudes fill the graves."

" Only by this vehicle—the coffin—can we enter Hades."

" As the floating grass is blown by the gentle breeze, or the glancing ripples of autumn disappear when the sun goes down, or as a ship returns to her old shore— so is life. It is a vapor, a morning-tide."

" Buddha himself wishes to hear the name of the deceased that he may enter life."

" He who has left humanity is now perfected by Buddha's name, as the withered moss by the dew."

" Life is like a candle in the wind."

" The wise make our halls illustrious, and their monuments endure for ages."

" What permanency is there to the glory of the world ?

It goes from the sight like hoar-frost in the sun."

" If men wish to enter the joys of heavenly light, Let them smell the fragrance of the law of Buddha."

" Whoever wishes to have his merit reach even to

the abode of demons, let him, with us, and all living, become perfect in the doctrine."

[36] Rev. C. B. Hawarth in the *New York Independent,* January 18, 1894.

[37] In 781 the Buddhist monk Kéi-shun dedicated a chapel to Jizo, on whom he conferred the epithet of Sho-gun or general, to suit the warlike tastes of the Japanese people.—S. and H., p. 384. So also Hachiman became the god of war because adopted as the patron deity of the Genji warriors.—S. and H., p. [70.]

[38] Corea, the Hermit Nation, p. 96.

[39] Dixon's Japan, p. 41 ; S. and H., Japan, *passim ;* Rein's Japan ; Story of the Nations, Japan, by David Murray, p. 201, note ; Dening's life of Toyotomi Hidéyoshi ; M. E., Chapters XV., XVI., XX., XXIII., XXIV. ; Gazetteer of Echizen ; Shiga's History of Nations, Tōkiō, 1888, pp. 115, 118 ; T. A. S. J., Vol. VIII., pp. 94, 134, 143.

[40] T. A. S. J., Vol. VIII., Hidéyoshi and the Satsuma Clan in the Sixteenth Century, by J. H. Gubbins ; The Times of Taikō, by R. Brinkley, in *The Japan Times.*

[41] The Copy of the Buddhist Tripitaka, or Northern Collection, made by order of the Emperor, Wan-Li, in the sixteenth century, when the Chinese capital (King) was changed from the South (Nan) to the North (Pe), was reproduced in Japan in 1679, and again in 1681–83, and in over two thousand volumes, making a pile a hundred feet high, was presented by the Japanese Government, through the Junior Prime Minister, Mr. Tomomi Iwakura, to the Library of the India Office. See Samuel Beal's The Buddhist Tripitaka, as it is known in China and Japan, A Catalogue and Compen-

dious Report, London, 1876.   The library has been re-
arranged by Mr. Bunyin Nanjio, who has published
the result of his labors, with Sanskrit equivalents of the
titles and with notes of the highest value.

[42] " Neither country (China or Japan) has had the
independence and mental force to produce a literature
of its own, and to add anything but a chapter of decay
to the history of this religion."—Professor William D.
Whitney, in review of Anecdota Oxoniensia, Buddhist
Texts from Japan, in *The Nation*, No. 875.

[43] Education in Japan, A series of papers by the
writer, printed in *The Japan Mail* of 1873–74, and re-
printed in the educational journals of the United States.
A digest of these papers is given in the appendix of F.
O. Adams's History of Japan ; Life of Sir Harry
Parkes, Vol. II., pp. 305, 306.

[44] Japan : in Literature, Folk-Lore, and Art, p. 77.

[45] Japanese Education at the Philadelphia Exposition, New York, 1876.

[46] See Japanese Literature, by E. M. Satow, in The
American Cyclopædia.

[47] The word bonze (Japanese *bon-so* or *bozu*, Chinese
fan-sung) means an ordinary member of the congregation, just as the Japanese term *bon-yo* or *bon-zoku* means
common people or the ordinary folks.   The word came
into European use from the Portuguese missionaries,
who heard the Japanese thus pronounce the Chinese
term *fan*, which, as *bon*, is applied to anything in the
mass not out of the common.

[48] See On the Early History of Printing in Japan, by
E. M. Satow, T. A. S. J., Vol. X., Part I., p. 48 ;
Part II., p. 252.

[49] Japanese mediæval monastery life has been ably

pictured in English fiction by a scholar of imagination and literary power, withal a military critic and a veteran in Japanese lore. " The Times of Taikō," in the defunct Japanese Times (1878), deserves reprint as a book, being founded on Japanese historical and descriptive works. In Mr. Edward's Greey's A Captive of Love, Boston, 1886, the idea of ingwa (the effects in this life of the actions in a former state of existence), is illustrated. See also S. and H., p. 29 ; T. J., p. 360.

⁵⁰ It is curious that while the anti-Christian polemics of the Japanese Buddhists have used the words of Jesus, " I came to send not peace but a sword," Matt. x. 34, and " If any man . . . . hate not his father and mother," etc., Luke xiv. 26, as a branding iron with which to stamp the religion of Jesus as gross immorality and dangerous to the state, they justify Gautama in his " renunciation " of marital and paternal duties.

⁵¹ See Public Charity in Japan, Japan Mail, 1893 ; and The Annual (Appleton's) Cyclopædia for 1893.

⁵² I have some good reasons for making this suggestion. Yokoi Héishiro had dwelt for some time in Fukui, a few rods away from the house in which I lived, and the ideas he promulgated among the Echizen clansmen in his lectures on Confucianism, were not only Christian in spirit but, by their own statement, these ideas could not be found in the texts of the Chinese sage or of his commentators. Although the volume (edited by his son, Rev. J. F. Yokoi) of his Life and Letters shows him to have been an intense and at times almost bigoted Confucianist, he, in one of his later letters, prophesied that when Christianity

should be taught by the missionaries, it would win the hearts of the young men of Japan. See also Satow's Kinsé Shiriaku, p. 133; Adams's History of Japan; and in fiction, see Honda The Samurai, p. 242, and succeeding chapters.

[53] In the colorless and unsentimental language of government publications, the Japanese edict of emancipation, issued to the local authorities in October, 1871, ran as follows: "The designations of eta and hinin are abolished. Those who bore them are to be added to the general registers of the population and their social position and methods of gaining a livelihood are to be identical with the rest of the people. As they have been entitled to immunity from the land tax and other burdens of immemorial custom, you will inquire how this may be reformed and report to the Board of Finance." (Signed) Council of State.

[54] In English fiction, see The Eta Maiden and the Hatamoto, in Mitford's Tales of Old Japan, Vol. I., pp. 210-245. Discussions as to the origin of the Eta are to be found in Adams's History of Japan, Vol. I., p. 77; M. E., index; T. J., p. 147; S. and H., p. 36; Honda the Samurai, pp. 246, 247; Mitford's Tales of Old Japan, Vol. I., pp. 210-245. The literature concerning the Ainos is already voluminous. See Chamberlain's Aino Studies, with bibliography; and Rev. John Batchelor's Ainu Grammar, published by The Imperial University of Tōkiō; T. A. S. J., Vols. X., XI., XVI., XVIII., XX.; The Ainu of Japan, New York, 1892, by J. Batchelor (who has also translated the Book of Common Prayer, and portions of the Bible into the Ainu tongue); M. E., Chap. II.; T. A. S. J., Vol. X., and following volumes; Unbeaten Tracks in

Japan, Vol. II.; Life with Trans-Siberian Savages, London, 1893.

[55] " Then the venerable Sāriputra said to that daughter of Sagara, the Nāga-king : ' Thou hast conceived the idea of enlightenment, young lady of good family, without sliding back, and art gifted with immense wisdom, but supreme, perfect enlightenment is not easily won. It may happen, sister, that a woman displays an unflagging energy, performs good works for many thousands of Aeons, and fulfils the six perfect virtues (Pāramitās), but as yet there is no example of her having reached Buddhaship, and that because a woman cannot occupy the five ranks, viz., 1, the rank of Brahma ; 2, the rank of Indra ; 3, the rank of a chief guardian of the four quarters ; 4, the rank of Kakravartin ; 5, the rank of a Bodhisattva incapable of sliding back," Saddharma Pundarika, Kern's Translation, p. 252.

[56] " Chiū-jō-himé was the first Japanese nun, and the only woman who is commemorated by an idol. She extracted the fibres of the lotus root, and wove them with silk to make tapestry for altars." Fuso Mimi Bukuro, p. 128. Her romantic and marvellous story is given in S. and H., p. 397. "The practice of giving ranks to women was commenced by Jito Tennō (an empress, 690–705)." Many women shaved their heads and became nuns "on becoming widows, as well as on being forsaken by, or after leaving their husbands. Others were orphans." One of the most famous nuns (on account of her rank) was the Nii no Ama, widow of Kiyomori and grandmother of the Emperor Antoku, who were both drowned near Shimonoséki, in the great naval battle of 1185 A.D. Adams's History of Japan, Vol. I., p. 37 ; M. E., p. 137.

[57] M. E., p. 213 ; Japanese Women, World's Columbian Exhibition, Chicago, 1893, Chap. III.

[58] There is no passage in the original Greek texts, or in the Revised Version of the New Testament which ascribes wings to the *aggelos*, or angel. In Rev. xii. 14, a woman is "given two wings of a great eagle."

[59] Japanese Women in Politics, Chap. I., Japanese Women, Chicago, 1893 ; Japanese Girls and Women, Chapters VI. and VII.

[60] Bakin's novels are dominated by this idea, while also preaching in fiction strict Confucianism. See A Captive of Love, by Edward Greey.

[61] " Fate is one of the great words of the East. *Japan's language is loaded and overloaded with it.* Parents are forever saying before their children, ' There's no help for it.' I once remarked to a school-teacher, ' Of course you love to teach children.' His quick reply was, ' Of course I don't. I do it merely because there is no help for it.' Moralists here deplore the prosperity of the houses of ill-fame and then add with a sigh, ' There's no help for it.' All society reverberates with this phrase with reference to questions that need the application of moral power, will power." —J. H. De Forest.

" I do not say there is no will power in the East, for there is. Nor do I say there is no weak yielding to fate in lands that have the doctrine of the Creator, for there is. But, putting the East and West side by side, one need not hesitate to affirm that the reason the will power of the East is weak cannot be fully explained by any mere doctrine of environment, but must also have some vital connection with the fact that the idea of a personal almighty Creator has for long ages been

wanting. And one reason why western nations have an aggressive character that ventures bold things and tends to defy difficulties cannot be wholly laid to environment but must have something to do with the fact that leads millions daily reverently to say ' I believe in the Almighty Father, Maker of Heaven and Earth.' "
—J. H. De Forest.

STATISTICS OF BUDDHISM IN JAPAN.

(From the official "Résumé Statistique de l'Empire du Japon," Tōkiō, 1894.)

In 1891 there were 71,859 temples within city or town limits, and 35,959 in the rural districts, or 117,718 in all, under the charges of 51,791 principal priests and 720 principal priestesses, or 52,511 in all.

The number of temples, classified by sects, were as follows : Tendai, with 3 sub-sects, 4,808 ; Shingon, with 2 sub-sects, 12,821, of which 45 belonged to the Hossō shu ; Jō-do, with 2 sub-sects, 8,323, of which 21 were of the Ké-gon shu; Zen, with 3 sub-sects, 20,882, of which 6,146 were of the Rin-Zai shu; 14,072 of the Sō-dō shu, and 604 of the Ō-baku shu; Shin, with 10 sub-sects, 19,146 ; Nichiren, with 7 sub-sects, 5,066 ; Ji shu, 515 ; Yu-dzū Nembutsu, 358 ; total, 38 sects and 71,859 temples.

The official reports required by the government from the various sects, show that there are 38 administrative heads of sects ; 52,638 priest-preachers and 44,123 ordinary priests or monks ; and 8,668 male and 328 female, or a total of 8,996, students for the grade of monk or nun. In comparison with 1886, the number of priest-preachers was 39,261, ordinary priests 38,-189 ; male students, 21,966 ; female students, 642.

CHAPTER XI

ROMAN CHRISTIANITY IN THE SEVENTEENTH CENTURY.

[1] See for a fine example of this, Mr. C. Meriwether's Life of Daté Masamuné, T. A. S. J., Vol. XXI., pp. 3–106. See also The Christianity of Early Japan, by Koji Inaba, in The Japan Evangelist, Yokohama, 1893–94; Mr. E. Satow's papers in T. A. S. J.

[2] See M. E., p. 280; Rein's Japan, p. 312; Shigétaka Shiga's History of Nations, p. 139, quoting from M. E. (p. 258).

[3] M. E., 195.

[4] The Japan Mail of April and May, 1894, contains a translation from the Japanese, with but little new matter, however, of a work entitled Paul Anjiro.

[5] The "Firando" of the old books. See Cock's Diary. It is difficult at first to recognize the Japanese originals of some of the names which figure in the writings of Charlevoix, Léon Pagés, and the European missionaries, owing to their use of local pronunciation, and their spelling, which seems peculiar. One of the brilliant identifications of Mr. Ernest Satow, now H. B. M. Minister at Tangier, is that of Kuroda in the "Kondera" of the Jesuits.

[6] See Mr. E. M. Satow's Vicissitudes of the Church at Yamaguchi. T. A. S. J., Vol. VII., pp. 131–156.

[7] Nobunaga was Nai Dai Jin, Inner (Junior) Prime Minister, one in the triple premiership, peculiar to Korea and Old Japan, but was never Shōgun, as some foreign writers have supposed.

[8] See The Jesuit Mission Press in Japan, by E.

Satow, 1591–1610 (privately printed, London, 1888). Review of the same by B. H. Chamberlain, T. A. S. J., Vol. XVII., p. 91.

[9] Histoire de l'Église, Vol. I., p. 490 ; Rein, p. 277. Takayama is spoken of in the Jesuit Records as Jûsto Ucondono. A curious book entitled Justo Ucondono, Prince of Japan, in which the writer, who is " less attentive to points of style than to matters of faith," labors to show that " the Bible alone " is " found wanting," and only the "Teaching Church " is worthy of trust, was published in Baltimore, in 1854.

[10] How Hidéyoshi made use of the Shin sect of Buddhists to betray the Satsuma clansmen is graphically told in Mr. J. H. Gubbin's paper, Hidéyoshi and the Satsuma Clan, T. A. S. J., Vol. VIII., pp. 124–128, 143.

[11] Corea the Hermit Nation, Chaps. XII.–XXI., pp. 121–123 ; Mr. W. G. Aston's Hidéyoshi's Invasion of Korea, T. A. S. J., Vol. VI., p. 227 ; IX., pp. 87, 213 ; XI., p. 117 ; Rev. G. H. Jones's The Japanese Invasion, The Korean Repository, Seoul, 1892.

[12] Brave Little Holland and What She Taught Us, Boston, 1893, p. 247.

[13] See picture and description of this temple— " fairly typical of Japanese Buddhist architecture," Chamberlain's Handbook for Japan, p. 26 ; G. A. Cobbold's, Religion in Japan, London, 1894, p. 72.

[14] T. A. S. J., see Vol. VI., pp. 46–51, for the text of the edicts.

[15] M. E., p. 262, Chamberlain's Handbook for Japan, p. 59.

[16] The Origin of Spanish and Portuguese Rivalry in Japan, by E. M. Satow, T. A. S. J., Vol. XVIII., p. 133.

[17] See Chapter VIII., W. G. Dixon's Gleanings from Japan.

[18] T. A. S. J., Vol. VI., pp. 48–50.

[19] In the inscription upon the great bell, at the temple containing the image of Dai Butsŭ or Great Buddha, reared by Hidéyori and his mother, one sentence contained the phrase *Kokka anko*, *ka* and *ko* being Chinese for *Iyé* and *yasŭ*, which the Yedo ruler professed to believe mockery. In another sentence, "On the East it welcomes the bright moon, and on the West bids farewell to the setting sun," Iyéyasŭ discovered treason. He considered himself the rising sun, and Hidéyori the setting moon.—Chamberlain's Hand-book for Japan, p. 300.

[20] I have found the Astor Library in New York especially rich in works of this sort.

[21] Nitobé's United States and Japan, p. 13, note.

[22] This insurrection has received literary treatment at the hands of the Japanese in Shimabara, translated in The Far East for 1872 ; Woolley's Historical Notes on Nagasaki, T. A. S. J., Vol. IX., p. 125 ; Koeckebakker and the Arima Rebellion, by Dr. A. J. C. Geerts, T. A. S. J., Vol. XI., 51 ; Inscriptions on Shimabara and Amakusa, by Henry Stout, T. A. S. J., Vol. VII., p. 185.

[23] " Persecution extirpated Christianity from Japan." —History of Rationalism, Vol. II., p. 15.

[24] T. A. S. J., Vol. VI., Part I., p. 62 ; M. E. pp. 531, 573.

[25] Political, despite the attempt of many earnest members of the order to check this tendency to intermeddle in politics ; see Dr. Murray's Japan, p. 245, note, 246.

[26] See abundant illustration in Léon Pagés' Histoire de la Religion Chrétienne en Japon, a book which the author read while in Japan amid the scenes described.
[27] *The Japan Evangelist,* Vol. I., No. 2, p. 96.

CHAPTER XII

TWO CENTURIES OF SILENCE

[1] See Diary of Richard Cocks, and Introduction by R. M. Thompson, Hakluyt Publications, 1883.

[2] For the extent of Japanese influence abroad, see M. E., p. 246 ; Rein, Nitobe, and Hildreth ; Modern Japanese Adventurers, T. A. S. J., Vol. VII., p. 191 ; The Intercourse between Japan and Siam in the Seventeenth Century, by E. M. Satow, T. A. S. J., Vol. XIII., p. 139 ; Voyage of the Dutch Ship Grol, T. A. S. J., Vol. XI., p. 180.

[3] The United States and Japan, p. 16.

[4] See Professor J. H. Wigmore's elaborate work, Materials for the Study of Private Law in Old Japan, T. A. S. J., Tōkiō, 1892.

[5] See the Legacy of Iyéyasŭ, by John Frederic Lowder, Yokohama, 1874, with criticisms and discussions by E. M. Satow and others in the *Japan Mail ;* Dixon's Japan, Chapter VII. ; Professor W. E. Grigsby, in T. A. S. J., Vol. III., Part II., p. 131, gives another version, with analysis, notes, and comments ; Rein's Japan, pp. 314, 315.

[6] Old Japan in the days of its inclusiveness was a secret society on a vast scale, with every variety and degree of selfishness, mystery, secrecy, close-corpora-

tionism, and tomfoolery. See article Esotericism in T. J., p. 143.

[7] Since the abolition of feudalism, with the increase of the means of transportation, the larger freedom, and, at many points, improved morality, the population of Japan shows an unprecedented rate of increase. The census taken in 1744 gave, as the total number of souls in the empire, 26,080,000 (E. J. Reed's Japan, Vol. I., p. 236); that of 1872, 33,110,825; that of 1892, 41,-089,940, showing a greater increase during the past twenty years than in the one hundred and thirty-eight years previous. See Résumé Statistique de l'Empire du Japon, Tōkiō, 1894; Professor Garrett Droppers' paper on The Population of Japan during the Tokugawa Period, read June 27th, 1894; T. A. S. J., Vol. XXII.

[8] For the notable instance of Pere Sidotti, see M. E., p. 63; Séí Yō Ki Bun, by S. R. Brown, D.D., a translation of Arai Hakuséki's narrative, Yedo, 1710, T. N. C. A. S.; Capture and Captivity of Pere Sidotti, T. A. S. J., Vol. IX., p. 156; Christian Valley, T. A. S. J., Vol. XVI., p. 207.

[9] T. A. S. J., Vol. I., p. 78, Vol. VII., p. 323.

[10] See Matthew Calbraith Perry, Boston, 1887.

[11] See the author's Townsend Harris, First American Minister to Japan, *The Atlantic Monthly*, August, 1891.

[12] See Honda the Samurai, Boston, 1890; Nitobé's United States and Japan; The Japan Mail *passim;* Dr. G. F. Verbeck's History of Protestant Missions in Japan, Yokohama, 1883; Dr. George Wm. Knox's papers on Japanese Philosophy, T. A. S. J., Vol. XX., p. 158, etc. Recent Japanese literature, of which the

writer has a small shelfful, biographies, biographical dictionaries, the histories of New Japan, Life of Yoshida Shoin, and recent issues of The Nation's Friend (Kokumin no Tomo), are very rich on this fascinating subject.

[13] A typical instance was that of Rin Shihéi, born 1737, author of *San Koku Tsu Ran to Setsu*, translated into French by Klaproth, Paris, 1832. Rin learned much from the Dutch and Prussians, and wrote books which had a great sale. He was cast into prison, whence he never emerged. The (wooden) plates of his publications were confiscated and destroyed. In 1876, the Mikado visited his grave in Sendai, and ordered a monument erected to the honor of this far-seeing patriot.

[14] Rein, pp. 336, 337

[15] Rein, p. 339; The Early Study of Dutch in Japan, by K. Mitsukuri, T. A. S. J., Vol. V., p. 209; History of the Progress of Medicine in Japan, T. A. S. J., Vol. XII., p. 245; Vijf Jaren in Japan, J. L. C. Pompe van Meerdervoort, 2d Ed., Leyden, 1868.

[16] Honda the Samurai, pp. 249–251; Nitobé, 25–27.

[17] The Tokugawa Princes of Mito, by Professor E. W. Clement, T. A. S. J., Vol. XVIII., p. 14; Nitobé's United States and Japan, p. 25, note.

[18] M. E. (6 Ed.), p. 608; Adams's History of Japan, Vol. II., p. 171.

[19] See the text of the anti-Christian edicts, M. E., p. 369.

[20] T. A. S. J., Vol. XX., p. 17.

[21] T. A. S. J., Vol. IX., p. 134.

[22] Tales of Old Japan, Vol. II., p. 125; A Japanese

Buddhist Preacher, by Professor M. K. Shimomura, in
the New York Independent; other sermons have been
printed in The Japan Mail ; Kino Dowa, two sermons
and vocabulary, has been edited by Rev. C. S. Eby,
Yokohama.

[23] On Sunday, November 29, 1857, Mr. Harris, rest-
ing at Kawasaki, over Sunday, on his way to Yedo and
audience of the Shōgun, having Mr. Heusken as his
audience and fellow-worshipper, read service from the
Book of Common Prayer.

[24] See a paper written by the author and read at the
World's Columbian Exhibition Congress of Missions,
Chicago, September, 1893, on The Citizen Rights of
Missionaries.

[25] This embassy was planned and first proposed to
the Junior premier, Tomomi Iwakura, and the route
arranged by the Rev. Guido F. Verbeck, then President of the Imperial University. One half of the
members of the embassy had been Dr. Verbeck's pupils at Nagasaki.

[26] A somewhat voluminous native Japanese literature is the result of the various embassies and individual pilgrimages abroad, since 1860. Immeasurably
superior to all other publications, in the practical influence over his fellow-countrymen, is the Séiyo Jijo
(The Condition of Western Countries) by Fukuzawa,
author, educator, editor, decliner of numerously proffered
political offices, and "the intellectual father of one-half
of the young men who now fill the middle and lower
posts in the government of Japan." For the foreign
side, see The Japanese in America, by Charles Lan-
man, New York, 1872, and in The Life of Sir Harry
Parkes, London, 1894, and for an amusing piece of

literary ventriloquism, Japanese Letters, Eastern Impressions of Western Men and Manners, London and New York, 1891.

See History of Protestant Missions in Japan, by G. F. Verbeck, Yokohama, 1893.

29

INDEX